Iowa
324.273   Cook
              Baptism of fire
C773
                                    950387

DATE DUE			

Learning Resource Center
Marshalltown Community College
Marshalltown, Iowa 50158

GAYLORD

Baptism of Fire

Baptism of Fire

THE REPUBLICAN PARTY IN IOWA, 1838–1878

Robert Cook

Iowa State University Press / Ames

ROBERT COOK is lecturer in American History at the University of Sheffield, United Kingdom.

©1994 Iowa State University Press, Ames, Iowa 50014
All rights reserved

Authorization to photocopy items for internal or personal use, or the internal or personal use of specific clients, is granted by Iowa State University Press, provided that the base fee of $.10 per copy is paid directly to the Copyright Clearance Center, 27 Congress Street, Salem, MA 01970. For those organizations that gave been granted a photocopy license by CCC, a separate system of payments has been arranged. The fee code for users of the Transactional Reporting Service is 0-8138-1938-5/94 $.10.

∞ Printed on acid-free paper in the United States of America

First edition, 1994

Library of Congress Cataloging-in-Publication Data

Cook, Robert (Robert J.)
   Baptism of Fire: the Republican Party in Iowa, 1838–1878 / Robert Cook.—1st ed.
     p.   cm.
   Includes bibliographical references and index.
   ISBN 0-8138-1938-5 (acid-free paper)
   1. Republican Party (Iowa)—History—19th century. 2. Slavery—Iowa—Anti-slavery movements—History—19th century. I. Title.
JK2358.I83 1994   93-31825
324.2777'04'09034—dc20

The Colton map of the STATE OF IOWA, 1867, is reprinted by permission of the British Library.

FOR MY MOTHER AND FATHER

Contents

PREFACE   xi

INTRODUCTION

1   Republicanism in the Civil War Era: Iowa as a Test Case   3

1 ORIGINS

2   The Second Party System on the Frontier, 1838–1846   15

3   Defeat of the Democracy, 1846–1854   31

4   Formation of the Republican Party in Iowa, 1854–1856   52

2 LEGITIMIZATION

5   The Race Question in the Campaign of 1857   75

6   The Impact of Recession on Local Politics, 1858–1859   95

7   Iowa and the Coming of the Civil War, 1859–1861   116

8   The Union in Peril, 1861–1865   136

3 CONSOLIDATION

9   Black Suffrage and the Intraparty Crisis of 1865–1866   159

10   The Waning of Reconstruction, 1867–1872   183

11   The Railroad Question during the 1870s   203

12   End of an Era, 1876–1877   227

CONCLUSION

13 The Party of Progress and Humanity   237

APPENDIX   249
NOTES   253
BIBLIOGRAPHY   279
INDEX   299

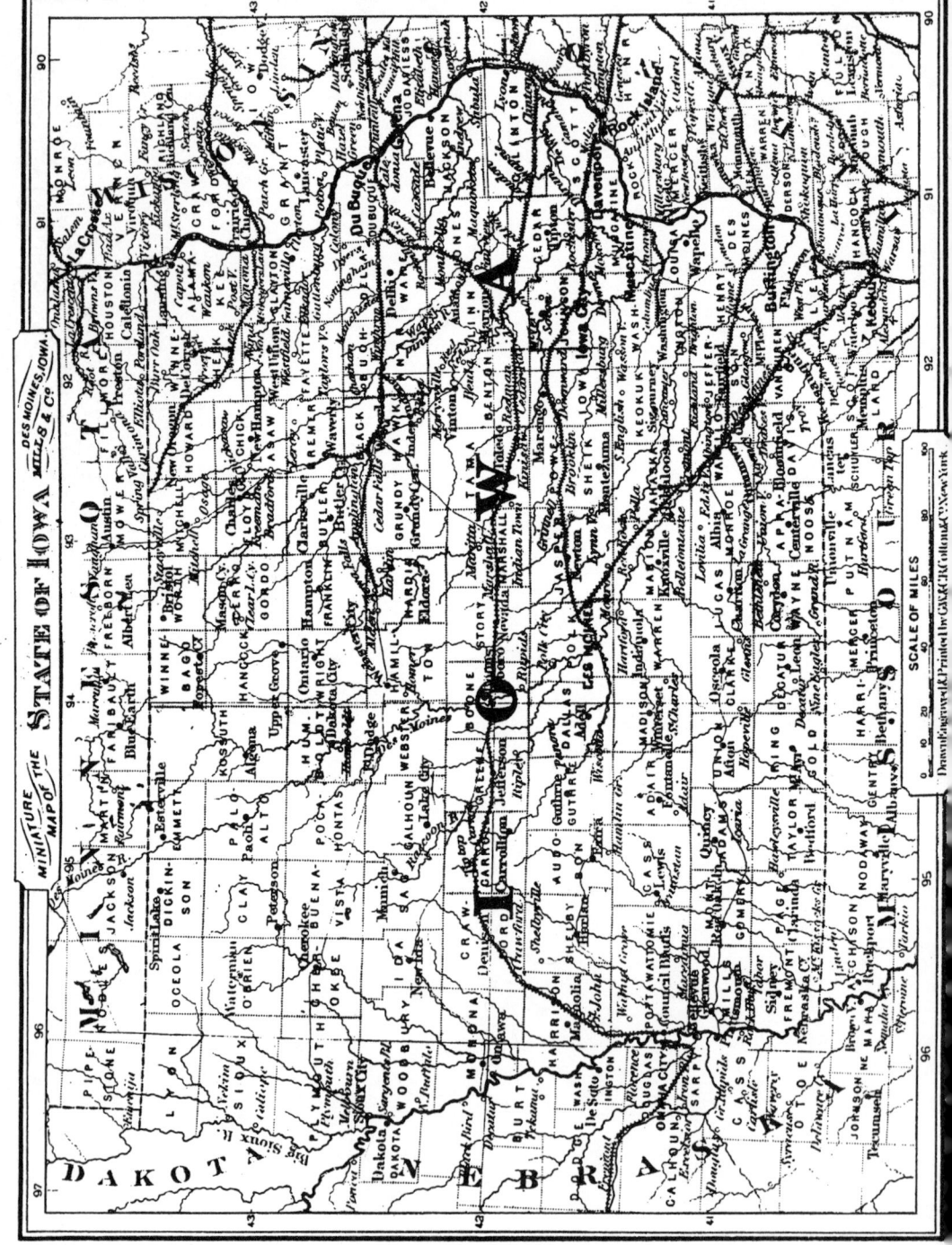

Preface

This book has been a long time—too long—in the making. My interest in Iowa, its people, and its past began on a bitterly cold December day in 1976 when I arrived in the state to begin work in a paint store owned by relatives in Cedar Falls. The purpose was to gain greater experience of the wider world beyond the confines of my suburban home in England before embarking on a history degree at the University of Warwick. I spent eight months stocking shelves, making new friends, and once in a while, journeying by car through the countryside of northeastern Iowa. Notwithstanding occasional pangs of homesickness and bleak winter days when it seemed as if spring would never come, the sojourn was a happy one. Never before had I seen a landscape so broad, a sky so vast, or girls' basketball on television. It was all very different from my childhood days in the industrial English midlands.

Back home at the university I took a number of courses in U.S. history. I learned about the Founding Fathers and Franklin Roosevelt, about European immigration and the rise of big business, about slavery in the South and the substantial achievements of the civil rights movement. A keen interest in race led me to focus on the sectional crisis of the mid-nineteenth century, for it seemed to me that the events of that era had settled the destiny of African-Americans for nearly a century. After investigating the efforts of the abolitionists to break down prejudice in the North, I was struck by the realization that it was not they who had freed the slaves but the young and vibrant Republican party of Abraham Lincoln. I turned then to the antislavery coalition of the 1850s and 1860s and began to ask why a mass political party in the Victorian era succeeded not only in freeing four million black bondsmen and women but also in granting them substantive civil and political rights.

Discovering that nineteenth-century Iowans were at the forefront of the movement to grant equal rights to blacks, I chose to use my adopted state as an arena in which to study the political antislavery movement. By the summer of 1979 I was doing research at the University of Northern Iowa in preparation for an undergraduate dissertation on the state's first Republicans.

One day an elderly gentleman approached the desk at which I was working. He introduced himself as Leland Sage and proffered some expert advice on a subject with which I was still hopelessly unfamiliar. Little did I know that I would soon be devoting a large chunk of my life to the characters, themes, and events covered so thoroughly by Professor Sage in his biography of William B. Allison and valuable modern history of Iowa.

When I decided to begin work on a doctorate at Oxford University in 1980, it never really occurred to me that I should study anything other than the early political, cultural, and socioeconomic development of Iowa. I remember a fleeting thought that the South might be warmer during the winter and therefore a touch more conducive to a year's archival research. However, memories of friendships made and ideas only half formed drew me back to the prairies. Thus began the project of which this book is the final outcome.

Many individuals have helped, indirectly as well as directly, in the preparation of both the doctoral thesis and the substantially revised chapters that follow this preface. Although they are not to be blamed for any errors, this study could not have been completed without them. My supervisor at Oxford, Jack Pole, kept a watchful eye on its progress and taught me the significance of legal history and roll call analysis. William Dusinberre of Warwick University stimulated my interest in the Middle Period and frequently supplied me with clear-sighted criticism and much-needed encouragement. An admirer of Henry Adams's classic account of the early national period, he sought to impress upon me the dangers of overblown prose. I also wish to thank a number of other scholars for their advice at various stages in the development of this book, notably Richard Carwardine, Bruce Collins, Edward Countryman, Valerie Cromwell, Charlotte Erickson, J. Morgan Kousser, David Montgomery, and John Rowatt. Special thanks must go to Paul Salotti and Clive Osmond, who provided the technical expertise for the computer-assisted survey of the state legislature; to the friendly and efficient staff at the Library of Congress, the National Archives, the Iowa State Historical Department, and the State Historical Society of Iowa; and to my editor, Jane Zaring, and my copy editor, Betsy Hovey, at Iowa State University Press. A fellowship from the Paul Mellon Fund at Cambridge University and a grant from the British Academy supplied indispensable financial backing for the final stages of the project.

Friends at home and abroad gave me vital moral support and material help during the extensive duration of this work. In America: Mary Beveridge, Jennifer Borton, Julianne Borton, Jim Christenson, Doris and Max Crandall, Joy and Roy Harvey, Barbara Holmlund, Phyllis McLaughlin, Val Shaw, Betty and Ben Webster (modern day Iowa Republicans who generously opened their home to me for nearly a year in 1981–82), Betty

Wells, Cathy Wright and her family, and John Zeller and his family; in England: Ray Amesbury, Ian Archer, Sarah Barber, Anne Bennett, Cathie Cook, Alison and Howard Greenaway, Trevor Griffiths, and Garry Owen Hughes. Finally, I should like to thank my parents. Even if they did not always understand my interest in nineteenth-century Iowa history, their love and encouragement kept me going throughout.

Introduction

1
Republicanism in the Civil War Era: Iowa as a Test Case

*ppletons' Hand-Book of American Travel* for 1873 described Iowa as a state "with no very notable history, beyond the usual adventure and hardship of a forest-life among savage tribes."[1] Although Victorian tourists journeying westward across the prairies en route for the Pacific would have found this judgment unremarkable, it was both unfair and inaccurate. For during the middle decades of the nineteenth century, Iowa played a distinctive role in the history of the American republic.

In the late 1830s the United States bequeathed to the fertile country between the Mississippi and Missouri rivers a unique system of government designed to protect white settlers from the evils of arbitrary power. The bequest proved a harsh one for the Indians who had roamed the grasslands for hundreds of years, but to the pioneers it was an inevitable corollary of progress. Washington did not disagree fundamentally with this analysis. It extinguished Indian titles to the land, gave preemption rights to those it called the people, and donated what was left of the public domain to local politicians for purposes of social and economic development. Admitted to the Union in 1846 Iowa was, by the outbreak of the Civil War, less a raw frontier territory than a fast-maturing state ready to contribute significantly to the nation's welfare.

Between 1861 and 1865 Iowa paid its debts to the United States. Over seventy thousand of her sons fought to suppress the Southern rebellion and preserve intact the federal Union, which they, like Lincoln, regarded as "the last, best hope of earth." Thirteen thousand of them surrendered their lives in the process—elegiac testimony to the force of American nationalism at the time of its greatest trial. For those Iowans who emerged from the war relatively unscathed, the North's triumph confirmed the superiority of free labor democracy over rival systems of government.

Aside from the sheer weight and tenacity of the Union effort, there were sound reasons for this conviction. No more liberal commonwealth existed on the face of the earth. Indians may not have been convinced of its benefits, but for native whites and Old World migrants the United States—and particularly the rural North—represented a land of equal opportunity, extensive political rights, and economic independence. After the Civil War even African-Americans had good reason to partake of the faith: in 1868 white Iowans registered their support for an amendment to the state constitution conferring upon the few thousand local blacks the right to vote.

In economic terms Iowa made impressive strides during the mid-nineteenth century. After being admitted to the Union at a time when the transformation from an agrarian to an industrial republic was well underway, the state developed rapidly as a center of commercial agriculture. Proximity to the Mississippi River, the advent of railroads, and a preponderance of fertile prairie soil gave Iowa significant advantages over its rivals in the market for farm products. Surpluses of corn, wheat, and pork were already being shipped eastwards by the time the Confederates bombarded Fort Sumter, and as early as 1870 Iowa was one of the largest corn-producing states in the Union. Although the region was to be dogged by relatively low rates of urbanization and industrialization, commercial agriculture alone brought riches to an area that, as elderly pioneers were always fond of pointing out, had been a wilderness within living memory.

While the economic achievement was impressive, growing pains were often acute. Many of the first settlers were suspicious of the agencies of a modern capitalist economy: banks, credit, moneyed corporations. Ultimately most of these doubts were swamped by the tantalizing prospect of economic gain held out by involvement in the market. However, the same capitalist institutions that liberated Iowans from the thralldom of preindustrial conditions contained within them the seeds of a new dependence on chaotic market forces. Throughout their early history Iowans struggled to come to terms with the consequences of the "market revolution."[2] Although they flirted briefly with state regulation of railroad rates, the final outcome of their battle was the same as that in the wider nation: a compromise between republican values and the new economy that legitimized the latter and left the former changed beyond measure from the days when Andrew Jackson was president and Iowa a hunting ground for the Indian.

One of the most important agencies linking early Iowa to the nation that gave it birth was the political party. Scholars have yet to agree on the primary role of this institution in modern society, but in the context of pre–Civil War America it seems clear that national parties worked to integrate disparate geographical and economic regions into a national community. That they failed to prevent the nightmare of 1861–65 should not allow us to forget that the parties of the antebellum era continue to dominate the political landscape of today. They may no longer excite the passions of the electorate to the extent they once did, but their primary function remains an essentially integrative one. Certainly the ill-fated second party system (which lasted from the mid-1830s to the mid-1850s) and the more successful third, which followed it, did much to contain the inevitable tensions that accompanied the development of the United States.

After an early period of Democratic domination, Iowa became a stronghold of the Republican party. During the eighty years spanning their first electoral triumph in 1854 and the onset of the Great Depression, Republicans won every gubernatorial contest in the state except two. Between 1856 and 1878 they swept seventy-one congressional races out of seventy-four, the only Democratic successes arising out of fusion with third parties. Over the same period the ratio of Republicans to opposition members in the state legislature was nearly three to one. Only once, in 1874, did Democrats manage to obtain parity in a chamber, and here again this was a consequence of fusion tactics. On a national scale Iowa ranked as the eighth most solidly Republican state in the country between 1856 and 1896. Only a handful of New England and trans-Mississippi states were more committed to the cause.

Historians have spent much time debating the precise role of the Republican party during the first twenty-five years of its existence. The reasons why are not hard to discover. Republicanism burst into the political arena at a time when sectional cleavages were threatening to sunder the Union and the nation seemed to be on the verge of industrial takeoff. Civil war and industrial revolution are compelling themes, and when they appear to be linked by the emergence of an organization representing specific interest groups in society, the fascination becomes particularly strong.

Southern slaveholders were the first to contend that Republicanism was a vehicle for narrow class interests—primarily those of industrial capitalists based in the Northeast. Extolling the virtues of their own racially exclusive forced labor system, they accused Republican leaders of promoting sectional discord in an effort to seize control of the federal government.

Progressive historians built on the claims of reactionary secessionists and the contemporary observations of Karl Marx to contend that the early

Republican party was the agency through which the American bourgeoisie (with the help of free midwestern farmers) finally triumphed over a seemingly entrenched landed aristocracy. In their classic survey of American history written in the 1920s Charles A. and Mary R. Beard argue that the Civil War constituted the nation's real revolution. Rejecting the standard picture of the Republican party as a vehicle for moral antislavery, they describe how that organization's rapid rise to power resulted in the emergence of today's modern industrial state. By destroying the power of the planter class Republicans were able to pass legislation conducive to the growth of advanced capitalism. Protective tariffs, a national banking system, federal aid for infrastructural development, and the due process clause of the Fourteenth Amendment are seen by the Beards as concrete results of what they call "a social war, ending in the unquestioned establishment of a new power in the government, making vast changes in the arrangements of classes, in the accumulation and distribution of wealth, in the course of industrial development, and in the Constitution inherited from the Fathers."[3]

The details of this analysis have not been borne out entirely by modern scholarship, but the kernel of the Progressive argument remains the starting point for much of the continuing debate over early national politics and society. Those historians labeled "cultural Marxists" by Richard L. McCormick have drawn on a variety of intellectual sources to produce a much more sophisticated version of the Beards' thesis.[4] Arguing that an extended process of economic change was underway in the United States by the end of the Revolutionary period, Eric Foner, Sean Wilentz, Bruce Laurie, and others have suggested that the main source of political conflict in mid-nineteenth-century America was an emerging social cleavage between, on the one hand, a dynamic commercial-industrial capitalism and, on the other, a more static, traditionalist agrarianism.[5] In their view, American republicanism with its reputed emphasis on civic virtue and communal values was gradually subverted by agencies of the market revolution: individualism, credit, wage labor, and evangelical Protestantism (to name but a few). Their ability to link politics with social change and to take into account the impact of religion on American life renders the work of these historians particularly impressive. Joined to that of David Brion Davis (who contends that antislavery agitation worked to legitimize the nascent capitalist economy), it throws up a nuanced picture of the Republican party and its precursor, the national Whig organization, as primary agents of bourgeois civilization.[6]

Persuasive though this account may be, it has not gone unassailed. The old image of Republicans as antislavery crusaders remains a powerful one. Embattled liberal members of the late twentieth-century party have drawn on the heritage of Lincoln's Emancipation Proclamation in their efforts to resist the challenge posed by the religious right.[7] Scholars during the civil rights years discovered that the racial achievements of the previous century were largely the work of radical Republicans and lavished fulsome praise upon their efforts.[8] While this generous verdict on the early GOP was initially the work of contemporary partisans and obscures the complex political environment in which the organization originated, it remains a challenge to those who regard the process of history as a series of triumphs for cynical elites.

But perhaps the most persuasive alternative to the class-based analysis of America in the Civil War era is the "modernization synthesis." Samuel P. Hays, Richard D. Brown, and Robert Wiebe agree that it is essential to delineate the social context for political development.[9] However, they reject a Marxian mode of analysis in favor of one that posits that the undeniable transformation of American society between 1790 and 1900 was rooted in scientific and technological progress rather than commercial and industrial growth. Fully aware of the relationship between grass-roots conflict and partisan allegiance, their emphasis is on political culture as a response to the strains imposed by modernization. Hays, for example, contends that the antebellum parties played a vital communalizing role at a time when alternative larger social relationships had not yet emerged.[10]

One of the advantages that this model has over some of its Progressive rivals is that it is better able to cope with the growing influence of ethnic diversity on American life during the course of the nineteenth century. As European immigrants, Catholic and Protestant, flooded into the United States, American parties responded in different ways to the altered electorates that confronted them. Some historians have argued that ethnocultural factors actually defined voter allegiance in many areas of the North after 1830.[11] Neither Hays, Brown, nor Wiebe would agree with this view in its entirety, but clearly their own account of national development has the capacity to embrace social conflict along vertical as well as horizontal lines.

Although the modernization synthesis does not discount the notion of economic cleavage, it does tend toward the consensus school of American historiography on this point. Much of the debate over the progress of the United States during the nineteenth century is concerned with the problem of popular support for capitalism. Whereas Marxist and Progressive historians see the new economy as the primary source of political disaffection among key social groups—notably Southern slaveholders, Northern workingmen, and subsistence farmers throughout the nation—Hays and his colleagues are inclined to insist that most Americans were receptive to the dictates of the market. Thus, while Brown accepts that modernization was an uneven process, he contends that the majority of Northerners, workers as well as farmers, responded positively to the opportunities offered by commercial expansion.[12] Hays, too, insists that Americans were united on capitalist fundamentals. For him what linked voters to the mass parties of the nineteenth century were divergent political cultures produced by scientific progress, commercial growth, and demographic and religious change.[13] The Republicans and Democrats of the third party system were thus divided not so much by capitalism but by different views on how to promote the economic growth of the nation within a capitalist framework.

What follows is an attempt to examine some of the preceding issues through the medium of the early Republican party in Iowa. On the face of things Iowa might seem a distinctly unsatisfactory vehicle with which to undertake this task. It was, after all, a peripheral state of the Union between 1846 and 1878. Its citizens proved loyal defenders of the nation's territorial integrity, but very few of them played a significant role in national politics. As well as being geographically remote from the main power centers in Victorian America, the state was overwhelmingly rural and agricultural, and its ruling Republican organization relatively insignificant in the eyes of eastern party notables.

This said, it is essential not to view nineteenth-century Iowa through modern eyes. Most of the Northern states remained predominantly rural long after Appomattox. In 1860, 40 percent of Northerners lived on farms. Another 30 percent resided in rural communities containing less than twenty-five hundred people.[14] Urbanization and industrialization were proceeding apace in southern New England and portions of the mid-Atlantic region before the Civil War, but the Beards exaggerated the impact of these factors on the antebellum United States. Even in those areas most affected by industrial development, a majority of workers labored in small economic units. The traditional master-apprentice relationship coexisted with the expanding factory system throughout the cities of the Northeast, although the balance between the two was certainly changing in favor of the latter. In economic terms Iowa, with its commercial towns and villages surrounded by agricultural hinterlands, was by no means out of step with the other states of the North. The United States was in flux during the mid-nineteenth century, and few people then could have predicted the extent to which Iowa would eventually be bypassed by the forces of industrialism.

In geopolitical terms early Iowa's real significance lay in its position as a constituent element of the expanding western section of the Union. Most contemporaries, at least those who were willing to set aside their prejudices against newly settled portions of the globe, professed to believe that the destiny of the nation lay in the Mississippi Valley. One perceptive English journalist wrote that the great prairie region was "pre-eminently the country of the future." Centuries would have to pass, he mused, "before absolute want is known in the West by any class, or before it ceases to be the granary of the New World, if not of the Old also."[15]

Many Americans viewed the West through political eyes. Southerners, for example, insisted that free western farmers were their natural allies against the Northeast. Senator Stephen Douglas of Illinois, on the other hand, regarded his adopted home as the potential salvation of the whole country. It was, he said, "the mission of the great Mississippi Valley, the heart and soul of the nation and the continent" to preserve the Union by defusing the North-South conflict with its own vital brand of American nationalism.[16] Admittedly this statement was designed to bolster his own presidential ambitions, but there were sound reasons for his professed optimism.

Between 1820 and 1860 the free West's share of the electoral college vote increased from 6 to 24.1 percent. Over the same period the South's percentage declined from 45.3 to 39.6, the Northeast's from 48.7 to 36.3. Manifestly the burgeoning section was coming to hold the balance of power within the Union. Why, indeed, should it not have used its position to promote national goals? As Douglas well knew and the historian Frederick Jackson Turner later reiterated, the region was being settled by easterners and Southerners. Here the sections came together and supposedly unique American values were being created. The principle on which Douglas built his political career, popular sovereignty, was a western solution to the problem of slavery expansion. Nonsectional in tenor, it should have swept the nation and carried Douglas into the White House. It did neither.

The West did prove to be the arbiter of the sectional struggle, but it helped to save the Union in a manner not envisaged by the Illinoisan. It did so by supplying a Republican president in 1860 and successfully investing the Confederate stronghold of Vicksburg two and a half years later. Douglas correctly perceived that the West might determine the outcome of the sectional conflict. Where he erred was in thinking that such an immature region could do so on its own terms.

Economic backwardness was at the heart of Iowa's problems during the period in question. How the state's political leaders responded to the challenge of growth depended to a very large extent on how the electorate perceived the prospect of development along capitalist lines. If this reads like a paean to American democracy, it should be emphasized that politicians frequently sought to manipulate economic policy-making to their own advantage while simultaneously appearing responsive to the people through the use of a culturally resonant political rhetoric. Yet in truth they could seldom be confident of maintaining popular support in this manner, particularly during an era that witnessed sudden upswings and downturns in the economy. The sectional crisis and the growing strength of evangelical Protestantism, moreover, injected new issues into political debate, forcing party leaders to be even more imaginative in their handling of voter concerns. Those who directed mutable grass-roots fears and demands into popular channels could be sure of obtaining their reward at the polls. Those who misjudged the mood of the electorate at a particular juncture in history—as did the leadership of Iowa's Democratic party during the mid-1850s—could find themselves cast out into the political wilderness.

Notwithstanding the significance of political culture as an element of linkage between voters and party elites, it would be naive to suppose that nineteenth-century Americans responded solely to the rhetoric of their elected representatives. Although they often possessed rank prejudices and harbored deep fears about the locus of power in society, Northerners were a practical people. They demanded action as well as words. Action on the economy, on race, on public morality, and on treason against the federal Union. Regardless of whether the action they demanded was positive or negative, they were, being highly literate in comparison with contemporary Europeans, well able to read the detailed reports of congressional and local legislative debates contained in the newspapers of the day. If a politician voted the wrong way on a specific motion or committed the sometimes graver sin of dodging a controversial issue, the voters were likely to find out sooner rather than later. Access to political information was by no means perfect. Accounts of legislative proceedings were always filtered through the medium of a partisan press and official legislative journals did not contain comprehensive reports of voting behavior. Yet in the context of the time mid-nineteenth-century American politicians had sounder reasons than their counterparts elsewhere to respond to popular pressures with deeds as well as words.

The following chapters trace the initial progress of the Republican party in Iowa. They are based on the conviction that issues such as economic growth and slavery expansion were of vital practical import as well as mere cultural resonance to the local population (including many people, particularly women, who were not members of political society). As Jerome M. Clubb, William H. Flanigan, and Nancy Zingale have suggested, policy formation was central to the political process.[17] Iowa's coalition builders recognized the significance of particular issues and labored hard, both in Des Moines and Washington, to champion those they considered attractive to electoral majorities and to ignore or neutralize those that portended defeat at the polls.

The Republicans succeeded where the Democrats failed because they perceived that after 1854 voters no longer wished the slavery question to be compromised at the expense of Northern rights. They also developed a powerful progressive image by adopting popular stances on key economic and ethnocultural issues such as railroad construction, nativism, and temperance. All of these issues, however, were essentially nonsectional. They were therefore regarded as expendable by Republican leaders who knew that the North-South conflict provided the underlying dynamic for party competition in mid-nineteenth-century America.

The following three chapters of this study chart the origins of Republicanism in Iowa. They reveal how a majoritarian Democratic party lost power because of the declining salience of its traditional issues and failure to respond effectively to the crisis brought on by the opening of Kansas to slavery. That crisis, it is argued, gave birth to the sectionally orientated Republican coalition dedicated to combating the pernicious influence of the South's avowedly despotic and retrograde planter class. Practical and rhetorical support for high-profile issues is shown to have played a major role in paving the way for disparate groups to unite under the banner of nonextension. Chapters 5-8 examine the way Republicans legitimized their rule during the late 1850s and early 1860s. The leadership's attitude to race and railroads is investigated in detail and its pragmatic responses to both viewed as having contributed to intraparty solidarity and the retention of an electoral majority. The Civil War is held to have been the crucible in which lasting voter allegiance to the party was finally forged. Chapters 9-12 describe the means by which Iowa Republicans consolidated their position during the postbellum years when Reconstruction and economic depression might well have brought the Democrats back to power. The emphasis throughout is on the way sectionalism worked to the benefit of men who would never have reaped the rewards of political success without the presence of the "slave power" as an antipodal force in a Manichaean world.

Frank J. Sorauf has described American political parties as "great and overt conspiracies for the capture of public office."[18] This sweeping statement is not entirely borne out by the findings of this study. For although there is plenty of evidence that power hungry elites did attempt to manipulate events to their own advantage during the mid-nineteenth century, it is equally clear that some historians have been too quick to deny that a strong moral imperative contributed to the genesis of the third party system. Try as they might, professional politicians were unable to ignore the fact that within the political society of the day existed a vocal body of opinion opposed to slavery as a sin against God and humanity. Even if it does not provide a complete explanation for the organization's role in the development of the United States, the presence of large numbers of antislavery men in the Republican ranks accounts not only for much of the historical profession's continuing fascination with this subject but also for the party's surprisingly tenacious support for basic black rights. That, however, is to anticipate the discussion in later chapters. Back in the territorial period nothing could have been further from the minds of the vast majority of Iowans than the plight of African-Americans.

1
Origins

2
The Second Party System on the Frontier, 1838–1846

hen President Martin Van Buren signed the act creating Iowa Territory on 12 June 1838 the population of the settled counties on the west bank of the Mississippi numbered just over twenty thousand.[1] Although some of these pioneers had been living in the area as traders and miners for over a decade, most of them had crossed the river after the defeat of the Sauk Indians in 1832. Virgin land was the magnet that drew them to the frontier, for with land went the alluring vision of a prosperous, independent future.

Because U.S. law required that public land be surveyed prior to being offered for sale at auction at the minimum price of $1.25 per acre, white Americans who set up shanties on Iowa soil in the wake of the Black Hawk Purchase were technically squatters. Their primary concern, aside from eking out an initial existence as subsistence farmers, was to protect their claims until the surveying process had been completed and they possessed sufficient cash to afford the purchase price. Predictably the most live political issue in early Iowa was that of preemption rights for settlers, and local politicians (primarily Jacksonian Democrats) were quick to champion what was clearly a popular cause.

Although politicians bombarded the settlers with flattery, the gap between word and deed was enormous. The vast acreage made available for private purchase by a government intent on land disposal rather than land management combined with a capital-starved economy to create favorable conditions for speculation.[2] Notwithstanding the passage of a national preemption act in 1841, large tracts of Iowa grass- and timberland fell into the hands of speculators. Even genuine pioneers who united to form claim clubs were frequently intent not so much on securing a family homestead as on profiteering from the sale of the land to which they staked a claim, for it was common knowledge that land values increased with population density and economic improvements.[3] Merchants and lawyers who had ready access to capital found themselves particularly well placed to take advantage of this equation.

In 1842 the federal government responded to grass-roots expansionist pressure by concluding its final treaty with the Sauk and Fox in Iowa. The Indians ceded 11.8 million acres in central and southern Iowa in return for a lump sum of $800,000, annuities of 5 percent of that amount, limited assumption of Indian debts by the United States, and the dubious guarantee of a new home on the Missouri River or its tributaries.[4] The following spring witnessed the first great land rush in American history as thousands of white settlers broke across the old treaty line to lay claim to some of the most fertile farmland in the world.

It has been estimated that 31.5 percent of buyers purchased nearly three-quarters of Congress land in this the largest of Iowa's Indian cessions. Of this group of more than 12,000 buyers, 9,886 bought up to 600 acres and 2,475 secured acreage above this figure. Some of the largest buyers would play an important role in urban development and later exert an influence on local politics.[5] No doubt these speculators made a positive contribution to the community by providing credit for less-wealthy settlers and swelling the coffers of county treasuries through their payment of taxes. But the fact that large capitalists found it so easy to purchase enormous portions of the public domain indicates that the egalitarian rhetoric of Jacksonian-era politicians masked the central government's abandonment of responsibility for land distribution to affluent middlemen.

Between 1846 and 1851 the United States extinguished the remaining Indian titles to the region bounded by the Mississippi and Missouri rivers. The stage was then set for a steady influx of migrants from the more-settled parts of the republic. By the time Iowa was admitted to the Union in 1846 the state's population was around 150,000. Within eight years it had more than doubled to 326,500.[6] Most of these settlers purchased land from speculators, making use of the credit facilities offered by private individuals and land agents.

During the territorial period the migrants came primarily from the mid-Atlantic states, the Old Northwest, and the upper South. Initially they followed the course of the local river systems, settling along the Mississippi and its major tributaries. This gave them access to rich alluvial land and placed them within easy reach of the oak and hickory forests that grew along the banks of the watercourses. In consequence the first counties to be settled were those in eastern and southern Iowa. Settlement of the open prairies was largely delayed until the advent of the railroad in the 1850s.

The country to which the flatboats and wagons came in the late 1830s and 1840s was fertile beyond the wildest dreams of any Yankee farm boy reared on the rocky soils of New England. True the undulating terrain of southern Iowa did not prove to be as productive as the flat expanses of northern prairie, but the clayey, planosol soil of that region was well able to support a thriving commercial agriculture during the mid-nineteenth century. The climate, though harsh and uninviting during the bitter cold winter months, was a major factor in farm productivity. While frozen ground prevented soil erosion and leaching, heavy spring rains and hot, humid summers provided ideal conditions for cereal (particularly corn) cultivation.

After staking a claim to a tract or tracts of land, the pioneers' primary objectives were to construct a rudimentary shelter for the family group, clear and break the land, then sow crops of wheat and corn in order that they could at least subsist for their first few months in the West. Most of them, however, were not prepared to remain subsistence farmers for very long. The rapid pace of urbanization in southern New England and the mid-Atlantic states (as well as parts of the Midwest itself) had wrought a transformation in the outlook of American farmers by the late 1830s. No longer content with securing a mere living from the soil, increasing numbers of them recognized that the development of a market beyond their immediate locality opened up the prospect of material success. While they did not abandon the Jeffersonian equation of agriculture with independence, their vision of the future was increasingly shaped by the price of farm products on the nascent American and international market.[7]

Although the majority of pioneers were members of farming families, urban growth constituted a significant factor in the development of the territory. Dubuque, a center of the old lead-mining district on the Upper Mississippi, and Burlington, the territorial capital until 1841, led the way in this respect, but other river towns, notably Keokuk, Bloomington (Muscatine), Davenport, and Clinton, grew up quickly as entrepôts for local food commodities and incoming supplies. These principal towns (harboring, for the most part, populations of less than ten thousand until after the Civil War) and smaller urban communities such as Fort Madison and Ottumwa were therefore integral cogs in what was, throughout the last two-thirds of the nineteenth century, a predominantly agricultural economy.

The importance of the river towns in early Iowa was social as well as economic. From the outset each of them was dominated by a small and relatively wealthy elite that took the lead in trying to ensure that their adopted home did not fall behind its rivals in the race to dominate the trade of the backcountry. Most members of this privileged group were either merchants or lawyers. Some were self-made; others had inherited their wealth or at least had the advantage of a college education in one of the older states. Virtually all speculated extensively in western land and town lots—the latter an increasingly profitable exercise as population pressures built up on the urban frontier.

Iowa's urban elite did not constitute an exclusive social class, for Northern society was more fluid than ever before owing to spatial expansion and economic diversification. Nevertheless, greater access to wealth, education, and status enabled local merchants and lawyers to exercise an inordinate influence on the communities in which they dwelt. The primary means by which they made this influence felt was involvement in political life.

During the late 1830s Iowa was a frontier bastion of Jacksonian Democracy. This was hardly surprising, for at that time Martin Van Buren's Democratic party was the country's dominant political force.

The popularity of Jacksonian Democracy was grounded in the expansive worldview that it embodied. Reflecting the self-confidence and insecurity of a chosen race breaking down with miraculous speed the barriers imposed by geography, custom, and technological backwardness, Democratic ideology lauded the sovereignty of the people, the primacy of the individual, and the role of negative government in preserving battle-won liberties. By identifying the Bank of the United States as a prime source of corruption within the nation, Andrew Jackson had successfully defined his party's role as the defender of true republicanism against the potential tyranny of the "money power." It was a popular stance, for symbols of corruption, decay, and arbitrary power were potent ones for a people reared on tales of patriot heroes and warnings of the fragility of historical republics. Urging constant vigilance as a solution to the problem of internal subversion and adept at using class-war rhetoric to berate their "aristocratic" opponents, Jacksonians successfully portrayed themselves as the only reliable conservators of the Revolutionary faith.

Aside from the crucial fact that Democracy was at one with the zeitgeist, Jacksonianism in Iowa was bolstered by federal patronage and support given to preemption by prominent western members of the party, particularly Senator Thomas Hart Benton of Missouri. Iowa Whigs, branded conservatives, aristocrats, and Federalists by their opponents, were poorly placed to take popular ground on preemption because of the national party's support for public land distribution to the states rather than to squatters.

However, after a succession of Jacksonian victories at the polls in the late 1830s, Democratic hegemony in Iowa began to come under threat. The occasion for this turn of events was the presidential campaign of 1840.

Although the citizens of U.S. territories were not permitted to vote in national elections, those resident on the west bank of the Upper Mississippi were no less excited by the famous Harrison–Van Buren contest than their fellow Americans in the states. The election, fought as it was against a backdrop of economic depression, promoted voter mobilization on an unprecedented scale throughout the country.[8]

The Democrats were the first to respond to the demands of the hour by pressing a series of blatantly partisan resolutions in the 1840 assembly. These lauded the recent message of President Martin Van Buren on the need for an independent subtreasury in which to deposit federal revenues, expressed support for the Little Magician's efforts to combat the depression with tight monetary policies, and praised the administration's stance on western settlement as "liberal beyond example."[9] The popularity of preemption with Iowa voters prevented Whigs from uniting against the resolves, but fewer than half their number in the house could bring themselves to vote in favor of passage.[10]

On 10 June southeast Iowa Whigs gathered at Wapello to commence battle. A local lawyer, Francis Springer, introduced resolutions that charged the Democrats with lighting the "smouldering fires" of party in the territory and throwing down "the gauntlet of defiance" at the feet of their opponents.[11] The Whigs, however, made no attempt to disguise their own partisan commitments. Recognizing the importance of swift organization, they appointed a committee of five to write to political friends in other parts of Iowa on the subject of holding a territorial Whig convention later in the summer. Predictably the presidential candidacy of General William Henry Harrison was endorsed in no uncertain terms.

Pursuant to this gathering and two similar ones in Des Moines and Muscatine counties, a "Congress of the People" assembled in Bloomington on 29 July. In spite of the high-sounding label, most of those present were prominent Iowa Whig politicians. No platform was adopted, but the delegates nominated a candidate for the territory's representative to Congress, appointed a central committee of five to oversee party organization, and directed another group of individuals to draft an address to the public. Whigs throughout the territory were urged to appoint committees of vigilance and correspondence.[12]

The hard cider and log cabin campaign run by American Whigs in 1840 was long seen as the artful response of conservative politicians to the imperatives of the new democratic era. More recently, however, scholars have begun to argue that the second party system was underpinned by divergent cultural and economic orientations among Whigs and Democrats. Jacksonian-era voters are now generally held to have responded consciously to the political rhetoric and specific policy stances of the major parties.

Whiggery is not an easy phenomenon to define. The best description of its earliest adherents is that they were opponents of the Jacksonian Democracy (although some of them had originally been members of that organization during the late 1820s and early 1830s). The Whig party as it emerged in the course of the latter decade was thus a complex amalgam of disaffected elite politicians, Southern nullifiers, National Republicans, Anti-Masonic evangelical Protestants, and, perhaps most significantly of all, ordinary American voters alarmed by what they saw as the disastrous impact of Jacksonian monetary policy on the national economy. Significantly most Whigs held the Democrats responsible for the crash of 1837 and the serious depression that followed it. Their party's fortunes during the late 1830s waxed and waned with the state of the economy. Three-fifths of new voters joined the ranks of the anti-Jacksonian coalition at this time primarily because they believed Whiggery offered the best hope of material regeneration.[13]

Whereas Democrats trumpeted the virtues of negative government and located the money power as the principal source of corruption in American society, their opponents believed that individual and national energies could best be released by judicious government support for economic endeavors. Whigs, therefore, were strong proponents of positive action on the part of state and federal governments. Specifically they backed the retention of a national bank to regulate the currency, the creation of an extensive transportation network funded by the sale of public lands, and the passage of a high tariff to protect nascent American industry from British imports. Confronted by the spectre of bank failures and economic stagnation, many voters regarded forthright government action as a much better option than Van Buren's commitment to an independent subtreasury.

Almost entirely undeveloped in 1840, Iowa was not as seriously affected by the depression as the states. Nonetheless, the Whig address (drafted by, among others, a young Burlington lawyer named James W. Grimes) concentrated its fire on the economic failings of the incumbent national administration. This prolix document reviewed what the Whigs regarded as the irresponsible financial policies of the Democracy and denounced Van Burenism as a threat to national prosperity. "All the evils," it concluded, "to be apprehended from a continuance of the present dominant party in power, and the good that we believe will result to the nation by the election of Gen. Harrison to the Presidency, we share in common with our fellow citizens throughout the country."[14]

In the late summer of 1840 Iowa Whigs discovered that their distinctive brand of economic nationalism was at last beginning to take root on the prairies: for the first (and as it turned out, only) time, they won control of the territory's upper house or council. And when Harrison was elected president later in the year, paving the way for the appointment of a Whig as territorial governor, the party at last seemed to be on the verge of gaining the ascendancy.

Yet Whiggery in Iowa never lived up to the promise of 1840. Internal bickering and a lack of genuinely popular issues rendered it a minority political force for more than a decade. To a large extent the same was true nationally. Harrison died after a month in office, leaving Vice-President John Tyler, a states' rights Virginian, to obstruct the party's program for economic recovery. By the mid-1840s returning prosperity and an expansionist war against Mexico had combined with internal Whig dissension to place Democracy in the driving seat once again.

Ostensibly the most significant issue in territorial Iowa was that of statehood. On the wisdom of this the parties had differing views. Democrats were generally united in favor of the region's swift admission into the Union. In relatively firm control of the local government, they had nothing to fear and everything—so far as patronage was concerned—to gain from statehood. Thus the Jacksonian governor, Robert Lucas (1838–41), had no qualms in seeking to promote that end during his two years in office. Iowa Whigs were less enthusiastic. Their own minority status impelled them to oppose statehood until they could monopolize the plums of office that accompanied membership of the Union. Thus they remained content with the territory's semicolonial status, while simultaneously laboring to build on the successes of 1840.

Given their opposition to statehood, it was ironic that the only Whig governor of Iowa Territory, John Chambers, proved to be an ardent advocate of the measure. Appointed to the executive office by President Harrison, Chambers, a Kentuckian who had once served under the general, appears to have viewed his role in terms of the national welfare rather than the good of the local party. After his former commander's death, moreover, he was the servant of a president for whom most regular Whigs had only utter contempt. Both of these factors brought him into conflict with his copartisans in the territory.

Internally divided and outgunned though they appeared to be on the statehood issue, local Whigs were aided by majority support among the electorate. Anticipating an increase in taxes if federal funds for territorial government were withdrawn, Iowans twice defeated proposals for the holding of a constitutional convention during the early 1840s, thereby thwarting the plans of the executive. In 1844, however, backed by another recommendation from Chambers, the voters finally went to the polls to elect delegates to a prestatehood convention. As the Whigs had feared all along, most of the successful candidates were Democrats and many provisions of the resulting constitution unmistakably Jacksonian. Once again the people came to their rescue. When Congress insisted that Iowa be admitted with reduced boundaries, they responded to Whig and minority Democrat opposition by defeating statehood 7,019 to 6,023. This setback was an embarrassing one for Augustus C. Dodge, the territorial delegate who had acquiesced in the congressional maneuver. But with the help of Dodge's ally Stephen Douglas Iowa Democrats secured the passage of a revised bill making the Missouri River the western boundary of the new state. In May 1846 a second constitutional convention (again dominated by Democrats) accepted Congress's revised terms and on 3 August the voters endorsed statehood by a margin of 456 out of more than 18,000 votes. The Whigs had fought hard, but ultimately their attempts to control local patronage and policy had proved unsuccessful. Iowa entered the Union as a Democratic state.[15]

The closeness of the statehood contest masked the underlying weakness of the Whig position in Iowa. For beneath the debates over boundaries and taxes lay the real issues of the day. Those subjects that infused the second party system with such tremendous vitality were centered on the economic development of the republic.

Superficially Iowa Whigs were in a good position to dominate this field during the late territorial period. Westerners were clamorous for material progress, and the Whigs had the policies to match this demand. Yet even though economic issues were the driving force behind the politics of the early 1840s, Frank Springer and his allies failed to benefit from their promotion of banks, credit, and internal improvement ventures. Why was this the case and what light does the early debate over these topics shed on the nature of the second party system in Iowa?

One of the most live issues in frontier Iowa was banking. The first settlers, market orientated as most of them were, quickly discovered that business transactions required the existence of reliable financial institutions and a sound currency. As early as December 1836 one citizen complained that "[w]e have no Banking facilities & our territory is flooded with Bills on all the eastern Banks. . . . If we must have Bills give us Banks of our own."[16] Shortly afterwards Congress responded to such protests by chartering the Miners' Bank of Dubuque. Designed primarily to serve the interests of laborers and merchants in the lead-mining district, this institution furnished a much-needed circulating medium for the entire region. In 1839, however, it was caught up in the general economic depression, and by March 1841 the bank's officers had ordered a suspension of specie payments.[17] Just as two-party competition was beginning in earnest, the problem of the Miners' Bank's future arrived to test the mettle of aspiring politicians.

Between 1842 and 1845 local Whigs and Democrats became embroiled in a fierce struggle to determine the institution's fate. Imbued with memories of Jackson's fight against the Bank of the United States and, in many cases, convinced that financial institutions were responsible for the economic depression, the Democrats strove to repeal the bank's charter on the grounds that suspension of specie payments was illegal. The Whigs, on the other hand, contended that banks were essential to the prosperity of the territory. In spite of compelling evidence that the Dubuque concern had not fulfilled its legal requirements, they fought a determined rearguard action to protect what they saw as both a practical institution and an important symbol of their political philosophy. By 1845 it was clear that their efforts had been in vain. The Miners' Bank displayed no signs of recovering with the improved economic climate, and it was deeply unpopular with the voters. Equipped with overwhelming superiority in both chambers of the assembly, the Democrats moved quickly to repeal the charter. Even the handful of Whigs in the lower house could not bring themselves to defend a now moribund institution.[18]

Democrats at the previous year's constitutional convention held at Iowa City (capital of the territory since 1841) had already responded to ideological and political demands by requiring all bank charters to be ratified directly by the people before becoming law. Enervated by defeat of the "monster bank" at Dubuque, radical Democrats in the 1846 convention succeeded in placing a stringent prohibition against the creation of banks in the first state constitution. The Whigs' worst nightmares had come true.

Throughout the extended debate over the status of financial institutions in territorial Iowa, most Whigs contended that banking was an integral feature of economic life in the nineteenth century and that to obstruct this essential activity was to hamper the material prospects of the region. Many thousands of words were written and spoken on the subject in the course of the argument, but none were more potent than those of William Penn Clarke, a prominent Iowa City lawyer and journalist.[19] In a public letter of July 1846 Clarke summarized the arguments of his party against the proposed state constitution and the antibank clause that it incorporated.

The central tenet of Clarke's communication was that if the new constitution was adopted it would "prove greatly detrimental, if not entirely ruinous to the nearest and dearest interests of the people, by retarding the growth of the proposed State, in population, wealth and prosperity." The primary reason for this was the prohibition against banks. The latter, he urged, were "the inventions of trade . . . not only in all the States of this Union, but in every civilized nation of any commercial or political importance." Although like most Whigs Clarke believed in the advantages of a soundly backed paper currency over specie, he was astute enough to recognize that the Democrats had had the better of this issue in the past. Neatly sidestepping the controversy, he contended that the central question was not the "abstract" one of whether Iowa should have a specie-based currency, but whether or not the state should have banks and a currency of its own creation. Left to the tender mercies of foreign shinplasters Iowa would become "the plunder ground of the Union." With banks of its own, however, the region would attract desperately needed development capital to break up the virgin prairies. Counseled Clarke, "Where money is plenty, there labor is amply rewarded, and all classes of society flourish."[20]

Because William Penn Clarke was one of the founding fathers of Iowa's Republican party in the mid-1850s, his views on economic policy are particularly significant. It is true that the Marylander was far from being a principled ideologue. He and his political associates undoubtedly saw the bank issue as the best way of preventing their opponents from gaining control of the prospective state government. Nonetheless, it is important to recognize that the vast majority of leading Iowa Whigs, Clarke included, adhered to their faith in banks when they became Republicans. As propounded here, Clarke's ideas were perfectly illustrative of the deep-rooted conviction among Iowa Whigs that government encouragement of private capital offered the best hope of prosperity and social harmony in the future.

Notwithstanding their radical stance on banking in 1846, Iowa Democrats were less united on the subject than their opponents. Ultimately the war against the Miners' Bank won the support of most erstwhile Jacksonians, but this was owing primarily to the fact that the institution was rotten to the core and its destruction a popular cause. The blanket prohibition of all banks of issue proved to be a more contentious topic.

In the second week of the 1844 constitutional convention, delegates debated a majority report from the committee on incorporations proposing the creation of a state bank. Because the Whigs occupied less than a third of the seats in the chamber, they could do little except encourage divisions within the majority. The first to speak was Stephen Hempstead, a young Jacksonian lawyer from Dubuque. After moving that the convention adopt a minority report supporting a constitutional interdict against banking, Hempstead backed his position by contending that banks of issue were objectionable because they encouraged inflation and speculation through their circulation of "fictitious" paper currency. "Miners, farmers, and others, created; the Banks only traded and speculated upon what had been created," said the Dubuquer.[21] His populist stance was supported by other Democrats, one of whom denominated banks in general "a set of swindling machines."[22]

This was too much for those Jacksonians who distinguished between monster banks and well-regulated financial institutions set up to promote economic growth. Ex-governor Robert Lucas argued that the question was one of expediency—that while he was generally opposed to banks he was not in favor of tying the legislature's hands on the matter.[23] One of his colleagues agreed. Prohibiting banks was not, said a Lee County Democrat, a test of party loyalty.[24] Perilously close to ideological heresy for some Jacksonians, this assertion was immediately rebutted. "[I]f banking was not the rock on which the two parties split in this country," said another Dubuquer, Francis Gehon, "he was mistaken up to this age of his life."[25]

Faced with the prospect of a damaging party split on this central issue, the Democrats agreed to a compromise solution requiring popular consent to be given to individual banking corporations. Since Jacksonians were traditionally skeptical of the representative principle, this move could be defended comfortably as an extension of political democracy. The defeat of the first constitution, however, and the subsequent election of a second convention in 1846 returned the issue to the debating chamber. On this occasion probank Democrats were forced to accept prohibition after the radicals and minority Whigs worked successfully (for very different reasons) to defeat their proposals for limited banking.[26] In reality what appears on paper to have been a confident act of political faith on the part of Iowa's Democracy was a product of the need for internal party unity on an issue of crucial practical and symbolic importance.

The split within the ruling Jacksonian organization appears to corroborate the view that antebellum Democrats were divided between conservatives who acquiesced relatively happily in the development of the new market-dominated economy, and antientrepreneurial radicals who feared that the paraphernalia of liberal capitalism would have a destructive impact on republican virtues.[27]

One problem with this analysis is that it posits the existence of a fundamental cleavage within the Democratic party over progress along capitalist lines. While it is true that the national Jacksonian coalition did include substantial numbers of agrarian radicals (especially in the eastern cities and slave states), debates in Iowa indicate that the primary source of division, at least among western Democrats, was privilege rather than capitalism. What concerned many antibank Democrats in the Upper Mississippi Valley was the granting of special favors to promote development. As Jonathan C. Hall, an opponent of the state bank measure introduced into the 1844 constitutional convention, remarked, "The privilege of being equal is the only privilege that this State should ever sanction."[28] He objected not to the business of banking per se but to the creation of specially favored institutions like the Miners' Bank. In Hall's view the task of Democrats like himself was to create an economic environment in which laissez-faire rules would work to prevent speculation and ensure equality of opportunity for all white settlers, regardless of their status in life. Their aim, in short, was to democratize not to abolish capitalism.

One way to illustrate how this objective divided Whigs from Democrats and radicals from conservatives is to examine their divergent attitudes to business corporations in general.

The development of Iowa's virgin prairies was a key issue in local politics from the earliest days of settlement. The antibank Democrat Stephen Hempstead made that perfectly clear in a patriotic oration on 4 July 1836. The territory, he told Dubuquers, was already dotted with flourishing villages and thriving farms: "That spirit of enterprise which pervades our country, and which moves so swiftly upon the rail-way of time, is here seen to travel with a velocity heretofore unknown to any government."[29] As if to prove the accuracy of this observation, the existing territorial seal depicting a miner's forearm, pick in hand, and broken rocks on the ground, was quickly replaced by one highlighting symbols of river traffic and a prosperous-looking farmer equipped with horse-drawn plow.[30]

Delegates to the first Iowa legislature (1838–39) were as committed to economic progress as Hempstead. From one house committee came a memorial urging Congress to appropriate funds for the survey of local rivers flowing into the Mississippi. The latter, urged the committee's report, "furnishes all that part of our population, who live near its banks, a great highway for the transportation of their surplus produce and for the importation of whatever must necessarily be brought from a foreign market."[31] As well as asking the federal government for developmental aid, the assembly passed a number of practical measures designed to promote growth at home. One of these, an act to incorporate the Burlington and Des Moines Transportation Company, anticipated future railroad legislation by permitting the enterprise to take control of private property on the grounds that it furthered the public good. A majority of Democrats in both chambers supported the bill (which retained legislative control over the charter), although in the lower house six Jacksonians refused to give it their sanction. Whig backing for the scheme was virtually unanimous.[32]

In the course of the next six years the territorial assembly passed several laws chartering joint-stock corporations. While most of these measures met with stiff resistance from radical Jacksonians, they were generally pushed through by a combination of Whigs and conservative Democrats eager to encourage economic diversification. As long as the legislature reserved the power to repeal or amend the charters granted, conservatives were prepared to grant the privileges asked for by the incorporators. The Whig minority, less inclined to favor the insertion of repeal clauses for fear of alienating potential investors, acquiesced to their inclusion in order to defeat what it regarded as the ruinous policy of the radical "locofocos."

Although radical Democrats made no secret of their opposition to special privileges, their actions and public pronouncements revealed a strong commitment to laissez-faire commercial capitalism. In 1843 the territorial house debated a number of developmental measures. Among them were a resolution asserting the legislature's duty to encourage home manufactures and two bills, one to incorporate the Scott County Hydraulic Company (a manufacturing concern given wide powers to take water from the Mississippi), the other to fix the maximum rate of interest allowed on contracts. While Whigs and conservative Democrats displayed a pronounced enthusiasm for the first two measures, a core group of five radicals (one-third of the Jacksonian delegation in the chamber) voted against both of them.[33] On the usury bill a different pattern emerged. Whereas a majority of the Whig-conservative bloc opposed raising the interest rate ceiling, the locofocos gave the initiative their support.[34]

The reason for the radicals' stance on this matter was made plain by one of their spokesmen, Thomas Rogers, chairman of the Jacksonian-controlled judiciary committee to which the usury bill had been referred. In an unusually frank report Rogers stated the committee's belief that usury laws were injurious to borrower and lender alike, unenforceable in practice, and easily evaded. His main point was that interest rates could not be artificially regulated in a modern economy:

> Money, like every other exchangeable commodity, is subject to frequent fluctuation in value, being no more uniform in price, than cotton, tobacco, and other great staples of the country. Its worth depends on the state of the market, and is regulated by the great law of demand and supply. There is no more reason for arbitrarily establishing the rate for the use of money, than for the use of houses, lands, merchandize, and other property.[35]

It had long been settled policy, continued Rogers, to allow every person to accumulate property upon such terms as they could obtain. Why not apply the same principle to money? "Individuals are presumed to understand their own business better than legislatures. It will be soon enough for these grave bodies to interfere with private rights, and assume the control of the personal matters of others, when the people shall have proven themselves incompetent to manage their own affairs."[36]

This lucid articulation of radical Jacksonian ideology, accompanied by the locofocos' backing for Rogers's compromise proposition to double the interest rate ceiling to 20 percent, constitutes further evidence that laissez-faire, not agrarianism, was at the heart of antebellum Northern Democracy. Its avowed intent was to liberate Americans from burdensome legislation and privileged corporations, thereby enabling them to prosper materially within the framework of the market. Small wonder that this philosophy proved so popular with the independent-minded, entrepreneurial farming people of Iowa during the increasingly prosperous 1840s.

Although economic issues held sway throughout the territorial period, there was another dimension to party competition in early Iowa. Ethnocultural, rather than class based, this dimension was a facet of the intense religiosity of American society before the Civil War. Energized by the long series of revivals known collectively as the Second Great Awakening, evangelical Protestantism had taken a firm grip on the United States by 1840. In a rapidly changing social universe the promise of individual salvation via the traumatic experience of conversion held out the prospect of an ordered and useful life on earth. Practical people though they were, many of Iowa's first settlers were members of, or quickly absorbed into, the chief evangelical denominations of the day. In terms of sheer numbers the Methodists, Presbyterians, and Baptists led the way, followed rather a long way behind by Congregationalists and Quakers.[37] Determined to remake the world in their own image and to purge society as well as individuals of sin, these groups were destined to have a major impact on local politics.

Between 1838 and 1846 the second party system in Iowa contained the moral issues generated by crusading Protestants. One of the main reasons for this was the initial primacy of economic subjects. Banking, light manufacturing, and infrastructural development preoccupied politicians and voters alike largely to the exclusion of antislavery and temperance. This was not simply because such material topics were of more immediate relevance to a frontier community but also because the ideologies of the major parties were based on contrasting (if by no means irreconcilable) socioeconomic philosophies. Since their electoral constituencies transcended sectional and religious allegiances, it was also in the interest of party leaders to direct voter concerns into safe political channels. A final reason for the secondary importance of ethnocultural issues in the territory was the lack of institutional backing for moral reform. Local prohibitionists and antislavery activists lagged behind Whigs and Jacksonians in forming the political organizations necessary to mobilize individuals in a democratic age.

Yet while moral causes made no appearance in the earliest party platforms, evangelical Protestants were far from inactive during the territorial period. Prior to statehood their main concern was to create the ideal moral climate for the growth of a Christian society on the frontier. As the eastern denominations were flooding the West with pioneer ministers, western evangelicals petitioned their representatives for measures to prohibit gambling, Sabbath breaking, and even the keeping of stallions within sight of decent townsfolk.

At first, leaders of both major parties evinced a readiness to respond to pressure from perfectionists or to the dictates of their own conscience. In the winter of 1838–39 Governor Robert Lucas, a Democrat and practicing Congregationalist, appealed successfully for a law to ban gaming in the territory.[38] Four years later an additional measure to suppress gambling received majority backing from Whigs and Democrats in the legislature.[39]

Because locofocos regarded evangelical attempts to remold society as another dangerous threat to the rights of individuals, their increasing influence within the Iowa Democracy portended a swift breakdown of the initial consensus over moral issues. The gaming act of 1843 would never have been passed had not nonradical Democrats united with the Whigs to force it through the house of representatives. There was no rigid correlation between radical Jacksonianism and opposition to puritanical measures, but a trend in that direction was visible by the early 1840s. The core radicals in the 1843 house refused to vote not only for the gaming act but also a bill designed to protect the sanctity of the Sabbath.[40] Incensed by the majority's wording of the latter as an act to prevent "immoral practices," Thomas Rogers moved to add the words, "And to violate the Constitution of the United States and the rights of conscience."[41] The following year over 80 percent of Democrats in the first constitutional convention voted against a Whig motion that proceedings should be opened by prayer.[42] Haunted by the prospect of an antibusiness, deist constitution, Ralph P. Lowe of Muscatine, a millennial Presbyterian and future Republican governor, rose to denounce the opposition. "[T]he time would soon come," he was reported as saying, "when men of proper moral and religious sentiments would alone hold the offices of this country."[43]

The strength of rationalist, laissez-faire Jacksonianism in Iowa did much to undermine the influence of evangelicals like Lucas within the Democratic party. But in truth Whiggery was always likely to attract the greater number of moral reformers into its ranks. Once the perfectionist impulse had taken root among America's Arminian as well as Calvinist denominations, the party that offered evangelicals the best hope of reforming society through government action was bound to attract their support. Whereas the Democrats promised to create a liberal state in which white men were free to exercise their earthly talents in whatever directions they pleased, their opponents held out a vision of a more organic, regulated, and structured society in which conformity rather than license would hold sway. Whereas the Jacksonians sought to achieve their goals by keeping government intervention to an absolute minimum, Whigs regarded positive legislative action as an essential concomitant of private initiative. As Protestants began to crusade increasingly vociferously and professionally for temperance and antislavery reform, they naturally turned to the Whig party to enact the kind of legislation that would further their aims. In combination with an upsurge in sectionalism and a decline in salience of economic issues, ethnocultural divisions would soon play a major role in the destruction of the second party system and the rise of the Republican party.

3
Defeat of the Democracy, 1846–1854

ix months before Iowa entered the Union in December 1846 the United States declared war on Mexico. Within two years American troops under Generals Zachary Taylor and Winfield Scott had brought their sister republic to its knees, forcing it to surrender a massive tract of land in the Southwest that encompassed modern California, New Mexico, Arizona, Utah, Nevada, and Colorado. The victory, however, was to prove a costly one. In August 1846 a Pennsylvania Democrat, David Wilmot, introduced into the U.S. House of Representatives a joint resolution prohibiting the expansion of slavery into any territory seized from Mexico. By establishing the primacy of the slavery question in national politics, Wilmot opened up a Pandora's box of sectional tensions that would undermine Democratic hegemony and ultimately lead to civil war.

Reactions in Iowa to the Mexican War were determined largely by the fact that the conflict was masterminded by the Democratic administration of President James K. Polk. While taking care not to criticize the bravery of American soldiers, Whigs were generally united in their condemnation of the war as unjust and mismanaged.[1] Democrats, on the other hand, denounced their opponents as disloyal and lauded the supposedly humane and Christian manner in which the war was being waged.[2] On the whole they had the better of the argument, for a majority of Iowans shared the general western enthusiasm for Manifest Destiny—the notion that the United States had an almost divine mission to occupy the North American continent.

Internally the parties were less united on the Wilmot Proviso than they were on the war itself. Both organizations possessed free-soil wings. That belonging to the Whigs was of a decidedly more antislavery character than its Democratic counterpart. Even though the Whig party contained large numbers of migrants from the border states, many of these people had little affection for slavery and had come to Iowa to escape the debilitating competition of slave labor. Being opposed to the expansion of the peculiar institution, however, was not the same as being in favor of heightening sectional tensions. Large numbers of free-soil as well as conservative Whigs balked at endangering the Union and offending their Southern copartisans. The result was a determination on the part of Whig leaders to avoid controversy. Early in 1847 the organization's legislative caucus at Iowa City backed the presidential candidacy of General Zachary Taylor, a Louisiana slaveholder without known views on the Proviso.[3] Taylor's military exploits during the war were enough to make him the favorite choice of a party whose chief objective was the seizure of political power in 1848.

While many Democrats were scarcely less appalled by the prospect of slavery expansion than their opponents, party leaders like Augustus C. Dodge and George W. Jones were unwilling to support a measure vigorously opposed by their president and powerful Southern copartisans. These staunch supporters of the Polk administration were experienced midwestern politicians whose election to the U.S. Senate was delayed until December 1848 by a complex wrangle in the Iowa legislature. Determined to protect the integrity of the national party and unashamedly racist in outlook, they undoubtedly played a major role in preventing the assembly at Iowa City from passing a resolution in support of the Wilmot Proviso. Their efforts enabled them to pose as defenders of sectional harmony during a period of acute crisis for the Union, but undermined attempts by Democrats at home to bid for the support of independent free-soilers. To understand who these free-soilers were and why they were of such significance to Iowa politics, we must examine the local impact of the race question in more detail.

The vast majority of Iowa's first settlers had little affection for slavery, but even less for black people themselves. Migrating beyond the Mississippi they brought with them the cultural as well as the partisan prejudices of the eastern states. Racism was endemic throughout Jacksonian America. Enslaved in the South, deprived of substantive civil and political rights in most Northern states, and legally excluded from much of the Old Northwest, blacks were held in low esteem by their white contemporaries. Free blacks were particularly despised. They resided in the ghettos of the urban North, mired in poverty and often deprived of rudimentary educational opportunities. Their condition made a mockery of America's vaunted enthusiasm for meritocracy, yet few whites were prepared to take even faltering steps to improve the lot of a population generally viewed as degraded. For the most part free blacks were shunned by a society unwilling to live up to its fine ideals.

Party politics offered Northern blacks little hope during the 1830s and 1840s. Aside from New York (where propertied blacks were enfranchised) and a handful of New England states, they did not possess the right to vote. Those who could exercise that privilege generally voted the Whig ticket, for the simple reason that virulent racism was an integral component of Jacksonian Democracy. Although stridently egalitarian in tone, the latter was built on a foundation of racial exclusivity. The fact that blacks were enslaved or confined to the bottom of the social scale helped Jacksonians to posit that white American society was made up of independent and theoretically equal individuals. Their close affiliation with urban workingmen (the class of men whose position in the labor market was most threatened by the presence of free blacks) strengthened the Democrats' reliance on white supremacy, as indeed did the increasing strength of Southern influence within the party.

Northern Whiggery was less dependent on racism because its hierarchical and organic conception of society proved more able to accept the presence of racial minorities within the American polity. Because Whigs did not presume to believe that all white people were equal, they felt less need to trumpet the claims of a chosen race that they knew to be tarnished by the excesses of levelers and atheists. However, while close links with crusading Protestantism further weakened their reliance on racism, Whigs seldom took positive steps to improve the lot of American blacks. At best their attitude was patronizing; at worst, it was wholly indifferent to the plight of a downtrodden people.

The territorial census of 1838 recorded the presence of 188 blacks on the west bank of the Upper Mississippi. Fearing major additions to this total, the first Iowa legislature moved quickly to limit the ability of blacks to cross the river. "An Act to regulate Blacks and Mulattoes" was passed by the assembly in the winter of 1838-39 apparently with bipartisan support.[4] This statute required all blacks entering Iowa to produce legal proof of their freedom and to post bond of $500. It also required blacks entering Iowa illegally to be hired out for six months, permitted slaveholders to pass through the territory, and denied the right of appeal to persons claimed as fugitive slaves. Modeled primarily on the Indiana exclusion law of 1831, the statute was designed to prevent Iowa from becoming a haven for free blacks or a dumping ground for manumitted slaves.[5]

Although there was little support for slavery in early Iowa, only one group of whites sought to improve conditions for local blacks during the territorial period. These were abolitionists who resided in a cluster of villages in the agricultural hinterland of Burlington. One of the most important of these antislavery communities was the Congregational stronghold of Denmark in Des Moines County.⁶ Inhabited largely by New England migrants, Denmark quickly became a center of crusading Puritan morality on the prairies. The driving figure behind this development was a Yale-educated pioneer minister named Asa Turner. Originally dispatched to the West by the American Home Missionary Society, Turner proved to be a determined foe of sin in all its earthly guises. Of these the gravest was human bondage. Slavery, Turner was once heard to say, was "a cancer eating out the life of our body politic. *There is no remedy for it but the knife.*"⁷ Throughout his long career spreading the gospel of Congregationalism, the Yankee preacher worked to foster a spirit of grass-roots hostility to the South's peculiar institution—an endeavor that led him inevitably into the unholy realm of power politics.

Religion was the prime source of antislavery sentiment in four other Iowa villages. Salem in Henry County was founded by Southern-born Indiana Quakers in the mid-1830s. Heavily influenced by the immediatist traditions of their sect and the Garrisonian critique of slavery, a group of local Friends followed the example of the Denmark Congregationalists by forming a village antislavery society in February 1841. Two years later, the Salem men withdrew from the existing communion and set up their own antislavery meetinghouse in the village. Like Asa Turner, the Salem minister Thomas Frazier was a leading figure in Iowa's early abolition movement.

Three predominantly Presbyterian communities completed the territory's antislavery vanguard: the Associate Reformed (Seceder) village of Crawfordsville in Washington County, and the more orthodox settlements in the towns of Washington and Yellow Spring in Des Moines County. Here too local clergymen were instrumental in spreading the gospel of immediatism.

Aside from the involvement of Old School Presbyterians in Yellow Spring, the common link between these antislavery activists was a commitment to what ethnocultural historians have labeled pietistic religion—that is, an evangelical Protestant faith characterized by inner spirituality rather than an emphasis on liturgy and outward conformity.⁸ Their hatred of slavery was engendered by a profound conviction that salvation was open to everyone and that people had no right to hold despotic sway over the minds and bodies of their fellow human beings, all of whom had equal moral responsibilities in the sight of God. The relatively democratic form of church organization that prevailed among Quakers, Congregationalists, and Presbyterians increased the chances—though it did not guarantee—that members of these denominations would be at the forefront of the abolitionist crusade. Confronted by the need to preserve harmony within their transsectional communions, Methodist and Episcopalian hierarchies were less likely to acquiesce to antislavery preaching on the part of their ministers. Only when the Civil War undermined the necessity for intradenominational compromise did Iowa's dominant Methodist church join the evangelical phalanx against slavery.

In common with their eastern colleagues Iowa's first antislavery activists were committed opponents not only of slavery but also of the deep-rooted racial prejudice that was believed to bolster it. It was hardly surprising, therefore, that the 1839 regulatory act quickly became a target of their wrath. During the early 1840s abolitionists petitioned the legislature for the law's repeal. They found little support at the capital. Only a handful of predominantly Whig representatives from their own districts displayed any inclination to brook popular racism.[9]

Unimpressed by the assembly's negative response to their memorials, antislavery activists from southeast Iowa gathered at Yellow Spring in October 1843 to form a territorial abolition society. As opponents of the anticlerical immediatism practiced by the followers of the Massachusetts editor, William Lloyd Garrison, the assembled insurgents rejected a resolution stating that abolitionists could not belong to churches "not found in active opposition to slavery."[10] Instead they adopted declarations asserting the unconstitutionality of the peculiar institution and requiring abolitionists to abandon their existing partisan attachments. With the formation of separate antislavery parties already well underway in the Northern states, these moves pointed toward the swift organization of a Liberty organization in Iowa.

In fact it took four years for local abolitionists to found an independent party. There were several reasons why they lagged behind their colleagues elsewhere. Lack of sympathizers and funds helped to delay the project. So too did the fact that Iowa had no say in the 1844 presidential election (an important focus for Liberty party organization in the states). Most significant of all, however, was probably the reluctance of most antislavery men to obey the abolition society's dictate to sever existing party ties. Throughout the Northern states a substantial amount of soft support for abolition could be found within the Whig organization.[11] Iowa's antislavery communities were traditionally Whig in their voting allegiance—only the representatives of that party displayed any real willingness to associate themselves with immediatist goals.

But in spite of some sympathy for the key Liberty party aim of divorcing the federal government from slavery, most leading Iowa Whigs regarded the seizure of power as their primary goal. Their pragmatic decision to support the presidential candidacy of Zachary Taylor indicated that sincere abolitionists could not rely on Whiggery to combat slavery and its defenders. Late in 1847 Asa Turner and his fellow Denmark Congregationalist Dr. George Shedd joined other abolitionists at their society's annual meeting. Instead of simply adopting the usual resolutions, the antislavery men drew up plans for the formation of a state Liberty party. Both Turner and Shedd were appointed to the organization's central committee, and a proposal was adopted to set up a newspaper in preparation for the forthcoming presidential campaign.[12]

Plans to fight the 1848 elections were soon modified. In the summer of that year the Democrats' nomination of Lewis Cass for president prompted a mass secession of Van Burenites from the Jacksonian camp in New York. Because these Barnburners had thrown their weight behind the Wilmot Proviso a modicum of common ground existed upon which political abolitionists and free-soil Democrats could meet. Pressed by an increasingly influential group of Ohio Liberty men led by Salmon P. Chase, most antislavery activists in the West rallied behind the call for fusion. August saw the formation of a Free-Soil party dedicated to opposing further expansion of slavery. Although the decision of the organization's national convention to endorse the candidacy of ex-president Van Buren was hard for many abolitionists to stomach, an Iowa Free-Soiler reported from Crawfordsville that the prairies were on fire with excitement. "The friends of the slave here will unite with the Barnburners," contended the writer: "There is almost universal dissatisfaction among the Whigs, and a good degree of it in the Democratic ranks. How many will adhere to the party nominations cannot yet be told."[13]

That fall Iowa Liberty men joined a small minority of local Democrats and Whigs to contest the first presidential election to be held in the state. Few leading figures from the major parties defected to the Free-Soil movement. The main exception was William Penn Clarke, an Iowa City Whig disgruntled at the refusal of his party to further the presidential ambitions of Henry Clay.[14] In the election the independents met with only limited success, polling just over a thousand votes, most of them in traditionally abolitionist communities.[15] Whig defections were confined to a minimum by the state party's belated endorsement of the Wilmot Proviso, while free-soil Democrats seemed happy to accept Cass's insistence that territorial legislatures should be allowed to decide the slavery question for themselves.[16]

Although Iowa Democrats triumphed as usual in the local elections of 1848, Cass's victory in the state was not enough to carry him into the White House. Taylor's military record and conspicuous silence on the Proviso combined with his party's hydra-headed campaign (antislavery in the North, proslavery in the South) to place Whigs in control of the federal government once again. Jubilant, his Iowa supporters looked forward to their reward. Foremost among the recipients of executive largesse was the Burlington lawyer and capitalist, Fitz Henry Warren. Appointed to the position of assistant postmaster general in the Taylor administration for his campaign efforts, the balding Warren endeavored to protect his chief from the attacks directed against him by abolitionists, insistent that the president should announce his stance on slavery expansion. "It seems," he complained to the apostate William Penn Clarke in July 1849, "that without waiting for Gen[era]l Taylor to give any evidence of his position upon Free Soil he is to be assumed to be its enemy & so taunted."[17]

Warren was correct in thinking the Louisiana planter an opponent of slavery expansion, for Taylor soon announced his backing for the immediate admission of California as a free state (much to the anger of his Southern followers). This move strengthened the hand of those nonextension Whigs in Iowa who were already seeking to forge an alliance of convenience between their own party and the new Free-Soil organization. Warren himself was skeptical of fusion because of the antislavery men's determination to heap abuse on the president.[18] However, efforts to combine with the Free-Soilers in the local elections of 1849 resulted in the joint nomination of a candidate for secretary of the board of public works.[19] That summer the Whig state convention adopted a plank condemning slavery expansion and calling for legislation to relieve the federal government of responsibility for that institution "wherever it has the constitutional authority so to do."[20] Fusion did not bring victory to the coalitionists, but some inroads were made into Democratic strength.

Any hope Iowa Whigs might have had that the president could unite Americans behind his plan were dashed by the concerted opposition of frustrated Southerners and Taylor's untimely death in July 1850. With the Union itself imperiled by threats of secession, pressure for a permanent compromise of the slavery question became intense. The initiative rapidly passed to Congress, thereby allowing Iowa's two Democratic senators to take the high ground of American nationalism.

Neither Augustus C. Dodge nor George W. Jones played a major role in the complex debates that led ultimately to the Compromise of 1850. Nonetheless, both men made abundantly clear their opposition to disunionism of any kind by supporting the full set of measures advanced to neutralize the slavery issue. The Iowans were thus the only pair of free-state senators to register approval of the controversial Fugitive Slave Law regarded by Southerners as the litmus test of the North's fidelity to the Constitution.

A former classmate of Jefferson Davis, Jones came closest to toeing the Southern line on the slavery question. In a speech on 19 July he condemned "free-soilism, abolitionism, and every other ism which is calculated to distract and divide the American Democracy." Having resided in slave states the Dubuquer claimed to know from experience that bondsmen were no worse off than free blacks. Though his opinions were against the peculiar institution, he would not, he said, vote for "insulting enactments" or lend himself "to harass or excite the fears of those amongst whom it exists."[21]

Dodge proved more eager than his colleague to display his free-soil credentials and took care to distance himself from the South. When the Louisiana Democrat Pierre Soulé introduced an amendment providing for the establishment of a territorial government for Southern California, Dodge announced his readiness to support the measure in order to promote sectional harmony. This did not indicate any sympathy for slavery, he insisted, for he was opposed to contact with the senator's "black boys." In the race to people New Mexico and Utah, Dodge defied Soulé "to come on with his constituents as fast as he pleases, and with his negroes too," for, he continued, "without congressional conditions or restrictions, I and my constituents will beat him in numbers and in influence; and if not, we will go to the wall."[22]

In stating their position on the Compromise, Dodge and Jones laid down the Iowa Democracy's fundamental position on slavery extension. Anchored to the Cass doctrine of nonintervention (the precursor of Stephen Douglas's more astutely worded popular sovereignty), the position was a strong one as matters stood in the late summer of 1850. Most Iowans favored relegating the slavery question to the local domain, if only because they saw this as the best means of preserving the Union. Nonintervention had the additional advantage of being consistent with the doctrine of laissez-faire that lay at the center of Jacksonian ideology. What gave this policy particular force was the blatantly racist rhetoric used to communicate it to an electorate known to be antagonistic toward blacks. Tying popular racism to the extension problem enabled Democratic leaders to dramatize the issues involved. By pinpointing two key negative reference groups—blacks and their abolitionist allies—in the midst of a white population fearful of racial amalgamation and disunion, they could pose successfully as the defenders of a united, lily-white republic.

Inevitably this tactic served to enhance the significance of black rights at home. Shortly after the Compromise was approved by both houses of Congress, the Democratic-controlled legislature at Iowa City finally passed a Negro exclusion act.[23] Because it required publication in the state's only Free-Soil organ to take effect, this statute must be interpreted as an abusive gesture directed toward the abolition "fanatics" who had so recently brought the Union to the brink of disaster. As a symbolic measure it therefore had the effect of consolidating the position marked out the previous summer by Dodge and Jones.

For Iowa Whigs the Compromise of 1850 proved to be an unmitigated disaster. Having placed their faith first in the Wilmot Proviso and then in the statehood program of President Taylor, they now found themselves forced to support a popular Union-saving measure that, primarily because it included rigid provisions for the return of runaway slaves, was anathema to members of the party's free-soil wing. Since Taylor's successor, Millard Fillmore, had compromised his position by signing the Fugitive Slave Act, many Iowa

Whigs no longer saw the president as an ally against the Democracy. A disgruntled Fitz Henry Warren believed his new chief to be a lame duck. His intention was, he told William Penn Clarke in August 1851, to return home and become "a quiet observer of the ebb & flow of political fortunes."[24]

Most of the credit for the 1850 Compromise went to those local Democrats who had contributed toward its passage in Congress. This meant that Whigs had little alternative but to look around for different issues with which to assail their opponents in future elections. Any political advantage they might gain from chipping away at vulnerable elements of the Compromise was likely to be more than offset by the damage this would do to internal party unity (conservative Whigs were happy to endorse Fillmore's role in promoting sectional harmony) and the opportunity it would present to the Democrats to label Whigs as disunionists. The immediate result of the congressional peace treaty was thus to produce an uneasy consensus on the slavery question. In Iowa, as throughout the North, Free-Soilers remained as virtually the only public opponents of finality.

The most obvious campaign option available to Iowa Whigs in the wake of the Compromise was to renew their assault on the state's Jacksonian constitution, thereby restoring economic issues to the forefront of political debate. Superficially there seemed much to be gained from taking this route. The late 1840s and early 1850s were transitional years for the young state. Between 1847 and 1854 its population increased dramatically from 116,454 to 326,500.[25] One observer reported in June 1853 that much of the existing riparian timberland had already been taken up by speculators.[26] Consequently the second wave of Iowa settlers (the bulk of whom hailed from the Old Northwest, the mid-Atlantic states, and Europe) began fanning out onto the open prairies and undulating pastures in the northern and central parts of the state.[27] New urban communities sprang up rapidly, most notably Fort Des Moines, the site of a former U.S. army camp deep in the interior; Council Bluffs and Sioux City, Missouri River trading posts serving the plains country; and Waterloo and Cedar Rapids, significant grain-milling towns in the northeast. No less eager to secure prosperity and economic independence than the first pioneers, those who continued to settle in the bustling urban and rural places of the state were quick to demand contact with the maturing American and international market. If the Whig philosophy of positive government could not find favor in this environment, it was unlikely to meet with success anywhere.

There were two major obstacles to a revival of Whig fortunes on the back of economic issues. The first of these was that Iowa shared in the general prosperity of this period. Democratic leaders could therefore point to the way their antibank, antimonopoly program had liberated individuals from the yoke of government legislation and special privileges, thereby creating the kind of conditions in which free enterprise could thrive.

The second obstacle was the Democrats' readiness to temper their enthusiasm for laissez-faire when the subject concerned was internal improvements. The plain fact was that all Iowans wanted a better infrastructure as soon as possible, regardless of whether or not government intervention in the economy was necessary to bring this about. Conservative and radical Democrats alike tended to favor government support for transportation projects such as canals, plank roads, and railways. When President Polk vetoed a bill to provide federal funding for western river and harbor improvements in 1847, Iowa's Democratic representatives in Washington publicly announced their disapproval.[28] The Whig opposition might declaim against the retrogressive economic policies of the administration, but local Democrats worked hard to ensure that blame for Polk's veto could not be attached to themselves.

The most important of all antebellum internal improvement ventures was the railroad. Because radical Democrats had spent most of the territorial period limiting the powers of corporations, the Whigs might have expected locofocos to hinder the progress of the iron horse across Iowa. In fact many of those same liberals who had helped to prepare the laissez-faire climate of the 1840s proved to be enthusiastic supporters of railroad development. In 1851 the Jacksonian-dominated assembly passed several acts granting certain embryonic railroad companies the right of way across the public domain.[29] The following year the Democratic state convention ratified a campaign plank upholding the right of the United States to promote "improvements of a national character" with grants of federal land and money.[30] In 1853 Democrats in the legislature supported a general right-of-way act permitting railroad corporations to purchase private land without the owner's consent.[31] Sardonically, local Whigs rejoiced to see "our Democratic fellow-citizens . . . occupying a part of our political platform," but inwardly they must have cursed the ease with which the enemy encroached upon their works.[32]

Constitutional reform remained the strongest economic card the Whigs could play. Even though the state was prosperous, future economic expansion depended on the ability of local transportation and credit facilities to cope with increasing agricultural surpluses. Those east-central Iowa farmers who benefited from substantial British demand for American wheat during the Crimean War were able to take advantage of the situation because their grain could be shipped to Europe relatively easily via the Mississippi River.

However, if they and their counterparts in the interior were to exploit future opportunities in a competitive market, they required not only cheaper, faster transportation but also a sound currency and easy access to farm credit. While Democrats seemed prepared to foster infrastructural development, their opposition to banks of issue—reiterated by Governor Stephen Hempstead (1850–54)—forced Iowa farmers to deal in the dubious notes of out-of-state institutions. Among the latter were several wildcat banks in Nebraska founded by Iowa-based capitalists who had made their fortunes from land speculation.[33] Neither they nor the state banks of Georgia or Tennessee were capable of producing the sort of elastic and reliable currency demanded by the commercially orientated settlers of the great West. If Iowa's economic growth was to be sustained, it was clear the state's ramshackle financial system would have to be reformed.

Whig demands for a constitutional convention to remove the prohibition on banks were in tune with the times. Aside from prosperity, the reason why they did not sweep the party into power was that the Democrats' antibank stance had a potent symbolic resonance for the voters. It strengthened the ruling organization's popular image, helped to stigmatize its opponents as friends of monopoly capitalism, and reminded the faithful of Andrew Jackson's titanic struggle against the monster bank. Suspicious of concentrated power, Iowa's electorate remained wedded to this crucial tenet of party faith long after its utility had been undermined by the expansion of the local economy.

Because economic issues held out little hope of electoral success at the beginning of the 1850s, many local Whigs, like their copartisans in other Northern states, began to take a growing interest in ethnocultural questions. Crucial demographic changes had been underway since Iowa joined the Union, and these helped to change the political map of the state.

After the War of 1812 the United States became a magnet for vast numbers of European immigrants. Unlike earlier generations of migrants who were predominantly of British stock and absorbed into society with reasonable facility, the new transatlantic pioneers hailed largely from Ireland and the German states. They brought with them the customs and prejudices of the Old World, many of these founded on devotion to Catholicism, a religion long regarded with suspicion by American Protestants. Fanned by fears of economic competition as well as popery, anti-Catholic riots became a feature of urban life across the North during the 1830s and 1840s.[34]

Evangelical leaders including the New England revivalist Lyman Beecher played a prominent role in whipping up popular prejudices, and a bitter contest for religious mastery of the continent began. The West became a prime focus of interdenominational rivalry. Protestant institutions like the American Home Missionary Society sought desperately to fight off the Catholic challenge by sending well-trained, highly motivated ministers to the battlefront. The dispatch of a band of Andover-educated Congregationalists to the west bank of the Mississippi in 1843 was a signal that Iowans would not be allowed to fall prey to idolatry and superstition.[35]

Between 1850 and 1856 over fifty thousand foreign-born settlers arrived in Iowa, increasing that group's share of the total population from 10.9 to 15 percent.[36] Nearly forty thousand of these new arrivals had been born in Germany and Ireland. The rest came mainly from Britain, Canada, Scandinavia, and the Netherlands. While many joined the native-born Americans on the open prairies, large numbers of these immigrants found their way into the booming river towns. There they found employment in a variety of occupations, mostly, in the case of the impoverished Irish, unskilled or semiskilled ones.

The sudden influx into Iowa of thousands of foreign-born settlers generated two important issues. The first of these centered on the Europeans' political rights and influence. In general the Democrats adhered to the notion that America should be a haven for the oppressed of the Old World. Their secular, pluralistic ideology may have had white supremacist foundations, but it proved much more tolerant of the new immigrants than the politically conservative, evangelical ethos of their opponents. Traditionally Anglophile, anti–working class Whigs looked on the Irish with contempt and decried the way the republic was becoming a dumping ground for poverty-stricken Catholics. Whereas they tended to support tighter restrictions on the naturalization process, most Democrats favored rapid assimilation of the foreign-born into the local and national polity.

European immigration gave added potency to a second issue: prohibition. Liquor drinking had been the subject of intense debate in America since the general outburst of reform agitation in the 1830s. By the late 1840s temperance activists in Iowa had launched a determined campaign to persuade voters that alcohol was undermining the physical and moral well-being of the republic. Impatient with the legislature's relatively lax attitude about liquor dealing, radical members of the Sons of Temperance started to call for a complete government ban on the trade.[37]

Among those leading the crusade was Hiram Price, a self-made lawyer and capitalist who settled in Davenport in 1844. Like so many of those in the vanguard of the reform movement, Price was a fervent evangelical, his unwavering self-belief and intolerance of alternative opinions a product of the perfectionist impulse that lay at the core of his Methodist faith.[38] Unlike many Methodists, however, he was also a committed antislavery man. This was significant, for the vast majority of political abolitionists in Iowa (most of whom were evangelical Protestants) actively supported the antiliquor campaign. Scarcely less than slavery, drink was seen by local Free-Soilers as a bar to individual responsibility and a threat to republican virtue. Legislative action against both was regarded as essential.

The passage of a prohibitory liquor act in Maine in 1851 induced Iowa temperance men to redouble their attempts to reform the law at home. So too did the fact that many of those European immigrants flooding into the state regarded alcohol as an instrument of socialization. Accounts of heavy drinking among the Irish were legion, and there was deep resentment at the Sabbath-breaking practices of lager-swilling Germans. Nativism and temperance were by no means wholly synonymous, but there was a good deal of overlap between them. As these issues grew in importance in the eyes of the voters, Iowa politicians were forced to recognize that they could no longer ignore the ethnocultural problems of the day.

Prohibition was a particularly worrying issue for the major parties because both of them were vulnerable to internal fragmentation over the matter. During the 1840s Whigs and Democrats alike had sought to steer a middle course on the liquor issue. While the former were more inclined to adopt a protemperance stance, several leading Democrats, including ex-Governor Robert Lucas, were noted for their opposition to liquor drinking. Neither party could afford to alienate minority opinion (protemperance in the case of the Democrats, antiprohibition in that of the Whigs) within their ranks, and therefore both adopted a hands-off approach as long as they possibly could.

By the early 1850s a number of antislavery Whigs, notably the Burlington lawyer James W. Grimes, were coming to the conclusion that their party would have to abandon its policy of neutrality in favor of one that leaned toward prohibition.[39] This belief was rejected by party conservatives who feared the divisive consequences of such a move in the run-up to a vital presidential election. The popularity of the 1850 Compromise gave this latter group the initiative, and at the party's state convention in February 1852 the free-soilers accepted campaign planks endorsing the Fillmore administration and the finality of the sectional accord. The platform made no allusion to prohibition but did include the predictable Whig call for reform of the state constitution.[40] Unlike their colleagues in other Northern states Iowa Whigs issued no approbation of General Winfield Scott's presidential candidacy. Scott was the preferred choice of the party's free-soil wing. His absence from the platform was thus a victory for conservatives within the organization.

Three months later Iowa Democrats met at the state capitol to declare the Compromise "a final settlement" of the slavery question.[41] In spite of some factional problems consensus was the order of the day as the party faithful roundly condemned the traditional Whig shibboleths of a national bank and a protective tariff. Confident that voters were unsympathetic to the stirrings of nativism on the prairies, the convention also passed a resolution opposing any change in the country's naturalization laws. Although this was the first time one of the major parties had taken a positive stand on an ethnocultural issue, it was significant that the Democrats too remained silent over prohibition.

At their respective national conventions in the summer of 1852 Iowa Whigs and Democrats voted for the presidential candidates they believed would bring them the spoils in November. Iowa delegates to the Baltimore Whig gathering in June backed the pro-Compromise Millard Fillmore.[42] This brought Iowa into line with Southern Whig feeling on the presidential question but was not enough to prevent the election of Scott on the fifty-third ballot. This outcome did not constitute a complete disaster for conservatives, however, because the convention adopted a resolution endorsing the settlement of 1850.

Iowa's representatives at the national Democratic convention were no more successful in their choice of a presidential nominee. Led by the wealthy Burlington capitalist, William F. Coolbaugh, they divided their support between the candidacies of Lewis Cass and Stephen Douglas, the favorite son of expansionist elements in the West.[43] By no means unhappy with the party's pro-Compromise platform, Coolbaugh and his colleagues were yet forced to acquiesce in the nomination of Franklin Pierce, a personable Yankee whose views on the slavery question were acceptable to the increasingly dominant Southern wing of the Democracy.

These events wrecked whatever chances there had been earlier in the year for fusion between Free-Soilers and one of the major parties. In Iowa some antislavery leaders had been genuinely hopeful of cooperation between their own organization and the Whigs. George Shedd had written to William Penn Clarke of his readiness to seek common ground with Clarke's former friends, but the failure of free-soil Whigs to gain the upper hand within their party ended talk of fusion and induced Iowa Free-Soilers to support independent nominations for Congress.[44] At Pittsburgh in August they endorsed Senator John P. Hale of New Hampshire as the national party's presidential nominee.[45]

Although Whig hopes were high, Pierce carried the state in November by 17,763 votes to Scott's 15,856.[46] As Hale won 1,604 votes, this gave the Democrat a majority of 50.4 percent. Pierce's national triumph meant that Jones, Dodge, and their colleagues regained full control of the federal patronage at home, but his relatively unimpressive showing in Iowa presented the opposition with some crumbs of comfort. Particularly significant was the fact that the Free-Soilers had come close to holding the balance of power at the state level. Pragmatic and antislavery Whigs had only to do some simple arithmetic to conclude that fusion offered them the best hope of undermining Democratic hegemony in the future. To cooperate successfully with the abolitionists, however, they would need to counteract the spell cast on Iowa politics by the Compromise of 1850. Their enemies did the work for them.

On 4 January 1854 Stephen Douglas reported to the U.S. Senate a bill to organize the central plains region of America into a single Nebraska Territory.[47] It was couched in the language of the Compromise and provided that the power of the local assembly should extend to all rightful subjects of legislation consistent with the U.S. Constitution. The bill was a western measure, demanded by western men eager to roll back the frontier, crafted by the leading westerner in Congress, and incorporating the truly western notion of popular sovereignty. Yet Douglas was an ardent nationalist and Democrat, not an exponent of particularism. He believed the bill would promote the continental destiny of the United States by rallying majorities behind a popular, Democratic program of expansion. How ironic then that a profoundly patriotic and partisan measure should have initiated a train of events that culminated in the sundering of both country and party in 1860-61.

As soon as the bill arrived on the floor of the Senate, it came under fire from several quarters. Many Iowans hoped that their state would lie astride the proposed railroad to the Pacific and dominate the western slope of the Missouri River.[48] Fearing Southern opposition to both objectives they pressed strongly for a division of the new territory that would prevent the region from falling under the influence of St. Louis interests. Douglas was also pressured by key Southern senators to negate the existing prohibition of slavery expansion north of 36°30'. This demand threatened to open up Nebraska to the peculiar institution, but the need for party unity meant that it could not be ignored. On 23 January Douglas introduced a revised bill providing for the organization of two territories (Kansas and Nebraska) and incorporating an explicit repeal of the venerated Missouri Compromise of 1820.

Nearly a month after congressional Free-Soilers had issued a scathing protest against the measure and outlined the case for political realignment on a sectional basis, Iowa Whigs gathered to prepare for the forthcoming gubernatorial elections. Having met with another ignominious defeat in the previous year's state contests, antislavery elements within the party were no longer prepared to submit to conservative domination. News of the Kansas-Nebraska bill strengthened their determination to convert informal ties with Free-Soil leaders into a concrete alliance. The Whig platform that emerged from the Iowa City convention was the most radical ever ratified by the party, for it included both an emphatic condemnation of Douglas's measure and a call for the passage of a prohibitory liquor law.[49]

Listed among the Henry County delegation at the meeting was the Reverend Simeon Waters, a Congregational minister from Mount Pleasant whose late wife Frances had played an active role in the state's political antislavery movement.[50] Waters's presence was significant because he had been chosen as the Free-Soilers' gubernatorial candidate and was keen to effect an arrangement that would result in the triumph "of the friends of morality[,] humanity[,] & freedom in Iowa."[51] The Whigs nominated him for secretary of state and ratified the independents' choice for superintendent of public instruction, George Shedd. Along with the campaign pledges these nominations reflected the Whigs' own desire for fusion. The only drawback was that their efforts to appeal to abolitionists did not go far enough. Free-Soilers noted the absence of a plank condemning the Fugitive Slave Law and announced their refusal to cooperate on the terms laid down at the capital.[52]

The burden of saving the alliance fell upon the man at the head of the Whig ticket. A handsome figure in his youth, James W. Grimes was now approaching middle age. Born in New Hampshire in 1816, he had been educated at Hampton Academy and prestigious Dartmouth College.[53] In common with many of his peers he had undergone a religious conversion experience while a teenager. Although this brush with revivalism influenced his approach to moral issues in later life, it did not equip him with the self-discipline necessary to quell his wayward temperament. He fell foul of the authorities at Dartmouth in 1835 and left the school without graduating. The following year, after a brief apprenticeship in a Peterboro law office, he left New England for the West.

By the age of twenty-five Grimes was well established as a prosperous Burlington lawyer and land dealer. Between 1839 and 1852 he emerged as a leading figure in the state Whig party, serving three terms in the Iowa house of representatives and on each occasion proving himself a strong friend of government support for business ventures likely to promote economic growth in the region. His Congregational background brought him into close contact with antislavery clerics like Asa Turner and William Salter. It was the latter, a member of the Iowa Band, who officiated at Grimes's wedding ceremony in November 1846. This may well have been the turning point in the politician's life, for his spouse, Elizabeth Nealley, a pious, red-haired

Yankee, did much to improve his powers of application and to instill in him a greater appreciation of moral questions. She was, her husband once confessed, "a sort of moral thermometer for my guidance."[54] In 1848 Grimes attended the national Whig convention as a supporter of Judge John McLean of Ohio, the favorite candidate of those Northern Whigs who believed that only a positive ban on slavery expansion could stem the pernicious growth of Southern power within the Union.[55] His credentials as a nonextension Whig were thus impeccable. An effective speaker, wily tactician, and possessor of a genuine moral conscience, Grimes was an inspired choice to lead his party into the summer elections.

Shortly after the abolitionists announced their refusal to accept the Whigs' terms, Grimes journeyed to Denmark to confer with antislavery leaders.[56] His objective was to convince the backcountry insurgents that he was a committed foe of both slavery and intemperance. Aided by his New England origins, impressive political record, and Waters's eagerness to stand down, Grimes can have had little difficulty winning over Turner and his lay lieutenant, George Shedd. On 28 March the Free-Soilers reassembled at the Seceder Presbyterian Church in Crawfordsville and, after a "[v]ehement debate," chose him as their gubernatorial nominee.[57] Both sides had taken a calculated political gamble. The Free-Soilers risked their principles; the Whigs their Silver Grey (conservative) wing that deprecated sectional excitement.

In March 1854 the Kansas-Nebraska bill passed the upper chamber of Congress with the full backing of Iowa's Democratic senators. The response among moderate Whigs was electric, permeated with sectional hatred born of genuine anger at the South's perceived role in destroying a sacred compact. Fitz Henry Warren told Penn Clarke that "the Nebraska villainy" had aroused his ire. "You may call my party what you please," he wrote, "but where resistance to southern aggression is their aim & where the interests and honor of the North are to be sustained is my political organization."[58]

In April James W. Grimes issued a major campaign document entitled "To the People of Iowa."[59] This contained something for everyone. To traditional Jacksonian voters he offered an endorsement of popularly elected state supreme court judges. To straight-line Whigs and conservative Democrats he offered a call for banks to be legalized under proper restrictions. To temperance advocates in all parties he offered a promise not to veto any prohibitory liquor law passed by the general assembly. In order to counteract the damage this statement would do to potential support among the foreign-born, he offered his considered opinion that no change should be made to the country's existing naturalization laws. To all he offered his support for a national homestead law and federal investment in western internal improvements.

The tremendous unpopularity of the Kansas-Nebraska bill, however, enabled Grimes to devote the bulk of the document to the problem of slavery expansion. Though it was issued several weeks before the bill became law, the message was predicated on the assumption that the House Democratic majority would eventually pass the measure.

In the course of a carefully crafted paper Grimes developed the thesis that hitherto only federal legislation had managed to stem the westward march of the peculiar institution. He reaffirmed the inviolability of the Missouri Compromise and warned that both Kansas and Nebraska might become slave states because of the suitability of their soil and climate to cereal, hemp, and tobacco production, and their close proximity to Missouri and Arkansas. But for the Compromise of 1820 and the Northwest Ordinance, he claimed, Iowa itself would have become a haven for slavery. Maintenance of the former was essential to the material welfare of the region: "Bounded on two sides by slave states, we shall be intersected with underground railroads and continually distracted by slave hunts. . . . The energies of our people will be paralyzed, our works of internal improvement will languish, and the bright anticipations of the future greatness of Iowa forever blasted."[60] To conclude, Grimes reported that Alexander Stephens, a leading Southern Whig, had predicted that Iowa would become a slave state within fifteen years. Thus would the abandonment of 36°30' provoke "a contest for the mastery between freedom and slavery" on the west bank of the Mississippi.[61]

Although this message was designed to have maximum electoral effect, the Burlingtonian's main concern during the 1854 campaign was to ensure that Free-Soilers did not abandon the ticket. While the abolitionists sought to pressure their time-serving Whig allies by questioning candidates, Grimes made clear his own moral as well as material opposition to slavery. One Henry Clay Whig remembered hearing him speak at Des Moines after the spring rains. Noting Douglas's statement that he did not care whether slavery was voted up or down in the territories, Grimes told his listeners: "I do care. The American people care. Mr. Douglas might as well attempt to dam the Des Moines river with prairie hay as to try to eradicate the aspiration for universal freedom from the soul of every American who appreciates his own liberty."[62]

At one point, fearful of Democratic efforts to deemphasize Kansas-Nebraska as a bone of political contention, he sought letters from national Free-Soil leaders Salmon P. Chase and Joshua Giddings urging Louisa County abolitionists to support the anti-Nebraska ticket.[63]

Grimes's hard work paid off at the polls in August. He defeated his antibank, antiprohibition opponent, Stephen Hempstead, by a margin of

2,123 votes out of nearly 45,000 cast.[64] William E. Gienapp's regression analysis of county-level data indicates that the victorious candidate owed his election primarily to the votes of those Whigs who had endorsed Scott in 1852.[65] These were supplemented by the ballots of men who had not voted in the presidential contest and those of a majority of Free-Soilers. Roughly a third of foreign-born voters appear to have supported Grimes, most of these almost certainly British, Scandinavian, and German Protestants.[66] Over half the immigrant vote went to Hempstead, indicating that Grimes's efforts to capitalize on the prohibition issue without alienating Europeans had not been entirely successful. Most Silver Greys appear to have stayed at home, refusing to support an openly sectional candidate and thereby contributing to a relatively unspectacular turnout of around 75 percent.

Grimes's slender margin of victory was a remarkable achievement. Fourteen counties underwent a change in political allegiance from that registered in 1852. Twelve of those counties, six of them bordering the Cedar River in the east-central portion of the state, switched from the Democracy to the anti-Nebraska opposition, thereby offsetting the ruling party's successes in newly settled southwestern districts. Apart from Dubuque the northeast went strongly for Grimes.

A monocausal interpretation of this election will not suffice to explain the result. The role of European-born voters was clearly important, but the coalitions of both candidates were made up largely of native citizens. Of these, substantial numbers of evangelicals—particularly Southern- and western-born Methodists and Baptists in the lower counties—continued to express a preference for the Democracy, the party of national expansion and individual moral choice. One of the reasons they did so was doubtless that organization's strong image as the friend of the migrant farmer and opponent of monopoly capitalism. Grimes had sought to counter Jacksonianism not only by endorsing a homestead law and popularly elected judges but also by contending that regulated banks were essential to the economic well-being of a maturing community. In other words he sought to pose as the purveyor of growth along democratic lines. It was this message that proved particularly attractive to farmers in the state's main wheat-growing northeastern and east-central counties. Eager to improve local transport and credit facilities in order to exploit the opportunities opened up by the Crimean War, this group may well have supplied Grimes with crucial votes in the swing counties of the Cedar and Des Moines river valleys. Thus, although the anti-Nebraska candidate proved attractive to New Englanders and reform-minded and often anti-Catholic Protestants, his triumph was not exclusively an ethnocultural one.

Throughout his long campaign for the governorship, James Grimes emphasized above all else his profound opposition to the Kansas-Nebraska Act. Ever since the outbreak of the Mexican War increasing numbers of Iowans had begun to react negatively to what they perceived to be Southern efforts to dominate the Union through the acquisition of additional slave territory. Extensive support for the Wilmot Proviso among antislavery Whigs and free-soil Democrats was the most obvious manifestation of this developing sentiment. When Southern radicals threatened secession over the territorial issue, there were genuine fears that the breakup of the Union might be imminent. The Compromise of 1850 quieted these, forcing major party politicians to accept the congressional peace treaty as the crux of their public policy. This proved particularly onerous for large numbers of antiextension Whigs. Less subject to Southern domination than their Democratic opponents and more inclined to dislike slavery for moral reasons, this important political bloc remained suspicious of Southern intentions. The Kansas-Nebraska Act destroyed the consensus created by the Compromise, brought sectional feelings to the fore once again, and enabled free-soil Whigs to overturn conservative power within their own party.

Grimes's achievement in the 1854 election was to forge a winning coalition on the back of economic, ethnocultural, and sectional issues. The Kansas-Nebraska Act was the chief agent of fusion. It enabled Whiggery to transcend its politically conservative roots and associate the Democrats with a source of corruption that Iowans, increasingly amenable to the institutions of an expanding capitalist economy, were coming to perceive as a greater threat than the money power. Douglas's measure seemed to provide positive proof that the South's planter class was determined to maintain political control within the Union regardless of the moral and material costs to the republic. Almost overnight he handed the torch of progress to his enemies in the Northern states.

The process of fusion along sectional lines was aided by the decline of Southern influence within Iowa itself. The advent of railroad communications from the urban Northeast reduced the farmer's dependence on the Mississippi and brought increasing numbers of non-Southerners into the state. In 1850 over 16.5 percent of the local population had been born below the Mason-Dixon line. Six years later that proportion was down to 10.8 percent. By the eve of the Civil War fewer than one in twenty Iowans were Southerners.[67] Ultimately, however, it was the activities of Southerners outside the state that held the fusionists together, for during the second half of the 1850s a procession of events served to persuade the voters that a genuine conspiracy was underway to deprive them of their rights. Within a year and a half of

Grimes's election, fear of the "slave power" had converted Iowa's nascent anti-Nebraska coalition into a state Republican party of formidable strength and vitality.

4
Formation of the Republican Party in Iowa, 1854–1856

Iowa's Republican coalition did not solidify in the immediate aftermath of Grimes's election. State and national affairs remained in flux. "We have no longer any political parties in this country," wrote the new governor in August 1854. "Every man fights on his own back & works his own political gods out of just such materials as he chooses."[1] By the autumn Grimes was communicating frequently with Ohio's ambitious Free-Soil leader Salmon P. Chase. Both men were convinced that the Kansas-Nebraska Act had radicalized the North. When the Burlingtonian reported that his Whig colleagues had begun to learn that it no longer hurt them to be labeled "abolitionists" or "woolly-heads," Chase replied that the voters were "in advance of the politicians on the slavery question."[2]

The determination of both men to cooperate in the construction of a broad-based sectional organization on solid antislavery foundations was evident from the beginning. Conscious that Grimes could be of inestimable value to those most heavily engaged in fostering political realignment in the North, Chase was especially anxious that the governor's inaugural address should conform to Free-Soil policy. To this end he made a number of trenchant suggestions that Grimes appears to have noted. On perusing a draft of the message the Ohioan had no hesitation in pronouncing it "excellent."[3]

The December inaugural began with a ringing endorsement of the positive Christian state. "Government," intoned Grimes, "is established for the protection of the governed."

> But that protection does not consist merely in the enforcement of the laws against injury to the person and property. Men do not make a voluntary abnegation of their natural rights, simply that those rights may be protected by the body politic. It reaches more vital interests than those of property.

Its greatest object is to elevate and ennoble the citizen. . . . It is designed to foster the instincts of truth, justice and philanthropy, that are implanted in our very natures, and from which all constitutions and all laws derive their validity and value. It should afford moral as well as physical protection, by educating the rising generation; by encouraging industry and sobriety; by steadfastly adhering to the right, and by being ever true to the instincts of freedom and humanity.[4]

After proceeding from this Whiggish introduction to recommend the establishment of several tax-supported public institutions, the governor expressed his conviction that the assembly would pass a prohibitory liquor law, then moved on to the nub of his speech: the Kansas-Nebraska Act. Douglas's measure, he asserted, had reversed the nonextension policy of the Founding Fathers, thereby revealing that all compromises with slavery were "mere ropes of sand, to be broken by the first wave of passion or interest that may roll from the South." Let the national government divorce itself from the peculiar institution, he said, and all agitation of the subject would cease.[5] It was little wonder that Chase had been so impressed with the document, for these closing words encapsulated policy that had been at the center of Liberty party thought for nearly a decade.

Joshua Giddings, the spokesman for antislavery radicals on Ohio's Western Reserve, was overjoyed. "One thing more, and Iowa will lead the great Republican party," he counseled Grimes: "Let your legislature back up the Governor by resolutions, and your State . . . will stand in a most admirable position. The point you make is the true issue, and I wonder that our State legislatures have not taken it long since."[6] Giddings was to be disappointed in his hope that the general assembly would thrust Iowa into the forefront of the Republican movement now well underway in many midwestern states. This was largely because the Democratic majority of one in the senate provided a counterweight to the supporters of nonextension who dominated the house, thus precluding the passage of a joint resolution on national affairs. However, the legislature did send an anti-Nebraska Whig to the U.S. Senate to replace Augustus C. Dodge. The events preceding the election were as confused as the times and shed much light on the nature of the emerging Republican coalition.

The fifty-four non-Democrats in the assembly did not constitute a united front. Had they voted en bloc they could have elected their senatorial nominee on the first ballot of the joint convention. In fact a maximum of one-fifth of this grouping were pro-Compromise National Whigs, ill disposed toward sectional agitation. The rest were nonextension Whigs and, fewer in number, Free-Soilers and antislavery immediatists. Although they were agreed on the subject of free territories, the anti-Nebraska men were deeply divided over the senatorship, a position regarded as vital by ideologues and professional spoilsmen alike. Prominent among the latter was Fitz Henry Warren, Grimes's main rival for control of the fusion movement. The former U.S. assistant postmaster general appears to have considered this plum office his by right on account of his services to the Whig cause. Unfortunately for Warren, most of his copartisans did not share this estimation of his worth.

On the evening of 15 December President James Harlan of Iowa Wesleyan University at Mount Pleasant defeated Warren for the nomination of the anti-Nebraska caucus.[7] His name was brought out by Whig chiefs in the southeast who believed that his low political profile would attract some of the Silver Greys. Although their hopes were dampened the next morning when the joint convention adjourned to determine the new candidate's views on the slavery question, Harlan—an Indiana-born Methodist—remained in the race by refusing to be drawn publicly on the sensitive issue of reforming the Fugitive Slave Act.[8] Nonetheless, the outnumbered Democrats were able to sabotage the nominating process by uniting with seven National Whigs.[9] Political stalemate ensued.

At this point in the proceedings Grimes abandoned his avowed policy of neutrality and attempted to unite the Silver Greys and fusionists behind the candidacy of Timothy Davis of Dubuque.[10] Unfortunately, his negotiations with Milton Browning, the conservative Whig whose cooperation with the Democracy had prevented an election, collapsed because of Davis's Free-Soil proclivities.[11] On 6 January 1855, therefore, Grimes abandoned backstage diplomacy and entered the senate chamber to urge his dissident copartisans to support a Free-Soiler, Norman W. Isbell, for state supreme court judge.[12] His intervention brought some of the waverers into line. Fearful that their strategy was about to be defeated the Democratic majority in the upper chamber then secured an adjournment to prevent a meeting of the joint convention. An hour later senate Whigs entered the house and, following a walkout by incensed Democrats, proceeded to elect both Isbell and Harlan virtually unopposed.[13]

These irregular proceedings highlighted some of the main aspects of the fusion movement. The significance of Grimes's personal influence was clearly visible. So too was that of crusading Protestantism: at least two-thirds of those who voted for Harlan immediately after the anti-Nebraska caucus were evangelicals, compared to a figure of only 31 percent of those Whigs who opposed him.[14] The whole affair also indicated the underlying unity of the Whig–Free-Soil alliance. Although Fitz Henry Warren's friends resented Grimes's refusal to support their hero's candidacy (Warren himself would spend the next twelve years trying to settle his "small private account" with his fellow townsman), they regrouped solidly behind the official nominee.[15] Had they not backed Harlan, the anti-Nebraska forces might have fragmented before they had had a real chance to coalesce.

The legislature went on to pass several important measures during the early months of 1855. These included a Sabbath observation act and a prohibitory liquor law. While this action reflected the strong ethnocultural bias of the coalition, it did not indicate that antislavery activity and moral insurgency on a broader scale were indistinguishable. A substantial number of Democrats joined the fusionists in supporting both measures. Once a referendum amendment had been attached to the Maine Law bill, Democratic majorities in both chambers voted in favor of passage.[16] Nineteen out of twenty-seven Democrats in the house acquiesced in the passage of the Sabbatarian act prohibiting dancing, fishing, or hunting on the Lord's day.[17] Forty-three percent of senate Democrats voted for this measure, which predictably won the backing of most fusionists.[18]

The salience of moral issues in the 1854–55 legislature reflected evangelical attempts to keep Iowa on the path of godliness. Local Protestant clergymen convinced that the West was "the moral Thermopylae of the world" were now deeply concerned that their proselytizing endeavors might be thwarted by the rising tide of foreign immigration.[19]

At the beginning of the decade two Dubuque ministers submitted a report to the annual meeting of the state's Congregational Association in which they urged the necessity of undertaking missionary work among the region's burgeoning German population. The clerics alleged that the "tide is swelling that rolls in upon us, drifting to our shores, an incalculable amount of infidelity, superstition and error, which threatens to lay waste and destroy our institutions."[20] Lucien W. Berry, Harlan's successor as president of Iowa Wesleyan, openly assailed Catholicism as "the enemy of human progress" and the implacable foe of enlightened Protestant Republicanism.[21] The massive influx of papists instilled local sectarians with a keen sense of insecurity, which, coupled with their crusading zeal, forced them to redouble their efforts to impose Protestant conformity on a changing population. Sabbatarian and temperance activity were part and parcel of this movement. So too, to some degree, was political nativism, the scourge of foreign immigrants that had swept across the eastern states in the wake of Kansas-Nebraska.

Early in 1855 it seemed as if Iowa might escape the full force of the nativist upsurge. Eager to capitalize on anti-Nebraska sentiment, Grimes told Chase on 8 April that it was time to "thoroughly organize the Republican party" and spoke warmly of the

Ohioan's presidential chances in 1856. "The Know Nothings [i.e., political nativists]," he maintained, "have pretty well broken down the two old parties, and a new one, now organized, would draw largely from the foreign element that goes to make up those parties, while it will draw away one-half of the Know Nothings at least."[22]

Talk of institutionalizing nonextension sentiment was now rife in Iowa. On 20 January an antislavery gathering outside Des Moines had called for "a concentrated political League of Freedom, to administer the affairs of this Government in accordance with the principles set forth by the patriotic founders of this Republic," and three months later local Free-Soilers signified their willingness to cooperate with other elements in forming a state Republican party.[23] In spite of these encouraging developments, however, Grimes was mistaken in thinking that the way was now clear for political realignment.

That spring Iowa nativists began to flex their muscles, winning municipal elections in Keokuk, Muscatine, Davenport, and Iowa City.[24] The men behind these victories, no less conscious than Grimes that fusion was an essential prerequisite for success at the polls, opted on 1 March to support the slate of state-level candidates chosen by the anti-Democratic forces in the legislature.[25] Possibly the governor interpreted this as a sign of weakness. In fact, while Iowa's Know Nothing organization did not at any time acquire the influence of the eastern order, its sudden arrival on the political scene was to delay the foundation of the local Republican party for almost a year.

Political nativism was antislavery's principal rival for voter allegiance in the midst of the extended destruction of the second party system. Its appeal lay in its compelling diagnosis of what had gone wrong with government at the grass roots, an attractive antiparty and reformist image, and an easily understood delineation of foreigners and Catholics as the main threat to republican values.[26] Americanism in Iowa took off at a juncture when foreign immigration was reaching a peak and the Kansas-Nebraska issue had begun to lose some of its salience as a vote-winning issue.

Most of the original nativist leaders were Whigs, a motley group of opportunists and conservatives whose aim was to exploit the undercurrent of nativism in the community, and who were doubtless attracted by the order's support for Protestant causes, notably prohibition. Free-Soilers tended to remain aloof from the movement because they objected to its proscriptive tenets or viewed it as an unwanted obstacle to fusion on purely antislavery lines. The main exception was the irascible William Penn Clarke, who appears to have joined the new organization with a view to sectionalizing it. Democrats were inclined to be strong opponents of Know Nothingism, but large numbers of them entered the nativist ranks as the movement grew in popularity.[27] Geographically the party's power bases in Iowa were the river towns below Dubuque and the lower-tier counties close to the Missouri border. This indicates that Know Nothingism appealed not only to evangelicals but also to urbanites (quite possibly native-born artisans) most affected by the new immigration and rural, Southern-stock voters who saw nativism as a counter to the increasingly sectional tenor of U.S. politics.

The relationship between Republicanism and Americanism in Iowa, as throughout the North, was symbiotic. Both of the anti-Nebraska congressional candidates in 1854, James Thorington and Rufus Clarke, allied themselves to the nativist cause, as did a number of other future Republican leaders. But though fusion was heavily tainted with nativism, it was the Know Nothings who were eventually forced to join the Republican party on terms dictated by the free-soilers. The key to this development lies in the unbending commitment of figures like Grimes and Chase to political realignment on sectional grounds and in the corroding strength of the American movement itself.

Western Republicans were determined to build a successful political coalition on a foundation of nonextension. As a result they were particularly keen to lure large numbers of liberal Protestant Germans away from their allegiance to the Democracy.[28] The trick was to attract as many immigrants as possible without alienating anti-Southern nativists. Chase himself was the supreme architect of the recently founded Ohio Republican organization, his achievement the product of an alliance with Know Nothing leaders whose confidence had begun to evaporate after bloody nativist riots in Cincinnati. The platform on which Chase was to run for governor in the fall of 1855 bristled with nonextension resolutions and made no mention of nativist goals. In spite of the risk of falling between two stools, the combination of vigorous opposition to the spread of slavery and silence on the naturalization question enabled Chase to win a plurality over his two opponents.[29] The lesson provided by the success of the Ohio Plan was not lost on party builders in other states.

In October 1855 the pro-Chase Washington, D.C., *National Era* reported that while Iowa had been wrested from the administration by an anti-Nebraska majority composed of Whigs, Free-Soilers, and Know Nothings, no Republican organization had yet been formed.[30] On this subject the editor published a letter from a local Free-Soiler that affirmed his colleagues' readiness to participate in the founding of such a party. "Our work would be easy and success certain," stated the correspondent, "were it not for the competition thrown in our way by the element of Know Nothingism."[31]

The insurgent's frustration was understandable. In spite of Whig calls for fusion on the sole issue of nonextension and the establishment of Republican and People's organizations at the county level, Iowa nativists had declined to throw in their lot with the sectionalists. In the local elections in August they registered a number of victories. Events, however, were no longer on their side. Kansas issues were already pushing their way to the forefront of the political agenda, and several American triumphs at the polls would not have been achieved without recourse to sectional rhetoric.[32]

In November Iowa's Know Nothing Grand Council adopted a set of resolutions intended to provide a basis for fusion. One of them looked forward to a modification of the country's five-year naturalization law and called for a free Bible and free (i.e., non-Catholic) schools. Five were blatantly sectional in tone, nonextensionist, and deeply critical of federal policy in the territories. Another invited the citizens of Iowa to unite with the American party in "the cause of freedom."[33]

This call for a Know Nothing–Republican alliance on nativist terms was viewed with distrust by antislavery men. One American leader told William Penn Clarke that free-soilers were fearful, "that while we invite them onto our platform . . . we have got it underlain with pipes in every direction to subserve our own purposes. They are timid. They have misgivings about becoming a part and parcel of us in the coming campaign."[34]

The writer was correct in supposing nonextensionists reluctant to play second fiddle in a coalition, but wrong in his assumption that Clarke shared his determination to fashion Republicanism in the image of the Grand Council. Early in January 1856 the *Mount Pleasant Observer* published a call for a Republican state convention to meet on Washington's birthday. It contained no reference to nativist objectives and concentrated solely on the issue of slavery extension.[35] Clarke later claimed to be the author of this document—an assertion that, if true, makes clear his tenuous commitment to orthodox Americanism.[36]

The ubiquitous Iowa City Free-Soiler declined to attend the state's first Republican convention but went east instead to officiate at a preliminary national Republican gathering in Pittsburgh that rejected cooperation with nativists.[37] He then moved on to Philadelphia to join a secession of Northern delegates from the national Know Nothing convention. The majority of these men planned to force the Republicans to nominate the Massachusetts nativist Nathaniel P. Banks as their standard-bearer, and to this end they called for an assemblage of North Americans to meet at New York in June. Clarke demurred. With five other delegates he signed a statement rejecting the majority call and averring that "the whole North ought to unite in a common organization to resist the aggressions of Slavery."[38] Small wonder that when Clarke returned home, his name was offensive to Know Nothing ears.[39]

While Clarke was in Pittsburgh listening to speeches denouncing Southern atrocities in Kansas, around four hundred of his fellow Iowans were meeting at the capital to organize a state Republican party.[40] The bulk of the delegates were lawyers, farmers, and newspaper editors. Except for Grimes and Harlan most of the region's leading nonextension Whigs were in attendance: Fitz Henry Warren and his powerful ally Francis Springer; Alvin Saunders, one of Harlan's principal backers in the winter of 1854–55; James B. Howell of the Keokuk *Gate City,* a future U.S. senator; and the English-born Dubuque attorney, William W. Hamilton. Also present were a fair number of anti-Nebraska Democrats (notably Samuel J. Kirkwood, a homespun Iowa City capitalist, and the temperance leader, Hiram Price), Free-Soilers, and a handful of outright abolitionists. Equally prominent were several Know Nothing chieftains, keen to effect an alliance on the best possible terms. It was they who were most disappointed with a party platform that was devoted entirely to sectional matters.

The latter began by reciting the life, liberty, and pursuit of happiness creed contained in the Declaration of Independence (a fundamental prop of the abolitionist movement). It then proceeded to affirm the party's commitment to state sovereignty, the perpetuity of the Union, and nonextension. In addition there were demands for the federal government to "relieve itself of all responsibility for the existence of Slavery," and for the speedy admission of Kansas as a free state.[41]

Significantly, the platform contained no reference to the liquor issue. Although the state supreme court had recently declared the 1855 Maine Law unconstitutional because it contained a referendum provision, the Republican convention defeated an attempt by Hiram Price to commit the new party to prohibition.[42] A reluctance to alienate antitemperance voters (47 percent of the electorate had opposed the Maine Law) bolstered the delegates' determination to sidestep an issue that had wreaked such havoc in the early part of the decade.

Virtually no mention was made of nativist objectives. Silence on the key American goal of naturalization law reform mirrored the tone of the Ohio Republican platform but ran contrary to the wishes of Governor Grimes who had hoped for an explicit affirmation of the existing laws in order to impress German voters.[43] The convention, however, did not reject outright the Grand Council's November advances. By choosing several nativist Republicans to represent the party in the forthcoming state elections, the convention made a blatant bid for Know Nothing support.[44] Only time would tell whether or not this attempt to forge a catchall coalition between disparate groups would be successful.

In fact, like its counterpart in Ohio, the first Iowa Republican platform came close to alienating those it was meant to attract. Shortly after the convention local Germans announced their determination to withhold support from the new party until it ceased to temporize on the nativist issue. And on 5 March an American gathering at Iowa City ratified the Know Nothings' nomination of Millard Fillmore for president, though it declined to endorse the pro-Southern national platform.[45] The Republican state ticket was also approved, but there was no move to abandon the local Know Nothing organization. Grimes was infuriated by the Americans' "want of good faith" and "ignorance of all political arithmetic."[46] Their decision to back Fillmore, he told Chase, rendered the state doubtful for Republicanism in November.[47]

The issue that did most to quell Grimes's fears and promote Republican organization during the mid-1850s was of direct interest to the citizens of Iowa. During the summer of 1854 George G. Rice, a Congregational minister based in the Missouri River town of Council Bluffs, reported disturbing news from the west. "People of Missouri & Arkansas are making into Kansas with their slaves," he wrote on 10 July. "If Kansas & Nebraska are not both made slave territory it will be no thanks to the administration or the Southern people."[48] By mid-August Rice had modified his views, possibly through watching wagon loads of free-staters pass through the frontier settlement on their way to the virgin land across the river. "I do not think much of an effort will be made to establish slavery in Nebraska," he predicted on the 22nd. "The war on that subject will be in Kansas."[49]

The minister was right. In less than eighteen months Kansas had become the battleground of the crumbling Union. Without this issue Iowa's Republican coalition could not have solidified as smoothly as it did in the winter of 1855–56. The call for a Republican state convention was issued only days after the beginning of all-out hostilities in Kansas between proslavery Lecomptonites and free-staters—antagonism that had been widely reported in Iowa's anti-Nebraska press as part of the campaign to sectionalize the Know Nothing order.

James Harlan was one of several politicians who cut their congressional teeth over Kansas. In his maiden speech on 27 March 1856 Iowa's new Republican senator accused President Pierce of reintroducing the slavery question into national politics and emphasized the conservative nature of the free-soil movement by outlining the historical precedents for nonextension.[50] He also sought to ridicule the Democrats' policy of popular sovereignty by insisting that Kansas-Nebraska itself had been based on the assumption that Congress was the ultimate source of sovereignty in the territories. At one stage during his oration the Republican moderate sounded like an abolitionist. Perceived black inferiority, he asserted, was a consequence of slavery, not genetics. Naked power was the only real justification for the Anglo-Saxon's claim over the black race.[51] As these points were integral elements in the ideological armory of antislavery radicals, their enunciation in Congress did nothing to calm the sectional excitement that Harlan claimed to deprecate.

The motivation underlying this speech epitomizes the ambiguous nature of Republican thinking on Kansas. Early in January Harlan had told his former college patron, the influential Methodist bishop Matthew Simpson, that he was planning to make an anti-Nebraska speech in the Senate.[52] Fearing an increase in sectional tension at a time when he was anxious to retain the allegiance of border-state Methodists, Simpson advised Harlan to proceed cautiously. This, replied the politician, would not be entirely possible, for conditions at home required him to speak out. "We elect a new Legislature in August next," he wrote. "A *Whig* Legislature in Iowa will be a quietus to opposition to me here. At least I think so. And my voice must be heard in that contest to prevent my falling into contempt with my friends at home."[53]

Harlan's speech was thus designed to further his own political career. His main themes—the inherent conservatism of nonextension and the immorality of slavery—were crafted to satisfy moderate and radical opinion in Iowa. Yet in spite of the somewhat cynical motives underlying the rhetoric, the speech was not entirely a product of careerism. In the same letter in which he detailed his personal reasons for speaking out, Harlan reported that proslavery forces were preparing to crush free-state resistance in Kansas. Within ninety days, he wrote, "there will have commenced a terrible struggle on the soil of Kansas between her *bonafide* citizens and armed marauders from southern states."[54] Even a sanctimonious and ambitious Whig like James Harlan possessed genuine fears that the slave power had taken the offensive.

The senator's prediction of bloodshed was well founded. Three weeks before his speech two leading figures in the free-state Topeka movement, James H. Lane and Dr. Charles Robinson, had written to Governor Grimes requesting immediate assistance to forestall an invasion attempt by Southern bushwackers. Because President Pierce was about to brand their opposition to the proslavery Lecompton government as revolutionary and to rebuff their pleas for federal aid, a request for Northern state intervention was perfectly logical. The letter was given prominence in the Iowa press and helped to raise public excitement to fever pitch.[55]

Although events in Kansas did not come to a head immediately, the situation deteriorated dramatically during the spring of 1856. In May a federal district court at Lecompton indicted several free-state officials (Lane and Robinson among them) for high treason—a move that led directly to the sack of Lawrence and John Brown's brutal revenge killing of five proslavery men at Ossawatamie. Full-scale war ensued, leaving many Iowa Republicans in no doubt that their assistance was essential if, in Harlan's words, the storm was "to end in the promotion of the permanent welfare of the human family, and the highest interests of the Kingdom of Christ."[56]

Iowa's contribution to the cause of freedom was not confined to rhetorical flourishes in Congress. It was solidly practical. Most effective of all were the efforts of local Republicans to speed the flow of men and munitions into the troubled territory. Harlan's ally, William Penn Clarke, spearheaded logistical activities after using his national reputation to forge links with prominent Topeka men. As chairman of the state's Kansas Aid Committee (an extension of his own political clique at the capital), Clarke was instrumental in having the Lane Trail designated the main emigrant thoroughfare across Iowa.[57] His involvement with the Mississippi & Missouri River Railroad Company made him especially useful to the free-staters because he was able to direct the transportation of guns from Chicago to the railhead at Iowa City.[58] Hiram Price, an official of the same corporation, aided Clarke from his office in Davenport.[59] Helping these men to supply the Kansans with arms was the governor himself. During the spring Grimes requisitioned nearly two thousand muskets and fifty Colt revolvers from the U.S. ordnance depot at St. Louis.[60] When they arrived, he allowed all or part of the consignment to fall into the hands of Lane's men.[61]

After mid-1856, when proslavery forces sought to impede Northern emigration to Kansas by blockading the Missouri River, Iowa became a focal point for free-state activity. The village of Tabor on the Nebraska border was converted into a camp for Lane's motley army and was the base for his forays into Kansas during August and September. The resident Congregational minister John Todd participated enthusiastically in the logistics effort, as did a number of his fellow clerics in other parts of the state.[62] That summer the prairies were afire with military activity and ghastly tales of Southern atrocities in Kansas.[63] Republicans gorged on the resulting tension.

The extent to which Kansas had radicalized public opinion was evidenced by the almost complete inaction of federal officers in Iowa. U.S. District Attorney Joseph C. Knapp declined to harass "the Abolition scoundrels now prowling around through the state" on the grounds that any attempt by him "to punish these murderers as their crimes deserve, would add another *plank* to the beutiful [sic] platform of Republicanism."[64] For all their determination to label their opponents as treasonous, Iowa Democrats were confronted with the fact that sectional agitation was beginning to win more votes than it lost. Widely seen as pro-Southern, federal policy was deeply unpopular among the electorate, and the Democrats responded to free-state maneuvers with justifiable caution.

Although Judge Knapp may not have been entirely aware of the precise identity of the scoundrels roaming the countryside, his epithet "Abolition" was close to the mark. After the dispersal of the Topeka legislature by U.S.

dragoons on Independence Day 1856, Northern free-state activists grew fearful of a Washington-backed proslavery triumph in Kansas. As a result several prominent New England abolitionists journeyed west as representatives of the various aid organizations. Their main objective was to increase the flow of trans-Mississippi settlement by ascertaining at first hand the most favorable emigrant routes through southern Iowa and establishing contacts with free-state sympathizers in the field. Among these Yankee sojourners were two militant antislavery activists from Massachusetts, Thomas Wentworth Higginson and Franklin D. Sanborn.

Higginson came to Iowa in the summer of 1856 convinced that the best way to defeat the votaries of human bondage was for Northern patriots to declare war on U.S. forces in Kansas. He told Penn Clarke shortly before setting out for the territory that New Englanders were prepared to fight the army. He considered that it would "be necessary to do it, first or last," and that when was "a mere question of policy."[65]

Sanborn's views were less extreme than Higginson's, but there was no denying his commitment to a free Kansas and the ultimate destruction of the peculiar institution. He too was anxious to persuade westerners of the need for radical action and, on arriving in Iowa, lost no time in seeking out men he could trust.[66] At the capital in early August he had an interview with Clarke and discussed the purloined state arms with the adjutant general. On the 10th he was in Burlington sipping tea with Governor Grimes, an acquaintance of his father-in-law. Next day Fitz Henry Warren gave Sanborn a free pass over the Burlington & Missouri to Mount Pleasant, an assembly point for Kansas emigrants. From there he traveled in filthy, ponderous stagecoaches across the rolling southern counties to the Missouri River and the fringes of the guerrilla war.[67]

Sanborn and Higginson were soon to become members of the clandestine abolitionist clique that provided backing for John Brown's raid on Harpers Ferry.[68] The easy familiarity that characterized relations between these insurgents and Iowa's foremost Republicans suggests that there were broad areas of agreement between both sets of men.

Kansas had done much to unite them. Although Iowa Republicans held themselves up publicly as opponents of disunion, their conception of state sovereignty was brought into sharper focus by Pierce's clumsy territorial policy. It therefore accorded well with the Yankees' burning hatred of a morally bankrupt national Democratic administration. James W. Grimes was incensed by Washington's refusal to intervene positively on the side of Northern settlers in Kansas. In August 1856 he wrote a strongly worded letter to the president detailing the putative sufferings of emigrant Iowans at the hands of "outlaws" and U.S. officers, and demanding that the pioneers receive immediate protection from the federal government. "In the event of a non-compliance . . . ," he warned, "a case will have arisen clearly within the principle laid down by Mr. Madison in the Virginia Resolutions of 1798, when it will be the duty of the States 'to interpose to arrest the progress of evils' in that Territory."[69]

Grimes probably chose his words for maximum political effect (he quickly gave Chase permission to quote from the letter).[70] Yet there is no doubt that his suspicion of Washington was sincere, for it was a leitmotif of his political career. Not all Republicans were violent opponents of central government per se. The majority of them proved to be rather less critical of central power when they gained control of the national administration in 1860. What is important is the degree to which Washington's mishandling of the situation in Kansas instilled a deep-rooted antipathy toward the federal government that sometimes found treasonable expression.

Republicans and abolitionists shared not only a dislike of Washington but also, and more significantly, a profound conviction that the South's slaveholding minority was conspiring to seize control of the U.S. government and reverse the nonextension policy of the Founding Fathers. Fear of the slave power undoubtedly exerted a potent influence on the Northern psyche, ever watchful of attempts to subvert battle-won liberties, but to what extent was Republican sectionalism grounded in the same abolitionist roots as that of Higginson and Sanborn?[71]

In May 1856 the New York editor Horace Greeley counseled a group of Rhode Island Republicans to disseminate the idea that the new party was "defensive, not aggressive [sic]; conservative of Freedom, rather than destructive of Slavery."[72] Many scholars have taken the chief policy objective of nonextension at face value and suggested that the Republicans had little interest in touching slavery where it lawfully existed.

Some contemporaries held that nonextension itself posed a direct threat to the survival of the peculiar institution. The one condition of slavery's vitality and profitableness, contended one newspaper, "is constant extension of territory. Once draw a cordon round it, beyond which it cannot pass, and Slavery would soon become utterly profitless within that cordon. It is only virgin soils which can be profitably cultivated by Slave labour."[73] Most Iowa Republicans perceived the South to be economically regressive and spatially dynamic, a view based on the dubious assumption that slavery was inefficient and cotton exhaustive of soil. Ralph P. Lowe of Muscatine, a prominent former Whig, contrasted the North's progressive free-labor system with slavery, which, he maintained, "brings premature decrepitude upon the country, by its wasteful and exhausting tillage, and to live must not only enlarge but often change the field of its operations."[74]

Whether or not most Republicans consciously regarded nonextension as a weapon of antislavery gradualism is debatable. Iowans seldom dwelt on the specifics of the expand-or-die theory, more often than not contenting themselves with bland assertions that Republican policy would place slavery on the slow road to extinction. Not all party activists, however, were willing to accept the complacent notion that a deep-rooted socioeconomic institution would eventually fade away like the Indians. While those prepared to take positive steps against slavery on moral grounds were generally former Liberty men and Free-Soilers, many leading nonradical Republicans evinced a readiness to participate in the abolitionist crusade.

On 23 June 1855 Dr. Edwin James, an elderly Yankee botanist and political immediatist whose farmhouse outside Burlington served as a refuge for fugitive slaves, was halted on the Illinois side of the Mississippi by two armed Southerners.[75] The Southerners were interested in the doctor's companion, a black man who they claimed was a runaway from Missouri. Together they made their way to the Burlington post office where, in the midst of an excited crowd, a writ was issued for the slave's arrest and the unfortunate captive was consigned to the city jail.[76]

One individual deeply disturbed by this affront to natural justice was Governor James W. Grimes. After informing his wife on 24 August that, "if not in office, I am inclined to think that I should be a law-breaker," the executive requested his political associates to attend the trial.[77] The response was overwhelming. Friends of the bondsman packed into the courtroom, and many others waited expectantly outside. Among those speaking in defense of the fugitive were David Rorer and Marcellus Crocker, prominent Iowa Democrats; Grimes's Whiggish law partner, William H. Starr; and two local anti-Nebraska men, Fitz Henry Warren and the Methodist preacher William F. Cowles. District Judge Ralph P. Lowe was waiting in the wings with a writ of habeas corpus, but it was not needed. The court ruled that there was insufficient evidence to order a rendition. "When the decision was made," recorded Grimes the next day, "such a shout went up as was never heard in that hall before . . . and the whole town reverberated."[78]

Relieved that there had been no humiliating rendition of a runaway slave in his hometown, the jubilant governor considered the rapid change in public opinion that had taken place since the passage of the 1850 Compromise. Whereas, four years previously, only a few of his fellow citizens had dared express contempt for the Fugitive Slave Act, now "three fourths of the reading and reflecting people of the county agree with me in my sentiments on the law, and a slave could not be returned from Des Moines County into slavery." Concluded Grimes, "It is a blessed thing that there is no ebb to the principles and progress of freedom: it is always a flood tide."[79]

This event highlighted the extent to which abolitionists, free-soil Whigs, and even a number of nonextension Democrats were brought into confederation by their antipathy toward slavery and the South. The Republican coalition as it emerged from the political turmoil of the 1850s was an amalgam of disparate groups. Its primary aim, like that of all major parties in American history, was to win elections. As such it could not have afforded to alienate majority feeling with calls for the immediate destruction of the peculiar institution even if its leaders had that object in mind. Within the organization's ranks in Iowa, however, the old Liberty–Free-Soil element strove consistently to ensure that the predominantly Whig leadership did not forget the terms of the pact agreed on at Crawfordsville in 1854. A minority though they were, pious individuals such as George W. Ells, a Davenporter with links to Salmon P. Chase, believed that agitation was "the principle that keeps everything pure, as well in the physical as in the moral world."[80] The radicals did not balk at taking unconstitutional action to promote the antislavery cause. They opened up their homes to Missouri runaways, vented their wrath against the Fugitive Slave Law, and gave succor to revolutionary disunionists. Highly motivated Christian men and women, they provided the underlying dynamic of early Iowa Republicanism and, in so doing, did much to substantiate Jefferson Davis's pithy observation that "bodies in motion will overcome bodies at rest."[81]

This said, the dramatic events of 1855-56 revealed that nonradical Republicans could be equally active in the politics of the antebellum era. If this amorphous bloc proved amenable to pressure from the party's antislavery wing, it did so out of self-interest and ideological compatibility with the radicals. Inevitably tension existed between the two groups. Republicans who did not think primarily in terms of moral imperatives sometimes regarded the antislavery men as impractical and deficient in manly virtues. William W. Hamilton once described John Teesdale, a zealous free-soil Whig and fellow Englishman who edited the Des Moines *Iowa State Register,* as a "good old woman wrapped up in Congregational clothing."[82] On the whole, however, the ties that bound the two groups were far stronger than those dividing them.

Historians generally distinguish between moderate and conservative Republicans. Although there was no clear demarcation line within the nonradical bloc, most leading Iowa Republicans can best be described as centrists. Their readiness to respond to public opinion at specific moments in history damned them as pragmatists in the eyes of many radicals, and it is certainly true that the primary aim of men like Grimes and Harlan was to retain power at the polls, not abolish slavery or pass controversial prohibitory laws. Yet the moderates, most of whom had been free-soil Whigs or anti-Nebraska Democrats, were by no means devoid of principles. Their opposition to the slave power was perfectly genuine and it was this that often led them to act with the radicals. Many of them, however, did sympathize with the antislavery wing's moral opposition to slavery, even if they tended to place more emphasis on the defense of the North's free labor system than on black freedom.

Those who hailed from the border states possessed firsthand experience of the peculiar institution. Charles C. Nourse, a Whiggish attorney and staunch Methodist "grounded in the theory that our fathers . . . had established a government with all the essential attributes of sovereignty," remembered leaving his hometown church in Kentucky and hearing the pathetic cries of a black woman as she was being lashed for giving offense to her mistress.[83] "The contrast between the quiet worshippers at the church," he wrote, "and the horrible cries that filled the air from the unfortunate negro slave woman was a comment on the injustice and brutality of the institution, that made an impression upon my mind that has never been erased."[84] Judge Samuel F. Miller of Keokuk, another Whig-Republican moderate and Kentucky native, denounced slavery as "the most stupendous wrong, and the most prolific source of human misery, both to the master and the slave, that the sun shines upon in his daily circuit around the globe."[85]

James W. Grimes, the most influential nonradical in the party, was unfamiliar with the daily workings of the South's labor system, but his personal involvement in the Burlington fugitive slave case indicated that he identified himself strongly with its opponents. Like many centrists he did not share the religious radical's determination to purge the world of sin. In spite of his early conversion experience, Congregational background, and sentimental disposition, he was a liberal in religion, inclining heavily toward Unitarianism in his later life.[86] A pragmatic party builder whose own personal ambition was, like that of Chase, inextricably linked with the Republican crusade to defeat the slave power, Grimes's strong moral sense led him to respond positively to radical pressure emanating from individuals like his wife, Elizabeth, and his avowed political godfather, Asa Turner.[87]

Just how radical these influences made him were revealed in late 1856 when the Garrisonian abolitionist Wendell Phillips delivered a lecture at the state capitol in Iowa City. After Phillips had finished speaking Josiah B. Grinnell (an antislavery Republican member of the general assembly) asked him to expound his views on slavery and disunion.[88] Phillips consented and proceeded to compare the U.S. Constitution to a box in which the acorn of liberty had been planted. The safety of the box, he said, was irrelevant. The germ, he hoped, would develop into an oak tree. The watching Grimes was delighted with the speech. "This is another evidence of the progress of antislavery sentiment," he told Elizabeth. "Let us thank God that the world moves."[89]

While the difference between moderates and radicals was often a matter of degree, it would be fallacious to suggest that all Republican centrists were closet abolitionists. What is important is that those who were not guided primarily by feelings of gut humanity—men like Harlan and Grimes's close ally, Samuel J. Kirkwood—were frequently induced to assume antislavery positions because of the pressure of events, their growing hatred of the South, and the stridency of the radical voice.

At times, of course, they had to respond to countervailing sentiments emanating from the party's conservative wing. This grouping, composed mainly of National Whigs and sectionalized Know Nothings, was interested almost solely in curbing the political and economic power of the South within the Union and downgraded the moral import of the slavery issue. Often overtly racist and anti-immigrant, conservative Republicans had no sympathy for the radicals' determination to elevate the status of American blacks. Because of the dramatic impact on Iowa of the Kansas-Nebraska Act and the guerrilla war in Kansas only a handful of genuine conservatives could be found among the local Republican elite. Judge George G. Wright of Keosauqua, an Indiana-born Whig, was probably the most prominent, but even he was carried along by the sectional tide in the late 1850s. "Fogeyism," as the radically inclined liked to call it, was more pronounced at grass-roots level, particularly in the southern counties where Unionist and nativist sentiment acted as a break on party extremism. On the whole though, the weakness of Silver Grey influence within Iowa's anti-Nebraska coalition worked against the development of a powerful conservative wing comparable to that in Pennsylvania. It was thus left to the pragmatists to determine the direction of party policy.

A month before Wendell Phillips's visit to Iowa City, local Republicans witnessed a major political triumph. John C. Frémont, the national party's presidential candidate, carried the state with a plurality of 49.1 percent over Buchanan and Fillmore, his Democrat and Know Nothing opponents who garnered 40.4 and 10.5 percent of the popular vote respectively.[90] It was the first time that the Democrats' presidential nominee had been defeated in Iowa and clear evidence that the old Jacksonian hegemony had been totally shattered by the growing sectional crisis and the economic and ethnocultural currents underlying state politics in the antebellum period.

Although strong Southern support sent Buchanan to the White House, Frémont's showing boded ill for the administration party. In Iowa Democratic strength was confined largely to Dubuque and the lower-tier counties.[91] The fast-growing northeastern quarter of the state went strongly for Frémont, and the central belt of counties running west of the Mississippi bend between Dubuque and Muscatine also turned in Republican majorities. The emerging sectional division of the state between a strongly Republican north, a less staunchly Republican center, and a faintly Democratic south mirrored that in Illinois, Indiana, and Ohio.

To some extent this pattern was a product of conscious settlement choices among the population. Whereas Southern-born migrants tended to favor the lower third of the state, New Englanders settled predominantly in the northeastern counties outside Dubuque. In very few areas did these two groups overlap, a fact indicative of a profound mutual antipathy. New Englanders perceived Southerners as indolent, backward, and frequently amoral, while the latter held Yankees to be puritanical, overbearing, and foes of a constitutional Union. Not only did they shun each other in many areas of the Midwest but they also tended to vote for different political parties.

William E. Gienapp's analysis of the 1856 presidential election indicates that Frémont received the backing of the vast majority of Yankees in Iowa but was largely rejected by Southerners who voted for Buchanan and Fillmore.[92] Amos Harris, an Ohio-born Democrat, blamed his party's poor performance on the presence in northern Iowa of large numbers of New Englanders, who, "educated to all the quisickal & busy body notions of their fathers," were prepared "to believe any story any ranting rifle Beecher clergyman may tell them."[93] A resident of Centerville on the Missouri border, Harris was venting the ethnocultural prejudices of most inhabitants of the lower-tier counties. Had he been a more dispassionate observer of events, he might have placed more blame for Buchanan's local defeat on the substantial number of Southern-born voters in his vicinity who abandoned Democracy for nativism in 1855–56.

Other ethnic groups voting Republican in disproportionate numbers in the presidential contest were British and Scandinavian immigrants.[94] Catholic Irishmen voted unanimously for Buchanan. Less predictable was the failure of many Germans to support the Frémont ticket. Although Grimes had hoped to bring German Protestants into the anti-Nebraska fold, the Republicans' endorsement of nativist candidates earlier in the year appears to have alienated this important bloc of voters. More than two-thirds of foreign-born Iowans chose to back the Democratic ticket, compared to 32 percent of native whites (a plurality of whom voted for Frémont).

Aside from the Germans, most of those who supported Grimes in 1854 remained loyal to the Republican cause.[95] The same was true of Iowans who had sanctioned the state's Maine Law by a popular majority of 53 percent in 1855. Prohibition was regarded by most European- and Southern-stock voters as an unacceptable attempt by Yankeefied politicians to impose their own rigid moral standards on the community. Because a close relationship pertained between the anti–Maine Law vote and support for Buchanan, it is clear that the two major parties in Iowa were now split along discernible ethnocultural lines.[96] There had been signs of such a division in the days of the second party system, but the events of the early 1850s polarized matters to a much greater degree.

This finding does not prove that ethnic and religious factors were the only determinants of party allegiance before the Civil War. Regression statistics indicate that there may also have been an occupational basis to partisanship. Gienapp suggests that Frémont won the backing of an inordinate number of skilled workers in Iowa—a particularly interesting contention in view of the fact that several modern historians have pointed to artisan support as a crucial prop of British and American abolitionism during the early phase of the industrial revolution.[97] No doubt many of these mechanics were responding to the homestead and protectionist planks in the national Republican platform. However, it is not impossible that the threat to their own economic status posed by the new industrialism rendered them sympathetic to the dependent position of Southern slaves. Although one reason why 86 percent of artisans voted Republican compared with only 13 percent of unskilled workers was that the latter were generally foreign immigrants and the former native-born Americans, the Republican inclinations of artisans and commercial farmers hint at a class as well as ethnocultural dimension to the party's success.

The period 1854-56 witnessed the transformation of James Grimes's anti-Nebraska coalition into an institutionalized political party. A multiplicity of factors contributed to this development. Of these the most important was the increasingly explosive sectional crisis between the Northern and Southern sections of the Union. The outbreak of a vicious guerrilla war in neighboring Kansas was the most serious manifestation of this crisis. It brought white Americans to blows with one another for the first time since the Revolutionary era and induced normally peaceable men in both sections to suppose that their purportedly distinctive civilizations were under threat from the enemies of republican liberty. More than that it paved the way for political realignment along wholly sectional lines.

Realignment had been the objective of most nonextensionists after the passage of the Kansas-Nebraska Act, but its accomplishment was thwarted by the rise of the Know Nothing movement. The annus mirabilis of Iowa nativism was 1855. That year Iowans flocked to the American standard, perceiving its superpatriotism and reformist policies as an antidote to the political ills of the day. However, reports of attacks on free-state migrants to Kansas by bands of ruffians from Missouri combined with the blatantly proslavery policy of the Pierce administration to give substance to the slave power rhetoric of opposition leaders. In February 1856 former Liberty men, Free-Soilers, anti-Nebraska Democrats, and nonextension Whigs were emboldened by these events to meet at Iowa City to form a state Republican party. Although the organization's first platform eschewed Know Nothing goals, the convention's decision to support nativist candidates in local elections reflected a readiness to cooperate with the Americans. The ongoing sectional crisis that split the national Know Nothing movement shortly afterwards ensured that cooperation would be on Republican terms. By November 1856 large numbers of nativists had been assimilated into the new party leaving mainly Southern-born voters in the lower-tier counties to vote for Fillmore. Most of them, it seems, were looking for a middle way out of the sectional crisis, rather than proscription of foreign-born immigrants.

Frémont's plurality in the presidential election confirmed the arrival of the Republican party as a major political force in Iowa. Its strengths were many: a dynamic radical wing made up largely of political abolitionists; a pragmatic centrist leadership that responded creatively to internal and external pressures; and a progressive moral and material image that appealed especially to reformist, native-born Protestants and middling, commercially orientated elements within the community who rejected laissez-faire Democracy as an adequate political ideology for the modern era. Most important of all, Republicanism offered a persuasive critique of the nation's problems: one that depicted the South's slaveholding minority as the most dangerous threat to all that these groups held dear—free labor, the Union, the constitutional rights of the North, even, in some cases, the liberties of black men. Southern actions during the mid-1850s made that critique persuasive, and because the national Democratic party was so closely associated with them, Iowa's ruling Jacksonians were forced to surrender power to their enemies. There was nothing inevitable about Republican hegemony, however. Between 1857 and 1860 local Democrats battled to restore their lost fortunes. They chose strong ground on which to fight: race, railroads, and the safety of the federal Union. To these issues we now turn.

2
Legitimization

5
The Race Question in the Campaign of 1857

ne of James W. Grimes's most important acts as governor of Iowa was to affix his signature to a bill providing for a referendum on the question of revising the 1846 constitution. Because that measure received substantial support from Democrats as well as anti-Nebraska men in the 1854–55 legislature, it must be regarded as firm evidence that the state's Jacksonian constitution was now regarded by all but the most ardent locofoco as outmoded.[1] The prohibition against banking had proved its principal weak point, for as the first railroads arrived from the east, popular demand for adequate financial institutions became irresistible. The voters approved the reform proposal by 32,790 votes to 14,162.[2] Elections for a constitutional convention to be held at Iowa City in early 1857 ensured that that body would be dominated by Republicans.

Iowa's third constitutional convention in thirteen years produced a document more in keeping with the Age of Capital. The delegates' primary achievements were to legalize banks of issue and facilitate state and local government investment in infrastructural improvements. These economic moves are discussed in detail in the next chapter.[3] The convention also decided that the state capital should be transferred to Des Moines, empowered a state board of education to oversee the common schools, reduced the gubernatorial term from four to two years, and doubled the residency requirement for voters in the counties. Although its economic content was decidedly Whiggish, the constitution retained legislative control over corporate charters and provided for popular election of supreme court judges. These provisions reflected the presence of ex-Democrats within the Republican ranks and the determination of the party leadership not to antagonize what had been until 1854 a predominantly Jacksonian electorate. Although the constitution's probank clauses were likely to endanger its ratification if the Democrats decided to oppose the work of the convention, it was the race issue that so nearly proved the document's undoing.

Relatively few black people dwelt in Iowa in the mid-nineteenth century. The slow pace of urbanization and industrialization combined with white hostility to limit Iowa's free black population to just over a thousand on the eve of the Civil War.[4] Nearly a third of them resided in the Mississippi River towns of Keokuk, Muscatine, and Dubuque.[5] The rest were scattered across the prairies in the agricultural communities of eastern and southern Iowa. In the urban areas they found employment as laborers and domestics. In the countryside they worked on farms or, occasionally, exploited their skills as artisans. The blacks were predominantly young (three-quarters of them were aged thirty or under), Southern- or eastern-born, and poor. Out of 258 adult males located in the 1860 federal census, 106 (41 percent) owned no property whatsoever. Only a quarter possessed any real property, and the median total estate was a paltry $50.

Although these figures indicate that Iowa blacks were a severely disadvantaged minority, the latter did not form a homogeneous underclass. Over a third of those in employment were engaged in middling occupations. Some, like the Reverend George Watrous's colony of Illinois and border-state blacks in Fayette County, were reasonably prosperous farmers.[6] Others displayed evidence of an entrepreneurial spirit by opening up barber shops in the towns. Among this group was Alexander Clark, a Muscatine native of mixed ancestry who made his fortune by investing the profits of his tonsorial enterprise in timberland and then contracting to supply local steamboat companies with wood.[7] While Clark benefited from the lightness of his skin, his free-born origins, and atypical grammar school education, his success was proof of the existence of a fragile black elite. Clark, a prominent member of the African Methodist Episcopal church, was his people's foremost spokesman in Iowa. Like most local blacks he recognized the limitations on independent action by working within the confines of the existing white-dominated political system.

Although it was not dependent on racism as a fundamental dynamic, the second party system had offered little hope to Alexander Clark (who arrived in Muscatine as a young man in May 1842). Jacksonian Democrats frequently labeled their opponents as friends of the black race, forcing free-soil Whigs onto the defensive and associating them with abolitionism in the public mind. Sectional concerns and lily-white locofocoism made most local Democrats unremitting foes of racial reform. In Iowa only politicians with significant numbers of antislavery constituents dared to champion the cause of black rights during the 1840s. The enactment of a more rigorous fugitive slave law in 1850 may have elicited popular sympathy for the bondsman, but as the passage of a local exclusion measure the following year revealed, very little of that sympathy rubbed off onto the free black.

While exclusion sentiment was far from synonymous with proslavery feeling, Democratic oratory sometimes hinted at a connection. In April 1856 Iowa's senior U.S. senator, George W. Jones, rebutted the statement of his Republican colleague James Harlan that slavery was the sole cause of black inferiority. In all his limited reading, said Jones, he had found no evidence that blacks had been created the equals of white men. The former, he contended, were "the veritable descendants of Ham, cursed in his son Canaan by the Almighty, driven out from the presence of his father with the vengeance of God marked upon his brow and doomed to be the servant of servants forever."[8] He went on to deny that the Declaration of Independence sanctioned racial equality and taunted Harlan with the last Iowa general assembly's failure to improve the lot of local blacks. "Though labour was in great demand," he announced, "and domestics could scarcely be had at any price, an abolition legislature, with all their inextinguishable fires of sympathy, would not allow negroes to emigrate to Iowa, or exercise the right of suffrage."[9]

The 1854–55 assembly to which Jones alluded was not "an abolition legislature" by any stretch of the imagination. Democrats possessed a majority of one in the senate, and the house was controlled by a coalition of nonextension Whigs and antislavery radicals. It was, however, the fusionists who had sent Harlan to Congress to enunciate environmental theories of racial equality, and Senator Jones was correct in thinking many of the legislators were concerned for the welfare of black people.

Midway through the turbulent winter session, Dr. Reasin Pritchard, an anti-Nebraska Whig from Muscatine, presented to the house a petition praying for repeal of the exclusion law. The signatories were described as "free colored persons," and the list was headed by Alexander Clark. Immediately, one of the leading Democrats in the house moved to lay the document on the table. The motion was approved by thirty-nine votes to twenty-six.[10] Of those registering their desire to receive the petition, twenty-five were fusionists.

Shortly afterwards, on 21 January 1855, a controversial senate bill came up for discussion in the lower chamber. This provided for the dispensing of state subsidies to Iowa blacks who wished to emigrate to Liberia under the aegis of the American Colonization Society.[11] It was well suited to tap racist and benevolent support for repatriation amongst the electorate, but unlikely to find favor with men sympathetic to the long-running abolitionist assault on the society.

As soon as the senate proposal was introduced, it drew the fire of problack legislators. After an abortive attempt by the latter to have the measure indefinitely postponed, Jacob Wentworth Rogers, a combative Fayette County abolitionist, offered to amend the bill by substituting immigrants for blacks.[12] This move highlighted not only the coalitionists' dislike of colonization but also the correlation between ethnocentrism and civil rights activism that was to have an important impact on state politics over the next decade. In spite of Rogers's failure to defeat the colonization bill, humanitarians in Iowa would continue to use foreigners (most notably Catholic Irishmen whose hatred of African-Americans was well known) as negative reference symbols in order to improve the black man's public image.

Senate File 141 passed the house the next day by thirty-five votes to twenty-five.[13] Ordinarily this action would have been followed by executive endorsement, and the bill would have become law. On this occasion Governor James W. Grimes withheld his approval. His action, which was enough to kill the state colonization scheme, was almost certainly impelled by his own personal dislike of the measure and by the fact that nearly two-thirds of the fusionists had opposed the bill on final passage.[14] Grimes's dependence on antislavery men during the mid-1850s has already been noted. Their unambiguous stance on colonization in the Iowa house could hardly have been ignored by an emerging party leader whose inclinations on the subject were scarcely less progressive than their own.

As shown in figure 5.1, motions relating to the exclusion law petition and the colonization bill united the Democratic minority and divided the opposition. Twenty representatives, all of them anti-Nebraska men, opposed the tabling of the Muscatine free black petition and voted consistently against the colonization bill. At least three-quarters of them were evangelical Protestants (predominantly Methodists and Presbyterians).[15] Sixty-five percent had been born in mid-Atlantic or western states. Although they tended to be slightly older than their Democratic opponents, they were, on average, six years younger than the nonhumanitarian Whigs in the house. This latter bloc contained most of the Silver Greys who had spurned Harlan's candidacy in the recent joint convention to elect a U.S. senator. Half of its number were nonevangelicals; half were Southern-born. The pro- and anti–civil rights factions were almost unanimous in their support for a prohibitory liquor law with or without a popular referendum—evidence that neoabolitionist and temperance activity were not quite part and parcel of the same all-encompassing "moral" ideology.[16]

The concern evinced by western radicals for local blacks was, as Senator Jones intimated, an adjunct of their commitment to political abolitionism.

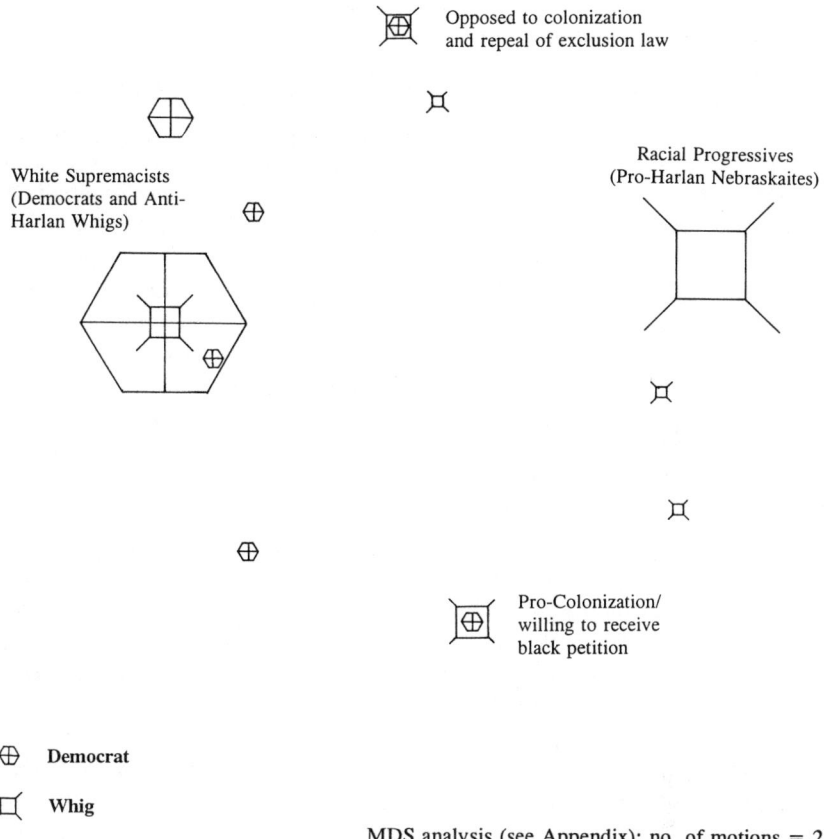

Fig. 5.1 Iowa House, 1854: Voting behavior on local black rights motions.

While the antislavery insurgents constituted a powerful humanitarian lobby within the new Republican organization, they did not control the party machinery. This remained in the grasp of free-soil Whigs like Grimes and Harlan—men who supported some of the radicals' objectives, but who recognized the fault lines of the coalition and worked tirelessly to promote unity among potentially discordant elements. Racial reform was closer to the center of antebellum Republicanism than some historians have suggested. But because it touched the prejudices of politicians and voters alike, it was an issue to be treated with care.

The presence of seasoned antislavery men in the Republican camp induced frustrated Democrats to rely increasingly on outright racism as a means of placing their opponents on the defensive. With no sign of majority support among the electorate for problack measures there were sound tactical reasons for greater emphasis on this issue. Pragmatic Republican leaders appreciated this fact and worked to balance the growing radical demand for black rights (including suffrage) with the need to construct winning coalitions among the electorate at large.

Caution was evident in the 1856–57 session of the general assembly when the vast majority of Republicans in both chambers voted to repeal the ban on black testimony in state courts but shied away from other measures that smacked of amalgamation. In the senate they lined up twenty to one against a Democratic attempt to embarrass them by adding the words "without distinction of color" to a resolution demanding the preservation of the national domain for "Free Homes" and "Free Men."[17]

House Republicans evinced a similar disposition to temporize on the race question. Most worrying to the delegates were fears that the constitutional convention (then sitting concurrently with the legislature) might tamper with the franchise. When a Dubuque Democrat introduced a resolution expressing the house's opposition to black suffrage, only five Republicans voted in the negative.[18] Republican members of the convention were thus left in no doubt as to the party's feeling on the suffrage question.

Iowa's third constitutional convention was called primarily to repeal the state's Jacksonian prohibition on banking. That it spent much of its time debating black rights testified to the salience of the slavery question in all its guises. Most of the twenty-one Republicans present were moderates on this issue. Particularly conspicuous was James F. Wilson, a promising young Fairfield lawyer described by one objective Democrat as "an intellectual giant" destined to make "a still greater mark in the future."[19] An effective orator and astute tactician, Wilson would soon emerge as one of Governor Grimes's principal allies in the state and, after the Civil War, as a major Republican power broker in his own right. The leading radicals in attendance at Iowa City were William Penn Clarke, the former Whig turned Free-Soiler who had organized Iowa's Kansas aid effort the previous summer, and George W. Ells, a onetime Liberty party organizer in Ohio.

The full range of Republican opinion on racial matters was evident in the debates of the 1857 constitutional convention. Four major civil rights issues were discussed at length by this body: black property ownership, legal testimony, suffrage, and personal security. Only the latter elicited a united response from the Republican majority.

At a gathering in Denmark to laud the activities of the defense counsel in the Burlington fugitive slave case of 1855, the Reverend Asa Turner had offered a toast looking forward to the enactment of a personal liberty law to protect free blacks and runaways from Southern slave catchers.[20] Several Northern states had already passed such measures, much to the annoyance of the South, which regarded them as unconstitutional and subversive of the 1850 Compromise. The Iowa legislature took no action in this direction and left the matter to the constitutional convention.

On 30 January 1857 George W. Ells, the chairman of the bill of rights committee (dominated, as were all the convention's important committees, by Republicans), introduced an amendment to the draft declaration on fundamental liberties. This additional section stated that no person should be deprived of life, liberty, or property without due process of law, and that everyone had the right to a speedy trial, legal counsel, and an impartial jury.[21] That Ells, a friend of Salmon P. Chase and "an ardent opponent of Slavery," intended the amendment as an abolitionist measure was made manifest when he expressed his desire to see the new constitution contain "every guarantee for freedom that words can express."[22] Then, he said, "that infamous Fugitive Slave Law will become a nul[l]ity, and the American people will trample its odious enactments in the dust."[23]

The sectional intent of Ells's maneuver led the minority Democrats to move that the words "and in all cases involving the life of an individual" be stricken out on the grounds that they were illegal.[24] Republicans of all stripes rallied to defend the clause as it stood. The progressive John T. Clark argued that without the existing phraseology "we cannot protect every individual member of society. Without this right we cease to be a sovereignty, and become dependent on some other power."[25] His centrist colleague James F. Wilson pronounced the Fugitive Slave Act unconstitutional and averred that he did not care if the provision under consideration should conflict with federal law.[26] These comments revealed how an unpalatable U.S. statute touched critical elements of Republican ideology, fusing genuine humanitarian zeal, suspicion of Washington, and deep-rooted sectional prejudices into consolidated opposition to an integral prop of the Union. It was also a prime source of political competition. When the discussion ended, the Democrats' motion was defeated by a strict party vote.[27]

The general Republican enthusiasm for inserting a personal liberty clause into the constitution was primarily a consequence of the party's sectional orientation, of its commitment to Northern—as opposed to black—rights. In a series of blatant stump speeches toward the close of the convention's deliberations, conservative, moderate, and radical Republican delegates expressed their hatred of the slave power and contempt for the Democrats' alleged subserviency thereto. John Edwards, a Kentucky-born conservative from southern Iowa, denounced slavery as "inconsistent and incompatible with the genius and spirit of our free institutions."

> [W]hen the south attempts to force this obnoxious institution upon free and northern soil, we, who are patriots and who love liberty and ground consecrated to liberty, can say to this slave oligarchy as the Maker of the universe said to the waves—thus far shalt thou go and no farther. . . . The true policy is to hem it in, and it will work its own cure.[28]

Although Jonathan C. Hall, a Burlington Democrat who had been a member of the 1844 constitutional convention, accused Edwards of fomenting sectional tension and sliding rapidly into the abolitionist camp, these criticisms had no impact on nonhumanitarian Republicans.[29] John A. Parvin, a protemperance nativist and ex-Democrat from Muscatine, launched into another campaign oration in which he accused the Democrats of being sectionalists for trying to force slavery into the territories.[30] William Penn Clarke concurred. In a speech taking up sixteen sides of the convention journal he explained how the South had forced Northern Democrats to abandon popular sovereignty in favor of federal support for slavery expansion.[31] Such remarks left no doubt about the Republican position on the territorial question. However, when that issue was not linked obviously with equal rights for local blacks, the party's stance became more ambiguous.

The fact that a minority of radical whites in the party were lobbying hard to improve the legal status of Iowa's tiny free black population confronted Republican leaders with a difficult dilemma: How could the demands of the antislavery wing be reconciled with the reality that there was relatively little support for equal rights among the electorate at large? The determination of delegates representing radical constituencies to press this issue upon the convention ensured that the problem could not be ignored.

On 31 January Rufus Clarke offered an amendment to the draft bill of rights giving "foreigners *and other persons not being citizens*" the same property-holding privileges as native-born residents.[32] Something of a shadowy figure in Iowa politics, Clarke did not have a reputation as a problack radical. He was born in Connecticut, educated in New York state, and had been living in Iowa for only six years. Like Fitz Henry Warren, whose ally he appears to have been, his manners were too refined to make him popular, but neither they nor his unstable financial situation had yet combined to obstruct his political career, first as a Whig, then as an unsuccessful nativist candidate for Congress.[33] Even though his inclinations were conservative (he did confess his prejudice against blacks and a penchant, in the abstract, for colonization), the presence of significant numbers of antislavery radicals in his Henry County constituency helped to make him one of the most outspoken radicals at the convention.[34]

Clarke's amendment stirred up a hornet's nest. Recognizing that the measure was designed primarily to benefit free blacks, opposition members were appalled. George Gillaspy of Ottumwa stated his opposition to holding out inducements to black immigration. He would, he said, "vote [today] for a proposition, if it was before this Convention, to exclude the negro forever from coming into this State."[35] His colleague Amos Harris agreed. "I am proud," he announced, "to think that the party to which I belong is the white man's party, and seeks to promote the interests of the white man."[36]

Most of the Republicans chose to remain quiet on this issue, leaving Clarke to defend his amendment as best he could. This he did by trying to establish the connection between white supremacy and support for slavery expansion. Were members of the opposition, he asked, so much in favor of "that Illinois slave law" (the Kansas-Nebraska Act) that they would violate all their campaign pledges and carry "this cursed system of slavery" into the territories? "Are they who are so much in favor of having the negro as a slave, so afraid to allow him to come here as a free man?"[37] The canny James F. Wilson came part of the way to his aid by arguing that the legislature's power to prevent black in-migration made a nonsense of Democratic fears, but when the amendment was put to the vote, only eight delegates gave it their assent.[38]

Rufus Clarke did not dwell long upon this failure. Two days later he moved that a provision for black testimony and officeholding be inserted into the proposed constitution.[39] On this occasion a few of his colleagues did speak up in favor of the measure, even though they were confronted by a predictable barrage of criticism from the opposition. Jonathan C. Hall warned them that their efforts to brook popular racism were unwise: "It is a prejudice of centuries standing, that is deeply imbedded in the minds of the people."[40] This truism did not prevent ten Republicans from voting for the amendment—their courage no doubt strengthened by the knowledge that the general assembly had already passed a law providing for black testimony.[41]

The redoubtable Clarke immediately reintroduced his amendment with the officeholding provision stricken out.[42] Why was it, he asked, that fellow Republicans were afraid to incorporate the legislature's action on black testimony into the constitution? James F. Wilson answered that his constituents (Democrats, Republicans, and nativists) had opposed any change in the racial complexion of the state's fundamental law.[43] To draw party lines on this issue was to endanger ratification. John Edwards was of a similar mind. While claiming to agree with Clarke's principles, he was both opposed to encumbering the constitution with measures that might lead to its rejection and unwilling to shock "the moral sensibilities" of those entertaining prejudices against blacks.[44] The Democrat George Gillaspy intervened at this point to dare his opponents to introduce this provision: "I say to them here if they do it that my county [Wapello], believing that the white man is better than the negro, will give a thousand majority against the constitution."[45]

John T. Clark led the opposition's counterattack. Democrats, he maintained, had the Republicans over a barrel on this issue because they could label his copartisans as abolitionists or hypocrites depending on which way they voted. "[T]he negro," said Clark, "by nature is just as good as the white man." Although slavery degraded the former in the South, the U.S. Constitution guaranteed free black citizens of all the states the right to come to Iowa and enjoy the same privileges as local whites: "Now I ask gentlemen . . . shall we as a republican majority sustain the principle which we in our hearts endorse, or shall we refuse to support it simply because we do not deem it expedient to incorporate it into the constitution?"[46]

Despite being wary of the race question, William Penn Clarke was convinced that Republicans could not afford to retreat from a position already mapped out by the legislature. His party, he claimed, was founded on one principle: "I believe that principle to be one that is incorporated into the Declaration of Independence, that all men are created free and equal; that all men have the same natural rights." The convention chamber, continued Clarke rather oddly, was the proper place to decide on these rights. "I say we are in danger of losing all the moral influence of the Republican party, unless we take a high and noble stand upon this testimony."[47]

The two radical speeches failed to rally the party faithful behind the amendment under discussion. Rufus Clarke's provision was referred to the bill of rights committee and subsequently watered down to authorize litigants to take the testimony of "any other person not interested in the subject matter of the suit, who may be cognizant of any fact material to the case."[48] This phraseology was acceptable to most of Clarke's colleagues because it permitted whites to call black witnesses in their defense and could thus be sold to the electorate as a means of strengthening the legal rights of the racial majority. Black testimony, however, was not the main issue on the radical agenda in 1857. The chief demand of antislavery voters was that local blacks be enfranchised.

Before proceedings began on 19 January a majority of Republican delegates would have been willing to take the legislature's advice and sidestep this subject. Any hopes that it could be avoided, however, were dashed at the end of the first week when the Republican-controlled committee on suffrage reported in favor of the status quo. Immediately, Rufus Clarke introduced a resolution instructing the committee to investigate the expediency of a popular referendum on black suffrage.[49] This was quickly laid on the table by twenty-four votes to ten, just over half of his copartisans voting with the Democrats.[50]

On 4 February, shortly after John A. Parvin had presented a franchise petition signed by thirty-three of his black constituents, the convention voted narrowly to refer the original report of the suffrage committee to a select body of five containing Rufus Clarke and two other Republican progressives.[51] Nearly three weeks later the majority submitted a resolution providing for a separate popular referendum on the question of eliminating the word *white* from the proposed constitution.[52] A furious debate ensued.

The Democrat Jonathan C. Hall led off by submitting the minority report written by himself and his colleague, Daniel Price of Council Bluffs. This document contended that to submit this question to the people would be "to keep up agitation, to furnish material and forbidding sentiment, that is fraught with evil to the Indian, negro, and Anglo-American races." Arguing that suffrage was an artificial rather than a natural right, the report pointed out that many groups in American society, notably women and minors, were denied the electoral franchise.

> In forming or maintaining a government, it is the privilege and duty of those who have or are about to associate together for that purpose, to modify and limit the rights, or wholly exclude from the association, any and every specie of persons who would endanger, lessen, or in the least impair the enjoyment of these rights. We have seen that the application of this principle limits the rights of our sons, modifies the privileges of our wives and daughters, and would not be unjust if it excluded the negro altogether. . . . True, these persons may be unfortunate, but the government is not unjust.[53]

Hall and Price concluded their critique of equal rights with the warning that franchise reform would prompt a massive influx of blacks from less liberal states, leading ultimately to race war and amalgamation.

The Democrats' readiness to raise the spectre of swamping and miscegenation forced Republican delegates onto the defensive on this issue. William Penn Clarke spoke out against a Democratic motion to print both the majority and minority reports of the suffrage committee. He did not, he said, believe that "the great mass" of Iowans anticipated action to admit blacks to all the rights of citizenship, or that "all the dread evils" predicted by Hall and Price were likely to ensue from such action. Printing, he claimed (with justification), would allow the Democratic press to conceal the fact that "not five members of this convention are with the gentleman from Henry."[54] Although John T. Clark, already accused of being an amalgamationist in the *Keokuk Evening Times,* boldly contended that the voters were "too intelligent to be humbugged" by the kind of "trash" thrown up by the Democrats, virtually all of his Republican colleagues concluded that discretion was the best part of valor and voted to reject the printing of the reports.[55]

This show of unity did not prevent an intraparty squabble over the tactical and ideological import of eliminating all racially restrictive provisions from the constitution. For the most part delegates who were themselves radicals or whose constituencies contained active proponents of the measure backed the idea of a referendum, while pragmatists and conservatives opposed it or sought to limit the damage it might cause.

William Penn Clarke denied that his party had ever favored black suffrage and counseled against the adoption of a measure that, he averred, would alienate one-half of the Republican organization.[56] Although similar arguments would be propounded by Iowa Republicans for years to come, a majority of Penn Clarke's colleagues took the view that a referendum was the only way to satisfy grass-roots pressure for reform. Parvin confessed his own preference for colonization but said that he was perfectly willing to give his radical constituents a chance to register their opinions on the suffrage issue.[57] George W. Ells, one of the few Republicans present to venture the assertion that "the right of suffrage should be as broad as the universe of God," emphasized the importance of religious ultras in his Scott County district—"old Scotch Covenanters and Presbyterians," men "who hold themselves strictly accountable to a Higher Being for everything they do."[58] It was left to Rufus Clarke to put the issue most bluntly. The main reason why the matter should be submitted to the people, he urged, was that "at least a very respectable minority request it of us. A large number of the people of this State would be deprived, on account of conscientious scruples, from voting for this constitution, unless they are permitted to vote upon a side question of this nature."[59]

Not all the arguments were based on political arithmetic. There was a widespread feeling that the issue of equal rights lay close to the moral core of Republicanism and that to oppose a referendum would endanger the party's ideological integrity. A.H. Marvin, a Jones County farmer and ex-

Democrat, asked his fellow Republicans,

> What do you suppose compelled us to make war upon the old Democratic party, if it was not for the principles of freedom and equal rights, which we considered were trampled under foot by that party? I acknowledge with pride, that I could not have occupied this place, had it not been conferred upon me by those who are in love with the great principles of freedom and the equal rights of all men. It is because I am fondly attached to these principles that I am a Republican to-day. If we are to lose sight of these great principles, and prove recreant to the trust confided to us by the people, it will require no prophet's tongue to foretell that our doom as a party is sealed.[60]

It was, urged Marvin, an act of justice to allow the people to vote on this question.

It was left to the man described by James W. Grimes as "prudent, cautious, [and] sagacious" to fashion a compromise proposal that would suit all parties.[61] In order to reassure those Republicans who feared that any mention of black suffrage would defeat the new constitution and divide the party, James F. Wilson offered an amendment voiding a prosuffrage decision at the election if it failed to equal the majority vote on the constitution.[62] This paved the way for a referendum, but as Wilson must have known, the same provision had negated a narrow victory for franchise extension in neighboring Wisconsin eight years earlier.[63] The passage of his amendment killed any remote possibility of a surprise vote in August, enabled the Republicans to straddle the race question, and, most significantly of all, imposed a measure of unity on his copartisans. The referendum clause as amended was agreed to by a strict party vote, with even the timid William Penn Clarke supporting it.[64]

Notwithstanding James F. Wilson's attempt to limit the damage caused by black suffrage, the divisions apparent in the convention were soon reflected across the state as the 1857 campaign got underway. Race was not the only barrier to a Republican triumph in the summer and fall elections. The general assembly had reinjected the emotive temperance issue into the political arena by amending the state's prohibitory liquor act with a provision for county referenda on the alternative of a license law.[65] Local option was seen by Republicans eager to attract the German vote as a means of neutralizing this burdensome subject. Instead, as the party's low cohesion on the amendment revealed, it served only to anger moralists within the organization. Because the Democrats were also wary of the temperance question, they devoted most of their energies toward defeating the new constitution at the August referendum. Branded as a partisan document, the constitution rapidly assumed symbolic form, its demise perceived by the opposition as an essential prerequisite for the election of a Democratic governor in October. Two aspects of the constitution were deemed particularly obnoxious by the opposition. The first was its Whiggish economic character; the second, its attempt to force equal rights down the throats of an unwilling populace.[66] Among those forced to contend with the controversial work of the legislature and convention were the inhabitants of West Union in Fayette County.

As they anticipated another stifling summer on the Iowa prairie, the citizens of this fifteen hundred–strong farming community could have been but dimly aware that they were basking in the late evening sunshine of the agrarian age. No railroad connected the village with the outside world, and the ambitious traveler would have had to journey seventy miles southeast to Dubuque to find any real manifestations of industrialism. Yet life for the majority was tolerable enough. True, the recently settled township was not exactly a shining example of frontier democracy in action. Four percent of the adult male population owned nearly one-third of the aggregate wealth.[67] In part this reflected the prowess of the tiny commercial elite that not only handled the food surpluses produced by the district's commercial farmers but also supplied the village and its agricultural hinterland with essential goods and luxuries.

Class conflict, however, was a minor factor in village life, possibly because property holding appears in large measure to have increased with age. Ethnic homogeneity should have reduced further the divisions within the community. Nine-tenths of the population were white, native-born Americans, and only a tiny proportion of these were Southerners. Most were migrants from New York, Pennsylvania, and the Old Northwest. There were some Irishmen in the township, but generally speaking, they were farmers not nascent proletarians. West Union might have been a model Northern village, relatively prosperous and socially cohesive as it was. That it was not blessed with internal peace was due entirely to an explosive combination of issue-orientated politics and party factionalism.

The Republican organization in West Union was ill equipped to cope with the problems of the 1857 campaign, for it was seriously split by an internal struggle for power between rival factions. The leaders of these two groups were both members of the village's elite. Jacob Wentworth Rogers was a rich New Hampshire–born lawyer and merchant who had migrated to the West as a young man in 1843. After teaching school in Illinois and

Wisconsin, he moved to northeastern Iowa in September 1849 and, setting up a grocery store alongside Otter Creek on the open prairies, helped to lay out the townsite of West Union.[68]

His rival, Carmen A. Newcomb, held the post of county judge (a position of some power created by the Democratic Code of 1851).[69] A native Pennsylvanian he was, in Rogers's eyes, the unprincipled head of the courthouse clique that was scheming to establish total control over the local Republican party. At thirty Newcomb was seven years younger than his opponent. His election to Fayette County's most prestigious office augured well for the future and must have rankled keenly with Rogers. After all, the latter had been a founding member of the party in July 1854 and already spent one term in the legislature. The battle for supremacy focused specifically on the election of a new county judge on the same day in August as the constitutional referendum.

On 11 July West Union Republicans gathered in convention at the Baptist church. There, Rogers's opponents failed to prevent the appointment of a committee to report names of delegates to the party's county assemblage.[70] Not all of the men subsequently chosen were friends of Rogers, but those who were combined with his supporters in outlying townships to secure his nomination as county judge two days later.[71]

Newcomb and his allies were less than overjoyed. Their immediate response was to induce Republicans from the neighboring (and rival) village of Fayette to promote their candidate for the position, arguing that if Rogers was elected he would favor his hometown at Fayette's expense.[72] The county's outnumbered Democrats encouraged this development, hoping that an opposition split would let in their own man, William McClintock. Shortly before the election LeRoy Templeton was announced as an independent candidate for the judgeship. Rogers was convinced that McClintock's Democratic friends and their soreheaded Republican allies were behind the maneuver.[73] If they were, they came very close to success. Rogers carried Fayette County on 10 August by the narrowest of margins. His majority of twenty-nine was over three hundred behind that of the Republican candidate for prosecuting attorney.[74] Two hundred of those missing votes were located in Fayette where Templeton was the first choice. Intervillage rivalry and party factionalism had nearly conspired to place a Democrat in the courthouse.

If power had been the only prize at stake in this contest, the events of 1857 could be dismissed as empty political feuding. Yet this was not the case, for Rogers was not simply a petty Republican chieftain determined to stave off the challenge of an ambitious rival. He was a confirmed moralist. Three weeks before the election the Democratic *Fayette County Pioneer* contained the following indictment of the Republican candidate for county judge: "As to his impartiality, whatever Mr. Rogers enlists in he advocates to the extent of his means and ability, and is blind to all opposition, deaf to all evidence to the contrary, and no argument can be introduced strong enough to convince him of his error."[75]

Even accounting for the fierce partisanship of the age, this description was an accurate one. Rogers was, as the hostile editorial implied, a self-righteous, self-opinionated ideologue. He seldom questioned the correctness of his own views and was always prepared to believe the worst about his opponents. Nothing delighted him more than the prurient discovery that one of Newcomb's associates had been guilty of adultery while a citizen of New York state.[76] His willingness to see conspirators behind every fence post sometimes bordered on the pathological. In 1878 he shot and wounded an enemy in broad daylight.[77] His obsession with intrigue and cabal may have been partly a product of anti-Masonic views. Always when he ran for office he charged that the Masons were working for his defeat.[78]

This particular preoccupation, however, does not explain Rogers's paramount concerns of temperance and abolitionism. He was, first and foremost, a devout Universalist. Often passed over lightly as a relatively insignificant liberal branch of Protestantism, American Universalism was originally a product of schisms within New England churches at the end of the eighteenth century.[79] Like Unitarians its adherents rejected the doctrine of the Trinity, but in contrast to the relatively elite Boston-based religionists, their emphasis was on the ultimate salvation of all mankind. No less affected by the tide of evangelicalism than members of the mainstream denominations, Universalists were often found alongside Quakers, Congregationalists, Free-Will Baptists, and Presbyterians in the vanguard of the Protestant reform movement. A small but radical body of Christians, Iowa Universalists had already made known their feelings on the important issues of the day. In 1849 their state convention had passed resolutions condemning "offensive war," capital punishment, intemperance, and slavery ("a grievous wrong" and "palpable usurpation . . . at war with the principles of Christianity and genuine Republicanism"). It was, contended the assembled delegates, "the duty of every friend of Christianity and human liberty to use lawful and honorable means to do away with oppression and injustice, wherever they exist, and in all their forms."[80]

Jacob Wentworth Rogers adhered rigidly to this injunction. He was a leading organizer of the local temperance society founded in January 1857 to do battle with the supporters of local option.[81] As a lawyer he also spearheaded efforts to enforce the state's Maine Law, bringing suits against persons violating that controversial statute. His war against this particular manifestation of evil came to a temporary halt in early July. So confused was the state of the law after the enactment of local option that prohibitionists were unwilling to bring further prosecutions until the Iowa supreme court handed down a ruling on the subject.[82] Rogers was also wary of Democratic charges that "temperance fanatics" were squandering public money on antiliquor suits.[83] Such accusations could only have damaged his chances in the August election.

Rogers, however, was a reluctant temporizer. Anyone who had been a radical antislavery man since his majority was unlikely to have acquiesced gladly in a compromise of principle. His views on the South's peculiar institution were essentially those of the voluntarist school of political abolitionists centered in the heavily evangelized Burned-over district of New York.[84] Specifically he endorsed Alvan Stewart's antislavery interpretation of the U.S. Constitution, which held that due process gave the federal government authority to abolish slavery in the states. Given widespread publicity in the writings of William Goodell (writings with which Rogers was familiar), this doctrine enabled the Iowan to conclude that a compromise between liberty and slavery was impossible. "One might as well give [the] devil States rights control in one part of his heart—God in another & the whole made a union of these powers," he reflected in his diary.[85] Events in Kansas and the buildup to the U.S. Supreme Court's decision in the Dred Scott case strengthened this conviction. "While Slavery is admitted Constitutional in any State of the Union," he wrote early in 1857, "that very admission gives slavery a strong position from which to argue for extension, and to combat any opposition to slavery. The tendency of federal laws favorable to slavery is alarming of late—& will be more so, if not checked."[86]

This firm commitment to immediatism was a prime factor behind Rogers's efforts on behalf of the Republican party. At the first ever meeting of that organization in Fayette County on 8 July 1854 he submitted resolutions "expressing opposition to slavery in all its forms, and devotion to the principle of equal natural, political, and social rights," and asserting that "all other political questions sink into insignificance when compared with the overshadowing evils of slavery."[87] These early declarations of party faith (which were adopted unanimously by the delegates in West Union's Methodist church) evinced strong support for the cause of black rights. This was characteristic of Rogers, who, as an ex-Liberty party activist in the 1854-55 legislature, had made no secret of his dislike of colonization.

Given the Democracy's racist onslaught on the new constitution (the *Pioneer* thought it looked toward the "equality and final amalgamation" of the races), one might have expected local Republicans to deemphasize the slavery issue.[88] Some of them did. At an Independence Day picnic at West Union in 1857 Carmen A. Newcomb led off the ritual speech making without a single reference to the subject. Rogers was disgusted. Without an indictment of the peculiar institution the day was, in his view, "but a mockery—a sham—a disgrace," and he contrasted his rival's cowardice with the antislavery offering of A.K. Moulton, a Free-Will Baptist preacher.[89]

While Newcomb remained silent on the race question, his antagonist made no attempt to evade the issue. During the short campaign for the judgeship, Rogers spoke out in favor of equal rights for Iowa blacks. At the outlying hamlet of Taylorville on 1 August he told an audience that he would vote to strike the word *white* from the proposed constitution.[90] He also mentioned a rumor that there were some ex-slaves in Fayette County (presumably members of the Watrous colony in Westfield Township). These blacks, he said, "were respectable—associated with white people in equal terms—and the word white if rumor was correct—would disgrace them—throw them out of the pale of society—which was wrong."[91]

At the same election that elevated Rogers to the judgeship, Fayette County voters rejected black suffrage by a ratio of two and a half to one.[92] The people of West Union gave it even shorter shrift. Only one in four voters approved franchise reform there. The victorious candidate must have known that his backing for such an unpopular issue would win him few votes—that it may even have cost him the election. Something more than a cynical quest for office was thus involved in the summer campaign of 1857. Something that showed Jacob Rogers to be a crusading radical Republican. "I shall not swerve for friend or foe," he confided on the day he assumed office. "I am unpledged—right shall be my aim."[93]

The events of 1857 shed important light on the interrelationship between race and Republicanism in early Iowa. They indicated clearly that immediatist ideology was a prime source of friction at state and local levels, that Protestant reformers within the Republican party were prepared to champion equal rights in spite of the potentially damaging electoral consequences, and that even moderate Republicans (like those in the legislature who supported black testimony) were willing to make some inroads into the racist polity.

Yet for all their efforts on behalf of human progress, the fact remains that most key members of the party were anxious to protect themselves, with one hand at least, from Democratic charges of abolitionism. The August referendum results suggest that the Republican members of the constitutional convention had fashioned the right policy for the hour. In a largely partisan plebiscite Iowans ratified the new charter by 40,311 votes to 38,701.[94] Considering that 69 percent of the electorate had called for a convention in the first place, the margin of victory was narrow—a tribute to the force of Democratic opposition and the impact of the race question. Black suffrage was defeated by the crushing margin of nine to one.[95] The prosuffrage vote amounted to nearly a fifth of Frémont's total in 1856—a rough guide to the proportionate strength of antislavery radicalism within Iowa's Republican ranks and substantial justification for the action of the convention. The 89.6 percent majority in favor of the status quo, on the other hand, demonstrated the wisdom of the Republican leadership's pragmatic stance on the franchise issue during the summer.

Concrete proof of popular opposition to racial reform relegated civil rights to the second rank of Republican policy aims. The party did enter the October gubernatorial contest with a plank condemning the Dred Scott decision for "reducing to the condition of chattels, those who are recognized by the [U.S.] Constitution as men, belying the sentiments of the Declaration of Independence."[96] But there was no expression of support for local black rights, and the bulk of the platform dealt with the efforts of the slave power (aided and abetted by the federal government) to foster the expansion of the peculiar institution at the expense of the Constitution and state rights. The Democrats, in contrast, largely eschewed embarrassing national issues (though they did demand compliance with the Dred Scott ruling) and concentrated their fire on the "Black Republicans" for attempting to abolitionize the state and "subvert the distinction between the black and white races."[97] Their unashamedly racist campaign nearly paid off. Ralph P. Lowe of Muscatine, an amiable Whig-Republican and land speculator, scraped through against his dangerous Democratic rival, Benjamin Samuels of Dubuque, by only 2,410 votes.[98] This represented a drop of more than 5,000 from the majority gained by the Republicans in 1856—further evidence, if any was needed, that equal rights was no vote winner in antebellum Iowa.

During the late 1850s the gap between the major parties was too small and the problems of the economy and the nation too pressing to permit the Republicans further brushes with racial egalitarianism. A conservative reaction took place as party leaders sought to shed the organization's abolitionist image in preparation for the crucial presidential election of 1860. As a result local blacks continued to be deprived of the vote and excluded from white schools. For moderate Republican policymakers like James Harlan and Samuel J. Kirkwood (both of whom expressed support for colonization in 1860) these injustices were inevitable. For radicals like Jacob Wentworth Rogers of West Union they were blots on the state's escutcheon to be removed immediately upon the development of the right sentiment.

The actions of Iowa Republicans on the race question during 1857 highlighted the party's ambivalent stance on this matter. The ambivalence was a product of the organization's coalitional makeup and the prevalence of racial prejudice among the electorate. Although free blacks like Alexander Clark petitioned hard for an improvement in their legal status, it was pressure from radical whites on the antislavery wing of the party that induced Republican politicians to take faltering steps on the road toward equal rights. The personal liberty clause of the bill of rights and the legalization of black testimony by the general assembly must be seen as positive steps in view of Iowa's hitherto bleak record on civil rights and an indication that moderate Republicans were by no means wedded to the racial status quo. These two measures, however, were defensible on grounds that were acceptable to white voters. The personal liberty provision could be depicted as a device to protect state sovereignty against slave power aggressions; black testimony as a means of providing whites with a greater measure of justice in the courts. On issues that could be labeled amalgamationist by the Democrats, nonhumanitarian Republicans evinced a distinct reluctance to antagonize public opinion. Pragmatic radicals such as William Penn Clarke and hard-nosed centrists like James F. Wilson recognized—quite rightly, if, perhaps, all too readily—that most Iowans did not share the reformers' sympathy for blacks. And yet, while the suffrage referendum was little more than a sop to the radicals, one has a sense from the debates of the constitutional convention that equal rights lay much closer than nativism or temperance to the core of Republican ideology. This was because, as Rufus Clarke rightly urged, slavery and racism were interlinked. As long as the Republicans made opposition to the slave power and slavery expansion the focus of their electoral campaigns, they would be forced (by the radicals, if not by their own moral sense) to tackle the notion of racial oppression in a supposedly free society. In the middle of the nineteenth century the black Iowan's best hope of securing justice lay with a continuation of the sectional crisis. The Civil War would make this abundantly clear, but between the defeat of black suffrage and Fort Sumter loomed the economic recession of the late 1850s.

6
The Impact of Recession on Local Politics, 1858–1859

he Republicans' narrow victory in the gubernatorial contest of 1857 revealed the tenuous nature of the new party's hold on power. Over the next two years the process of legitimization would be further undermined by the onset of economic recession late in 1857, the growth of internal factionalism, and damaging revelations about the corrupt activities of Republican state officials. Several factors enabled the organization to retain control of the government during this difficult period, including divisions within the rival Democratic camp and the continuing salience of sectional issues. But probably the single most important reason for the party's crucial success in the elections of 1858–59 was the leadership's pragmatic response to the political problems thrown up by a sharp downturn in the state's economic fortunes.

Notwithstanding the troubles in neighboring Kansas, Iowa prospered for most of the antebellum decade. American and European immigrants flocked into the state in greater numbers than ever. Between 1850 and 1860 the local population more than trebled to 674,913.[1] Over 15 percent of that figure had been born outside the United States. The new arrivals swelled the size of the river cities and occupied the empty spaces of the interior. Population density grew rapidly from only 4.1 persons per square mile in 1852 to 12.2 on the eve of secession.[2] By the time Iowans went to war only the swampy northwestern quarter of the state remained sparsely settled.

In spite of sporadic lynchings (usually of horse thieves) and the occasional Sioux Indian depredation, Iowa was beginning to take on a more mature look, its system of justice now well established and infrastructural development seriously underway. For the landless, the restless, and the ambitious, the open prairies offered a prospect of unbridled opportunity and self-fulfillment. One contemporary English handbook noted that Iowa "is emphatically a 'Land of Promise' to the emigrant, and is now perhaps attracting more attention and filling up more rapidly than any other State in the Union." Blessed with fertile soil and a healthy climate, rich in game and minerals, "easily accessible, and free from many of the dangers incident to newly settled countries," the region was hailed as offering "the greatest inducements to emigrants and others to make it their home." The vision of a thriving commercial agriculture was probably the chief inducement to emigrants. The same pamphlet contended that the settled portions of the state were already dotted with good roads, and predicted that several railways in the course of construction would "soon find a ready market for the surplus produce of the country."[3]

While such effusive language ignored the harsh reality of life in the western country, there was plenty of truth in the assertion that "[p]robably no country in the world . . . is more promising to the agriculturist."[4] Within fifteen years of its admission into the Union, Iowa had become one of the most productive farm states in the republic. In 1859 its bountiful soil yielded more than forty-two million bushels of corn and eight million of wheat.[5] Nine hundred thousand pigs were fattened for local and supralocal consumption.[6] The cash value of farms increased more than sevenfold during the 1850s, and the ratio of improved acreage to unimproved land grew steadily.[7] All these figures confirm the state's rapid integration into the market. Modern research suggests that Iowa farms produced some of the largest meat and grain surpluses in the antebellum North. In 1859 only 11 percent of the Iowa townships analyzed by Fred Bateman and Jeremy Atack had food deficits of any kind compared with 56 percent in Michigan and 69 percent in New Hampshire. Rates of profit were respectable: perhaps eleven cents on the dollar.[8] Combined with the social independence that farm ownership seemed to offer, commercial agriculture on the Iowa prairies constituted an attractive alternative to the cramped economic conditions experienced by many whites in the eastern states and western Europe.

Towns as well as countryside benefited from the boom years of the mid-1850s. Members of the state's urban elite continued to speculate enthusiastically in town lots, their returns impressive in the wake of spectacular demographic and commercial growth. President Pierce's commissioner of patents, Charles Mason, returned from Washington in the summer of 1855 to find his hometown of Burlington "greatly improved since last spring" and the populace "crazy about prices." One local resident offered him $200 per acre for a farm he owned within the city limits. "I am informed I can sell my farm in small lots of from one to ten acres at something like that price," noted the erstwhile Jacksonian Democrat. "If so I shall be for letting it go pretty soon."[9]

Although soil fertility was a prime factor in the rapid growth of the local farm economy, the advent of the railroad played a major role in stimulating immigration and dramatically improving Iowa's links with the market. During the 1840s most of the region's food surpluses had reached out-of-state consumers via the Mississippi River. While some of this grain and pork went to supply Southern plantations, much of it was destined for the lucrative urban market in the Northeast.[10] The same decade also witnessed the rapid expansion of America's railroad network across the Old Northwest. The iron horse made the East more accessible to the food products of western farmers and built up great cities on the prairies. Mercantile elites in Iowa's river towns looked enviously on the rise of Chicago and Detroit and began taking active steps to secure railroad communications for themselves. Their aim was to dominate the trade of their immediate agricultural hinterlands and, if possible, that of neighboring commercial centers as well. By the early 1850s a fierce struggle was underway between Dubuque and Davenport, Burlington and Keokuk, to link themselves to the national rail network.

This parochial competition for commercial supremacy cut across party lines. Leading Whigs and Democrats joined together in an effort to promote the development of their adopted communities. This was particularly evident in Burlington where James W. Grimes cooperated enthusiastically with Democrats Charles Mason, William F. Coolbaugh, and Jonathan C. Hall to secure a railroad connection with Chicago via Quincy, Illinois.[11] Locofoco suspicions of business corporations were tempered by the general enthusiasm for the new technology. As already observed, Iowa Democrats passed legislation to encourage track construction in the state, their efforts applauded by farmers eager to compete in the marketplace with their rivals in Illinois, Ohio, and Indiana. George W. Jones and Augustus C. Dodge worked tirelessly in Congress to secure the passage of a federal land-grant act that would open up Iowa's fertile interior to the railroad companies. While Dodge shared Stephen Douglas's enthusiasm for a Pacific railroad, Jones's chief objective was a rail link between his hometown, Dubuque, and Keokuk. This latter goal antagonized the Burlington Democrats and helped to undermine Jones's position at the head of the state party—a position rendered increasingly precarious by his unwavering loyalty to Pierce and Buchanan during the course of the decade.[12]

By the end of 1855 neither the efforts of the state's congressional delegation nor those of the general assembly had yet produced the comprehensive land-grant bill that politicians of all parties regarded as the solution to Iowa's infrastructural problems. In the spring of 1856, however, eastern opposition to this measure finally evaporated, enabling Jones and his colleagues to push through a bill granting to the state more than four million acres of prime agricultural land.[13] The act provided for the construction of four east-west lines between Lyons, Dubuque, Davenport, Burlington, and the Missouri River. Only Keokuk interests were left out in the cold.

As soon as the act had been passed, Governor Grimes called a special session of the legislature to accept the federal grant and establish conditions for its disposal. An enthusiastic proponent of railroads, Grimes took care not to strike too Whiggish a note in his message to the assembly. The legislators' wisdom, he said on 3 July 1856, would doubtless "mature a system which, while it promotes the present material interests of the State by developing its resources and advancing its settlement by the construction of lines of intercommunication, will protect the people against the sometimes oppressive monopolizing tendencies of powerful corporations."[14] Having lived through the Jacksonian era, the governor recognized not only that ex-Democrats within the Republican party retained their suspicion of business corporations but also that public enthusiasm for railroads waxed and waned with the state of the local economy. He recommended that the assembly define the duties and responsibilities of the new transportation companies and regulate the speed of trains passing through built-up areas and across public highways.[15]

Keen to attract European and American risk capital into the state, the Republican-controlled legislature ignored Grimes's recommendations. However, it did place time limits on construction and subjected the four land-grant roads "to such rules and regulations as may from time to time be enacted and provided for by the General Assembly of Iowa."[16] By the middle of 1857 the Mississippi & Missouri, the Burlington & Missouri, the Iowa Central Air Line, and the Dubuque & Pacific railroad companies had constructed several hundred miles of track in eastern Iowa. A fifth corporation was building between Keokuk and Des Moines.

The same prosperity and market requirements that brought about a consensus on railroad development in the early 1850s produced a rising chorus of opinion in favor of banks of issue. Neither the credit facilities provided by local land agencies nor the notes of out-of-state banks provided the kind of elastic, plentiful, and reliable currency demanded by urban merchants and commercial farmers. As early as 1852 Democrats in the legislature were calling for a constitutional convention to repeal the prohibition on banks of issue.[17] Although Governor Stephen Hempstead vetoed an act providing for a referendum on the issue, the coming to power of the Whig-dominated Republican party ensured passage of a similar measure in the winter of 1854–55. The crushing margin by which the voters approved a constitutional convention testified to the strength of grass-roots support for economic growth. Most of the delegates who attended the gathering at Iowa City in early 1857 favored a change in the law on banks.

In spite of a general conviction that something had to be done, there was little unity on this question among partisans of either stripe at the convention. On 9 February debate began on the report of the committee on incorporations, a body consisting of three probank Republicans, one conservative Democrat, and one antibank Democrat. The report recommended that the general assembly be empowered to enact legislation setting up free (i.e., private) and state banking systems.[18] It also required popular referenda to be held on both measures before either could be put into operation and contained a number of restrictive clauses designed to safeguard billholders. The committee's proposal represented an attempt to forge a compromise between the advocates of two ostensibly different forms of banking, both of which had been tried and tested in the older states. Consensus, however, did not prove easy to achieve.

A small number of Democrats adhered to the traditional Jacksonian view that banks were enemies of the people. One of them looked upon banking as "nothing more or less than a series of tricks of adroit swindlers, invented by ingenious financiers, to rob the laboring man of the fruits of his labor."[19] This view was rejected not only by the Republican majority but also by conservative Democrats like George Gillaspy of Ottumwa. Gillaspy responded to suggestions that banking was inflationary by contending that his southern Iowa constituents were not burdened by the problem of too much money. Their trouble, he said, "has been that they have not had enough of it."[20] Although most of Gillaspy's colleagues expressed a decided preference for hard money, they generally shared his contempt for the prevailing system of finance. Amos Harris, another Democrat representing counties on the Missouri border, confessed that he was not a special friend of banks but argued that most Iowans would prefer to borrow money from responsible capitalists rather than pay interest on "the worthless trash" then being circulated in the state.[21] While the few locofocos in the chamber insisted that free banking was at least preferable to the creation of a monopolistic state institution, the conservatives tended to support the latter on the grounds that it would promote more responsible banking.

Republicans had no doubt that economic progress required that the Jacksonian incubus on banking be removed, but they too were divided over the system to be erected in its stead. Diametrically opposed to the views of the locofocos were those of William Penn Clarke, the former Free-Soil Whig who proved to be the most outspoken advocate of growth along capitalist lines at the convention. Denouncing what he regarded as an overly restrictive liability clause in the report of the incorporations committee, Clarke insisted that Iowa must compete for scarce capital resources if its economic advance was to continue. "Our object," he said, "should be to provide such a banking system that people will bring in capital here, and thus enhance our business facilities. Without capital there can be no business."[22]

Other Republicans claimed to have less faith in business corporations. Rufus Clarke of Mount Pleasant asserted that he looked on banking as "a great evil," but "a necessary one, demanded by the necessities of the people."[23] Several ex-Democrats in the Republican ranks expressed an antipathy for easy money or avowedly monopolistic state banks. John A. Parvin of Muscatine, for example, insisted that billholders had to be protected from the designs of avaricious moneylenders. He shared Amos Harris's belief that the establishment of a state bank was the best method to procure a sound currency. Other Republicans, Rufus Clarke and George W. Ells included, agreed with H.D. Gibson, a Tennessee-born merchant from southern Iowa, that this would only encourage monopoly.[24]

James F. Wilson opposed the incorporation of statute law into the constitution. Avowing his antipathy toward a further expansion of wildcat banking in Iowa, Wilson proclaimed that the people must have some protection against the exercise of what he called "the money power."[25] The best way to do this, he continued, was to allow the legislature to provide for a combination of state and free banking, and then allow the people to decide. The young Ohioan's use of Jacksonian rhetoric to attack the prevailing locofoco system of finance was the work of a master politician. Wilson was no enemy of banks, but like Grimes, he knew that economic development (as well as party unity) could best be promoted by subtle means.

After much debate during which it became clear that the Republicans were less in favor of building restrictive features into the constitution than their opponents, the report was referred to a select committee of five. This body, which was dominated by four strongly probank delegates, recommended that the legislature alone should regulate the operations of the banks. Cautious Republicans and conservative Democrats then united to add a number of constitutional restrictions to the section under review and finally approved the report of the select committee as amended by thirty votes to five.[26]

The fact that a majority of Republicans and Democrats backed this measure indicated the extent to which commercial imperatives had removed the economy as a primary dynamic of partisan competition. Notwithstanding the persistence of hard money sentiment among the Democrats, the eclipse of locofocoism enabled conservatives to make common cause with the Republicans on the bank provisions of the new constitution. Had the opposition been guided by strident Whigs like William Penn Clarke (who voted against the bank report because he deemed it too restrictive), cooperation might not have been possible. As it was, the refusal of ex-Democrats like Parvin and Ells to abandon their suspicion of banks ensured that pragmatic Republicans (who also had one eye on the Jacksonian proclivities of the electorate) would follow Grimes's example and temper any enthusiasm they might have had for the institutions of corporate capitalism.

A similar pattern was evident during debates over the right of localities to issue bonds for railroad construction. Since the early 1850s voters in the eastern counties had subscribed enthusiastically for such bonds on the assumption that the advantages of infrastructural improvement would vastly outweigh the disadvantage of increased taxes. Although these issues had been upheld by the state supreme court in 1853, there was a general feeling in the convention that some ceiling should be placed on local indebtedness (estimated at more than $7 million by Governor Grimes).[27] This provision would fully legitimize the activities of substate governmental entities and at the same time prevent them from incurring the kind of massive debts that could not possibly be serviced and which might prompt a popular reaction against those politicians who had allowed the debts to be incurred in the first place.

Predictably William Penn Clarke was the only Republican to oppose the erection of a debt ceiling. In an impassioned speech on 9 February he again championed the Whig philosophy of economic growth by contending that it was the government's duty "to promote the morality and the intelligence, as well as the physical condition of man." Because railroads were an important agent of human progress, it followed that the convention had no right to restrict counties and municipalities from investing in their expansion across the prairies. "To say that you will not have internal improvements," said Clarke, "is to say, that you will place Iowa in the position of a desert island, surrounded by oceans for miles around, to cut off all communications between her and the world. We are compelled to have them, for if we do not, we will cease to be a part of the world, so far as things are in this age."[28] An official of the Mississippi & Missouri Railroad Company, Clarke could not be accused of concealing his bullish views for reasons of political expediency.

This was less true of some of the other delegates at Iowa City. The antibank Democrat J.H. Emerson, a Dubuque real estate dealer, professed his opposition to government tax aid to railroads for traditional laissez-faire reasons. His attempts to take the moral high ground, however, were undermined by a fellow Democrat who observed pointedly that Emerson was a director of the Dubuque & Pacific Railroad, a beneficiary of the recent U.S. land grant.[29] A number of Republicans expressed their antipathy toward the new business corporations. Rufus Clarke, often keen to establish his radical credentials, insisted that "the power which corporations may exist for evil is very great"—an assertion that was probably no more sincere than his much-vaunted fondness for equal rights.[30] More genuine was probably

John A. Parvin's fear "that by inviting these railroad companies among us, we are placing ourselves . . . in their power, and that we are creating a monopoly that will wield an influence over our cities and counties, that we will in due time have occasion to regret."[31]

In spite of the divisions among themselves Republican delegates opted to support a compromise proposal prohibiting localities from investing in internal improvements at a rate exceeding 5 percent on the taxable property within their boundaries. The state itself was barred from becoming a stockholder in any company, and the property of all profit-making corporations was deemed subject to taxation at the same rate as that of individuals. Although most Democrats had opposed the provision for a 5 percent debt ceiling, the majority of them supported the article on incorporations when it came up for a final vote on 4 March.[32]

The draft constitution submitted to the voters in August 1857 represented an attempt to balance Jacksonian fears of special privilege with Whiggish concern for the needs of a modern economy. However, while the bulk of its provisions had elicited bipartisan support at Iowa City, the state Democratic organization moved swiftly to condemn the proposed charter as a Republican document. As well as pointing out the obnoxious "abolitionist" features of the constitution, Democratic editors across the state focused attention on its banking clauses.[33] These, it was alleged, contravened traditional Jacksonian doctrine and portended the triumph of old-time Whiggery. Although some of the party's leaders endeavored to show that the constitution was as much a Democratic achievement as a Republican one, it was clear that the seriously riven Dubuque organization that dominated the state party was determined to use the document to regenerate political competition in Iowa.[34] The narrowness of the constitution's ratification and the near defeat of the Republican candidate in the October gubernatorial contest merely intensified the efforts of local Democrats to exploit economic issues for their own ends. Their cause was greatly helped by the onset of economic recession.

In August 1857 a crash on the New York securities market prompted a sudden contraction of business activity throughout the United States. As early as September eastern railroad magnates were making arrangements with subcontractors to lay off men and halt expansion west of the Mississippi. By Christmas all track construction in Iowa had ceased. That winter saw a dramatic plunge in real estate prices and the steady eastward drift of currency as out-of-state banks began to call in their loans. Although a bountiful harvest cushioned Iowans against the worst effects of the panic, Governor Ralph P. Lowe told the general assembly on 13 January 1858 that the nation was "smitten as with a palsy." He lambasted that "spirit of cupidity and reckless speculation" that was widely believed to have caused the recession and asserted that the only sure way of ensuring prosperity was "to conduct the affairs of the State upon Christian principles."[35] Despite being a fervent Presbyterian, Lowe was not prepared to trust everything to faith. As well as pressing upon the legislators the need for a state banking system, he observed that railroad development was an essential precondition for healthy economic growth. "The practical experience of the whole country," he said, attested to the "indispensable utility" of these corporations:

> Although diffusive in the benefits they bestow, extending themselves to every class in [the] community, yet the country is indebted for the most part, to individual capital and enterprise for their construction. This fact should bear down with great urgency upon the mind of both the State and National Government, to hold up the hands and encourage the hearts of the noble and self-sacrificing few, who manifest a willingness to peril much of their fortunes, to push forward a description of improvement that marks one of the great features of the age.[36]

Lowe's thinly veiled endorsement of government aid for troubled business enterprises was good Whig doctrine, but it contrasted sharply with the outgoing executive's silence on the issue. In his final address to the legislature, Grimes had concentrated largely on national questions—principally on the iniquity of the Dred Scott decision and President Buchanan's efforts to force a proslavery constitution on Kansas. His only reference to business corporations had been an assertion "that banks are to be established to secure the public welfare, and not to promote the purposes of stockholders and capitalists; and that it is far better that banks should realize small profits, than that the public should be liable to injury by their suspension or failure."[37] With popular enthusiasm for banking increasingly susceptible to an anticorporate backlash, Grimes had revealed an awareness of grass-roots feeling that the genial Lowe did not possess. True, the bank provisions of the new constitution were defensible as an essential means of promoting economic recovery, but the shrewd Burlington lawyer knew well that Democrats would seek to exploit antibusiness sentiment for all it was worth.

Figure 6.1 highlights the extent to which banking was a major party unifier in the Iowa house of representatives that winter. The Democratic minority in the lower chamber fought to graft hard money and regulatory provisions onto the state- and free-banking bills under discussion, finally

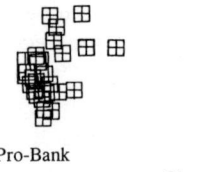

⊞ Republican

⊕ Democrat

MDS analysis (see Appendix); no. of motions = 30
SOURCE: *Ia. Hse. Jnl.* (1858), pp. 69, 593–97, 599– 600, 628; 451–52, 473–74, 514–16, 519, 531–34, 536– 40, 587–88.

Fig. 6.1 Iowa House, 1858: Voting behavior on state and free bank motions.

voting eighteen to eight and twenty-four to three against both measures respectively.[38] The balance between pro- and antibank forces was reversed in the senate, but taken as a whole, the Democratic stance on these bills contrasted sharply with the Republicans' almost unanimous support.[39]

Had the fundamental motivation behind antibank sentiment been opposition to capitalism, one might have expected house Democrats to register their dislike of internal improvements. In fact they voted unanimously in favor of resolutions urging Congress to aid several midwestern railroads with grants of land, and, by a two-thirds majority, joined the Republicans in reducing the individual liability of stockholders for corporate debts.[40] Those Iowa Democrats who opposed the establishment of a banking system did so as much for political as economic reasons.

Aside from passing measures to promote banking and railroad development, the Republican-controlled legislature did little to alleviate the effects of the panic. Its only positive move was to authorize the state to borrow $200,000 in order to replenish a depleted treasury. Hawkins Taylor, a prominent Whig-Republican leader in Keokuk, bemoaned the assembly's failure to enact substantive relief measures. This, he told a colleague, had "very much weakened the ardor of thousands of the best working Republican mechanics who are now involved in debt."[41]

The reluctance of Taylor's copartisans to countenance welfare legislation stemmed from a variety of sources, notably the ideological and political constraints on state intervention, and their religious-based conviction that the recession was basically a product of human greed. Although some Democrats sought to take advantage of Republican inaction with Jacksonian class-war rhetoric, their party's ability to exploit local issues was undermined by its own commitment to negative government and the Republicans' steadfast determination to distance themselves from increasingly unpopular railroad companies.

The electorate's ambivalent attitude toward eastern railroad magnates became apparent during the spring of 1858. With no sign of an upturn in economic conditions or a renewal of railroad construction, farmers in the southeastern counties began to vent their frustration against the business companies into which they had poured so many of their precious tax dollars. Accusations of corporate tyranny started to appear in the newspapers of both parties, and county judges in several areas refused to issue bonds to fund new assessments on their locality's railroad stock.[42] As many members of the constitutional convention had feared, it now seemed likely that too close an attachment to the iron horse might become an electoral liability.

Before investigating how the Republicans responded to the growing anti-monopoly prejudices of the grass roots, it would be well to take a closer look at the precise relationship between the party and the railroad companies. The latter had a revolutionary impact on the mid-nineteenth-century United States, cutting days off traveling times between the Mississippi River and the eastern seaboard, opening up new markets for farmers and entrepreneurs in all sections, and inspiring visions of a vast American empire peacefully acquired through the workings of trade. Inevitably Iowans spent much time and energy considering the possibilities engendered by this supreme achievement of modern science (most especially the idea of an iron thoroughfare to the Pacific). Although the delegates at the 1857 constitutional convention were by no means agreed on the merits of the new technology, all of them recognized that they were living "at the advent of a railroad era."[43] Some of them shared the common view that this greatest of all industrial innovations would strengthen the bonds of Union. The Davenport merchant and radical Republican George W. Ells went so far as to suggest that railroads would "do vastly more to remove the jealousy now existing between the two sections, and ultimately destroy that infernal curse, African slavery, than any other single agency in our country."[44]

A welter of ties united Iowa Republican leaders with the transportation companies that began to traverse the western prairies in the mid-1850s. Many of the party's leading figures found remunerative employment as legal counsel. Others worked as lobbyists for the eastern magnates who provided much of the initial capital for the trans-Mississippi roads. As members of the state's urban elite, they acted as civic boosters for their respective communities, assuming, albeit naively, that the arrival of the iron horse would guarantee local prosperity for years to come.

Self-interest was a major factor in their efforts. Railroad expansion augmented land values and enabled many Iowans to garner substantial profits from moderate investments. The greatest rewards often went to those who possessed reliable inside information on proposed transportation routes. When Josiah B. Grinnell, a Congregational minister domiciled in New York during the early 1850s, decided to found a New England colony in Iowa, he sought advice on its location from officials of the Mississippi & Missouri Railroad Company. Granted access to this vital information, Grinnell purchased 160 acres in Poweshiek County on which he thought the town and its projected railroad depot would be sited. This, he told his wife in May 1854, "will be fortune enough for us if the RR is built within two years of which there is little doubt. . . . O pray for us that we may not be too worldly."[45]

One evangelical who was less disturbed by the profits to be made from land speculation was Senator James Harlan. In November 1856 the Mount Pleasant politician informed a leading local capitalist that he could provide detailed information on the planned line between Keokuk and Des Moines. "I can know *in advance* where the road will be established, and also the location of every *depot,*" he wrote. "This, if embraced, will cost you *one half of the clear profits* growing out of the investment."[46]

Grinnell and Harlan were just two of the state's Republican chieftains with close connections to the railroad companies. There were many others. Hiram Price and William Penn Clarke, for example, were affiliated with the Mississippi & Missouri.[47] Before the Civil War, however, the most important Republican leader working closely with the corporations to promote railroad development was James W. Grimes.

On 25 January 1858 Republican votes in the general assembly sent Grimes to the U.S. Senate. This very public triumph at the new statehouse in Des Moines masked his private activities on behalf of the railroads. Throughout the winter of 1857–58 the Republican leader was in close contact with James F. Joy, a well-educated Detroit lawyer who had tutored Grimes during his college days at Dartmouth.[48] An employee since 1846 of the Boston merchant-capitalist John Murray Forbes, Joy had become reacquainted with his former student six years later when seeking to link Burlington with Forbes's burgeoning railroad system. Like many of the river town's civic leaders Grimes participated enthusiastically in the development of what rapidly became the Forbes-owned Burlington & Missouri Railroad. In March 1857 he was named a director of the company along with Joy, Forbes, and several local notables.[49]

When the recession hit Iowa later that year, Grimes, a prominent real estate dealer as well as politician and lawyer, found himself heavily in debt as a result of overextensive speculation and lending during the property boom. Unlike many other Iowans who found themselves in the same situation, the ex-governor found a ready avenue of escape from the slough of bankruptcy. On 18 December he informed Joy that he owed his creditors $20,000. "The amount is not very great in proportion to my property," he wrote, "but it is enough to give me some perplexity."[50] Promising to give any amount of security at 10 percent interest, Grimes asked his acquaintance for $15,000, half payable at once, the rest by 1 March 1858. Joy agreed not only to this request but also to a slightly later demand for an extra $5,000.[51] His action was not, one suspects, entirely a product of altruism. For Joy was an astute businessman who recognized the importance of having such an influential politician tied to his apron strings.

Over the next few months, while still negotiating for this loan, Grimes worked clandestinely to further the interests of the land-grant companies—each of them keen to pressure the state into providing remedial help (legal if not economic) for their stymied operations. Resident in Burlington for most of that winter's session of the general assembly, he communicated his personal views on railroad legislation in a confidential letter that he placed in the hands of his fellow townsman, William F. Coolbaugh. Coolbaugh, a director of the Burlington & Missouri and one of the leading Democrats in the state senate, was instructed to show the letter to influential assemblymen if the political climate at the capitol grew hostile to the railroads. Grimes told Joy on 18 February 1858 that he did not think Coolbaugh should have any trouble, but he warned his Detroit confidant that representatives from the Mississippi & Missouri should also be present at Des Moines.[52]

The following month Grimes reported that a bill drawn up by Joy had passed the senate.[53] Joy appears to have drafted several pieces of legislation for the 1858 legislature. This particular bill may well have been one allowing the railroads to issue bonds secured by mortgages on their as yet unearned real estate and freeing the corporations from the individual liability clause of the Iowa Code. On 18 March another dispatch to Joy indicated that his "tax law" (possibly a measure limiting the state's ability to tax the land grants) had been introduced into the senate by Lyman Cook, a Burlington banker and Republican. Unfortunately, wrote Grimes, Coolbaugh had declined to present it himself, thus diminishing its chances of receiving Democratic support. The senator-elect was contemptuous of Coolbaugh's role: "Deposite with him & buy & sell him exchange & he will be a great friend until adversity overtakes you."[54] Four days later Grimes reported that two bills placed in "the hopper" earlier in the session would be "satisfactorily ground out." Again, he was unsure of the tax bill. Coolbaugh, he thought, could secure passage if he really wanted it to go through: "Almost anything can be done in the last day or two of a session by a cool, shrewd parliamentarian. Coolbaugh is shrewd enough, but he has other 'fish of his own to fry.'"[55]

The correspondence between Grimes and Joy during the winter of 1857-58 indicates the extent of business influence on Iowa politics before the Civil War. It is also suggestive of the gap that existed between word and deed in nineteenth-century America. As governor, James W. Grimes had issued several warnings against corporate power. Like many of his fellow politicians he was obviously less of a people's man than he claimed to be in public. There is no evidence of a corrupt bargain between the two men. The new senator had been an advocate of internal improvements since the Jacksonian era, and he had lobbied hard for Burlington railroad interests in the early 1850s. He was still representing the interests of the Burlington & Missouri in Congress long after he had paid his debts to Joy and Forbes. But if $20,000 did not actually purchase Grimes's political influence, it certainly helped to strengthen a relationship between an ambitious politician and an aggressive businessman that most Iowa voters would have regarded as unhealthily close.

Of course, Grimes was not the only practitioner of demagoguery in Victorian America. Anticorporate rhetoric frequently veiled probusiness activism during the second and third party systems. Mercantile and industrial capitalists seldom had any difficulty coopting wealthy middle-class politicians who already had a substantial stake in the expanding market economy. The party affiliation of the coopted was largely irrelevant. In Iowa Democrats as well as Republicans enjoyed close links with the railroads. It is clear from the Grimes-Joy correspondence that William F. Coolbaugh was expected to promote the interests of the Burlington & Missouri at Des Moines. If he did not do so in this particular instance, it was, as Grimes intimated, because he had his own political reasons for not wanting to appear a friend of the corporations.

The situation in which Grimes found himself, however, was certainly ambivalent. He was responsible not only to the people who had indirectly elected him to Congress but also to an eastern-controlled business corporation whose interests were not entirely consonant with those of western farmers. The best that can be said of Grimes's closet relationship with Joy is that he sought to use his position to promote the economic development of the state. In January 1859 he warned his creditor that unless the Burlington & Missouri started to build westward at once it would lose business to the more aggressive Mississippi & Missouri Railroad. All that was needed, he insisted, was for Joy to give the project his encouragement: "It will secure prosperity to your road. Without it, I would not give a farthing for your stock." Continued Grimes, "I am really the most indifferent man in the world on this subject. I am as deeply interested in Muscatine as in Burlington—I think the preponderance is in favor of Muscatine if it is either way. But I have some predilections in favor of your company, soul[l]ess and selfish as all rail road companies are known to be."[56]

The ex-governor's attempt to paint himself a friend of the whole state was not entirely convincing, but clearly he wished to place some distance between himself and Joy. There were two main reasons for this. Firstly, Grimes was genuinely keen to defend the sovereignty of the state, whether it be against the encroachments of the federal government, the slave power, or "selfish" corporations. If he sided too closely with the railroads, that was partly because he believed—along with most other Iowans—that their growth was essential for the general good. Secondly, he was astute enough to recognize that antimonopoly sentiment ran deep in Iowa and that the economic recession had brought this to the surface in many southeastern counties of the state. With the onset of hard times all members of Iowa's political elite, regardless of party affiliation, were confronted with the fact that a hitherto popular form of transportation in which they had invested considerable political and material capital had suddenly become less than popular because of the downturn in the economy. This was a problem that Grimes, no less than William F. Coolbaugh, had to face during the final years of the 1850s. Judging by the way he reacted to the antebellum economic crisis, it would appear that he too had fish to fry.

At the same time that the voters began to vent their wrath against the transportation companies, Platt Smith, an officer of the Dubuque & Pacific Railroad, was canvassing opinion on the possibility of state aid for internal improvements. In the spring of 1858 he wrote to several leading politicians including Grimes and Coolbaugh.[57] Because both of these men were aware of the drift of public opinion and, equally significantly, allies of the rival Burlington & Missouri that had no interest in such a project, Smith received little encouragement from this quarter. In June, however, the Dubuquer elicited a more favorable response from Governor Lowe.

Notwithstanding his opposition to Smith's suggestion that he call a special session of the legislature to discuss state aid, Lowe outlined a more-limited scheme that, he assured the railroad man, would be fully within the terms of the new constitution. This involved the purchase of several million dollars worth of railroad iron by the state, in return for which the corporations would pay bonds bearing at least 1 percent more interest than those issued by the state to buy the iron. Only after the roadbed had been prepared would the companies be eligible to exchange bonds for iron. To the naively Whiggish governor, this plan represented the most politically feasible way of promoting economic recovery. To his fellow Republicans it seemed like a recipe for political disaster.

The ruling party went into the local and congressional elections of 1858 with its reformist and progressive image greatly tarnished. Early in the year Republican legislators made an open bid to attract German voters into the coalition by permitting the manufacture and sale of beer, cider, and wine made from local fruits. While this measure dismayed prohibitionists by driving a coach and horses through the Maine Law, the defalcation of the superintendent of public instruction undermined Republican efforts to attack the corruption of the Buchanan administration. So too did indications that bribery had been involved in the location of the new capitol on the east side of the Des Moines River. There were even rumors that ex-Governor Grimes was a party in this latter scandal. The former Free-Soil leader George Shedd reported being told that Grimes was indeed deeply embroiled in "the astounding frauds & corruption" in Des Moines, though he confessed that his informant (a friend of Fitz Henry Warren) might be somewhat biased. Nonetheless, wrote Shedd, "I do not know that I shall soon be as much out with the honesty & morality of the Republican party as I was with the old Whig party & am now with the Pres.[ident] and his trucklers."[58]

Evidence of corruption and probusiness leanings did not lead to Republican defeats in October 1858. Federal policy in Kansas came to the party's rescue once again, elevating sectional issues to the fore and sundering the local Democratic party in two. While both Republican congressional nominees were elected, most of the candidates on the party's state ticket secured majorities of over three thousand. These results were an improvement on the perilously narrow margin of victory in 1857 and fully justified the Republican state convention's determination to fight the election on national issues. The voters ratified the state- and free-bank laws passed by the legislature by majorities of 91.8 and 74.4 percent respectively, thereby indicating the widespread faith among the electorate that modern, domestic financial institutions would help to promote economic recovery.[59]

Prosperity, however, showed no signs of returning in the second half of 1858. An abnormally wet growing season reduced crop yields across the state, portending hardship for many Iowans that winter. Only thirty-five miles of railroad were built during the entire year, frustrating those people who had looked to the new technology for economic salvation. As the corporations began to lobby hard once again for state aid, Republican leaders like James Harlan warned Governor Lowe not to consider calling a special session of the assembly for that purpose. Such a call, wrote Harlan in November, might well damage the party's electoral prospects in 1859.[60] The governor's secretary, Thomas F. Withrow, advised his friends to pressure Lowe into rejecting state aid. His fear was that opportunistic Democrats would take advantage of a special session to help force through prorailroad legislation and then blame the Republicans for reckless expenditure at a time of acute economic crisis. "We must keep our skirts clear of this thing," he urged.[61]

The following month a convention of railroad men gathered at Iowa City to endorse a plan for a judicious system of state aid to railroads of regional importance. Significantly, the former Democrat Samuel J. Kirkwood wrote a strongly worded minority report condemning the proposal on constitutional grounds.[62] This represented what was by now mainstream Republican thinking on the state aid issue. Even Governor Lowe had no desire to brook the opinion of the party leadership.[63]

The recession bit heavily during the savagely cold months of December, January, and February. In the countryside there was widespread distress.

Farmers throughout the state thought only of subsistence. One elderly pioneer recalled that during the winter of 1858–59 many residents of southeastern Iowa "were sore pressed to obtain the mere necessaries of life. I knew families to live for weeks on corn bread and water."[64] Life was easier for the middling classes in the towns and cities, but even here business closures were common and negotiable currency scarce. Several municipal and private corporations issued their own scrip in order to keep afloat. The urban poor (many of them immigrant workingmen) experienced severe hardships and were frequently dependent on the philanthropy of the rich.[65]

The parlous state of the local economy forced Republicans to think hard about their gubernatorial candidate for 1859. While Dubuque railroad interests led by Platt Smith pressed for Lowe's renomination and a measure of state aid for their moribund project, key Republicans began to see the governor as an electoral liability. Some, like William W. Hamilton of Dubuque, thought him too soft.[66] Others, notably John A. Kasson, a gifted Des Moines lawyer who had recently been appointed party chairman, considered him too Whiggish.[67] Most worrying of all was Lowe's much-publicized fondness for government aid to railroad corporations. James W. Grimes was shocked to hear reports that some Republicans were hoping to secure an endorsement of state aid by the party convention in June. "No man with a thimble full of brains, . . ." he told Kirkwood,

> would seek to have our convention embrace in any way, either directly or indirectly, such a scheme. It would blow us at once to the d__l. . . . I am a republican upon principle, but my republicanism does not require me to become instrumental in a great scheme of state & private swindling as in Minnesota. Our policy is to say nothing about it, pro or con, and this, you will find will be the view of the convention when assembled.

Burlington Democrats, added Grimes, were all hoping for Lowe's renomination so that they could take advantage of the state aid scheme. But, he continued, "outside of Lee, Polk & DuBuque counties I do not know any body in favor of his nomination in our party."[68] Kirkwood was Grimes's choice for the governorship. The two men had become close political allies, and Grimes was well aware that the Iowa City businessman's laissez-faire inclinations were best suited to the times.

That spring Republican leaders pressured Lowe to stand down as governor. As a sop to his injured pride they offered him an appointment as chief justice of the state supreme court. Although Lowe proved amenable to this idea, a factional dispute over the succession threatened to damage the party's chances in October. The possibility of internal wrangling over Kirkwood's candidacy, however, was reduced by James Harlan's refusal to endorse the ambitious William Penn Clarke as an alternative nominee. Clarke and Kirkwood were engaged in a battle for control of the party organization in Iowa City, and Harlan might well have taken this opportunity to thwart Grimes's efforts to entrench his friends in power. Luckily Harlan regarded internal harmony as an essential precondition for his own reelection to the U.S. Senate in 1860, and he warned Clarke not to rock the boat.[69] The threat of an open split between Iowa's two leading politicians finally receded in July when Harlan announced his acquiescence in Kirkwood's candidacy. He told the former Democrat, "Let us pull together—elect the State ticket and the legislature, and the consequences will take care of themselves."[70]

Shortly before Iowa Republicans met at Des Moines on 22 June 1859, Lowe made it known that he would not be seeking renomination. His relieved copartisans then nominated him for supreme court justice and chose Kirkwood to fight the gubernatorial contest. As Grimes had hoped, the Republican platform ignored the state aid question entirely. Instead it focused largely on tried and tested national issues. The "Africanized Democracy" was attacked for its corrupt administration of the federal government, and there was predictable criticism of fire-eating Southern demands for a reopening of the slave trade and a national slave code for the territories.[71] More surprising was a plank opposing any abridgement of the existing U.S. naturalization law. Local Republicans had been acutely embarrassed by the anti-immigrant stance of their nativist-inclined counterparts in Massachusetts, and this measure represented another attempt to persuade the foreign-born in Iowa that their rights were safe in the hands of the ruling party.[72] That it was directed specifically at German Protestants was made clear when Nicholas Rusch, a liberal refugee from Schleswig-Holstein, was nominated for lieutenant governor. This move was unpopular with nativists and prohibitionists in the Republican ranks, but the prospect of defeat at the hands of the Democracy imposed a fragile unity on the local party.

Just how great a threat the Democrats were likely to be in October became apparent the following day when the opposition met at the capital to endorse what was probably the party's strongest policy statement of the decade. Having already wrested control of the state organization from its proadministration wing, supporters of Stephen Douglas proceeded to formulate a platform containing a judicious mix of national and local issues. On the one hand the Democrats made a bold attempt to neutralize the sectional appeal of Republicanism. A ringing endorsement of popular sovereignty announced that the territories were "justly entitled to self-government and the undisturbed regulation of their own domestic or local affairs."[73] Such language could be interpreted as criticism of the Buchanan administration's abortive attempt to impose the proslavery Lecompton constitution on Kansas. Even more outspoken were planks condemning the

Dred Scott decision and plans to reopen the African slave trade. The latter's revival, it was argued, would not only "renew those cruelties which once provoked the indignation of the civilized world" but also "entail a foul blot on our country's fair escutcheon."[74]

As well as distancing themselves from the unpopular national administration and proslavery Southern wing of the party, Iowa Democrats concentrated their fire on state issues—widely regarded as the Republicans' weak link. It was here that the decision to replace Lowe with Kirkwood may have been crucial. For while the Democratic platform contained several planks condemning Republicans for supposedly trying to encourage black immigration and racial integration, there was no mention of the controversial state aid plan. Had Lowe been nominated, it is likely that his Whiggish endorsement of government help for unpopular railroad corporations would have found a prominent place in the Democratic platform. As it was, Kirkwood's nomination deprived the opposition of what could well have been a master card. Proponents of laissez-faire, Democrats were left with no economic initiatives to offer the hard-pressed electorate beyond calls for retrenchment and criticism of recent tax increases. Since both of these planks were mirrored in the Republican platform, it was clear that Grimes and his colleagues had beaten the Democrats at their own game.

The combination of popular sovereignty, racism, and opposition to the state's prohibitory liquor law failed to secure victory for Augustus C. Dodge, the Democrats' gubernatorial candidate. Returning from Madrid where he had been American minister, the former U.S. senator cut a poor figure beside the homespun Kirkwood, who was adeptly packaged as a man of the people by the Republican central committee.[75] At the October election Dodge went down to defeat by a margin of 3,170 votes, his cause undoubtedly harmed by his support for Cuban annexation and less than impressive record as a defender of Northern rights.[76] Once again the Democrats failed to register significant gains outside their traditional strongholds in the Dubuque area, the southeastern river cities, and the southern and western counties. Nicholas Rusch appears to have brought few Germans into the Republican camp, but equally significantly, his candidacy failed to alienate Republican nativists (the majority of whom were unlikely to have been impressed with Dodge's Catholic allegiance) to any major degree.[77]

Kirkwood's narrow triumph and the election of yet another Republican-dominated legislature were severe blows to Democratic ambitions. Dodge was an experienced campaigner, a pioneer western man respected by members of both wings of the party. If he could not defeat the opposition at a time when the state debt had mushroomed to over $300,000, when taxes were relatively high, when the economy had still not fully recovered from the recession, and when the wellspring of popular racism was full, his party was clearly in danger of being permanently marginalized. The Republicans, in contrast, had good reason to feel buoyant. In spite of all their problems over recent years, they had succeeded in fighting off the Democratic challenge. One reason for this was their ability to circumvent potentially damaging questions of local import: prohibition, black suffrage, banking, and now state aid for railroad development.

Although a number of historians have suggested that the rise of the Republican organization in Iowa was intrinsically connected with its support for railroad development, it seems clear that the relationship between the party and the corporations was an essentially ambivalent one.[78] Notwithstanding the existence of close links between men like Grimes and James F. Joy, the uneven progress of the market economy, the fluctuating nature of public opinion, and a measure of ideological commitment prevented those bonds from becoming too incestuous. To contend that Republican railroad policy was the crucial factor in the organization's success is to ignore the fact that the opposition was also in favor of key developmental measures such as land grants, tax incentives, and local investment. The truth is that until the recession of the late 1850s virtually everyone in the state supported railroad expansion. Even bank reform was generally popular until political necessity induced the Democrats to oppose it in the 1857 campaign. Significantly, both major parties reacted in precisely the same manner to the onset of hard times: that is to say they drew back from their unqualified endorsement of railroads and displayed a cynical willingness to heap opprobrium on eastern capitalists—always useful scapegoats for hard-pressed western politicians.

The real reason for the rise of the Republican party in Iowa was the sectional crisis. That that organization came close to relinquishing power between 1857 and 1859 was due largely to the relative decline in salience of that issue. Yet in spite of the Democrats' concerted efforts to neutralize the vote-winning potential of slave power rhetoric, sectionalism remained an important factor in state politics throughout this period. The South, the Buchanan administration, and a Northern abolitionist named John Brown made sure of that. As America's regional split moved toward a bloody climax, Iowa's Republican leaders prepared to play their part in seizing control of the national government.

7
Iowa and the Coming of the Civil War, 1859–1861

otwithstanding the importance of state issues in the campaigns of 1857–59, the underlying dynamic of party competition in antebellum Iowa remained the sectional crisis. As the presidential election of 1860 approached, national concerns began to push their way to the fore once again. Because Republicanism fed on anti-Southern passions, this development was of tremendous value to men like Grimes and Harlan. For all their efforts to depict the opposition as treasonous, Iowa Democrats had repeatedly found out to their cost that Unionism was a less potent political force than sectionalism. The South's aggressive posture during the middle and late 1850s alienated the middle ground and drew normally moderate men into alliance with hitherto marginalized antislavery activists. By 1860 Stephen Douglas's split with the Buchanan administration over its Kansas policy had helped not only to divide the national Democratic party along sectional lines but also to sunder the organization in Iowa. Benjamin Samuels's defeat of George W. Jones for the senatorial nomination of the Democratic legislative caucus early in 1858 marked the triumph of Douglas's supporters over those of the administration. However, the intraparty feud continued to preoccupy Iowa Democrats over the next three years, sapping the local organization's energies and undermining its attempts to take advantage of the economic recession.

Although the Douglasites' adherence to popular sovereignty had substantial appeal for those seeking a middle way out of the sectional crisis, Lincoln's triumph in 1860 revealed that a majority of the electorate did not regard it as a strong enough bulwark against slave power designs. In spite of increasing signs of incipient factionalism within their own ranks and more than a modicum of discomfort caused by John Brown's rash attempt to spark off a slave insurrection in Virginia, Iowa Republicans held on to power by adhering to their policy of nonextension. The secession crisis of 1860–61 placed great strains on that commitment, but as their reluctance to forge another humiliating sectional compromise revealed, they were ultimately prepared to go to war rather than submit to the will of the planter class.

Several factors helped to keep sectional passions alive during the late 1850s. The first of these was President Buchanan's ill-judged territorial policy. Convinced that deference to Southern opinion was the price that had to be paid for national and Democratic unity, Buchanan announced his support for the admission of Kansas as a slave state on 2 February 1858. Republican legislators in the Iowa house had already anticipated this move by passing a joint resolution condemning both the proslavery Lecompton constitution and the president in no uncertain terms—an undisguised attempt to force the Democratic minority into a corner over Kansas.[1] The fraudulent constitution was held in contempt by most Iowans, and few Democrats had any desire to endorse it. On the other hand they could hardly sanction opposition resolutions arraigning national party leaders. House Democrats therefore voted against the Republican measure and, with the exception of five proadministration delegates, signed their own declaration on the subject. This denied the assembly's right to pass judgment on the president, but affirmed that Congress possessed authority to investigate the circumstances behind the ratification of Lecompton and that the admission of Kansas under that constitution would be a violation of popular sovereignty.[2]

In spite of the large degree of bipartisan agreement over Kansas throughout the North, Republican politicians, worried about the impact of the recession on their shaky hegemony, endeavored to keep Lecompton alive as a bone of electoral contention. James W. Grimes, unimpressed with the legislature's response to the economic crisis, told Samuel J. Kirkwood in March 1858 that "after this winter[']s work at Des Moines, the passage of the Lecompton bill will be the only thing that can save our party. If I believed . . . that the end [just]ified the means I think I should pray for its adoption."[3]

Although the senator's words indicated a cynical readiness on the part of Republican leaders to manipulate this issue for their own selfish ends, there is no denying that genuine sectional passions underlay their opposition to Lecompton. Grimes and his colleagues regarded themselves as the guardians of Northern rights and the republican legacy of the Founding Fathers. So incensed was Francis Springer at federal policy in Kansas that he urged Governor Ralph P. Lowe to throw his weight behind the free state cause in that benighted region of the country. Kansans, said Springer, were ready to defy "the power of the central government, its standing army, assisted perhaps by regiments of volunteers from the fire eating states of the South." The question of whether or not they would fight alone was now up to Northern "patriots" to decide. Iowa, he continued, should dispatch "men and munitions of war." "The cause is not alone theirs. If conquered they will be but common sufferers in a common catastrophe. The wave of despotism which will be suffered to overwhelm the people, may be expected in its reflex to overwhelm us also."[4] Just as it had done in 1856, the Kansas issue was again tapping fears of centralization and unrestrained power located deep within the American psyche. Once more Iowa Republicans were prepared to flirt with treason to protect themselves against a government widely believed to be controlled by the South's planter class.

Hopes that Lecompton would keep the party afloat during 1858 were dashed during the summer by congressional Democrats who passed a compromise measure over the opposition of the Republican minority. When Kansans rejected statehood in August the issue was dead and buried, much to the relief of Douglas's followers in Iowa.

Fortunately for the Republicans, the "English swindle" angered Southern separatists who had always viewed Lecompton as the best means of protecting their section's rights in Kansas. A few of them began to demand the reopening of the African slave trade, but more important was the call for a federal slave code for the territories. This provided a rallying point for states' rights men and, after Harpers Ferry, won the support of most Southern Democrats.

Coming as they did close on the heels of Dred Scott and Lecompton, these new and extreme objectives provided further evidence that the slave power was bent on warping the national destiny. Republican pronouncements became more stridently anti-Southern. An editorial in the *Fairfield Ledger* prefaced the 1859 campaign by warning that in spite of Northern vigilance the slave power had succeeded in breaking down all legislative and judicial obstructions to slavery expansion except those relating to the external slave trade. Must the North be punished for giving succor to the "panting fugitive," it asked, "and the South go unwhipped of justice while engaged in violation of law importing slaves by the hundred?"[5] In a speech written for the same contest Cyrus Clay Carpenter of Fort Dodge, a moderate pro-Grimes Republican, contended that slaveholders had begun an offensive war against free institutions. "All things," he said, "point towards a general absorption of power by a class who propose and are determined to make this government the cringing supple tool of Pro Slavery Fire Eaters." The latter were already seeking to purchase Cuba and to keep the territories barren until they had reopened the slave trade. "Every man," he thundered, "should be at his post, with armor on, & bayonet fixed for action."⁶

The third source of sectional antagonism was the Fugitive Slave Act of 1850. As well as prompting the insertion of a personal liberty clause into the new Iowa constitution, this controversial measure was the source of well-publicized events in other midwestern states that served to remind politicians and voters alike of the barbarity of the peculiar institution.

Early in 1859 several citizens of Oberlin, Ohio, were imprisoned for attempting to rescue a runaway black man. Pro-Chase radicals like James Ashley and Joshua Giddings participated in mass meetings denouncing the Fugitive Slave Law and the federal courts and calling for the preservation of state sovereignty.⁷ An agitated Senator Grimes told Chase on 30 May that he hoped the Ohio supreme court would soon declare the hated statute unconstitutional. "Our government," he wrote, "must become a great consolidated elective monarchy in a few years, supported mainly for the purpose of breeding & importing African slaves unless something interposes to check its present tendencies, and I know no instrumentalities than [sic] can be so safely used to this end as the judiciaries of the several states."⁸ The Iowan's belief that state institutions were the North's best defense against the Southern-dominated central government had been a keynote of his career for most of the decade. Like many moderate free-soilers he had been radicalized by the perceived and actual aggressions of the South. The Fugitive Slave Act encapsulated those aggressions for thousands of other nonradicals and would continue to do so until the outbreak of the Civil War.

The efforts of Republican leaders to respond creatively to local issues and yet simultaneously to emphasize the primacy of the sectional crisis were both hindered and abetted by John Brown's surprise attack on the U.S. arsenal at Harpers Ferry, West Virginia, in October 1859. Initially it seemed that the raid would have a detrimental impact on Republican chances in the forthcoming presidential election. Charles Aldrich, the editor of a free-soil newspaper in remote Webster City, recognized as much when he asserted that, if the conspirators were guilty of even half the offenses attributed to them, "the authorities did no more than their duty in dealing with them as sternly and summarily as they have done." On the other hand Aldrich's readiness in the same editorial to condemn slavery as "a magazine of evil" and to recount Brown's sufferings in Kansas betrayed the Republicans' ambivalent attitude to the outrage.⁹ As many of them realized, the martyred abolitionist had an important part to play in the maintenance of sectional tension.

This is not to say that Brown was merely perceived as a political pawn in Iowa, for the dead man's cause meant more to some local Republicans than they cared to admit in public. During the winter of 1857–58 the veteran guerrilla fighter had removed his headquarters from Tabor on the border with Nebraska to the hamlet of Springdale, one of a cluster of Quaker settlements outside Iowa City.[10] Leaving his armed followers ensconced in the farmhouse of a trusted spiritualist, Brown journeyed east to acquaint black activists and revolutionary white immediatists of his plan to invade the South. He returned to Springdale in April 1858, gathered up his men, and proceeded to Canada West to consolidate the organization of his prospective maroon state in the Appalachians. Although the invasion attempt was imminent, fears of betrayal induced Brown to engage in diversionary maneuvers. In December he led a spectacular assault on two northwest Missouri plantations, freeing eleven slaves and killing one of their owners in the process. The band then retreated eastward across Iowa.

After a markedly cool reception at Tabor on 5 February 1859 Brown's men reached the Des Moines River nine days later. The radical editor John Teesdale paid the ferriage. He was not the only prominent Republican to abet the outlaws and their train of liberated blacks. Josiah B. Grinnell gave them shelter and heard Brown allude to his "mission" before a crowded town meeting.[11] While his guests were evading the Democratic postmaster at Iowa City and journeying on to the Springdale area, Grinnell went to Chicago to procure a boxcar in which they could be smuggled out of the state. Although it proved to be a fruitless journey (the Rock Island official with whom he conferred feared being prosecuted under the Fugitive Slave Act), Grinnell's fellow activist William Penn Clarke took charge of the escape plans. With the help of several local Republicans including Dr. Jesse Bowen (soon to be elected to the state senate) and the Davenport Methodist Hiram Price, Clarke arranged transportation for Brown's troop (four of whom were Iowans) to Chicago.[12] Some time after their departure John H. Painter, a justice of the peace in the Quaker hamlet of Pedee, boxed up the captain's weapons and shipped them off to Maryland. Thus did the antislavery zealots of Iowa play an integral role in the events leading up to Harpers Ferry.

If the radicals' involvement with Brown was unsurprising in the light of their previous record on Kansas and slavery, the reaction of more-conservative Republicans to Harpers Ferry was less predictable. Instead of recoiling with horror at what was clearly an unconstitutional and premeditated attack on the rights of the Southern states, many of them evinced a pronounced reluctance to heap criticism on the Puritan revolutionary. Governor Kirkwood's centrist organ at Iowa City reported on 30 November 1860 that Brown was preparing for his execution with the same "calm courage," "steady nerve," and "unwavering consciousness of moral rectitude" that had marked his life on earth. He was, contended the same paper, ready to meet his fate "like a true hero."[13] Hawkins Taylor, a moderate Republican leader in Keokuk, contended that Brown had shown noble generosity to his Southern prisoners in the besieged engine house, even though he was generally conceded to be "crazy on the slavery subject." A former Kentucky Whig raised to hate the abolitionists after their reputed defeat of Henry Clay in 1844, Taylor now avowed himself willing to "vote for the meanest of them all in prefference [sic] to any Doughface who has endorsed the inhumanity of the late trial of Brown and his associates and attempted to attach the Harpers Ferry outrage on the Republicans."[14]

Rather than fend off Democratic attempts to label them as traitors and disunionists, local Republicans took the offensive by depicting Brown as a misguided but principled abolitionist fighting the injustices of slavery. They also blamed Southern leaders for trying to make political capital out of the affair. L.A. Duncan, coeditor of the Iowa City *Republican,* visited Virginia shortly after the martyred abolitionist had been hung. Although he found the Southern populace "very courteous and obliging," he insisted that the state governor had magnified the raid's importance to improve his presidential chances. There was, claimed Duncan, general ignorance about the Republican party, for Southerners were duped by their leaders into equating Republicanism with abolitionism. If only the people would consult the 1856 Philadelphia platform for themselves, they would discover that "there is about as little sympathy between these parties as between the Abolition and African Democratic parties."[15]

Such efforts to distance Republicanism from the cause that Brown represented were not entirely convincing. Just how boldly nonradicals reacted to the Brown raid was revealed that winter by Samuel J. Kirkwood himself. On 17 December 1859 Barclay Coppoc, the youngest Iowan to participate in the Harpers Ferry conspiracy, arrived back at his Springdale home after a lengthy flight from Southern justice. While his elder brother Edwin had taken part in the raid itself, Barclay had been posted on the Maryland side of the Potomac to guard the attackers' Northern escape route. After Brown's surrender he fled into the mountains in a desperate effort to evade the noose. Within days of his return to Springdale he was the subject of a requisition attempt by the state of Virginia.

Two weeks into the new session of the general assembly, two antislavery Republicans of Quaker stock, Benjamin F. Gue and Ed Wright, entered the executive office at Des Moines to find an agent of the Old Dominion berating Governor Kirkwood for his lack of zeal in tracking down Coppoc. The two legislators lost no time in convening a meeting with their radical colleagues at the capitol, prominent among whom were Grinnell and the former Free-Soil-Democrat Jonathan W. Cattell. After some discussion the informal radical caucus dispatched a messenger to Springdale to warn Coppoc of the danger. Kirkwood, meanwhile, discovered technical grounds for refusing to order the fugitive's arrest. By the time a watertight requisition arrived, the bird had flown.[16]

The Republicans' involvement with John Brown suggests that their efforts to play down their sectional leanings in the aftermath of Harpers Ferry were tactically motivated. Local Democrats were under no illusions about the opposition's real feelings on the raid. Augustus C. Dodge, still smarting from his gubernatorial defeat, commented privately: "They (Republicans) sympathise with 'old Brown' & yet seek to deny it. The whole party are as false to their professions as they are to their Constitutional obligations and oaths. If they would only show their hand fully we would have little difficulty in beating them at the approaching [presidential] election."[17]

During the winter of 1859–60 Democratic legislators sought to probe the circumstances behind Coppoc's abrupt disappearance, but the Republicans closed ranks and prevented any damaging investigation into the affair.[18] The former also condemned the sectional tenor of Governor Kirkwood's inaugural address—a one-sided view of a carefully crafted speech that, with its tempered criticism of Harpers Ferry, predictable condemnation of Lecompton and Southern filibustering in Central America, astute advocacy of colonization, and uncompromising restatement of Jackson's stance during the nullification crisis, was clearly designed to unite all elements of the party behind an essentially nonradical position.[19]

This said, it is difficult not to agree with Dodge's analysis of Republican fundamentals. Underneath the reassuring gloss provided by such phrases as "our southern brethren" and "reason will resume its sway" lay a profound unwillingness on the part of most Iowa Republicans to mend sectional fences on Southern terms.[20] The conservative centrist Kirkwood revealed as much when he obstructed Governor John Letcher's attempts to have Coppoc returned to Virginia. In spite of being a Democrat Letcher was no states' rights extremist. The granting of his request would have furnished tangible evidence that Republicans were sympathetic to Southern fears, and improved the position of Upper South Unionists vis-à-vis the separatists. But moderate Northerners like Kirkwood were not in the business of reassuring their Southern counterparts. How could they be when they themselves viewed the latter as arrogant and despotic, and their own radical wing was eager to meddle practically with the institution on which Southern society was founded? Behind the public protestations of constitutional conservatism lay the mailed fist of abolition.

Republican members of the eighth Iowa general assembly (January–March 1860) did more than thwart Democratic attempts to tar them with the brush of disunionism. As well as reelecting James Harlan to the U.S. Senate, they responded positively to grass-roots economic grievances by enacting legislation curbing the powers of county judges (long held up as local embodiments of the centralizing tendencies of modern Democracy) and providing temporary relief against foreclosure.[21] James F. Wilson, moreover, announced his support for a bill to regulate railroad rates, but Democratic opposition to such an interventionist measure consigned it to defeat.[22] Such overt manifestations of anti-monopoly sentiment in the legislature must have alarmed the sizable railroad lobby present in Des Moines, even if they were products of political necessity rather than ideological commitment. In November 1859 John Murray Forbes had asked U.S. Senator James W. Grimes to keep the railroads out of state politics.[23] Clearly there were limits to the Republicans' ability to brook popular discontent with the corporations.

By the beginning of 1860, however, most Republicans were preoccupied less by local matters than with the absorbing question of who should be the national party's presidential candidate in the November elections. After Frémont's fine showing in 1856 and the subsequent disarray within the Democratic organization, there was a general feeling that Republicans could secure control of the federal government if they chose the right man as their standard-bearer. Victory would deal a death blow to the slave power and coincidentally elevate Republican partisans to positions of untold influence and material reward.

At the height of the Coppoc excitement there appeared in the Des Moines *Iowa State Register* an open letter from the boy's mother to the governor of Virginia. In it she condemned his state's course of "insane revenge" against the conspirators and confirmed her willingness to surrender both her own life and that of Barclay, "if thereby the distressed bondsmen might be liberated and their masters purged of their sins."[24]

Three days earlier, on 20 February 1860, the publisher of this inflammatory epistle, John Teesdale, had urged the nomination of Senator William Henry Seward for president.[25] The majority of Iowa radicals shared Teesdale's enthusiasm for the exponent of "Higher Law" politics, their commitment unshaken by Seward's recent public displays of moderation. Although antislavery support for Seward was strong enough to convince James Harlan that the New Yorker should receive the Republican nomination at Chicago in May, other centrists were less sure.[26] Some considered that Seward's corrupt state machine, his Whiggery, and his pronounced opposition to nativism made him an electoral liability. Others disliked his radical image, either for personal reasons or because they thought it would lose the party thousands of votes in key Northern states.

Surprisingly few Republicans, however, were prepared to countenance a dilution of party principles in order to capture the presidency. Horace Greeley's attempts to promote the nomination of elderly Edward Bates on the grounds that the conservative Missourian was the only man who could carry the doubtful states found little favor in Iowa. Opined Fitz Henry Warren: "I go in for electing; but why go in to the bowels of Niggerdom for a candidate?" The nominee, he continued, must "be alive, and able to walk at least from parlor to dining-room."[27] Like most of his copartisans Warren paid little heed to the interests of border-state Republicans (for whom Bates would have been an ideal candidate). There was a general assumption that the election would be won in the North alone—proof, if any was still needed, that sectionalism was ingrained in the marrow of Iowa Republicanism.

Although there is little evidence of a ground swell of support for Abraham Lincoln in Iowa during the early months of 1860, his western background and availability meant that no one could discount his chances. The fact that he had performed so impressively against Stephen Douglas in the recent Illinois debates helped to strengthen his position as the conference season approached. Many local Republicans feared that a Douglas nomination at Charleston would undermine the party's strength and began to look on Lincoln as the only man who could compete successfully against the Little Giant in the West. Congressman Samuel Ryan Curtis of Keokuk numbered among those sympathetic to his cause. So too did some key conservative centrists, most notably Governor Kirkwood and the adept Mount Pleasant politician Alvin Saunders, a staunch ally of Senator Harlan.[28]

Early in the new year Iowa Republicans convened at Des Moines to select delegates for the national convention in May. Thirty-three men were chosen to represent the state at Chicago, a ridiculously large number in view of the fact that Iowa had only four votes to cast at the convention, but sufficient to encompass the wide range of intraparty opinion on the presidential question. There were several prominent names among the delegates elected, with radical supporters of Seward particularly in evidence. The diversity of opinions, however, made instruction impossible, and the majority of these Republicans traveled to the Wigwam "in favor of the strongest name, if that can be known."[29] The Democrats, meanwhile, selected a pro-Douglas delegation to attend their party's convention at Charleston.[30]

When the state's Republican delegates arrived in Chicago, they were generously entertained at their grandiosely named "Iowa Headquarters" made available at the Tremont House by William Penn Clarke. At the crowded wooden convention center nearby they finally announced their positions on the presidential nomination. Judging by the stances on the first ballot, only eight delegates believed that a conservative candidate could be elected. John A. Kasson, the dynamic chairman of the state central committee who played a major role in drafting the national platform, cast his initial vote for Edward Bates. Twelve men voted for Seward or Chase, the two radical candidates on show. They included some staunch antislavery activists: Jacob Butler and Henry O'Connor of Muscatine, the Free-Will Baptist minister John Johns, and possibly William Penn Clarke himself. Another twelve delegates plumped for Abraham Lincoln or Simon Cameron.[31] Among this moderate or pragmatic bloc was the Des Moines attorney Charles C. Nourse. Thinking Seward "a dangerous radical" who would alienate Iowa's Southern-born voters, he supported Lincoln on the grounds that he, "would represent and attract those in all the old parties who strongly opposed the extension of slavery and the aggressions of its leaders, and whose character and career would not suggest attacks upon the property rights of the southern slave owners."[32]

When it became clear that Seward could not garner sufficient votes to procure the nomination, the nonradical members of the Iowa delegation moved quickly into the Lincoln camp. Nourse recalled not only that Kirkwood and Saunders played an important role in this development but also that great whoops of joy went up from the Iowans when the rail-splitter was nominated on the third ballot.[33] As the Seward vote remained largely intact, it can be surmised that most of the enthusiasm came from centrists like Nourse. Whether it was they who drank most of the liquor available at the Iowa Headquarters (leaving the unfortunate William Penn Clarke to pick up the tab) is less certain, but clearly Lincoln's nomination represented a defeat for the more extreme antislavery elements in the Republican camp. Power resided with moderate pragmatists like Kirkwood and Saunders, and the two key players whom these men represented, Senators Grimes and Harlan.

The crucial event of that spring, however, was not Lincoln's nomination but the split within the national Democratic party at Charleston. Hindsight shows that the South's refusal to support Douglas's nomination greatly increased the chances of both a Republican victory in November and a formal dissolution of the Union. Iowa Democrats were forced to contend with the secession of the proadministration wing of their organization. In June the followers of George W. Jones (many of them federal officeholders) assembled at Davenport to ratify the presidential candidacy of John C. Breckinridge, the choice of the Southern Democracy. At their convention in August they made no state nominations but drew up a slate of presidential electors and a blatantly proslavery platform. Soon afterward a small group of conservative Whigs, fearful of impending crisis, met at Iowa City under the banner of the recently formed Constitutional Union party.[34] Press support for themselves and the Breckinridge faction was virtually nonexistent. The real choice before the voters in November lay between Lincoln and Douglas.

No new issues were raised when the campaign got underway during the summer. Both major parties pledged their support to the federal Union, to a national homestead law, and to retrenchment at home. The Republicans repeated their charges that Iowa Democrats were dupes of the slave power and insisted that Northern rights could only be maintained by prohibiting the spread of slavery into the territories. The Douglasites railed against "the hydra-headed monster, Congressional Intervention," lambasted their opponents as disunionists and abolitionists, and, still seeking to revive anti-bank fervor, called for "reasonable restrictions" to be placed on banking in Iowa.[35] Disillusioned with the whole political process, the eccentric Burlington Democrat David Rorer bemoaned the existing state of affairs:

> Conventions and party organizations managed mostly by professional & gambling politicians, have crushed out the thought and individuality of the people. These men excite party strife, by rubbing the heads of the people together, to make them quarrel for their benefit as the boys do the heads of dogs to make them fight, for boy's amusement.

Worried that Democrats in his own district were beginning "to deny that *slaves are property,*" the Kentucky-born lawyer announced his decision to support the Breckinridge ticket. If slavery was good, he reasoned, it ought to go into the territories. If it was bad "it had better be there, than where it is, & so it ought to go any how, & be farther off in case of trouble."[36]

The question of the status of slavery in the territories dominated the presidential campaign, much, one suspects, to the benefit of the Republicans whose nonextension policy constituted the most clear-cut solution to the whole problem. Popular sovereignty was promoted vigorously by the Little Giant himself on a brief visit to Iowa in October and by his friends on the stump.[37] Lecompton, however, had undermined its attractiveness to those concerned about the growing arrogance of the South, and neither the Freeport doctrine (Douglas's notion that territorial police powers were an adequate safeguard against slavery expansion) nor frequent doses of Democratic racism could outweigh the advantage held by the Republicans in their self-appointed role as defenders of Northern rights within the Union.

In the November election Lincoln won 54.9 percent of Iowa's popular vote against Douglas's 42.9. Bell and Breckinridge garnered less than three thousand votes between them.[38] As expected the rapidly growing northeastern counties provided the rail-splitter with his largest majorities, but even in the more densely populated southeast the Republican candidate emerged victorious.[39] Support for Douglas was heaviest in the Dubuque and Keokuk areas as well as in a number of southern and western counties, indicating a combined economic and ethnic explanation for the vote. Lincoln appears to have run strongly in the more-developed Yankee-orientated sections of the state, while Douglas attracted most support from voters farthest away from the market and from those fearful of the sectional and nativist leanings of the Republican party, principally the Southern- and foreign-born. Just as they had done in 1856, the vast majority of German immigrants (Catholics in particular) seem to have voted Democrat.[40] Although Davenport's German language weekly backed the Republican cause, neither its efforts nor those of men like James W. Grimes to attract significant numbers of Protestant Germans into the ruling coalition bore fruit before the Civil War.

Historians have differed over whether or not Lincoln's election—he carried every Northern state except New Jersey and won a plurality of 39.8 percent—represented a triumph for antislavery principles. Contemporary observers were equally divided. One man who thought it did was Grimes's mentor, the veteran abolitionist and black rights campaigner, Asa Turner. "We rejoice in the election of Lincoln now made certain by the telegraph," he wrote privately on 9 November 1860. "I have felt a deep interest in the election, and it is the first time in my life I ever cast my vote for a successful candidate."[41]

Nonradicals shared Turner's enthusiasm, but not for the same reason. The moderate Whig-Republican Samuel F. Miller (soon to be elevated to the U.S. Supreme Court) privately expressed his confidence in Lincoln's real conservatism to a Southern correspondent on 11 November.[42] Most of the judge's fellow centrists shared his view that the president-elect was a cautious man who would not attempt to antagonize the South after its defeat at the polls. Even so, Miller himself was farsighted enough to recognize that any amount of conservatism on Lincoln's part might not be enough to prevent the breakup of the Union. With the national government now in the hands of their enemies, Southern radicals were in no mood to acquiesce in the judgment of the American people. South Carolina fire-eaters were already preparing for secession when Miller volunteered the hope that matters could be settled amicably. "It is true we cannot permit a single State to set up for herself in our midst," he wrote, "but if enough join in the movement to make it creditable let the thing be done decently and in order."[43] Whether this acceptance of peaceable secession was typical of most Iowans is doubtful, but Miller was correct in thinking that a general withdrawal of Southern states from the Union was about to take place. Two days later the South Carolina legislature set that process in motion by issuing a call for a state secession convention to meet at Columbia.

The Republican response to the ensuing crisis was predictably confused. Lincoln was not inaugurated until March 1861, his party had never before held the reins of national power, and the distribution of the spoils often seemed a more-pressing problem than supposedly empty threats of disunion. Iowa's congressional delegation spent much of the winter dealing with federal appointments and keeping the dangerous Fitz Henry Warren out of the cabinet. Individual Republican reactions to the deepening crisis were often ambivalent, bearing witness not only to ideological divisions within the party and the complex pressures acting on inexperienced statesmen but also to the bewildering nature of the events themselves.

Iowa's Republican leaders quickly discovered that Lincoln's success was by no means an unmixed blessing for the local party. Those secondary level partisans who had labored for years to promote Republicanism assumed that their efforts would be amply rewarded during the winter of 1860–61 with the gift of a remunerative federal position. Since there were not enough offices available, many of the place-seekers were bound to be disappointed. Predictably, therefore, the appointment process antagonized substantial numbers of loyal Republicans and intensified the internal factionalism that had been simmering for several years.

By the end of 1860 many of Iowa's urban centers possessed rival Republican groupings based on personal rivalries and ideological differences. The bitterest of these was in Iowa City, where William Penn Clarke was embroiled in a furious faction fight with Governor Samuel J. Kirkwood. Clarke, repeatedly deprived of a meaningful office, had sought to strengthen his position by purchasing the Democratic Iowa City *Reporter* in July 1860. This move caused consternation among Douglas supporters and gave Clarke a powerful organ with which to rival the governor's generally moderate *Iowa Republican*.[44] During the secession crisis the *Reporter,* ably overseen by Clarke's handpicked editors, Lurton D. Ingersoll and Frederick Lloyd, became one of the most radical newspapers in the state, frequently critical of the governor for his pronouncements on the national situation. Clarke himself hoped to obtain a judgeship of the court of claims at Washington, but in this, as in so many other of his attempts to secure high office, he was ultimately frustrated by his failure to win the support of either Grimes (a close ally of Kirkwood) or Harlan (personally friendly toward Clarke, but unwilling to bring about a split within the state organization by promoting his career).

William Penn Clarke was one of yesterday's men. In Des Moines and Council Bluffs several of tomorrow's men were laying the foundations of their own political careers. Towards the end of 1859 James C. Savery, a conservative Des Moines businessman, complained to Governor Kirkwood that a coterie of politicians was slowly carving out an independent power base at the capital.⁴⁵ The principal target of Savery's wrath was John A. Kasson. A native of Vermont and graduate of the state university, Kasson had made a name for himself as a talented lawyer and free-soil politician during the antebellum years, first in New Bedford, Massachusetts, then in St. Louis as a member of the city's Blair faction, and most recently as chairman of the Republican central committee in Des Moines. He was a vain, foppish man, fond of shooting, contemptuous of blacks and Indians, and, later in the century, a fervent admirer of Bismarck. While many of his views were conservative, his brilliant legal abilities, organizational expertise, and personal charisma quickly made him one of the rising stars of the Republican party in Iowa.⁴⁶

Numbering among Kasson's friends was Grenville M. Dodge, a resident of Council Bluffs and another Yankee Republican of Democratic antecedents. Dodge, a trained civil engineer, had found employment with the Rock Island Railroad in 1852 and was soon working for its Iowa subsidiary, the Mississippi & Missouri. Along with the Council Bluffs merchant John T. Baldwin he founded a local land speculation and banking firm that benefited greatly from its railroad contacts.⁴⁷ In the late 1850s Dodge was working as a lobbyist for Henry Farnam, president of the Mississippi & Missouri. It may have been in this capacity that he first met Kasson, for the latter was a paid servant of the same corporation.⁴⁸ Dodge and Kasson joined a number of other young men along the Council Bluffs–Des Moines axis (principally Caleb Baldwin, a bulky Pennsylvania-born lawyer, and H.M. Hoxie, the latest chairman of the Republican central committee) in actively promoting their personal business and political interests. It was this group that Savery had in mind when he told Kirkwood that he looked "with distrust upon a class of new politicians located here at the capital who give early promise of a regency that may become notorious with like institutions in some of the older states."⁴⁹

Lincoln's election provided these ambitious railroad men with the opportunity they were looking for. Hopeful of receiving direct support from the new administration through their close ties with the president's manager, David Davis, they were determined to lay the foundations for their incipient political ring. Notwithstanding some disagreement over candidates for the strategically important federal posts opened up by Buchanan's defeat, Caleb Baldwin, now an Iowa supreme court judge, predicted on 9 December 1860 that "[w]ithin 4 years we will have Representatives[,] Senators[,] District judges, [and] perhaps a congressman."⁵⁰ Hoxie's appointment as U.S. marshal early in the new year represented a major victory for the railroad clique, but few of its members could have supposed that by the end of the decade they would be in a position to take control of the state Republican party.

While Hoxie's promotion was less than universally popular at home (one Republican denounced him as "suspicious, treacherous and as corrupt as the devil wants him to be"), the most important factional struggle during the Great Secession Winter involved attempts by the friends of Fitz Henry Warren to secure his appointment to the cabinet as postmaster general.[51] Spearheaded by Hawkins Taylor and Francis Springer, this campaign received much support from state officials.[52] Crucially, however, it was obstructed in Washington by members of Iowa's congressional delegation, all of whom recognized Warren to be a dangerous political rival.[53] The Burlington man's overbearing sense of pride and determination to settle his score with Grimes prevented him from accepting anything less than a full cabinet post.[54] He thus remained in the political wilderness and would do so for the duration of the Civil War.

If Iowa Republicans spent many hours during the final months of the Buchanan administration distributing the spoils, their chief concern was the crisis of the Union. The initial reaction of the state's political leaders to secessionist maneuvers was confused. One reason for this was the conflicting nature of the advice that they received from their constituents and the press. While most Republicans were earnest in their determination to stand up to the South, there was no real consensus over how to respond to specific events. Outwardly many of them dismissed secession threats as "all froth and fury, signifying nothing."[55] Southerners had long trumpeted their readiness to sunder the Union without ever taking serious steps to carry out that treasonous design. Surely secession calls had been an electoral ploy to frighten the voters and would be abandoned once it was discovered that Lincoln was not a black abolitionist?

Privately, many Republicans did realize that secession was a very real possibility. Some, like Samuel F. Miller and John A. Kasson, accepted it as inevitable and were prepared to let South Carolina and its sister states go in peace.[56] Others, almost certainly a substantial majority of Republicans, rejected the notion of peaceable secession and demanded that the federal government act positively to preserve the nation's territorial integrity.[57] Some of them may have dismissed the idea that the South would unleash civil war upon the country, but all were prepared to support measures that in fact made fratricidal conflict virtually inevitable. On the whole, conservatives (who abhorred the prospect of a brothers' war and sympathized to some extent with the South's position) and radicals (intent on preventing another humiliating compromise of the slavery question) were more likely to acquiesce in secession than staunchly pro-Union moderates.

A second reason for confusion (aside from the swift pace of events) was Lincoln's reluctance to give a strong lead to his party. Remaining silent until

Christmas, the president-elect left the field open for other influential Republicans to advance their own conflicting solutions to the burgeoning crisis. Even after his famous public statement of 22 December on the need to hold firm on slavery extension, he continued to allow his chosen secretary of state, William Henry Seward, to advance compromise measures that undermined the Chicago platform.

For all its inconsistencies Republican policy during this period was grounded solidly on existing premises. The basic free-soil image of the South as an expansionist, tyrannical section controlled by an amoral minority of blustering plantocrats continued to color the party's actions, causing most of its congressional leaders not only to exaggerate the extent of slave-state Unionism and underestimate the force of Southern nationalism but also to adopt a fairly defiant stance toward the secessionists.

Iowans in Washington, however, did not reject all forms of compromise. Shortly after Congress convened in December Representatives William Vandever and Samuel Ryan Curtis (both of them nonradicals) voted to set up a House committee to discuss the possibility of a political solution to the nation's problems.[58] Curtis himself was appointed a member of the Committee of Thirty-Three. Two days later he was one of only eight Republican members of the latter to approve a conciliatory resolution calling for the adoption of measures to guarantee the constitutional rights of the South. If, at this point, Curtis still harbored genuine hopes of a settlement, they were surely dashed by the subsequent appearance of a manifesto signed by thirty Southern congressmen declaring the argument exhausted.[59]

On 11 January 1861 Senator James Harlan referred approvingly to a compromise plan currently under review. Already championed by Seward and soon to receive cautious backing from Lincoln, the proposal to admit New Mexico as a slave state was designed to initiate a process of voluntary reconstruction under the leadership of the border South.[60] Harlan's colleague, Curtis, was also amenable to this controversial measure that was clearly in breach of the free-soil pledges made at Chicago.[61]

The motives of these men were mixed. Like most of their fellow moderates they articulated and shared the Northern people's semireligious devotion to the Union. As a result they usually combined conciliatory statements with thinly veiled threats of coercion and denunciations of the right of secession. Generally they recognized that the final outcome of the winter's deliberations might be civil war. As early as 16 December James W. Grimes (who was later reported to have applauded Seward's compromise utterings) was predicting that secession was bound to be followed by "war of a most bitter and sanguinary character."[62] Curtis, a former West Pointer and veteran of the Mexican campaign, wrote privately on 9 January that bloodshed was unavoidable "and therefor the sooner the appeal to arms be made the less extended will be the conflict and the sooner we may hope to see peace."[63] His willingness to abandon the principle of nonextension stemmed partly, like that of Harlan, from a desire to delay the plans of the rebels and to isolate the latter from reasonable men everywhere.

This said, it would be too cynical to accuse the moderates of mouthing compromise and plotting war. Their conciliatory stance (not only over New Mexico but also on a review of the North's personal liberty laws and the passage of a constitutional amendment guaranteeing slavery against federal interference) was, at least in part, a genuine attempt to meet some of the more palatable Southern demands with a view toward avoiding war and curbing future expansion of the peculiar institution. Harlan defended his support for the New Mexico scheme on the grounds that if the South accepted it as "an olive branch" the remaining territory below 36°30' would be organized at a stroke, "thus effectually limiting the number of Slave states, and leaving them forever in the minority."[64] Even Curtis entertained the possibility of a nonviolent end to the crisis in commenting that, "if it tends to peace or . . . to expose the obstancy [sic] of the revolutionists," the measure was worthy of his support in the House Committee of Thirty-Three.[65]

Iowa's moderate delegation in Congress came under a good deal of fire from radicals back home. Neoabolitionist ultras rejected what they saw as yet more degrading concessions to the slave power and, on occasions, could be found openly advocating peaceable separation. This latter position was wholly compatible with their antislavery critique of the Union and, in individual cases, a logical continuation of their backing for John Brown. On 23 January John Teesdale predicted that the dissolution of the Union would lead to the ultimate extinction of slavery. Arguing tendentiously that hitherto only the military power of the federal government had prevented a general slave insurrection, the devout Congregationalist submitted that "God Almighty" might have stricken the secessionists with "judicial blindness, that in their hot zeal for the dominance of slavery, and in their fierce lust for the wages of unhallowed ambition, HIS own right arm might be bared in the liberation of every captive."[66]

William Penn Clarke proved rather less eager to counsel disunion, but his new radical organ, the *Iowa State Reporter,* was swift to criticize Seward's much-publicized compromise speech of 12 January, which had been lauded by Grimes, Curtis, and Harlan. The New York senator had suggested that the nation's remaining territories be admitted immediately as two new states, and reiterated the call for a constitutional guarantee against emancipation. The *Reporter* rejected the former on the grounds that it would legalize slavery in the West, and dismissed the latter because no party "except the radical abolitionists, who are inconsiderable in numbers and influence," proposed to meddle with slavery in the states.[67]

Teesdale and Clarke had good reason to fear a Republican sellout, for some nonradical leaders seemed prepared to abandon the existing territories in the Southwest to slavery. Governor Kirkwood joined the ranks of the trimmers on 28 January by proposing that the Missouri Compromise line be restored, that the status of slavery in New Mexico and Utah be determined by the local settlers (as envisaged in 1850), and that no further territorial acquisitions be made by the United States. Recognizing the significance of the Fugitive Slave Law, he added that it be made less obnoxious to the North. "If something were done," suggested the governor (whose maxim on this subject was clearly *out of sight, out of mind*), "to modify it so as to require the alleged fugitive to be taken by the officer before the court of the county from which he is alleged to have fled, and there have a trial if he demands it, in my opinion the law would be much more effective than it is." As for the North's personal liberty laws, concluded Kirkwood, "I doubt not [they] would be repealed when the present excitement has passed away. Iowa has never had nor does she want one."[68]

Crucially, however, the party's moderate leadership refused to support the only plan that might have satisfied the South. In blocking the so-called Crittenden Compromise Iowa's congressmen remained loyal to their stated policy objective of hemming in the peculiar institution. The key element in this ill-fated proposal was a clause requiring federal protection for slavery in all present and future American territories existing south of 36°30'. For Republicans who remembered Southern filibustering expeditions to Central America during the mid-1850s and who believed that an expansionist dynamic underlay slave power aggressions, this was too much to stomach.

Late in January Senator Grimes issued a public condemnation of Crittenden's proposal. Far from involving a mere extension of the Missouri Compromise line, wrote Grimes, it envisaged a slave code for Mexico's northern provinces upon which the South had proven designs. Clearly the North was being asked to "change the Constitution into a genuine proslavery, slavery-extending empire." This demand could not possibly be met, he concluded: "It only remains for us now to obey and enforce the laws and to show to the world that this Government is strong enough to protect itself from rebellion within as well as from assault without."[69]

Fears that the South was bent on carving out new slave states below the Rio Grande meant that there was never any possibility that the Crittenden plan would be approved by Iowa Republicans. The most they were willing to accept was the *possibility* that slavery might take root in New Mexico and Utah as a result of the Compromise of 1850. Both Harlan and Curtis gave their support to the proposition of the Virginia-backed peace conference that slavery be tolerated south of 36°30' in the existing southwestern territories.[70]

None of the Iowans in Washington, however, were prepared to condone talk of a positive guarantee for the peculiar institution in this region, and by the beginning of March (when Senate Republicans finally laid Crittenden's scheme to rest) the party's position on secession had hardened. Vandever and Curtis, for example, supported the Bingham force bill, which looked toward the coercion of seceding states.[71] Although their colleagues in the Senate joined a minority of Republicans in voting for a constitutional amendment guaranteeing slavery in the states, this action was designed primarily to mollify the border.[72]

With the country on the verge of disaster, many Iowa Democrats had no hesitation in apportioning blame for the crisis. The prominent Keokuk attorney William Worth Belknap confided to Judge Charles Mason on 11 March that "[t]his infernal spirit of Abolitionism has ruined us."[73] A month later Confederate guns opened up on Fort Sumter in Charleston harbor. "Civil War is inaugurated," shuddered Mason. "God only knows the end."[74]

If one accepts that perception played a crucial role in the secession movement, then clearly men like Grimes and Harlan, Kirkwood and Penn Clarke, must bear some of the responsibility for the outbreak of the Civil War. Quite apart from the fact that they were not averse to manipulating popular prejudices for their own ends, they also possessed a deep-rooted suspicion of Southern politicians and institutions that worked against a peaceful outcome to the sectional crisis. There were, of course, good reasons for their fears about Southern expansionism, but the fact remains that their overblown slave power rhetoric (particularly in evidence during the 1859 gubernatorial campaign), thinly veiled and sometimes overt support for John Brown, and increasingly shrill condemnation of secession were bound to play into the hands of Southern radicals. For just as Republicans manufactured political capital out of fire-eating demands for a federal slave code and the revival of the African slave trade, Southern leaders bolstered their positions by pointing to the reluctance of Northern politicians to safeguard their constitutional rights. Governor Kirkwood's refusal to extradite Barclay Coppoc was a case in point. By the end of 1860 Republicans and Southern Democrats were arguing past one another. There was no longer any meaningful debate over slavery. One section considered the institution beneficial to humanity; the other, in the words of an editorial in the *Dubuque Times,* condemned it as "a gigantic crime against God and humanity, and a stain and disgrace to our civilization and our christianity."[75]

Although Lincoln's nomination at Chicago confirmed the primacy of nonradicals within the Republican party, the South could have taken little comfort from that fact even if it had sought to do so. Centrists did not always share the neoabolitionists' concern for blacks, free or slave, but they recognized that the outcome of the sectional power struggle was intertwined with the resolution of the slavery question. As Southern leaders well knew, their longstanding hegemony within the Union (not to mention their constitutional rights as they understood them) could not survive a Republican victory in the presidential election. Hence the decision to secede during the winter of 1860–61. After a brief period of confusion their opponents, Black Republicans all as far as the fire-eaters were concerned, became convinced that the prize was now theirs by right and that Southerners had no cause to annul the democratic decision of the American people, let alone break up the Union of the Fathers. Hence their refusal to acquiesce in the Crittenden plan.

Because the Civil War cost hundreds of thousands of lives, some historians have blamed congressional Republicans for failing to promote a peaceful solution to the secession crisis. While this judgment has some historical validity, it nevertheless smacks of ex post facto reasoning. Iowa's political leaders were not, as we have seen, entirely opposed to compromise. Much to the chagrin of antislavery radicals they were prepared to grant the theoretical right of the peculiar institution to exist in the southwestern territories. To have sanctioned federal protection of slavery, however, would have been to undermine the party's fundamental raison d'être. The Republican organization had come into being to contain the spread of slavery. Now it had triumphed at the polls (albeit by a plurality) and expected, like all victorious American parties before it, to put its principles into action and reap the rewards of political success. In fact proslavery Southern nationalism was no more amenable to compromise than antislavery Republicanism. As James W. Grimes told his wife in December 1860:

> No reasonable concession will satisfy the rebels. It is not that Lincoln is elected, or that there are personal liberty laws in some of the States, or that their negroes occasionally run off, that troubles them. They want to debauch the moral sentiment of the people of the North, by making them agree to the proposition that slavery is a benign, constitutional system, and that it shall be extended in the end all over this continent.[76]

Republicans, in short, refused to eat dirt to preserve a peace that, from their vantage point, was probably not worth keeping in the first place. Preservation of the Union on a Northern basis was a different matter. This was the daunting task that now confronted them.

8
The Union in Peril, 1861–1865

he prolonged military conflict that raged across the United States between 1861 and 1865 was a costly one. Nearly eighty thousand Iowans (48.8 percent of the adult white male population) fought for the North in the Civil War. Thirteen thousand of them died in the process.

The initial enthusiasm that most Iowans felt for the struggle to save the Union evaporated quickly as casualty figures mounted and the expected victories failed to materialize. Although morale never deteriorated to the point where most people were prepared to accept an independent Confederacy, the war placed enormous strains on individuals, families, and institutions. The economy was particularly hard hit during the early years and did not begin to exhibit signs of recovery until the summer of 1863. When the lack of material well-being is added to the mental burden imposed upon the populace by news of battlefield disasters and burgeoning casualty figures, it is perhaps remarkable (the strength of American nationalism notwithstanding) that most Iowans remained so doggedly committed to the attainment of a complete military victory over the South.

The war had two primary consequences. Firstly, it preserved the federal Union intact. Secondly, it resulted in the emancipation of four million black slaves. These developments were intertwined, and the Republican party was the chief agency of both.

The military denouement of the North-South split transformed the position of blacks in American life. Without the war there could have been no early emancipation of the slaves, no extension of the franchise, no decline in state racism in the North. The destiny of African-Americans had long been linked to the sectional conflict but, from the moment the carnage began, their fate became conjoined with that of the Union itself. The great patriotic Republican party was the instrument of national salvation. While that organization's response to secession was initially cautious and confused, it was, nevertheless, solidly practical and, in the final analysis, murderously effective. In no small way did this intensifying commitment to total war mirror the progress of Republican race policy.

During the early months of the Civil War Iowa's political leaders responded to President Lincoln's call to arms by mobilizing the limited financial and human resources of their debt-ridden state. As the success of this program was dependent on the maintenance of a popular anti-Southern consensus, they strove to cultivate an image of safe conservatism in readiness for the fall elections. Radical elements were swift to condemn reaction, but their attempts to commit the party to the abolition of slavery were blocked at the state convention in July 1861 when Governor Kirkwood was renominated on a platform that had much to say about the evils of secession, and nothing about the sin of human bondage.[1]

Particularly galling for the radicals was the failure of Elias H. Williams of McGregor to secure the nomination for supreme court judge. Williams, a talented Yale graduate, had spent some time as a teacher in South Carolina where he had "imbibed a strong feeling against the institution of slavery."[2] His rebuff delighted one of his local enemies, Eliphalet Price, a conservative Whig-Republican who abhorred the efforts being made to abolitionize the state organization into "a 'Wendel Philips' party." "What a calamity would have befallen us," Price told his friend Kirkwood after the convention, "had Williams been nominated. An out and out abolitionists [sic] who believes the Constitution to be a 'Covenant with hell' who has never been a Republican. I frankly believe that 2000 Republicans in this District would have wheeled from the sup[p]ort of the Ticket with disgust had he been nominated."[3]

The official Republican silence on slavery contrasted sharply with the public stance of Iowa's Congregationalists. In June 1861 that denomination's state association adopted a report declaring the war to be a contest between "Right and Wrong" that God had permitted in order "to open the eyes of the Nation and of the world to the inherent wickedness of Slavery; to punish us as a Nation for our collusion with and support of it, and in the end to exterminate it."[4]

Such outspoken words were anathema to conservatives, but they began to assume a more persuasive character after the Battle of Bull Run on 21 July. This humiliating federal defeat was witnessed by several congressmen, including Senator James W. Grimes.[5] For moderates like him the debacle was a sobering lesson in the realities of war and a salutary warning that the

North's vapid response to the rebel challenge was portentous of national destruction. It was, therefore, with much satisfaction that Grimes greeted Major General John C. Frémont's unilateral emancipation edict of 30 August and with corresponding disbelief that he received the news of Lincoln's countermand nearly a fortnight later.

Frémont's proclamation marked a watershed in the Republican party's attitude toward slavery. Until its issuance only the radical wing of the anti-Southern coalition had dared to champion immediatist doctrine. Frémont's action in Missouri transformed abolition into a moderate objective because it seemed to herald a more positive response to the rebellion. Lincoln's decision to rescind the edict and suspend Frémont from duty pending an investigation into allegations of misconduct at his headquarters infuriated many Iowa Unionists. Grimes informed his close friend U.S. Senator William Pitt Fessenden of Maine that Washington's action was having a disastrous effect on enlistments in Iowa. The general's proclamation, he said, had been described by Mrs. Grimes as, "the only real noble and true thing done during this war. . . . Everybody of every sect, party, sex and color, approves it in the Northwest, and it will not do for the Administration to causelessly tamper with the man who had the sublime moral courage to issue it."[6] The administration did more than tamper with Frémont's position. On 24 October Lincoln ordered the general's dismissal after receiving reports of jobbery and tactical ineptitude from his subordinates, prominent among whom was Keokuk's ambitious soldier-politician Samuel Ryan Curtis.[7]

Once again Republicans vented their wrath on the administration. Grimes blamed the powerful Blair family for engineering Frémont's downfall and belittled the allegations of misconduct. "I do not question that Fremont made some unfortunate selections of agents," he told the more cautious Fessenden. "So too has the Secy. of War, Mr. Seward, Gov. Chase & it is shrewdly suspected that even the Father of the faithful has sinned in this way."[8]

Fortunately for Grimes's copartisans at home, their opponents were far more divided over the drift of events. After a brief period of enthusiasm for the war effort Iowa Democrats began to split into those broadly supportive of Washington's efforts to suppress the rebellion and those increasingly critical of what they perceived to be a war to subjugate the South. Although many Peace Democrats (derided first as "Tories" and later as "Copperheads") had belonged to the old Jones wing of the party, it did not follow that all Douglas Democrats supported their leader's call to rally behind the Lincoln administration. Dennis A. Mahoney, a pugnacious Irishman who edited the *Dubuque Herald,* was just one of many Douglas men who came out against "subjugation" in the summer of 1861.[9] However, neither his efforts nor those of his friends to promote the gubernatorial candidacy of Judge Charles Mason on a virulently antiabolitionist platform were enough to prevent Kirkwood from being comfortably reelected in October. The Republican garnered 55.5 percent of the vote, a significant improvement on his performance against Augustus C. Dodge two years previously.[10]

The scudding snows of January 1862 brought cold comfort to Iowa farmers, hard hit by another season of poor crop prices. Prospects of a swift Northern victory, so bright the previous spring, had faded with the year. The first ever national Republican administration seemed incapable of seizing the initiative. In his annual message to Congress, Lincoln had again ruled out the possibility of federal emancipation by saying that he did not want the war to degenerate into "a violent and remorseless revolutionary struggle."[11]

This reluctance to attack the cornerstone of Southern society was no longer shared by moderate Iowa Unionists. In his second inaugural address on 15 January 1862 Governor Kirkwood outlined his belief "that to prosecute this war successfully, we must strike directly at Slavery."[12] The executive's belated conversion to immediatism was significant, for he had not previously shown any interest in the question. His policy statement to the assembly indicated that the sectional crisis was continuing to radicalize the middle ground. Charles Clarke of Fairfield declared himself much pleased with Kirkwood's views and predicted that Lincoln would eventually come up to the mark. "I have," he said, "great faith in the educator, War."[13]

Clarke was right. As a pedagogue Mars had no superior. In Washington, Iowa's seasoned U.S. senators Grimes and Harlan signaled their intention to act with the radical bloc in Congress by supporting a bill to abolish slavery in the District of Columbia. This measure had long been a prime objective of political abolitionists who argued that the central government had full authority to eradicate the peculiar institution in the nation's capital. Because of its symbolic significance and lack of bearing on the military situation, the bill was vigorously opposed by Senate conservatives as needlessly antagonistic of border state opinion. This objection did not prevent the Iowans from supporting abolition in the District, although Harlan did approve a colonization amendment attached to it by the advocates of caution.[14]

The Mount Pleasant Methodist was reluctant to alienate conservative sentiment at home. When the Delaware Democrat Willard Saulsbury introduced an amendment providing for the removal of liberated Washington slaves to Northern free states, Harlan was quick to respond. Such a proposal was untenable, he said, because men like Saulsbury were well aware "that there is in all the free states a deep-seated prejudice against an association with the colored population—a prejudice that does not exist in the slave states." Although Harlan proceeded to refute the notion of a postemancipation race war in the language of Christian love, his failure to act on spoken principle must have convinced Saulsbury that the Republicans were hypocrites. What did Harlan know of free blacks, he retorted acidly? "The State of Iowa talking about the character of a free negro population . . . and she has not got free negroes enough to make milestones along one of the public roads, within her limits, perhaps!"[15]

Grimes's actions in the second session of the Thirty-seventh Congress showed him to be a more dependable advocate of abolitionist principles than Harlan. Allan G. Bogue's quantitative analysis of the Civil War Senate indicates that the Burlington politician was one of the most radical Republicans in the session, his innate fears of centralized power temporarily curbed by a newfound determination to secure a Northern military victory.[16] This latter development, which owed much to his appointment as a member of the Senate committee on naval affairs, proved a potent spur to action, particularly as it dovetailed neatly with his natural dislike of slavery.

In the summer of 1861 Grimes had played a major role in procuring the release of slaves from the infamous District of Columbia jail.[17] His support for emancipation at the capital the following year was thus a logical extension of this humanitarian act. But it was much more than that. For Grimes and other Senate radicals, District emancipation was both an end in itself and a preliminary to total emancipation. This greater goal induced Grimes to appeal vehemently for the use of black labor in the military service of the United States. He spoke so compellingly on the subject in April 1862 that one Garrisonian abolitionist was moved to praise his "spirit of humanity and love of justice."[18]

Early in May Secretary of the Navy Gideon Welles directed the enlistment of blacks in the maritime service. "This *must* be finally followed up by an army order sooner or later," Grimes told his wife, "and then comes the end of slavery. I regard the employment of colored persons in the Army and Navy as of vastly more importance in putting an end to slavery than all of the confiscation acts that could be devised by the ingenuity of man."[19] So confident was he that emancipation was inevitable that he received with stoical resignation the news that Lincoln had rescinded Major General David Hunter's edict freeing the slaves of South Carolina, Georgia, and Florida. The end must come, he reiterated to Elizabeth, protracted though it might be by "the obstinacy of rulers."[20]

On the whole these practical efforts on behalf of abolition accorded well with Republican feelings in Iowa. Frank W. Palmer, the new editor of the Des Moines *State Register,* alluded favorably to Grimes's speech on black labor and greeted the demise of Hunter's proclamation with the confident assertion that slavery would eventually "swamp in its own infamy."[21] Publicly, the only issue on which Palmer disagreed with the junior senator that spring was the formation of black regiments. For Grimes, whose amendment to Henry Wilson's militia bill in July provided for the liberation of black soldiers and their families, this policy represented yet another nail in slavery's coffin.[22] The *State Register,* however, rejected the proposed development on the grounds that racial prejudice would not sanction it and that blacks would not make good soldiers—a reaction that indicated that centrist Republicans were still acutely sensitive to Negrophobic feelings among the electorate.[23]

The party's state convention on 23 July issued no clarion call for black troops, and when Alexander Clark wrote to the governor suggesting the establishment of separate Negro companies, he was told bluntly that "you know your color would not be tolerated in one of our regiments."[24] Privately, though, most members of the Republican elite were ready to admit the necessity, if not the justice, of Grimes's stance on this matter. Three days before Clark's rebuff, Kirkwood expressed his support for contraband labor to General Henry Halleck, who commanded the Department of the Missouri. "I have but one remark to add," concluded the governor, "and that in regard to negroes fighting. . . . When this war is over & we have summed up the entire loss of life it has imposed on the country I shall not have any regrets if it is found that a part of the dead are *niggers* and that *all* are not white men."[25]

If public opinion in Iowa and in the field was not yet receptive to the idea of a black soldiery, it was now prepared to endorse emancipation as an urgently needed war measure. Born of impatience with the continuing military stalemate and Lincoln's reluctance to abandon his border state policy, this growing sentiment was fueled by a series of proconfiscation, proabolition speeches given by local Unionist leaders in the summer of 1862. Thomas F. Withrow, an intimate of Frank W. Palmer, told an audience at Saylorville on Independence Day that "[p]opular government must be based upon a surer foundation than human chattelism."[26] A week later Senator Harlan announced that emancipation had become a necessity. "We cannot," he said, "if we persist in our folly, thwart the ultimate purposes of the Almighty."[27]

At the end of July Iowa Republicans adopted a platform expressing undiminished confidence in the president of the United States and accepting, albeit in fairly conservative terms, the need for total abolition.[28] The blandness of this campaign document concealed a welter of pent-up frustration in the Republican ranks. Two days after the party convention, Judge Caleb Baldwin confessed privately that if he was a Union commander he would "make a clean swath of the [peculiar] institution" and "let the oppressed go free." The North, he continued, was "ripe for a bold strike and unless it is made soon there will be a decapitation in Washington."[29]

The strength of war-driven abolitionism west of the Mississippi was revealed the following month when southern Iowa Methodists convened for their annual conference. Traditionally cautious in their public stance on slavery, they adopted resolutions supportive of emancipation and the use of blacks to defeat the South. "Our country," intoned one of the church's policy statements, "can never have permanent peace while the great cause of this rebellion continues." Another concluded that if the president should announce the abolition of slavery, he would be sustained by the "moral convictions and patriotism" of the United States and give "a 'great idea' to our armies, inspire them with sentiments of justice."[30] As Methodism was by far the most popular religious denomination in Iowa at this time, these pronouncements must be regarded as a sign that the grass roots were now ready to accept racial change of the most radical kind.

Soon afterwards Lincoln finally moved to satisfy moderate Unionist opinion in the Northern states by issuing a preliminary emancipation proclamation. In so doing an astute politician cut the ground from under the feet of his critics. "Better than fifty ordinary victories on the field of battle," declared the Des Moines *State Register*. "The Nation and the World will sing hallelujahs, for the great day of Jubilee is near."[31] Caleb Baldwin was equally pleased, although more inclined toward understatement. "I think it is very opportune," he told his friend, General Grenville M. Dodge, now a rising star in the Union army thanks to the efforts of Baldwin and the Iowa delegation in Congress.[32]

If these reactions seem to indicate that the proclamation was well received by the Republican elite, the results of the midterm elections in October 1862 suggest that it was equally acceptable to the majority of Iowa voters. Aided by the ballots of soldiers in the field (who voted as they shot throughout the war) and the enthusiastic efforts of U.S. Marshal H.M. Hoxie to secure the arrest of allegedly treasonous Democratic politicians, the Republicans made a clean sweep of all six congressional contests—an impressive success given that it was achieved against a backdrop of economic stagnation and military stalemate, and that nationally the elections were a disaster for the party. Among those elected to Congress to promote the Union cause were Grimes's lieutenant, James F. Wilson (a U.S. representative since 1861); two important allies of the Dodge clique, John A. Kasson and William B. Allison; and two genuine antislavery veterans, Hiram Price and Josiah B. Grinnell.

These various expressions of support for a tougher war policy should not be allowed to obscure the fact that some local Republicans were dissatisfied with attempts to promote the emancipation proclamation as a bill of lading.

Early in the new year a mass meeting in Des Moines ratified Lincoln's official edict of 1 January 1863 declaring forever free all slaves in rebel-held districts. The assembled Unionists, many of them War Democrats, passed a resolution upholding the measure as "a Military and Governmental Necessity."[33] Although this was a relatively enlightened move on the part of the capital's traditionally conservative citizens, Charles C. Nourse did not consider the resolution sufficiently progressive. In a letter read before the assemblage, Iowa's attorney general argued that, far from being a base expedient, the proclamation was "a glorious consummation" of God's plan to destroy slavery. A prominent lay Methodist and supporter of Senator Harlan, Nourse was determined to fire a warning shot at those who sought to deny the religious roots of abolition. Too many of his countrymen, he said, had sought justice and liberty for whites and ignored the rights of the black race. "We will all yet learn, in our terrible experience," he continued, "that as a Nation we are under the moral government of a God, who is not satisfied with such selfish purposes."[34] As an evangelical Nourse needed no persuading that the Civil War was an instrument of divine retribution, inflicted on Americans as a punishment for their complacent tolerance of human bondage.

Although the attorney general's words evinced concern for Southern blacks, his concluding assertion that emancipated slaves would have no desire to move northwards betrayed the politician's sensitivity to racial prejudice. In fact, some freedmen had already begun to find their way into the Midwest as a result of the farmers' increasing demand for labor and the War Department's readiness to supply them with Southern "contrabands." This minor population movement had major political consequences in Iowa, for it caused nonradical Republicans like Charles C. Nourse to confront the race question at home.

During the winter of 1862-63 there were several reports in the Iowa press that local farmers were hiring out-of-state blacks in preparation for the new crop season.[35] The war had seriously depleted the area's white labor pool, and blacks were regarded by some employers as a cheap solution to the labor shortage. Those wishing to take advantage of this alternative were faced with two problems. The first was the racial prejudice of their neighbors; the second, the 1851 exclusion law, which, in theory at least, still prohibited free blacks from entering the state. Together, these two factors played an important role in the hounding of Archie P. Webb, a black youth from Arkansas who had secured employment on a farm in Delaware Township outside Des Moines.

On 20 January 1863, several days after he had been ordered to leave the neighborhood, Webb was arrested in accordance with the exclusion act, fined $12 plus costs, and incarcerated in the Polk County jail until he either paid the money or consented to leave the state.[36] All the local officers involved were Democrats. Fortunately for Webb the Republican establishment at Des Moines was appalled by the treatment meted out to him. No less a figure than Secretary of State Ed Wright, a Cedar County Quaker, was present at his arrest to ensure that no harm befell him, Palmer's *Iowa State Register* damned as traitors all those who had instigated his persecution, and District Judge John H. Gray granted him a writ of habeas corpus pending his hearing on 26 January.[37]

At the trial the prosecution urged that Webb's imprisonment was legal because he had come to Iowa since the promulgation of the exclusion act, section two of which required all township and county officials to request immigrant blacks to leave the state within three days.[38] It was an argument that left Judge Gray little room to maneuver. Either he upheld the statute or negated it. The defense counsel did at least give him a chance to dodge the moral aspects of the case by contending that the law had been repealed by nonuser, but Gray ignored this avenue of escape and declared the statute inoperative and void on constitutional and technical grounds.[39]

The most interesting portion of his decision was a section dealing with the complex issue of black citizenship. Of course it was not the task of a secondary level Iowa judge to determine the status of blacks inside or outside the borders of the state. Nonetheless Judge Gray made it plain that this question would have to be ruled upon soon by the courts, and that as far as he was concerned, citizenship was a natural right of all free-born Americans. The arguments advanced to deprive free blacks of this right struck him as untenable, particularly the notion of inherent black inferiority. While this was more a problem of history than law, he asserted, "It may be submitted to the enlightened conscience of a Christian world whether a race of men forced from home to foreign shores, which they never sought, and sold into bondage, should be more despised than pitied." If blacks were citizens, continued Gray, the exclusion act violated the "privileges and immunities" clause of the U.S. Constitution by permitting blacks migrating to Iowa before 1851 to reside there, but denying that basic right to out-of-state blacks after the law's promulgation.[40] Although there had long been doubts about the efficacy and legality of the act, Gray's decision virtually extinguished Democratic attempts to revivify it.[41]

Cynics might argue that the judge's verdict was influenced by the farmers' pressing need for manpower. It is certainly true that Iowa's ability to take advantage of wartime demand for local foodstuffs was seriously threatened by the acute labor shortage. When the Ohio abolitionist Josephine S. Griffing appealed to Governor William M. Stone, Kirkwood's successor, to allow substantial numbers of Southern black refugees into the state, she claimed to have received a favorable response.[42] Because Stone, a former nativist Democrat, had no record as an equal rights advocate, it is not unreasonable to surmise that his support for Griffing's scheme of settling liberated slaves in Northern states was a product of economic necessity. The Des Moines *State Register*'s assertion during the Webb affair that "[a]ny man has a right as undoubted to employ a Negro to work for him, as he has to employ an Irishman or an American," certainly had capitalistic, free labor overtones.[43] On the other hand, blacks constituted a much less viable solution to the labor problem than the employment of women and improved farming techniques.[44] Not one of the Republican leaders involved in securing Webb's release can have believed that popular racial prejudice would have sanctioned a massive influx of blacks into the state, even if it was to promote economic prosperity. More likely their main objective was to protect a vulnerable fellow human being whose basic right to live and work in Iowa was being infringed by disloyal Copperheads. Justice Gray's own words contained no hint of an economic justification for his verdict. On the contrary, his analysis of citizenship bore all the hallmarks of the moral imperative. Talk of "enlightened conscience" and "a Christian world" marked him out as a devout evangelical (like Charles C. Nourse he was a Southern-born Methodist) whose charitable instincts toward the oppressed caused him to deny all sanction for a system that placed individual blacks beyond the pale of society.

The subtle shift in white racial attitudes that was taking place as a result of the war was most evident on the battlefield. As Union armies began to penetrate the South, Iowans were brought into contact with large numbers of blacks for the first time in their lives. Most of the midwestern troops harbored racist views before they enlisted and the sight of bedraggled groups of runaway slaves overrunning their camps merely intensified their prejudices. Generally speaking those racial beliefs appear to have had their roots in the popular minstrel culture of antebellum America, for the most prevalent attitude of these predominantly young, white male farm boys toward the unfortunates in their midst was one of derision.[45]

Typical were the remarks of Private Thomas L. Hoffman of Fairfield on witnessing some hungry contrabands at Corinth, Mississippi: "Was amused to see the scrable among the darkies to see who could get the most cabbage as they were being distributed to the colored population instead of the soldiers as they should have been."[46] Another Iowan, a Mount Pleasant youth serving in the U.S. Navy, shared the services of two young blacks who had been shipped up from South Carolina, early in the war. "Our boys," he told his father, a prominent Harlan Republican, "are good for one thing, they can grin & show ivory equal to any. . . . An amusing diversion is to test our powers of sword exercise on them. No danger of hitting them, they are experts at dodging."[47] Even self-confessed abolitionists like Private Alfred A. Rigby seemed unable to take the blacks seriously. In Arkansas he came across a contraband named Moses, who was probably more intelligent than Rigby realized. "I think it is rather doubtful about his possessing the meekness of his illustrious predecessor," quipped the Iowan, "for he is the quintessence of fun. . . . I asked him if he was afraid of us yankees. He replied, 'no, but dems massa be mighty feard.' He is a darky of the genuine stamp. For an hour he amused the boys by various negro antics."[48]

The black man was regarded by most Iowa volunteers as a clown—an immature, childlike figure whose role in life was to entertain and to be laughed at accordingly. There was little recognition of the freedman's plight, no hint of familiarity with enlightened environmental theories of racial development. But because blacks were not taken seriously by most of the soldiers, there was a very real prospect that the latter would not be overly alarmed by the prospect of emancipation, particularly when that policy was advanced as a war measure. By asserting that it was not he but his master who was afraid of the Yankees, Moses the contraband indicated that it was now the white slave owner who was under pressure.

Iowa's leading military officers had not been slow to find fault with the administration's less than vigorous attempts to suppress the rebellion. As early as January 1862 the War Democrat General Marcellus Crocker complained that there were not twenty loyal slaveholders in Missouri. "They are all Secesh, either openly or covertly," he told Secretary of State Elijah Sells. "I believe this to be the case everywhere in the South. . . . What I want is peace, so that I can come home to my wife and children. . . . The war spirit wants to be intensified."[49] A similar impatience pervaded the ranks. Even a pro-Lincoln moderate like Cyrus Clay Carpenter of Fort Dodge, who was initially opposed to freeing the slaves, hoped for tougher measures. "I do not care if they press every negro into service on the continent," he wrote from Iuka, Mississippi, in August 1862. "I believe that this war before it ends will become a 'violent and . . . revolutionary struggle' try to avoid [it] as presidents and Cabinets may."[50]

When the preliminary emancipation proclamation was issued the following month, most Iowa soldiers appear to have welcomed it. "[Y]ou wanted to know what I thought of the pr[o]clamation and confiscation bill," Private John Sharp addressed his wife on 8 October. "Well I think them the right thing in the right place and will do more to whip the rebs than fifty regimen[ts] of men[. I]t brakes the back of [the] rebelion[.] I am for it."[51] Another infantryman, Joseph Ruckman, concurred. "Things I think are ripe and ready for the proclamation," he reported. "It sets well with nearly all the soldiers. I have not seen one that complained at it while I have heard hundreds say it is the very thing."[52]

The antipathy that soldiers in the field came to feel for Southerners—particularly Southern slaveholders who, as Republican politicians continued to emphasize, were largely responsible for the rebellion—worked a subtle change in their attitude toward blacks. During the spring of 1863 substantial numbers of Iowa troops were campaigning with Grant's western armies in the fertile Mississippi Delta. On 8 April Lieutenant Alonzo A. Abernethy's unit encamped on Dr. Samuel Taylor's plantation above the Confederate stronghold of Vicksburg. Taylor, noted the young man, a Fayette County Baptist with a penchant for self-improvement, "has been an active rebel & when we came skedadled & deserted his place." Abernethy helped himself to some of the doctor's books. Then the mansion was razed to the ground. Crossing over a small creek he came upon the smokehouse. "Got a ham & shoulder," he recorded in his diary, "& had the pleasure of throwing out . . . a lot of meat to the begging and half-starved darkies."[53]

The Iowans garnered a great deal of satisfaction from hurting the enemy in this manner. One of them summarized the prevailing feeling in the army thus: "The soldiers believe in putting down the Rebellion and they argue everything from the Anti-Slavery stand point, not because they have any feeling on the moral question of slavery but because they think it a good joke on the Rebels to strike them through the Institution they cherish most."[54] By April 1863 Private Ruckman could write home that "[a]ll prejudice against arming the niggers has died out in the army. The only question asked is will the negro soldiers be effective[;] if they will let us have them."[55] As the war dragged on, the widely held grass-roots notion that "a good nigger is better than a bad traitor" played into the hands of radical Republicans, and enabled them to use Southerners, Copperheads, and supposedly disloyal Irishmen as potent negative reference symbols in their efforts to promote the cause of equal rights.

Although some conservative Iowa Republicans, notably Congressman John A. Kasson of Des Moines, continued to flirt with colonization as a solution to the race question, events continually drew the center away from a complacent acceptance of repatriation.[56] In February 1863 Congress finally paved the way for the enrollment of black volunteers. Fully cognizant of the mood in the field, Iowa Republicans generally welcomed the move, even though they sometimes felt obliged to justify it to a racist electorate. The *Cedar Falls Gazette* defended the measure in the same terms that Kirkwood had used to Halleck: "Provided the result would be the same, we would much rather that a regiment of blacks should lead a forlorn hope, than a regiment of our friends and brothers."[57]

The main reason why a majority of Iowans, civilians as well as volunteers, could now accept the idea of black troops was that the North was desperate to exploit its manpower advantage over the Confederacy. The seven and a half months between Antietam in September 1862 and Chancellorsville in May 1863 constituted the nadir of the Union war effort. Even General McClellan's dismissal and Grant's circumspect advances on Vicksburg failed to lift the gloom pervading Iowa Republican circles that winter. "I am discouraged and disheartened," wrote Governor Kirkwood on 3 February 1863, fearful that a disastrous assault on Vicksburg would close the Mississippi to Iowa grain and leave the people "at the mercy of Northern Rail Roads" for yet another year.[58]

If Lincoln's decision to pacify Missouri conservatives by relieving the enthusiastic confiscator General Samuel Ryan Curtis from his command at St. Louis merely intensified Republican disquiet, the prevailing sense of pessimism continued to convince the religiously inclined that the hand of a righteous God was behind events. After Hooker's catastrophic defeat at Chancellorsville, John W. Rankin, a moderate Keokuk Republican, told William Penn Clarke that the debacle was "only another evidence of the design of Providence to accomplish by the war, two results": the first being the abolition of slavery; the second "the eradication of the deep seated, damnable prejudice against Color."[59]

The enrollment of black soldiers was the most obvious link between military necessity and civil rights, for it presented Iowa blacks with the opportunity not only to fight for their country and the freedom of their brothers but also to prove their own manhood. In July the War Department issued special orders for the organization of Iowa's first (and only) black regiment.[60] Between then and December six companies were recruited at home, four in Missouri, comprising an aggregate strength of 911. The Sixtieth regiment of U.S. colored troops was employed mainly as a garrison force in the secondary southwestern theater. Only one of its contingent was killed in battle, but nearly a third of the regiment died of disease. In the summer of 1863, however, the prospects for glory seemed bright. The courageous attempt of the Fifty-fourth Massachusetts to take Fort Wagner near Charleston did more than any well-intentioned free labor experiment to convince Northern whites that the black man deserved his freedom. Progressives like Frank W. Palmer rejoiced at the way such heroism broke down prejudice and strove to hasten the process of enlightenment by contrasting black sacrifice with white treachery as it had recently manifested itself in the horrific New York City draft riots.[61]

The *State Register*'s assertiveness was symptomatic of the new sense of confidence now sweeping the state. This was partly a consequence of returning economic prosperity. Currency prices of Iowa farm products reached their highest levels since 1859 partly due to inflation but also because of rising demand from the army and Great Britain. The river cities, particularly Keokuk, benefited from the wartime increase in the pork-packing trade, although some urban merchants were unhappy at the way Chicago continued to siphon off this lucrative business. A more significant contribution to morale, however, was made by the brace of federal military successes at Vicksburg and Gettysburg in July. These costly triumphs restored the citizenry's faith in ultimate victory and may have prevented large-scale defections from the Republican party in the fall elections. But for radicals across the North this change in fortune portended no good. "I fear more from our victories than our defeats," remarked the Massachusetts senator, Charles Sumner. "If the Rebellion should suddenly collapse, democrats, copperheads & Seward would insist upon amnesty & the Union & 'no questions asked about Slavery.' God save us from any such calamity."[62]

The belief that racial progress could only be fueled by a continuation of the fighting was well-founded. In Iowa the existence of substantial numbers of conservative War Democrats within the Republican ranks meant that there was no party consensus on humanitarian reform in the second half of 1863. The choice of Major William M. Stone as the Republican gubernatorial nominee boded ill for the cause of equal rights. A wounded veteran and ex-Democrat, his views on the race question were no more progressive than those of Kirkwood or Kasson. Whether or not he would act on his prejudices would depend, as the radicals well knew, on the drift of events.

Sumner need not have worried about the possibility of a swift Union triumph, for there were many deaths to come yet. After Chickamauga, stalemate returned to the battlefield. Fortunately for the Republicans of Iowa (now officially reconstituted as Unionists to attract War Democrats) the state's loyal heart did not miss a beat. Stone was elected governor with 60.5

percent of the popular vote, 5 percentage points greater than Kirkwood's total in 1861.[63] Unionists also monopolized the legislative contests, securing overwhelming majorities in both chambers at Des Moines. The patriotic fervor engendered by the war was beginning to make Iowa a solid Republican state, at last giving party progressives room to maneuver.

There is no accurate way of gauging the strength of radical opinion within the antislavery coalition at this stage, but one possible indicator is the extent of internal opposition to Lincoln's renomination. Late in 1863 Rufus Clarke, the outspoken proponent of equal rights at the 1857 constitutional convention, made a brief tour of southeastern Iowa on a furlough from the treasury department in Washington (where he had found employment on the recommendation of Senator Harlan).[64] His brief was to sound out the views of local Republican leaders on the presidential aspirations of his political master, Secretary of the Treasury Salmon P. Chase.

In Burlington he had "a long and pleasant interview" with James Grimes. The senator was opposed to Lincoln's reelection and friendly toward Chase. "I say to you that he is thoroughly *radical* in sympathy & purpose & he boasts of Iowa as a Radical State," reported Clarke. At Mount Pleasant the latter found his patron, James Harlan, under the impression that a second term was inevitable. "I believe he is now satisfied that there is hope & salvation in another direction. . . ," Clarke informed Chase. "If the issue becomes fixed he will be with the radicals allways [sic] & ever. He is enthusiastically your friend & admirer."[65] In Muscatine the treasury agent spoke to Judge Francis Springer, one of Fitz Henry Warren's chief allies, and the irascible antislavery lawyer Jacob Butler. He discovered that both were "right" on all questions. Significantly Butler had been elected to the forthcoming general assembly, which Chase hoped would resolve to back his embryonic presidential candidacy. "The great work can & should be done at our Capital this winter," wrote Clarke. "Our friends the radicals are overpoweringly in the ascendant, & only need the gentle appliances which form the tree from the twig."[66]

The confident assurances of Chase's servant turned out to be misplaced. Early in February 1864 the Iowa house adopted a resolution endorsing the administration and calling for Lincoln's renomination.[67] Over 70 percent of the Unionist delegation voted for this measure, including the speaker, Jacob Butler. Of the twenty-two Unionists who found themselves in the minority, only thirteen (roughly a sixth of the party's total representation) backed a call for a congressional amendment abolishing slavery.[68] The rest were anti-Lincoln conservatives. By the time the resolution was introduced into the senate, Chase had already announced that he would not be standing for the presidency—a move occasioned by the refusal of the Ohio legislature to endorse his campaign.[69] Surprisingly this did not prevent a large proportion of Iowa senators from opposing the house's second-term resolution. When John G. Foote of Burlington introduced an amendment striking out the call for Lincoln's renomination, twenty-six Unionists (most of them apparently proemancipation moderates) voted to sustain it.[70] They included at least three well-known friends of Senator Harlan: Coker F. Clarkson, Theron W. Woolson, and Dr. Thomas Saunders. Although the practical consequences of this vote were nil, it was nonetheless an important expression of intraparty dissent. Whether it can be seen as a gesture of problack radicalism is debatable.

Neither Grimes nor Harlan displayed an unqualified commitment to equal rights in the opening session of the Thirty-eighth Congress. Their conduct marked them out as practical centrists, men reluctant to advance too far ahead of public opinion. On 13 February 1864 both senators opposed Charles Sumner's attempt to make retroactive a bill equalizing the pay of black soldiers with that of whites.[71] Grimes had never thought highly of the austere New Englander and was beginning to resent his arrogant assumption of moral superiority. Retroaction, said the Burlingtonian, would exhaust the treasury. What mattered was that henceforth black troops would receive the same salary as whites: "That is making great progress, that is an advance in the right direction; and with that, it seems to me, they [the blacks] ought to be satisfied."[72] The same view was held by Grimes's friend Fessenden. As the revolutionary implications of the war became increasingly apparent, these two powerful centrists were beginning to draw back from the kind of positive equal rights legislation demanded by congressional radicals.

Iowa's two senators also adopted an equivocal approach to the coming question of the day, black suffrage. Although they gave their backing to a bill providing for universal manhood suffrage in Montana Territory, Sumner's determination in late May to press the more germane issue of enfranchising blacks in Washington, D.C., caused Harlan successfully to limit the reform to veterans, and Grimes to oppose it altogether.[73] It is true that the latter was infuriated by the Bostonian's attempt to attach the suffrage amendment to a straightforward enrollment bill, and that he promised to support franchise extension as part of the forthcoming measure to organize a bureau for the relief of ex-slaves.[74] However, when that bill did come before the Senate, Grimes opposed it, much to Sumner's dismay.[75]

Although the Burlington politician was becoming embroiled in a power struggle between Republican moderates and radicals, he undoubtedly had genuine ideological objections to the establishment of a government department to oversee the transition from slavery to freedom. Always suspicious of federal power, he was now concerned about the centralizing impact of the war. This impelled him to undertake a long retreat from the doctrine of positive government that he had enunciated as governor of Iowa almost exactly a decade earlier. The laissez-faire, antimonopolistic tenor of his thought was revealed during a debate over the planned Pacific railroad that took place in the spring of 1864. After condemning the government-aided project as "the most stupendous monopoly that was ever devised on this continent," Grimes absented himself from the chamber when the bill to reorganize the corporation was read for a third time on 23 May.[76]

The following month saw him oppose the creation of a Freedmen's Bureau for reasons that were consistent with this stand. Arguing that such a body would introduce an element of unwarranted interference into the lives of supposedly free men, he insisted that the bill was "violative of some of the fundamental principles of the institutions of this country." State paternalism was not the way to improve the lot of Southern blacks, he continued: "They will be jostled as we are all being jostled through this life, but in a little while they will settle down into the position that Providence has designed that they shall occupy under the new condition of affairs in this country."[77] Perhaps Grimes meant well, but he surely underestimated the enormous problems facing the freedmen, uneducated and poverty stricken as most of them were. His stance on the Bureau was at variance with that of his fellow Iowans in Congress and, as Sumner bitterly observed, placed him firmly in the camp of ultraconservative border state men on this important issue.[78]

The actions of Iowa's U.S. senators on racial legislation during early 1864 indicate that radicalism as they understood it and apparently professed it to Rufus Clarke was not synonymous with an unflinching desire to promote the cause of equal rights, although manifestly their conduct was progressive in the dismal context of contemporary race relations. Their objection to Lincoln was not so much that he was failing in his duty toward blacks but rather that he had hampered the Union cause with what they regarded as his inept border-state policy and allied misuse of the patronage. To the increasingly misanthropic Grimes the president was an "incompetent" who did not merit his place.[79] For Harlan he was a well-meaning dullard, "an old line Whig of the fossil type."[80] The same war-driven radicalism was almost certainly the cause of anti-Lincoln feeling in the general assembly wherein sat the friends of both men.

There is, quite simply, no satisfactory means of determining the strength of humanitarian radicalism in Iowa in mid-1864. One can speculate that the pro–black suffrage fifth of 1857 had lost some of its relative influence because of the influx of War Democrats into the Republican party.[81] On the other hand, it is just as likely that this bloc had retained its strength by way of recruits won over to equal rights by the exigencies of war. Certainly radicals were delighted by the legislature's long overdue repeal of the 1851 exclusion act and praiseworthy decision to bring blacks within the purview of the state's poor law.[82] Their verdict on Lincoln's renomination at Baltimore in June was less positive, but as the opposition to the president had virtually evaporated, they were forced to accept the inevitable.

Some satisfaction may have been gleaned from the support given by six Iowa Republicans (Grimes, Harlan, Wilson, Price, Allison, and Nathaniel M. Hubbard) to the Wade-Davis bill in Congress.[83] This ill-fated piece of legislation struck at the basis of the president's plan for reconstructing the Union. Although his suggestion that 10 percent of loyal voters in a seceded state could initiate the reintegration process had initially won the backing of Iowa moderates, it was now deemed overly lenient by congressional Republicans who were seeking not only to delay Reconstruction until after the war but also to challenge the executive's role in policy-making. In the event the bill was pocket-vetoed by Lincoln—a move that incurred the wrath of outspoken radicals like Thaddeus Stevens of Pennsylvania, but one which was probably less damaging to party unity than many historians have supposed.

For all their dislike of Lincoln and the border state influence, Harlan, Grimes, and the rest of their dissatisfied copartisans back home could not fail to recognize that the present incumbent of the White House remained popular with the voters. He was, in addition, a more acceptable candidate than his Democratic opponent, General McClellan.

Riven by bitter infighting between pro- and antiwar factions, the Iowa Democracy sought to capitalize on the ground swell of discontent brought on by another season of bloodletting in Virginia. In June 1864 members of both intraparty groupings convened at Des Moines to nominate candidates for the forthcoming state elections. After much excited debate prowar activists succeeded in preventing the adoption of a party platform, leaving the local organization at the mercy of the national convention due to meet at Chicago in August.[84]

This uneasy compromise failed to satisfy Copperhead leaders whose opposition to the war had now become hysterical. Shortly before the Chicago convention Iowa Peace Democrats met in Iowa City and adopted an astonishing series of resolutions that reflected the impact of three years of militarization and centralization on traditional Jacksonian ideology. Fulminating against the manner in which "this abolition war" had led to the slaughter of American manhood and spawned "a multitude of usurpations, tyrannies and corruptions," the assembled Copperheads called for a negotiated peace to end the war. They also threatened to lead a counterrevolution if Lincoln was reelected with the help of 10 percent states like Louisiana and held fast to the doctrine of state rights. They also denounced the growing trend toward "negro equality," insisting that as "the African negro is not our equal in a political or social sense . . . every usurping attempt, by federal force, so to declare him, will meet with our determined resistance."[85] McClellan's subsequent nomination on a peace platform was generally held to constitute a victory for the Copperheads, and Republicans and Confederates alike looked to the presidential contest to decide the outcome of the war.

Just as they had been in 1863, the Republicans were saved by events on the battlefield. That autumn federal forces won spectacular victories in the Shenandoah Valley and the Southern heartland. The capture of Atlanta on 1 September dealt the Confederacy a hammer blow from which it never recovered. At the polls the electorate did much the same thing to the Copperhead cause. All six of Iowa's incumbent U.S. representatives were reelected for another term. Each of them secured over 60 percent of the vote, largely as a result of overwhelming support from local troops.[86] In November Lincoln carried the state by a majority of nearly forty thousand. Only Dubuque, Buchanan, and Allamakee counties in the east and a few sparsely populated counties in the west were won by McClellan.[87] Even southern Iowa rejected the general. A war that had brought private grief to many thousands of citizens had bolstered the position of the ruling Republican party, giving the latter a patriotic legitimacy that would help keep it in power for nearly three-quarters of a century.

As the war drew to a glorious close, reformist elements within Iowa's Unionist ranks began to renew their calls for black rights. Conservatives were horrified. Solon M. Langworthy, a wealthy Dubuque capitalist and nativist Republican, noted in his diary shortly after Lincoln's triumph that once slavery had been abolished, "we may expect to see political parties, divided upon the question of Free and Equal political rights & privileges." What he feared most after witnessing Democratic efforts to secure the Irish vote in Dubuque was that, once in the ascendant, Republicans "may in order to Continue in power seek to Confer upon the Freed men of the Country the Elective franchise." Such a move, he thought,

> would doubtless Create a division in the party and give to the opposition a Club well Calculated to Brake the Republican back for their are many true republicans, who tho they are decided Aponents to Slavery in any and Every form, are disposed to believe that the only way to maintain A free government is to adhere Strictly to the Revolutionary Test, is he Capable is he Honest.[88]

Although serious intraparty divisions over black suffrage were subsumed by the general determination to defeat the Confederacy, Iowa's Republican leaders were clearly aware that this was the coming question. Early in 1865 several Unionist editors expressed support for the enfranchisement of blacks, either for reasons of justice (primarily black loyalty to the government during the war) or national policy (the need to combat secessionist influence in the Southern states). Most radical of all was the suggestion of Edward Russell's *Davenport Gazette* that the word *white* should be expunged from the state constitution. Some kind of literacy qualification might be necessary, thought Russell, "[b]ut at any rate color of skin should no longer be a test tolerated and enforced in the free and enlightened State of Iowa."[89]

While this suggestion was not taken up by most of his editorial colleagues, many of them were prepared to support black suffrage in less specific terms. Shortly after Congress passed the Thirteenth Amendment preparing the way for the abolition of American slavery, the *Iowa State Register* contended that the issue of black rights "in a Republican and professedly Christian nation" would soon be at the forefront of the political agenda. "The War has upset many a silly and barbarous notion," opined the editorial, "and there is no telling how far traitorous aristocrats who have been accustomed to teach that the Ethiopian race are scarcely better than apes, may have their nerves shocked by revolutions in social and political franchises."[90]

The debate over this question and the closely related one of how to reconstruct the Union was interrupted in early April by the news that Lee had finally surrendered to Grant in Virginia. The wild rejoicing that ensued was short-lived. On Good Friday Abraham Lincoln was assassinated in Washington. Iowans responded with a mixture of sadness and anger. All talk of national reconciliation was quickly forgotten. Business in Des Moines had been suspended as a tribute to the fallen president, reported one eyewitness on 14 April. "[T]he city is draped in mourning, the bells are tolling & minute guns are firing. Every loyal heart is in tears. [O]ne word from a Copperhead would be the signal for a general butchery."[91] Shortly afterwards the nonradical Keokuk *Gate City* declared in favor of black suffrage: "[N]ow when the blood of Abraham Lincoln . . . swells the red current of the righteous atonement for the blood drawn by the lash from an oppressed race, the people cannot fail to believe that the negro has rights which God designs to compel white men to respect."[92] The long drawn-out struggle over Reconstruction was about to begin in earnest.

Hindsight suggests that the Civil War was a critical event, not only in the history of the United States but also in the development of the Republican party itself. There was nothing inevitable about the organization's rise to political prominence in the late nineteenth century—indeed there were many people who doubted whether or not a party that had come into existence to prevent the spread of slavery could survive the extinction of the peculiar institution. Together with Republicanism's undeniable moral force and purveyance of particular socioeconomic values, however, the triumphant crusade against the South converted a blatantly sectional party into a permanent and respectable feature of America's political landscape. The fact that that crusade had been an appallingly sanguinary one served only to deepen Northern voters' attachment to the creed.

But the war did more than simply confirm the newfound power and status of the Republican party. It also wrought a subtle and, in the context of the time, dramatic change in the way many whites regarded American blacks. Aside from the inhabitants of the South's hill country, black slaves had proved to be the only loyal Unionists in the Confederacy. Northern free blacks had fought and died for the Union. Why, asked many radical and centrist Republicans, should these people not enjoy the same political privileges as white men? It was true that many Northerners balked at the cumulative process of racial change that took place during the war. However, the combination of events and radical pressure was a potent one, and confiscation of rebel property was followed swiftly by the enlistment and emancipation of African-Americans. Although Iowa Copperheads played on racial prejudice in their efforts to exploit grass-roots dissatisfaction with the war, economic prosperity and military victories during the second half of 1864 left them politically stranded. The South, the bastion of American constitutional liberties in the eyes of many Peace Democrats, was defeated within six months of Lincoln's reelection. The dream of an independent Confederacy was gone, and with it went the institution on which the South's society and economy was based. Although Garrisonians, Liberty men, and Free-Soilers had all played their part in slavery's demise, there was much truth in the verdict of the *Iowa State Register* that "[a]s a successful Abolition Society, the Confederate League at Richmond has had no equal since the foundation of the world."[93]

3
Consolidation

9
Black Suffrage and the Intraparty Crisis of 1865–1866

he North's victory in the American Civil War raised as many questions as it answered. Two key problems confronted the administration of President Andrew Johnson. Firstly, the seceded states had to be reintegrated into the Union in such a way that they would never again pose a threat to the republic. The process of Reconstruction had begun during the war when Lincoln announced his 10 percent plan, but as we have seen, executive leadership had been challenged by the Republican-controlled Congress during the final months of the conflict. The administration party was also divided over the constitutional position of the Southern states. Radicals like Thaddeus Stevens of Pennsylvania deemed them out of the Union in order that they could be brought under the sway of the federal government. (Their wartime leaders could then be severely punished for treason, and their institutions remade in the image of the liberal North.) Although they agreed with the ultras on the importance of destroying slavery, moderate and conservative elements in the party were less inclined toward a punitive approach to Reconstruction and, opposing theories of "state suicide" and territorialization, sought to have Southern delegates readmitted to Congress as quickly as possible.

The second and by no means unrelated problem was what to do with the four million black slaves emancipated by the Thirteenth Amendment. Again Republicans were divided among themselves on this issue. Radicals saw the blacks as allies against the defeated planter class and, for reasons of natural justice and national policy, demanded that the freedmen be given equal rights (above all the privilege of the vote) so that they could counterbalance disloyal elements within Southern society. Conservative Republicans, on the other hand, were skeptical of black intellectual capacities and seemed more concerned with putting the freedmen back to work on the cotton plantations than granting them the franchise. Moderates held the balance of power in

Congress. Led informally by men like Fessenden and Grimes, they recognized that the ex-slaves had to be guaranteed some fundamental rights in order for them not only to bolster Southern Unionism but also to compete fairly in the race of life. However, they too were less than confident in the abilities of the uneducated freedmen, and many of them were willing to accept a postponement or dilution of black suffrage.

As nominal head of the Union party, President Johnson was bound to play a major role in the outcome of the Reconstruction debate. A Tennessee War Democrat who had been named as Lincoln's running mate in 1864 in order to enhance the attractiveness of the Republican ticket, Johnson was initially assumed to hold more extreme views on Reconstruction than his predecessor. In fact, as he revealed in two important proclamations of May 1865, he had much more in common with nonradicals on this issue than he did with Stevens and his allies. The discussion over national policy, however, was still very much in progress when Iowa Republicans convened at Des Moines on 14 June 1865 to formulate a platform for the coming state elections. During the course of this meeting local partisans contributed significantly to the ongoing debate over Reconstruction by deciding to give Iowa blacks the vote.

Seventy-two out of Iowa's ninety-nine counties were represented in the convention, the number of accredited delegates allowed to each one weighted heavily in favor of the most strongly Republican.[1] The 663 delegates present were authorized to cast a total of nearly 890 votes and included members from every branch of the Republican coalition. Several of the party's founding fathers were in attendance, including ex-Governor Kirkwood and Congressmen Hiram Price and Josiah B. Grinnell; well-known abolitionists and Free-Soilers like J.C. Jordan, Tom Mitchell, Jonathan W. Cattell, Henry O'Connor, and Edward Russell; scores of former Whigs and Democrats; and, importantly, a strong military presence led by one of Grant's most trusted subordinates, Major General Marcellus Crocker of Des Moines, a War Democrat.[2] Although some of the names were familiar, the majority of delegates were small-town politicians who had little to do with the actual running of the convention. Most of the business was conducted, as it always was at such gatherings, by a coterie of experienced politicians who, in the words of one eyewitness, "had shrewdness enough to compel the turning of the grind-stone in advance."[3]

Charged with the task of drafting the party's platform for the fall elections was the committee on resolutions, a body of twelve persons, one from each judicial district. As the task at hand was so important, most of its members were fairly prominent politicians. Five of the committee, George W. McCrary, Frank W. Palmer, James W. McDill, Nathaniel C. Deering, and Captain William Wolf, went on to become congressmen. Among the remaining six members (the abolitionist Benjamin F. Gue was removed from the committee after it was discovered that he was not an accredited delegate) were Harvey Tannehill, a future district judge from conservative Appanoose County; Edward Russell, the radical editor of the *Davenport Gazette;* Jacob Rich of Burlington, a close ally of Senator Grimes; and Christian Slagle, an intimate of Congressman James F. Wilson.

After some deliberation the committee adopted eight to one a plank declaring: "That with proper safeguards to the purity of the ballot-box, the franchise should be based upon loyalty to the Constitution and Union, recognizing and affirming the equality of all men before the law."[4] This ambiguous and merely declaratory expression of support for some form of black suffrage failed to satisfy the one dissenting committee member, Edward Russell. Russell, an English immigrant and artisan-turned-journalist, had joined Iowa's Republican party at its inception. According to his son, a well-known Progressive reformer, his experience at Victorian boarding school had implanted in him "a hatred for cruelty, a passionate love for justice and a sympathy with the oppressed that shaped all his after life."[5] Russell had certainly proved himself an inveterate foe of slavery as a Free-Soil editor, lay Congregationalist, and Underground Railroad operator in antebellum Scott County. Contemporaries testified to his moral worth. One described him as "a Christian editor—conscientious in his declarations, forming no compromise with heresy, preferring to be right rather than popular; free from the baseness and sycophancy of a debauched press, and evermore zealous for the enthronement of righteousness, and the overthrow of all forms of personal vice and political corruption."[6]

Although this description was not entirely accurate—Russell did evince a willingness to trim on the liquor issue to mollify Davenport's substantial German population—the Englishman was a committed antislavery radical with a clear vision of the Republican party's humanitarian mission. During the weeks preceding the convention he had been the local organization's staunchest advocate of franchise extension for Iowa blacks. When the platform came before the committee of the whole he immediately introduced the following amendment: "Therefore we are in favor of amending the Constitution of our State by striking out the word 'white' in the article on suffrage."[7] Realizing the potentially damaging electoral consequences of this amendment, Russell's opponents moved to lay it on the table. The convention's president, however, ruled that this motion would take the rest of the platform with it, and therefore the measure was thrown open for debate.

First to speak was Henry O'Connor, a bibulous Irish Protestant who had fought for freedom in Kansas and who had long been a crusader for equal rights. His address, which focused attention on the black man's devotion to the Union during the war, "fully enlisted the sympathy of his audience and aroused continuous approbation and applause."[8] After a counterspeech by Joshua Tracey, the new chairman of the state central committee, others entered the fray. Opposing the amendment were Edward Stiles, a conservative state legislator from Ottumwa; the Reverend William F. Cowles, a federal officeholder and Methodist minister in Oskaloosa; possibly Hugh Sample of Keokuk; and, most significantly of all, radical Congressman Josiah B. Grinnell.

According to Benjamin F. Gue, Grinnell and many other opponents of Russell agreed with his amendment in principle but protested that it would alienate large numbers of Republican voters.[9] This argument cut no ice with the Unitarian and former lieutenant governor Enoch Eastman, whose prosuffrage speech was reported as being "full of solid argument and withering sarcasm."[10] The most effective discourse in favor of Russell's amendment, however, was delivered by the Davenporter's close political ally Hiram Price. "The Republican party . . . ," urged Price,

> is strong enough to dare to do right, and cannot afford now, or at any other time, to shirk a duty. The colored men, North and South, were loyal and true to the Government in the days of its great peril. There was not a rebel or traitor to be found among them. They ask the privilege of citizenship now that slavery has been forever banished from our country. Why should the great freedom-loving State of Iowa longer deny them this right? Not one reason can be given that has not been used to bolster up slavery for the past hundred years. The war closed has swept that relic of barbarism from our land; let the Republican party have the courage to do justice. I have no fear of the result in a contest of this kind. We shall carry the election and have the satisfaction of wiping out the last vestige of the black code that has long been a disgrace to our State.[11]

Like Russell, Price was a Christian in politics—a crusading Methodist who "never waited to catch the drift of the popular breeze, but always led off, prompted only by his convictions of right and wrong."[12] His argument struck a chord among the assembled delegates who proceeded to ratify the Russell amendment by a majority of 67.9 percent.

There would seem to be two possible explanations for this remarkable decision. The first is that it was a consequence of burgeoning intraparty factionalism. Russell, Price, and O'Connor were all within the political orbit of James Harlan, Iowa's most prominent evangelical politician who had been appointed U.S. secretary of the interior shortly before Lincoln's assassination. Because radicalism was sometimes used as a political weapon by chameleonic Republican factions in the states, and since James Grimes had begun to distance himself from the Jacobins in Washington, it is possible that Harlan's friends were trying to use the suffrage issue as a means of isolating the Burlington senator from the party at home.[13]

Grimes was certainly no advocate of franchise extension in Iowa. While his main political organ, the *Burlington Hawk-Eye,* was a strong preconvention critic of such "fanciful questions," he personally remained silent on the subject until mid-September when he adjudged the party's action impolitic.[14] Harlan, moreover, was planning to use his cabinet post as a stepping-stone back to the Senate—a move that was to alienate Grimes and his allies, particularly Samuel J. Kirkwood who coveted the vacant long-term Senate place for himself.

The problem with a factional analysis of the convention's decision is that the latter proved an embarrassment to Harlan as well as Grimes. The secretary did not venture a public opinion on the subject until late summer, and when it finally appeared, it proved to be a rather faltering endorsement of impartial, rather than universal, suffrage.[15] As a centrist Republican whose congressional record was actually less radical than that of Grimes, Harlan was unlikely to have sanctioned the action of his allies at Des Moines. Besides, if his political future depended on successful manipulation of the federal patronage, he would hardly have been eager to antagonize the new president by sponsoring a burst of trans-Mississippi radicalism. Like Grinnell, Grimes and Harlan placed party unity above what they perceived to be a divisive display of principle. All of them regarded the national problem of Reconstruction as paramount.

The likelier explanation for what happened at the convention is that Iowa Republicans chose to endorse franchise extension because they wanted to. Russell and his supporters all had staunch antislavery records, and there seems little reason to doubt the sincerity of their rhetoric. The response of the committee of the whole is less easy to explain, yet in the context of the party's cumulative support for black rights and the fluid state of opinion on Reconstruction, it is far from incomprehensible. According to Frank W. Palmer's account of events, Russell's amendment was passed because the convention "was unwilling to stand committed even in appearance against the principle of negro suffrage." The prevailing opinion after adjournment, he wrote, "was that inasmuch as the issue must be squarely met, it might as well be this year as next."[16]

There are several reasons why the majority of delegates deemed a positive declaration on this controversial subject essential. One of them was the growing realization among Republicans that the precious fruits of a bloody conflict could only be preserved by counterbalancing Confederate voting power with the ballots of Southern freedmen. Many local partisans (moderates as well as radicals) believed quite genuinely that Iowa could not promote such a policy without putting its own house in order.

The party faithful must also have been aware of radical pressure for reform. Evidence of preconvention support for black suffrage does exist. In June 1864, for example, Iowa Congregationalists recommended, "still further perseverance in the effort to remove the prejudice of our people, and change the laws of our State, averse to the equal rights of the colored man—for we cannot expect the government in its measures in behalf of freedmen to advance beyond the spirit of our treatment of such among us."[17] Nearly a year later, on 30 May 1865, Edward Russell's *Davenport Gazette* noted that Republicans in Davenport's second ward had instructed their delegates to the Scott County convention to vote for franchise extension if the matter came before that body.[18] Given that reform was also a subject of debate among Iowa troops at the end of the war and that local blacks continued to press strongly for their services to the Union to be recognized, it is clear that there was significant political backing for a revision of the state constitution.[19]

Yet in spite of the importance of radical pressure, the most persuasive explanation for the party's action is that the mass of pragmatic, centrist Republicans were now willing to bestow the franchise on local blacks as an act of justice. When the Iowa journalist Lurton D. Ingersoll compiled an appreciation of Oskaloosa's fallen hero Brigadier General Samuel A. Rice in late 1864, he recalled how, at the battle of Jenkin's Ferry, Confederates had opened fire on the Twenty-ninth Iowa and a black regiment from Kansas. Rice ordered a charge, wrote Ingersoll, "and these two regiments of white men and black men, rushed forward with a shout, captured the guns, and triumphantly brought them off the field, through the deep mud."[20] Because black patriotism was a central theme of the prosuffrage orations at the Republican convention, there seems no reason to suppose that a battle-driven sense of obligation was not the chief factor behind the success of Russell's amendment.

The fact that Iowa Republicans felt emboldened to take such a positive stand on the race question was owing in large measure to the party's compelling Unionist image and consequent electoral lead over the treason-tainted Democracy. Between 1856 and 1864 the state Republican organization had increased its popular majority by over 15 percentage points. Its members were thus well placed to indulge in an expression of principle. Their counterparts in other "safe" Northern states—Maine, Vermont, Massachusetts, and Minnesota—also declared in favor of black suffrage that summer.[21] The development of a political system in which "a party worship their leaders and their leaders worship the nigger" was unpalatable to local

Democrats, but it provided a sound basis for ambitious political action.[22] If only the Democrats would nominate their old-stagers, boasted the *Burlington Hawk-Eye* on 21 June, "we could carry the State in favor of mule suffrage."[23]

Such outspoken confidence should not be taken to mean that the decision to embrace franchise extension was a no-risk strategy. The impassioned pleas of Grinnell, Stiles, and the others for sanity furnish abundant proof that some Republicans feared major losses if Russell's measure was passed. Returning veterans—those "brave boys in blue" who had voted to sustain the Union party by majorities of 78.3 to 91 percent during the worst years of the Civil War—were thought to be especially antagonistic toward equal rights.[24] Republican leaders usually set great store by the soldiers' views and might well have been expected to treat the race question with more caution.

In August 1865 a group of conservative Republican veterans registered their dissatisfaction with regular party policy by nominating a Soldiers' Anti-Negro Suffrage Ticket, which was quickly endorsed by the Democrats, desperate for any opportunity to regain the initiative. This move seemed to confirm the fears of the convention minority and forced Republican tacticians onto the defensive. Many of them took refuge in endorsements of impartial or qualified suffrage and emphasized that a constitutional amendment could not become law until it had been approved by two successive legislatures and then ratified by the people themselves. Significantly, however, the party did not abandon the strike-out clause of its platform, and when Governor Stone was reelected with a 56.4 percent majority in October, his triumph was taken as a popular endorsement of the Russell amendment.[25] At least twenty thousand Unionists either voted for the Soldiers' Ticket or stayed away from the polls.[26]

Although the Civil War had not worked a complete transformation in the racial attitudes of local whites, it had taught many of them to respect the patriotism of American blacks and, equally significantly, to despise the activities of disloyal Southerners and Copperheads. The changing attitudes of Cyrus Clay Carpenter toward the race question are a case in point. The Fort Dodge surveyor had gone to war as a nonradical Whig-Republican. (Like his hero Henry Clay he was an advocate of colonization.) With little faith in the capacity of blacks for self-improvement, he was far from optimistic about the consequences of Lincoln's preliminary emancipation proclamation and the enlistment of black troops.[27] Yet gradually his anger at the South's stubborn opposition to the government overcame his dislike of blacks. By April 1865 he was advocating the total destruction of slavery, "justice to the African race," and the banishment of Confederate leaders.[28] That summer he campaigned vigorously at home for black suffrage. Later in the year he delivered a lecture to the local literary society. Using Luke 3:16 as his text

(Carpenter was a practicing Methodist), he contended that the war had left the country "redeemed, regenerated, and disenthralled." In true millennial style he urged that if the nation was now reconstructed on the basis of equal and exact justice, it would act as a beacon of freedom and Christianity, thereby preparing the world for the second coming of "Him whose first visit to earth was so rapturously heralded by the preaching of John. . . . 'He shall baptize you with the HOLY GHOST and with FIRE.'" "Our late baptism of fire," said Carpenter, "has liberalized the American heart."[29] Though he spoke largely from personal experience and exaggerated the extent of the regeneration that had taken place in men's hearts, recent events seemed to demonstrate the truth of his statement.

Several weeks after Iowa Republicans voted to enfranchise local blacks, War Democrat Thomas Hart Benton, Jr., nephew of the great Missouri senator and the gubernatorial candidate of the Anti-Negro Suffrage forces, dispatched a confidential letter to Andrew Johnson. In it he warned the president that Republican leaders were pressuring federal officeholders into supporting Governor Stone and endorsing the reform plank of the June convention. "I am satisfied," wrote Benton, "that this resolution is incorporated in the platform to be used as a lever against you in your reconstruction policy."[30]

There is no evidence to support this assertion. Even if Edward Russell had intended his controversial resolution as a response to Johnson's conservative North Carolina proclamation of 29 May 1865, those delegates who voted for it would probably have been appalled if they thought they were censuring a man still regarded as testing the unknown waters of Southern opinion and described by Secretary Harlan on 12 June as "firm as a rock and inflexibly right on all points."[31] Yet while one must conclude that Benton's claim was designed primarily to add the president's weight to the conservative cause west of the Mississippi, the convention's action did reflect an early recognition on the part of most Iowa Republicans (moderates and radicals) that black suffrage had an integral role to play in federal Reconstruction policy.

Throughout the summer campaign ruling politicians like Samuel J. Kirkwood defended franchise extension at home on the grounds that the same measure would have to be applied to the South if Northern war gains were to be preserved.[32] The problem was that as they were trumpeting equal rights the Southern states were introducing Black Codes and electing ex-Confederates to Congress, and President Johnson (to whom the Iowa

Republican convention had extended "confidence and support") was failing to adapt his conciliation strategy accordingly.[33] Worried party leaders in Washington, James W. Grimes included, now began to seek a compromise solution to the growing internal crisis. "My impression," mused the Burlington Democrat Charles Mason in late December 1865, "is that a great effort will be made in Congress to harmonise the views of the President with those of the republican party so as to avoid a breach. It remains to be seen whether they will succeed in this. I think they will be willing to forego Negro suffrage."[34]

Mason's surmise that the opposition was planning to abandon franchise extension in an attempt to placate Johnson was soon put to the test not only by members of Congress but also by delegates to the Eleventh Iowa General Assembly, which convened at Des Moines on 8 January 1866. The importance of the state legislature at this crucial stage of Reconstruction lay in its mandate to initiate the complex process of constitutional reform. If Russell's measure were to become law, it would have to be affirmed by two consecutive sessions of the assembly and then ratified by the voters in a separate referendum. The Republicans who dominated both chambers of the new legislature could choose between several policy options. Firstly, they could renege on their campaign promises and abandon local franchise extension—a move that would alienate the radicals but possibly contribute toward national party unity. Secondly, they could carry out the directive of the Russell amendment by resolving to eliminate the word *white* from the article on suffrage in the state constitution. This would pave the way for a potentially divisive popular referendum on universal suffrage at home. The third and possibly most attractive option was some form of qualified or impartial suffrage that might satisfy party moderates and not antagonize the president.

On 17 November 1865 the *Burlington Hawk-Eye* printed a letter from "DES MOINES" that supported the third alternative. It was, asserted the writer, the settled conviction of the party's "best thinkers" that the next legislature should act promptly on the suffrage issue. "Let our own acts be the exact measure of our exactions of the South. If intelligence, loyalty or military service are allowed to qualify the suffrage of the black man, they should qualify the suffrage of the white man."[35] Although Governor Stone echoed this call for impartial suffrage in his second inaugural address, the assembly did not heed the voice of moderation.[36] Instead, its members decided on the second and more radical course. More than that, they opted to excise almost entirely the word *white* from the state's fundamental law.

Two weeks after Stone delivered his inaugural, Charles Dudley, a Republican representative from traditionally conservative Wapello County, introduced a complex resolution that, by extending the franchise to all adult

Union veterans and, after 1871, to all persons able to read, seemed to incorporate the wishes of both "DES MOINES" and the governor.[37] The measure was referred to the house committee on constitutional amendments. So too were a number of more radical proposals. On 30 January 1866 Charles Ben Darwin, a wild-eyed Oberlin graduate and prominent anti-Grimes lawyer from Burlington, offered five amendments to the Iowa constitution, striking out the word *white* from the articles on suffrage, apportionment of legislators, and eligibility for militia duty. Shortly afterwards the Fayette County Baptist and Union army veteran Alonzo A. Abernethy introduced his own set of measures. These encompassed the Darwin resolutions but added to them a provision for black membership of the legislature.[38] When the committee met to discuss the reform question, it thus had before it two proposals that looked beyond universal male suffrage to the near or, in the case of Abernethy's motion, total removal of racial distinctions from the Iowa constitution.

When William Hale, the chairman of the resolutions committee, rose to reveal that body's findings, it was to announce a preference for the more limited of the two radical measures. Perhaps as a result of the subject's controversial nature the report failed to review in detail the relative merits of the various proposals. Instead Hale simply urged that it was enough to know that "a considerable number" of Iowans were anxious for reform and that the dictates of democracy demanded that they be given an opportunity to vote on this issue.[39] This was the logic of 1857. Nine years on, however, many Republicans were less reticent about making their views known. At Abernethy's insistence the committee was induced to accept the additional resolution on legislative qualifications and on 30 March the six anti-discriminatory amendments came up for final consideration in the committee of the whole.[40]

At this point Samuel McNutt of Muscatine attempted to take some of the sting from the collective joint resolution by moving as a substitute his own proposal to remove the racial qualification from the article on suffrage alone. Twenty-eight Republicans (40.6 percent of those voting) supported the motion. The rest demanded an opportunity to register an opinion on the wider issues incorporated in the Darwin-Abernethy resolutions. These were then voted upon individually. All passed with substantial Republican backing and unanimous Democratic opposition except the amendment to eradicate the bar on nonwhite legislators.[41] Thirty-one members (43.1 percent) of the majority party refused to sanction the notion of blacks in government at home.

Initially the senate proved to be more willing to follow the lead provided by Governor Stone. In late March, however, Democrats and radicals combined to defeat a minority report that would have restricted black suffrage to Union veterans and those able to read and write. Forty-three percent of Republicans in the chamber approved the measure. Its defeat forced nonradicals like Edward Stiles and Theron W. Woolson to rally behind the house resolution as the only reform proposal that could now succeed, and the latter then passed with the opposition of only four Republicans.[42]

The legislature's decision to initiate root-and-branch reform of the state constitution at a time when a cautious approach to the subject of civil rights might have been more expedient reveals the strength of the antislavery dynamic underlying early Republican policy. But who were the men who thought fit to snub the moderate counsel of Governor Stone, what were their reasons for so doing, and how did their action relate to the crisis thrust upon the Union party by Andrew Johnson's veto of the Freedmen's Bureau bill on 19 February?

The radical forces at Des Moines were concentrated in the house. The membership of that chamber differed from that of the senate in several respects.[43] It contained few prominent Republicans; Speaker Ed Wright and Kirkwood's right-hand man Robert Finkbine were the most conspicuous. Present in the senate were some of the party's leading men: Fitz Henry Warren, Jonathan W. Cattell, Ezekiel Clark, and John A. Parvin to name but four. The average age of house delegates was 37.4 compared with 42.2 for members of the senate. This made it one of the youngest gatherings of legislators in the history of mid-nineteenth-century Iowa, a fact occasioned primarily by the large number of veterans in the hall. Over 44 percent of representatives had served with the Union armies. Most of these soldiers were in their late twenties and thirties, and the majority of them had been born in the Midwest. The senate, in contrast, appears to have been largely the preserve of civilian politicians.

While this comparison highlights the youthful and distinctly military complexion of the house, it obscures the subtle divisions that existed on the equal rights question among the chamber's substantial Republican majority. A multidimensional scaling analysis of McNutt's substitute and the six radical amendments indicates that there were four main Republican stances on this issue, all of which are revealed in figure 9.1. Bloc A contains twenty-seven legislators who opposed McNutt's measure and supported each of the anti-discriminatory resolutions. Those Republicans in bloc B also voted against the substitute but refused to countenance the idea of black legislators. The two remaining Republican groups initially favored restricting reform to the electoral franchise and then diverged over Abernethy's proposal, bloc C supporting it, bloc D opposing it. A fifth group, E, composed almost entirely of Democrats, voted against all the resolutions.

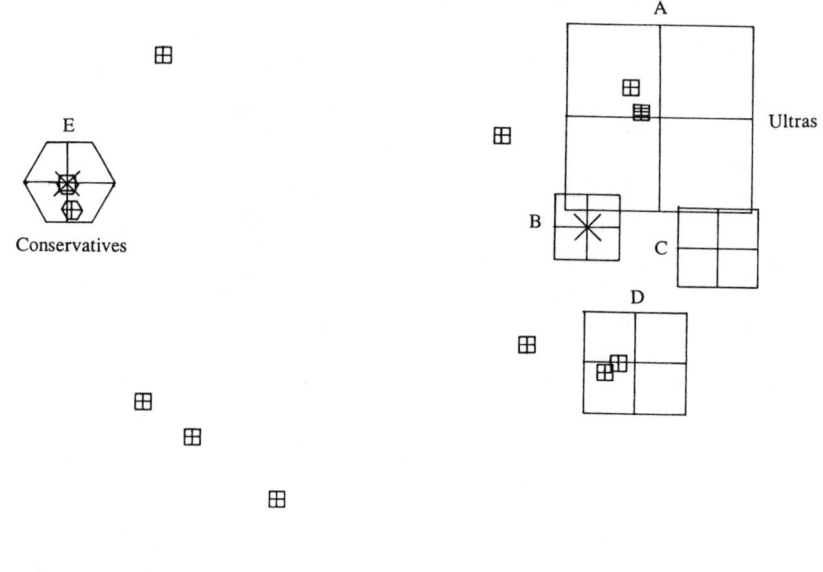

MDS analysis (see Appendix); no. of motions = 7
SOURCE: *Ia. Hse. Jnl.* (1866), pp. 644–47.

Fig. 9.1 Iowa House, 1866: Voting behavior on local black rights motions.

Highlighted in table 9.1 are the key differences between radicals (bloc A), moderates (blocs B, C, and D), and mainly Democratic conservatives (bloc E) in the lower chamber. It confirms Robert R. Dykstra's valuable assertion that there was a strong correlation between the antebellum referendum on franchise extension and the ultras' uncompromising endorsement of constitutional reform in 1866.[44] Nearly 60 percent of those in bloc A represented constituencies containing significant numbers of proven humanitarians, compared with 40.5 percent of moderates and a mere 16.7 percent of conservatives. This appears to indicate the importance of grass-roots radicalism to Republican policy, and to show that the latter was marked by a substantial degree of continuity.

Analysis of other variables also reveals that ultras were more likely than

Table 9.1. Iowa house, 1866: Characteristics of radicals, moderates, and conservatives

Variable	Radicals (N = 27)		Moderates (N = 42)		Conservatives (N = 18)	
	N	%	N	%	N	%
Birthplace						
New England	4	14.8	11	26.2	1	5.6
Mid-Atlantic	10	37.0	9	21.4	4	22.2
West	9	33.3	12	28.6	10	55.6
South	3	11.1	5	11.9	2	11.1
Europe	1	3.7	5	11.9	1	5.6
Religion						
Revival Calvinist	8	29.6	12	28.6	1	5.6
Evangelical Arminian	5	18.5	11	26.2	5	27.8
Nonevangelical Christian	4	22.2	2	4.8	5	27.8
Nondenominational Protestant	0	0.0	4	9.5	2	11.1
Liberal	7	25.9	7	16.7	3	16.7
Occupation						
Farmer	7	25.9	21	50.0	7	38.9
Professional	8	29.6	12	28.6	8	44.4
Farm elite	7	25.9	7	16.7	2	11.1
Union veteran	12	48.1	18	42.9	5	27.8
Aged forty-five plus	4	14.8	10	23.8	3	16.7
Constituency gave at least 15% support to black suffrage, 1857	16	59.3	17	40.5	3	16.7
Against liberalized liquor law	17	63.0	21	50.0	1	5.6
For state regulation of railroad rates	21	77.8	28	66.7	3	16.7
Against ban on Indian entry into Iowa	13	48.1	16	38.1	4	22.2

moderates not only to favor prohibition (as Dykstra found) but also to oppose restrictions on the entry of Indians into Iowa and to uphold the state's right to regulate railroad tariffs.[45] Since the moderates themselves were more inclined toward these positions than the Democrats, this would appear to suggest the existence of a political continuum with laissez-faire and interventionist poles and radicalism as the most concrete expression of state paternalism.

It is possible that the latter was partly a product of evangelical religious fervor—the civic manifestation of the crusading Protestants' drive for self-improvement. Although this theory is not entirely born out by the evidence (note the slight predominance of evangelicals within the moderate bloc), the radicals did contain the highest percentage of revival Calvinists, the most puritanical of all the Protestant groupings. And taken as a whole the reform contingent (blocs A, B, C, and D) did contain a much higher percentage of evangelicals (52.2) than the conservative grouping (33.3), the disparity between the respective proportions of Calvinistic legislators being particularly wide. The figures are not sufficient to prove the correlation between a loosely defined Puritanism and a clearly discernible state paternalism, but traces of that relationship are certainly evident. Religious liberals too, however, were prominent members of the radical bloc, indicating that statism in postbellum America had secular as well as evangelical roots. Moreover, the presence of large numbers of veterans in the chamber may also have played a significant role in the outcome of the debate on constitutional reform. War memories had been evoked to prompt the prosuffrage decision of June 1865 and soldier-politicians like Alonzo A. Abernethy had more reason than most to press for a practical tribute to black loyalty.

In figure 9.2 the extent of house Republican unity on national policy is revealed. With the exception of a few representatives who harbored reservations about specific aspects of that policy, moderates and ultras were united in their determination to support Congress's attempt to fashion a just and workable Reconstruction settlement. Iowa Republicans had won the fall election on a platform demanding that rebel leaders be brought to trial for their crimes against the nation, that proven traitors should be disfranchised, and that slavery should be abolished.[46] Their unanimity on a resolution calling for the execution of Jefferson Davis, an amendment to the Iowa constitution excluding "traitors and draft evaders" from the suffrage, and the ratification of the Thirteenth Amendment was thus wholly predictable.[47] Less so was their response to Andrew Johnson's veto of the Freedmen's Bureau bill.

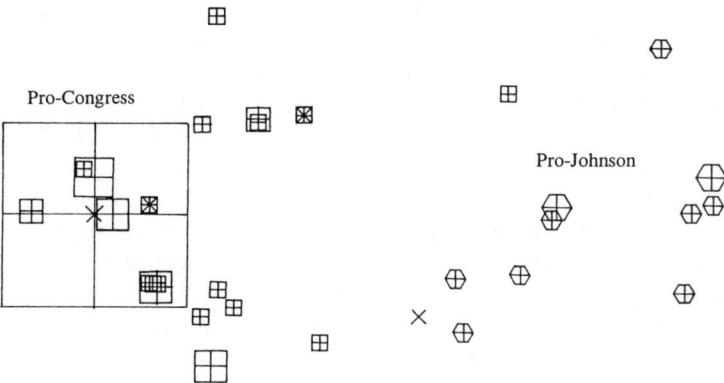

	Republican
	Democrat
×	Independent

MDS analysis (see Appendix); no. of motions = 6
SOURCE: *Ia. Hse. Jnl.* (1866), pp. 59, 97, 284, 364, 648, 756–57.

Fig. 9.2 Iowa House, 1866: Voting behavior on Reconstruction motions.

During the first part of January 1866 nonradical congressional Republicans labored to formulate a plan that would provide for the swift readmission of Southern delegates, guarantee the security of Unionists in the conquered section, and foster harmony between the president and his party. These objectives were particularly dear to the hearts of former Whigs who placed a high priority on organic progress—men like U.S. Supreme Court Justice Samuel F. Miller of Keokuk who believed that Johnson would "assent to almost any means of securing the civil rights of the negro, short of imposing negro suffrage on the states in rebellion against their will."[48] For most nonradicals the bill to extend the life and increase the powers of the Freedmen's Bureau was no more than a simple act of justice to the emancipated slave, one seemingly in full accordance with the president's recently stated views on the Southern problem. The executive veto on 19 February, therefore, came as a profound shock to most moderates.

In Iowa the Des Moines *State Register* labeled it "a weak, pettifogging document" that, because of its reliance on conservative theory, could have been written by any notorious Copperhead.[49] Such outspoken language provided an accurate reflection of majority opinion in the local legislature. Two days after the veto's publication General Fitz Henry Warren, the prominent anti-Grimes Republican who was now seeking to revive his political career by aligning himself with the president, moved to have the message read out in the senate. Only five of Warren's copartisans voted for the measure. The upper chamber then passed a resolution urging Iowa's congressional delegation to support the passage of the Freedmen's Bureau bill over Johnson's veto.[50] On this occasion only Warren and the outnumbered Democrats rallied around the president's standard. The same pattern was evident in the house where all but four Republicans gave their assent to the resolution and the Democrats were unanimous in their opposition.[51]

The assembly's unambiguous reaction to Johnson's act of bad faith was consistent with that body's stance on local black suffrage and indicated that Iowa Republicans were reluctant to abandon the freedmen for the sake of party unity. It did not, however, reveal whether these same legislators were ready to overcome constitutional scruples and reservations about the political aptitude of the former slaves in order to lobby Congress on behalf of universal suffrage in the South.

On 16 March senate Republicans passed a joint resolution on Reconstruction.[52] Eschewing the doctrine of conquered states as too controversial, it called on the Iowans at Washington to use their powers under the guarantee clause of the U.S. Constitution to work for a number of measures, the most germane of which was the securing of "the full rights of citizenship, civil and political," to all inhabitants of the late rebel states, "irrespective of race and color." The force of these words was tempered by an additional clause designed to ensure the support of nonradicals: "If any qualifications or restrictions of the rights of suffrage are deemed necessary for the safety and well-being of any State, such qualifications or restrictions shall be made without reference to the color or race of the persons to whom they shall apply."[53] Although the measure indicated that Iowa's senior politicians were still reluctant to endorse universal suffrage, there was little evidence here, beyond the use in the preamble of some of Johnson's more progressive rhetoric, that senators were prepared to compromise on his own terms.

Republicans in the lower chamber failed to address themselves to the senate directive on Reconstruction. Instead, toward the end of the session, they passed a joint resolution of their own urging Iowa congressmen to refuse admission to Southern delegates until "sufficient guarantees" had been provided for securing to the former bondsmen "the substantial enjoyments of all rights of freemen."[54] Why the house contented itself with this equivocal declaration is unclear. Is it possible that men who were determined to destroy the bulwarks of institutional racism in their own state were uninterested in securing the vote for Southern blacks? This is surely inconceivable given the radical, anti-Johnson complexion of the chamber. More likely these inexperienced legislators, knowing that the senate favored only limited franchise extension, were willing to entrust Iowa's Republican leaders in Congress with the task of finding a viable alternative to Johnson's discredited system of provisional governments, or the radicals and moderates were hopelessly divided over the relative merits of granting universal, impartial, or qualified suffrage to the former slaves.

Whatever the reasons for the lack of positive action in the lower chamber, the resolution failed to come up for debate in the senate. Thus the Republican-controlled assembly issued no binding declaration on Reconstruction except for its demand that Congress should pass the Freedmen's Bureau bill over Johnson's veto.

Although Iowa Republicans were largely united in their opposition to presidential Reconstruction during the winter of 1865–66, there were increasing signs of factionalism within the party. To a large extent internal disputes over patronage had been contained by the exigencies of war. Now various elements in the Union organization (disaffected politicians, army veterans, and ambitious party leaders) began either to seek their place in the sun or to consolidate their existing positions. Not surprisingly many of these people regarded Reconstruction as a stick with which to beat their opponents. Fitz Henry Warren was probably the most prominent Iowan to take up the president's cause in an effort to secure control of federal offices at home. More significant than Warren's maneuvers, however, was the emergence of an open rift between the supporters of Harlan and Grimes. Crucial to this development was the senatorial election of early 1866.

Several Republican chieftains hoped to obtain the long-term U.S. Senate position to be decided upon in the party's legislative caucus. (There were so few Democrats in the 1866 assembly that the nomination by joint convention was a mere formality, a rubber-stamping of the Republican caucus's decision.) Initially ex-Governor Samuel J. Kirkwood was the leading candidate. He had Grimes's full backing and was popular in many parts of the state because of his achievements as wartime executive.[55] During the summer of 1865 Kirkwood had hoped to be named Harlan's successor by Governor William M. Stone, but the latter failed to fulfill his tentative promises, possibly because he was planning to secure the long-term place for himself.[56] The other prime candidate for the great prize was Congressman John A. Kasson, one of the leading figures in the railroad ring at Des Moines. Kasson, however, made a number of patronage errors during 1865, the most costly being his failure to appoint General Grenville M. Dodge's splenetic young lackey George C. Tichenor as Des Moines postmaster. Vowing revenge on the conservative U.S. representative, Tichenor—a converted Breckinridge Democrat uncharitably described by one contemporary as "an infernal fool and shit ass"—gradually poisoned the general's mind against Kasson, thereby reducing the latter's chances of political promotion.[57]

Not until the fall of 1865 did another candidate enter the senatorial arena. This was Secretary James Harlan. Finding himself the member of an increasingly unpopular administration, the devious Mount Pleasant politician began making plans to return to the Senate in order to shore up his power base.[58] The battle was joined in early October when Harlan forces secured control of the *Burlington Hawk-Eye,* hitherto a firm supporter of the party's Grimes-Kirkwood wing.[59] Backed by the substantial patronage power of the interior department, a $10,000 campaign chest donated by Thomas Durant of the Union Pacific for services rendered to the transcontinental railroad, and letters of support from the influential Methodist bishop Matthew Simpson, Harlan defeated Kirkwood on the third ballot of the Republican caucus.[60]

Because the senatorial contest mobilized warring political cliques in the commercial towns and farming villages of Iowa, the local Republican party became increasingly bifurcated. Although Kirkwood may have been somewhat mollified by his nomination to the vacant short-term Senate place (made available by Harlan's cabinet appointment), his eclipse left a nasty taste in the mouths of his friends. While Reconstruction would impose a fragile unity on members of both the Harlan and Grimes-Kirkwood spheres of influence, the stage was set for a showdown between the two groupings.

By the spring of 1866 Andrew Johnson was an outcast within his own party. Instead of isolating the Jacobins by embracing Congress's attempt to graft a nonradical addendum onto his policy, he had alienated the center with his negation of the Freedmen's Bureau and civil rights bills, his untenable claim that market forces would guarantee the safety of Southern blacks, and his unwavering trust in men who, less than a year previously, had been engaged in a bloody revolt against the government. Dr. George Shedd, the Denmark Free-Soiler who had helped to engineer Iowa's anti-Nebraska coalition in March 1854, spoke for the majority of his fellow partisans when he told Samuel J. Kirkwood that he had read with pain Johnson's "slimpsy copperheadish objections" to the Freedmen's Bureau legislation. There were, he wrote, only a hundred voters in his village,

> yet we sent over 100 persons, soldier boys, into the war to put down the Rebel[l]ion. Many of these brave men lie buried in southern soil—few families here but have suffered the loss of dear ones. Was that all in vain? It seems to us so if the Pres⁵ policy is to prevail, traitors are to be whitewashed, then justified & restored to all the privileges & immunities of loyal citizens.

Shedd concluded his letter to Kirkwood with a piece of advice: "Stand firm to the end for the Right & your friends will stand by you."[61] As a veteran antislavery man the backcountry Congregationalist knew well that pragmatists like Kirkwood were capable of temporizing on important humanitarian questions, yet frequently responsive to pressure from radical elements within the Republican coalition. Iowa's war governor was not a racial progressive, but as he had shown during the Coppoc crisis, he recognized the dictates of sectionalism and the power of the abolitionist lobby. After his senatorial election by a manifestly reform-minded legislature at home, Kirkwood can have had little hesitation in voting to pass the Reconstruction bills over Johnson's vetoes. In doing so he was joined by the rest of Iowa's center-radical delegation in the Congress, including his increasingly erratic ally James W. Grimes.[62]

During the early months of 1866 Grimes was a member of the centrist-controlled Joint Committee on Reconstruction, which had been empowered to formulate an alternative to executive Reconstruction. The result was the Fourteenth Amendment, a distinctly moderate compromise between the Republican factions designed to reduce the Southern states' representation in Congress if they failed to permit the freedmen to vote. When the draft amendment emerged at the end of April the only section to which Grimes objected was one providing for the disfranchisement of former Confederates. It is possible that his objection to this clause was motivated by a continuing desire to promote a rapprochement with the president.[63] Although they were frustrated with Johnson's course, both he and his powerful friend Senator William Pitt Fessenden remained determined to prevent congressional radicals from dictating Southern policy. Neither of them were keen supporters of universal suffrage or unaware of the fact that the president had only to endorse the principle of impartial suffrage to regain the confidence of nonradical Republicans. The party's Senate caucus certainly evinced a disposition to keep open the channels of communication with the executive by endorsing a motion proposed by Grimes, Fessenden, and Jacob Howard of Michigan to replace the disenfranchisement prohibition with one on office holding.[64] If the Burlington politician was still intent on preserving party unity after the winter's vetoes, he was not alone in seeking to further that objective.

Whether intraparty reconciliation was uppermost in the minds of Grimes's Iowa colleagues at this stage is a different matter. Governor Stone informed Congressmen James F. Wilson and Hiram Price on 24 February that the state legislature had repudiated Johnson's veto of the Freedmen's Bureau bill. "The loyal heart of Iowa is warmed anew," he proclaimed. "No flattering here. The Radical majority in Congress will be triumphantly sustained. . . . Stand firm whatever the President may do."[65] Stone's uncompromising support for the opponents of executive Reconstruction contrasted sharply with his proadministration address of 11 January, indicating the extent to which Johnson's vetoes and the assembly's response had restricted his freedom of maneuver.[66] His message to Washington was also a signal to the congressmen that Iowa Republicans had lost patience with Johnson. Five out of six of the state's U.S. representatives voted for the revised constitutional amendment that passed the House on 13 June.[67]

The dangers of further association with the president were fully understood by his own secretary of the interior. During the second half of 1865 James Harlan had found himself in an increasingly uncomfortable position, sandwiched between a conservative master and a local party that had little faith in further unrequited acts of sectional reconciliation. Yet in spite of the risks involved in retaining his cabinet post, he declined to set his face publicly against the president, preferring instead to defend the latter's policy on the grounds that it was wholly compatible with Congress's right to fix the terms for readmission of the Southern states. His loyalty was not entirely a product of altruism.

Harlan needed to hold onto the office for two reasons. The first of these was his dependence on federal patronage as a weapon in the senatorial contest. The second was his desire to promote a variety of profitable business deals, the most spectacular of which was the sale of the Cherokee Neutral Tract in southern Kansas to the American Emigrant Company.[68] Described by one historian as "a land jobbing and scab-importing agency," this Connecticut-based corporation had invested heavily in the swamplands of northwestern Iowa and employed James C. Savery of Des Moines as one of its principal officers.[69] Because Savery, a fellow Methodist and former conservative Whig, was one of Harlan's closest political allies at home, it must be adjudged highly suspicious that the secretary—with the help of two other Iowa Methodists, Commissioner of Indian Affairs Dennis N. Cooley and Indian Superintendent Elijah Sells—negotiated a treaty providing for the cession of eighty thousand acres of cheap Cherokee land to the United States and then authorized the tract's sale to the American Emigrant Company under a clause (insisted on by Harlan) permitting resale to a single party without regard to squatters' rights. There is no proof that the need to conclude this deal forced the secretary to retain his cabinet post beyond the call of duty, but the timing casts serious doubt upon his actions.

At the end of January 1866, shortly after his election to the Senate, Harlan told a delegation of Iowa Republicans that he had no doubt that the freedmen were fit for citizenship. He had, he said, never disguised his belief "that it is much safer to trust an ignorant loyal man than a wise rebel."[70] This statement caused consternation among Johnson's supporters, and the president himself, failing to secure Harlan's endorsement of the Freedmen's Bureau bill veto, waited impatiently for his minister's resignation.[71] So too did the latter's friends and enemies at home. Harlan hung on desperately until midsummer. The Cherokees signed their Civil War settlement (incorporating the cession of the Neutral Tract) with the government on 19 July. On the 27th, over a month after the official call for a pro-Johnson National Union convention and only a day before he agreed to the sale of the Indian lands to the American Emigrant Company, Harlan finally drafted his letter of resignation.[72] He had left the move late, but not too late, it seems, to reap the rewards of office or to preserve his political reputation.

Harlan's resignation severed one of the last-remaining links between the president and Iowa's Republican organization. Apart from the disaffected Fitz Henry Warren, Congressman John A. Kasson was now left as the administration's only prominent Republican ally in the state. Unfortunately for Johnson, even this help proved to be of limited value. Kasson's patronage policy and support for executive Reconstruction alienated many of his political associates in Des Moines and Council Bluffs.[73] On 19 June these disgruntled elements, headed by Iowa's war hero, General Grenville M. Dodge, engineered his defeat at the fifth district congressional convention, thereby seriously undermining his capacity to aid the president's cause.[74]

The eclipse of Representative Josiah B. Grinnell in a neighboring district was less of a threat to the success of the National Union movement. Since his wavering on local black suffrage in 1865, the wealthy abolitionist had pursued a thoroughly radical line on Reconstruction and could in no sense have been mistaken for an apologist of the president. His defeat at the hands of William Loughridge came as a profound shock to his overconfident supporters.[75] In fact Loughridge, an Oskaloosa judge, had been plotting Grinnell's downfall for over a year, targeting his campaign on politically ambitious army veterans and office-seeking members of the legislature.[76] Although the nonradical, pro-Kirkwood delegation from Johnson County was the final arbiter of the nominating contest, Reconstruction issues did not play a role in the convention and Loughridge went to Washington a committed adherent of congressional policy.

Notwithstanding compelling evidence of Republican unity on the fundamentals of Reconstruction, Iowa Democrats were determined to exploit the break between Congress and the president and to rebuild their party's fortunes on the basis of amnesty and readmission. Charles Mason attended a meeting of the National Democratic Association in Washington on 8 April. This body passed several resolutions prepared by the Burlington Copperhead. These declared a reluctance to abandon the regular party organization but manifested "a willingness to come to the rescue of the President in solid column & without the hope of favor or reward from him leaving him free to bestow his patronage upon those who aided in his election."[77] The assumption was that Johnson would be forced to use his appointing power to galvanize the National Union movement, and that the Democrats had no alternative, at least initially, but to endorse the conservative Republicans that he would presumably find to replace unreliable "radical" officials.

While expectations of a patronage offensive were well-founded (it began in July after Congress adjourned), Mason and his colleagues were mistaken in their belief that such a blitz could prepare the ground for a Democratic resurgence. In the first place, Democrats and conservative Republicans failed to agree on tactics. Whereas the former—particularly ex-Peace Democrats—tended to insist on wholesale removals, conservatives were more likely to recommend that incumbent Republican officeholders should be retained until after the fall elections.[78] Both Kasson and Warren opposed indiscriminate purging because they recognized the dangers of making political martyrs and were loathe to surrender control of the Johnson movement into the hands of discredited Democrats.[79] Kasson told Montgomery Blair, like Mason a member of the National Union Executive Committee, that removals would only help his enemy, Grenville M. Dodge, whom he designated a "radical ignoramus." Significantly, the lame-duck congressman professed his loyalty to the party of Lincoln and warned his correspondent to "beware the advice of A.C. Dodge, Charles Mason, & other old fossil hardhead democrats"—politicians who "have been asleep for 10 years, & know nothing of the present living men and times."[80]

The Copperhead cause was further stymied, before and after the elections, by the duplicity of the officeholders themselves. Local assessors, collectors, and postmasters frequently pledged their support for Johnson in written communications to Washington, while simultaneously criticizing the president and his policy at home.[81] Such double-dealing infuriated Iowa Democrats, already disappointed by their failure to gain tangible rewards from the national Republican split. By the beginning of October Mason was drafting plans to resist any attempt by the radicals to impose a military despotism on the country.[82]

There was little chance that the Johnson forces would carry Iowa in the forthcoming state elections. Quite apart from the inherent limitations of the patronage weapon and the disagreements between conservatives and Democrats over how it should be used, the National Union movement suffered from the insurmountable problem of grass-roots unpopularity. Part of the reason for this was the essential moderation of the Republicans' electoral stance, four-square on the proposed amendment to the federal Constitution. Although some genuine radicals were unhappy with the compromise forged in Washington, there is no doubt that the amendment was a vote winner. Most realistic progressives, Edward Russell included, grudgingly conceded that the measure was the only one that could have united moderates and radicals in the Thirty-ninth Congress.[83]

The National Union movement was further hampered by the conduct of the president himself. His support for the opponents of Congress in Louisiana was regarded by many as a precipitating factor in the New Orleans massacre of July 1866—an event that came to symbolize the moral bankruptcy of executive policy. Not all voters were yet inclined to follow the lead of the Des Moines *Iowa State Register* and call for Johnson's impeachment, but they were certainly ready to deal the administration a crushing blow at the polls.[84] Colonel Ed Wright was reelected secretary of state with a majority twice as large as Stone's the previous year. In the congressional contests all six Republican candidates were returned without seriously being threatened by their opponents.[85] Grenville Dodge, his candidacy tellingly endorsed by Kasson shortly before the election, secured 59 percent of the vote in his traditionally conservative district. It was a clear illustration of how badly Johnson had misjudged the mood of the country.

The events of late 1865 and 1866 highlighted the extent to which the Republican party in Iowa had been radicalized by the Civil War. In August 1857 pragmatic centrists within the organization had successfully neutralized the issue of black suffrage through their use of the referendum. Eight years later centrist Republicans combined with radicals at the state convention in Des Moines to initiate the process of expunging racial qualifications from the Iowa constitution. Although concerns over national Reconstruction policy may have played a part in this development, the key reason for the convention's action was black loyalty to the Union during the war. President Johnson's lack of interest in the enfranchisement of Southern freedmen tested the local Union organization's fidelity to its controversial campaign pronouncement, but even those pragmatists and moderates who were unenthusiastic about black suffrage displayed little sign of abandoning the state platform in the 1866 legislature. Nor were they inclined to support a hasty program of national reconciliation. After hopes that executive and Congress could reach a compromise solution to the problem of Reconstruction, Johnson's determination to formulate his own conservative Southern policy led moderates and radicals to unite behind the Fourteenth Amendment as the only practical plan to lay before not only the states but also the voters of the North. For while centrists were skeptical of black enfranchisement, they were no less aware than their more extreme copartisans that presidential Reconstruction threatened to deprive them of the fruits of war. In spite of some worrying factional developments during early 1866, Iowa Republicans emerged victorious from the fall elections because, like them, the electorate refused to contemplate the readmission of Southern delegates to Congress without genuine signs of repentance from the vanquished section and concrete guarantees of good behavior in the future.

10
The Waning of Reconstruction, 1867–1872

lthough Iowa Republicans rejected the president's lenient Reconstruction policy and evinced a strong determination to confer equal rights on local blacks, there is no indication that they sought a revolutionary transformation of Southern society beyond the extension of the North's free labor system to the Confederacy. Modern historians have frequently blamed the Republicans for not bolstering the freedmen's position with land reform. In fact there is little evidence that land redistribution was regarded as a key to black freedom by any but the most-committed radical in Congress. Even the progressive Iowa legislature of 1866 failed to demand the breaking up of the plantation system and a reversal of Johnson's policy of returning confiscated land to the old master class. Like their copartisans in other Northern states, Iowa Republicans complacently assumed that the combination of wage-labor contracts and equal rights would secure the position of the former slaves by converting the latter into independent farm laborers subject to the meritocratic laws of the North's capitalistic democracy. Where most radical and many moderate Republicans differed from the president was in their willingness to use federal power to ensure that the freedmen were not prevented from competing fairly in the race of life by unrepentant Southern whites. While this determination meant that Reconstruction would remain at the head of the political agenda until the late 1860s, the Republicans' overriding preoccupation with equal civil and political rights left them ill equipped to deal with the myriad of economic problems facing both the freedmen and the South as a whole.

In 1867 Congress responded to the Confederate states' rejection of the Fourteenth Amendment by providing for military rule and black suffrage. Although the latter was a victory for congressional radicals, the Republican center remained wedded to the Fourteenth as the basis of Reconstruction.

Together with the rise of new issues, worsening factional strife, and burgeoning fears about the growth of federal power, this commitment helped to ensure that Reconstruction no longer dominated Iowa politics by the end of the decade.

While the president's supporters were left to lick their wounds after the annihilation of the National Union party, Iowa Republican leaders set about interpreting the election results. Inevitably the crushing victories at home and in other Northern states were regarded as a vindication of congressional Republican policy. Radicals and centrists, however, had very different ideas about the substance of that policy. Those who were unperturbed by the South's failure to ratify the Fourteenth Amendment during late 1866 were strengthened in their determination to impose a republican system of government on the uncowed section. Some of them endorsed the presidential ambitions of General Benjamin F. Butler, the controversial Massachusetts congressman whose calls for territorialization of the South made him anathema to party centrists.[1] Predictably the latter denied that Republican majorities constituted a green light for more radical action. James Harlan informed William Penn Clarke on 7 November of disappointing results in Ohio, Pennsylvania, and New York, and defeats in Maryland and Delaware. "This is not important," he wrote, "except on the question of the adoption of the impending Constitutional amendment. . . . But it teaches us the necessity of *impartial suffrage:* the Union cause in the lately rebel States can be secured in no other mode."[2]

Harlan was exceptionally keen to stress the dark side of what were really a promising set of election results. For him the results were a good reason to persevere with the moderate program on which Iowa Republicans had gone to the people during the summer—a program that, note the senator-elect's emphasis, incorporated the principle of limited, not universal, suffrage.

Harlan's main rival for control of the state organization, James W. Grimes, was equally insistent that the elections did not constitute a triumph for radicalism. He told Secretary of the Navy Gideon Welles that while there was widespread approbation for congressional Reconstruction, those who formulated the policy were not "exclusionists" as the secretary had termed them. They were, he said, "the men who elected Lincoln & Johnson & fought down the rebellion. They demand no blood, no penalties, no confiscation of property. They have proposed more lenient terms than were ever offered by conquerors to the conquered."[3] It was, continued Grimes, up to the president whether he accepted the popular verdict or ignored it and gave new impetus to the radicals.

Apart from the attitude of the president, the major problem confronting nonradicals during the winter of 1866-67 was the South's continued failure to exhibit signs of genuine repentance. Moderates like Justice Samuel F. Miller found this reluctance extremely disturbing, for it could only strengthen the hands of extremists within their own party. Miller told a Texan correspondent early in the new year that, although he was opposed to franchise extension on principle, the South would have to accept impartial suffrage before the reconciliation process could begin. "If I could be able to say tomorrow," confided the judge, "See here, they have hung a rebel in Texas for killing a negro, it would be the most effective speech that has been made since the war ended."[4]

Unfortunately for Miller every Southern state except Tennessee rejected the Fourteenth Amendment. By mid-November 1866 Republican newspapers in Iowa were demanding the obliteration of Johnson's provisional governments and the imposition of black suffrage on the South.[5] Brigadier General James A. Williamson of Des Moines, a onetime conservative War Democrat who was now looking to make a name for himself in local politics, launched his campaign for the Republican gubernatorial nomination with a call for territorialization. The South, he maintained, had rejected compromise "and released us from all obligations to stand by any. Our Senators and Representatives will not be slow to avail themselves of the opportunity thus offered, and now instead of compromises, all questions will be settled upon principles of eternal right and justice."[6] Williamson's lofty statement appeared in the *State Register* on 11 December. A week later an incident occurred that highlighted intraparty tension over Reconstruction, cast doubt on Iowa's devotion to eternal principles and yet, for all that, underlined the Republicans' stubborn refusal to backtrack on the race question.

On 19 December the U.S. Senate took up a bill providing for the admission of Nebraska into the Union. Two radicals, B. Gratz Brown of Missouri and Charles Sumner, had already assailed it on the grounds that it did not require black suffrage as a condition for statehood.[7] This upset Iowa's junior senator, Samuel J. Kirkwood, who testily pronounced the radical condemnation a slur on the constitution of his home state (which, of course, remained open to the same criticism). Sumner, he said, had declared Iowa's fundamental law offensive. It was none of his business: "The people of Iowa will deal with it in their own way when they see fit, and as a loyal people they have the right to do so; and so I apprehend have the people of Nebraska."[8]

The Bostonian responded to this indignant outburst in typically aggressive fashion. Since the Nebraska constitution did not give blacks the vote, it contained a reprehensible principle and Sumner doubted not that Kirkwood "would undertake to say that an exclusion from rights on account of color would be properly characterized as otherwise than odious and offensive."[9] Kirkwood, the only Republican senator who had voted for a recent literacy test amendment to a bill providing for black suffrage in the District of Columbia, undertook no such thing.[10]

When news of this bitter exchange reached home, Kirkwood's views were subjected to a good deal of hostile scrutiny. Sumner, contended Edward Russell's pro-Harlan *Davenport Gazette,* had always been at the forefront of the antislavery movement and Iowans were no less progressive. Kirkwood's views merely reflected his own "personal prejudices" and were consistent with his previous record on the suffrage issue. "Iowa," concluded the editorial, had no need for "trimming or dodging politicians."[11] The Des Moines *Iowa State Register*, which had no factional axe to grind, also took the governor to task. It could not be that Kirkwood was defending the existence of the word *white* in the Iowa constitution, urged an editorial on 29 December. Had not local Republicans already declared their opposition to that clause? "We are free to say," it went on,

> that *we* do not like the *color* disqualification in the Constitution of Nebraska, and as much as we would rejoice at the admission of the Congressional delegation elect from that State, it would teach the Republicans there a useful lesson to keep them out in the cold until they should voluntarily place all citizens, regardless of color, upon an equality.[12]

This outspoken criticism of one of Iowa's most-respected politicians did not impress those who held racial progressives in contempt. A number of conservatives rallied to Kirkwood's defense. George C. Tichenor, a longtime foe of abolitionism, congratulated the senator for his "'plucky' tilt with His Serene Theorist Sumner."[13] Judge George G. Wright advised Kirkwood to ignore the criticism being directed at him. "Be not alarmed about your 'Radicalism,'" he wrote. "But I know you are not. Thank God, there is something to sustain & give support & character to the Republican party beside the negro."[14]

Significantly, however, Kirkwood's views were disowned not only by the radical press but also by some of his conservative friends. The Des Moines engineer, Colonel John N. Dewey, opined tactfully that Sumner "had you at a slight disadvantage," and warned that "we are making history fast and what would have been deemed radical two years since is cold conservatism now."[15] Even more pointed was the advice of Congressman-elect Grenville M. Dodge, one of the senator's closest political allies. He told Kirkwood in a private letter that he knew him to be in favor of eliminating racial distinctions from the Iowa constitution. "You know we have got to meet this question," wrote the general bluntly, "and I have but one view of it[:] that is to take it early[,] fight for it on the ground of right, justice &c. and educate the people up to it."[16] Coming from a conservative ex-Democrat who had spent his youth hounding abolitionists and blacks in New England, this was remarkable advice.[17] When the Nebraska bill again came up for discussion, Kirkwood joined Sumner in voting for an amendment declaring it to be a fundamental condition of admission that within the new state there should be no abridgement of the elective franchise "by reason of race or color."[18] Evidently the pressure had told.

Although the response to Kirkwood's clash with Sumner may have persuaded a number of pragmatic Iowa politicians that it was time to move beyond the Fourteenth Amendment, the state's congressional delegation continued to seek a practical, popular solution to the ongoing crisis. On 28 January 1867 the House of Representatives debated a crucial motion to refer to the centrist-dominated Joint Committee of Fifteen Thaddeus Stevens's Reconstruction bill, which expressly extended the franchise to Southern blacks. Stevens and the Ohio radical James Ashley believed that this move would kill the measure and argued eloquently for its defeat. Grinnell, Price, Wilson, Kasson, and Allison joined the majority of their copartisans in opposing the (successful) motion to refer, but it would be wrong to see this unanimity as evidence that the state delegation had thrown in its lot with the Jacobins.[19] Shortly afterwards the House turned its attention to a new bill to provide the South with a system of military government. Three Iowans— Allison, Wilson, and Price—voted to recommit this measure to the House judiciary committee with instructions to report it back with an amendment linking readmission to ratification of the Fourteenth Amendment. Only Grinnell voted alongside core radicals like Stevens against the motion, which, partly because of conservative opposition, was defeated ninety-four to sixty-nine. The bill then passed unamended with the backing of most Republicans, Iowa's trimmers included.[20]

After first conceding the principles of military rule and black suffrage prior to the South's forthcoming constitutional convention elections, it was the Senate that now attempted to moderate congressional policy by adhering to the Fourteenth Amendment as the basis of Reconstruction. Both Grimes and Kirkwood voted for the same enabling clause that had been rejected in the House.[21] As national level politicians they shared Harlan's conviction that radicalism endangered the Republican cause in key Northern states. All of them had their eyes on the forthcoming presidential election.

When the amended bill returned to the House, the Massachusetts radical George Boutwell contended that because Johnson's provisional governments remained unscathed the way was now open for universal amnesty and the restoration to power of Southern traitors.[22] Among those opposing this view was James F. Wilson, the chairman of the judiciary committee. The bill, he averred, fell short of what he desired but was nonetheless a liberal plan of Reconstruction. It not only secured "equal suffrage" to loyalists but also presented "an affirmative policy . . . hostile to that of the President" and demonstrated "the ability of Congress to agree upon a given line of future action." Just as he had done in the 1857 constitutional convention, Wilson again proved himself a practical politician of the highest order. The Senate's action had made it clear that moderation would have to prevail and the Fairfield attorney was perfectly correct in suggesting that the amended bill reached "far beyond anything which the most sanguine of us hoped for a year ago."[23] Allison, Price, and Kasson accepted their colleague's reasoning and voted to concur in the Senate amendment. Grinnell joined the radicals in defeating the bill with conservative help.[24]

Fearing a complete stalemate, Wilson stepped into the breach the following day (20 February) with a measure prohibiting rebels barred from officeholding by the Fourteenth Amendment from voting in the constitutional elections.[25] This and a second amendment offered by Samuel Shellabarger of Ohio declaring the Johnson governments subject to modification or abolition united House Republicans behind the congressional program. The First Military Reconstruction Act then passed the lower chamber by 126 votes to 46, Kasson being the only Iowan present not to register an opinion.[26] The Senate concurred in the amendments on the same day. Kirkwood voted with the majority. Grimes was paired off with an opponent of the measure.[27]

Denounced by Charles Mason as the "Proconsular bill," this seminal piece of legislation divided all the Confederate states save Tennessee into five military districts under Union army control.[28] Because the former slaves were allowed to vote for delegates to the constitutional conventions, it paved the way for significant black involvement in Deep South states where the freedmen made up a sizable proportion of the population. However, while the act fostered a "unique and dramatic experiment in interracial democracy," its grounding in the Fourteenth Amendment and failure to provide a secure economic foundation for black freedom indicated that Congress was not prepared to deal as harshly with the South and act as justly toward the emancipated slaves as many radicals had hoped.[29]

There was little evidence during the spring and summer of 1867 that the majority of Iowa Republicans were disposed to quarrel with the compromise fashioned in Washington. Convening at Des Moines in June they ignored the claims of the proven radical Josiah B. Grinnell and nominated a moderate army veteran, Samuel F. Merrill, for governor. They also passed a set of unremarkable resolutions approving congressional policy and censuring an attempt by the U.S. attorney general to emasculate the Military Reconstruction Act.[30] It was not until August, when Johnson suspended from duty Secretary of War Edwin Stanton and removed General Phil Sheridan from his command in the Southwest, that a degree of passion returned to the Reconstruction debate. Those radicals who had been calling for the president's impeachment since the New Orleans and Memphis massacres found new voice and were joined by men who had previously shied away from such a revolutionary step. George C. Tichenor reported from Des Moines that Johnson's latest effort to obstruct congressional policy had provoked a widespread feeling in favor of impeachment.[31] Expectations grew in radical circles that justice was soon to be done.

Senator Grimes was equally hopeful that the nation's enemies were about to receive their just desserts. In his opinion, though, it was the radicals not the president who posed the greatest threat to public safety. That summer he observed the drift of national events from his residence at Burlington. He read angrily of Sumner's diatribe against his friend Fessenden in the *Boston Advertiser,* was mortified by Johnson's ill-conceived actions, and cursed attempts by the radicals to manufacture proimpeachment sentiment in the North.[32] Revolutionary and inflationary talk by men like Stevens and Ashley strengthened his commitment to stricter construction of the U.S. Constitution and hard money, laissez-faire economics. At times his mood was black. He told Fessenden shortly after the fall elections that he feared "another civil war & anarchy for a time."[33] Yet those same contests also enabled him to perceive a glimmer of light at the end of the tunnel. "The elections this autumn," he wrote more optimistically on 7 September, "will show in the north west a great reaction and any extreme radical will be beaten next year for the Presidency."[34]

In spite of the Iowa Democracy's efforts to exploit racial prejudice, constitutional conservatism, and antiprohibition feeling in the river towns, Merrill secured the governorship in October with 58.9 percent of the popular vote (a slight gain on Stone's majority two years previously), and his party won enough seats to retain its stranglehold over the assembly.[35] Farther east, however, in the key states of Ohio and New York, the Republicans suffered greatly because of their support for local black suffrage. The worst defeat was in Ohio where the Democrats won control of the legislature, thereby ensuring that radical leader Benjamin F. Wade would not be reelected to the U.S. Senate. Grimes was jubilant. "Wade & Co will be as meek as moses," he told Fessenden, with reference to the forthcoming session of Congress.[36] On this occasion, the senator's customary foresight let him down.

Soon after the new session of Congress had begun, it became evident that radical leaders were preparing to impeach the president in an attempt to seize control of the Republican party before the onset of sectional peace. At first it seemed that their rearguard action was doomed to failure. James F. Wilson took the lead in seeking to discredit the notion that impeachment could be employed as a political weapon against a man whose only crime was to oppose the will of Congress. He spoke the majority view. The House rejected a preliminary impeachment report on 7 December by 108 votes to 57.[37] Only two Iowans voted for the report: Grinnell's successor, William Loughridge, and the Davenport banker Hiram Price, one of the few contractionists who favored impeachment at this early stage.[38] The insurrection, it appeared, had been quelled.

From his outpost in Guatemala City (to which he had been dispatched by a grateful president) American minister Fitz Henry Warren reviewed the current state of politics at home. No more well disposed toward radical designs than his old rival, James W. Grimes, Warren looked forward to the nomination of Ulysses S. Grant for president as "the only solution of our present problems." The great general, he told Senator Elihu B. Washburne of Illinois (Grant's principal backer), would be sure to rein in extremist elements within the Republican party. "[I] say to you in all honesty," wrote the Iowan, "that you must place some limit to this wildness of theory. How long will the white men of the South be ruled by a majority of Negro[e]s, they in the majority of population and of voters. Just as long as *you* and *I* would, and no longer. What is to be the effect on the Negro? Evil and only evil." A reaction was sure to come, concluded Warren (now a firm believer in impartial suffrage), either through "a sharp financial *rip*" or disturbing events in the South: "*Radicalism* is *not* a normal or a natural condition of any people, but for periods of excitement."[39]

Warren's judgment in this instance was astute, but the excitement at home had not abated yet. In mid-November 1867 Frank W. Palmer's *State Register* demanded Johnson's impeachment on the grounds that he was a drunkard, had abetted the massacres at Memphis and New Orleans, and impeded congressional Reconstruction.[40] These were flimsy reasons for deposing a head of state in a legalistic-minded republic, and the vote in Congress recognized that fact. But eight weeks later the president altered the terms of engagement by ordering the dismissal of Secretary of War Edwin Stanton. This outrage, which seemed to many to constitute a blatant violation of the Tenure of Office Act, dispelled many lingering doubts about the lawfulness of impeachment. Coupled with evidence of further presidential obstructionism in the South, it united radicals and moderates behind a strategy of decapitation.

As Congress returned to the subject of impeachment, the members of

Iowa's twelfth general assembly were confronted by several problems: not only "the paramount question of reconstruction" but also demands for a revision of the laws on drink, for action to curb railroad power in the state, and for the submission of the black suffrage question to the people.[41] Impeachment, however, was the subject on everyone's lips. At the end of February 1868 news arrived that Iowa's six congressmen had endorsed this policy, thereby paving the way for the Senate to try the president for high crimes and misdemeanors.[42] Republicans in the Iowa house passed a resolution condemning Johnson's "dangerous and evil course" and expressing support for his removal.[43] Although the upper house proved more cautious, it too threw its weight behind Congress by urging the state's delegation in Washington to take such action as would "finally and effectually remove any and all organized opposition to the reconstruction policy of the nation."[44]

The assembly then acted to provide for a popular referendum on the Darwin resolutions of 1866. Iowa blacks had lobbied strongly for the Republicans to fulfill their campaign promises on this issue, and they were not disappointed.[45] Not one member of the ruling party voted against the provision for a referendum. In contrast, every Democrat bar one at the capitol opposed this precursor to constitutional reform (as they had done the Fourteenth Amendment, which was ratified earlier in the session), but Republican unanimity and their own paucity of numbers rendered this action purely symbolic.[46]

Notwithstanding the radical tenor of affairs at Des Moines, many conservative and moderate Republican leaders privately continued to voice their doubts about the wisdom of impeachment. Samuel J. Kirkwood told Hiram Price that he thought his courage better than his judgment on this issue.[47] Justice Samuel F. Miller was equally skeptical. "The political situation looks to me more gloomy than it has ever looked," he wrote on 19 January.

> [I]n the threatened collision between the Legislative branch of the government and the Executive and judicial branches I see consequences from which the cause of free government may never recover in my day. The worst feature I now see is the passion which governs the hour in all parties and all persons who have controlling influence.[48]

The problem for men like Miller was that their voices were temporarily drowned by the general clamor for Johnson's conviction. Most Northerners insisted that the president should be punished for seeking to revive the careers of Southern traitors, and there was enormous pressure on individual senators to vote for impeachment. It was thus with great alarm that Iowans greeted rumors that James W. Grimes was ready to acquit "the bold, bad man" in the White House.

At the Republican state convention in May, angry delegates listened approvingly to an impassioned speech given by a pro-Harlan radical, Attorney General Henry O'Connor, in which he declared that if Grimes voted against conviction he "would be the first in every doorstep, in every school house to denounce him as unfit to represent Iowa."[49] Given that the Burlington senator was one of the state organization's founding fathers, these were harsh words indeed. They came too late, however, to influence him.

Judge Charles Mason had visited James W. and Elizabeth Grimes in March and found them "tired of the folly & wickedness of the party."[50] It did not matter to the senator that many of his closest political associates were baying for his blood, nor did he care that his potential rival for control of the patronage, James Harlan, was ready to vote for conviction. On 11 May Grimes delivered his opinion in the impeachment case. Arguing that the president had every right to prompt judicial review of the Tenure of Office Act, he grounded his argument firmly in the notion of constitutional balance. "This Government," he averred, "can only be preserved and the liberty of the people maintained by preserving intact the coordinate branches of it. . . . I cannot agree to destroy the harmonious working of the Constitution for the sake of getting rid of an unacceptable President."[51] Even a severe attack of paralysis three days before the Senate sat in judgment failed to deter him from frustrating the hopes of his copartisans at home and preventing the elevation of Senate President Benjamin F. Wade to the White House. On 16 May Grimes joined Fessenden, five other Republican senators, and the Democratic minority to defeat impeachment.[52] Shorn permanently of his health and temporarily of his political reputation, the Iowan left Washington to recuperate in New England.

On Independence Day 1868 the national Republican organization nominated Ulysses S. Grant as its presidential candidate. Although the general was regarded with much suspicion in radical circles because of his Democratic background and close association with Johnson in 1866–67, he had successfully distanced himself from the apostate executive to become the obvious Republican choice after the watershed elections of late 1867. Together with the failure of impeachment, Grant's nomination at New York City virtually assured the demise of Radical Reconstruction.

If Iowa's Republican leaders were not unduly bothered by this prospect, they did at least refuse to backtrack on the suffrage question. There were, of course, renewed fears that this issue would prompt mass defections to the Democracy. These might well have occurred had not the leadership imposed a fairly stringent whip on the troops. Any wavering on the proposed constitutional amendments, warned Peter Melendy, the pro-Harlan chairman of the state central committee, would result in the "defeat of one of the acknowledged principles of the party" and leave the anticipated election victory "a partial triumph."⁵³

Grant's unrivaled popularity among Iowa veterans enabled Republican strategists to reemphasize the connection between black suffrage and national duty—a link that had to be established if the antireform vote of 1857 was to be reversed. In fact, as Robert R. Dykstra has demonstrated, the nucleus of a prosuffrage majority had already been created in 1865 when Governor Stone was reelected on a platform containing the pledge on franchise extension.⁵⁴ Passionate exhortations such as "[a] vote for Grant is *not a true, honest, Republican, vote,* unless it contain the clause striking the word 'white' from the Constitution" built on that foundation and produced a remarkable 56.5 percent prosuffrage majority in the November referendum.⁵⁵ Grant won a larger share of the poll (61.9 percent) and carried fourteen more counties (most of them in the south and west), but the achievement was impressive nonetheless.⁵⁶ Aside from the anomalous Wisconsin vote of 1848 it was the first time in U.S. history that the people of a state had approved en masse the extension of the elective franchise to blacks.

Interest in the Southern question waned perceptibly in Iowa, as it did throughout the North, after November 1868. There were several obvious causes of this development: war weariness and a growing desire for national reconciliation, the burgeoning debate over various aspects of the postwar economy, and the tendency of politicians and voters alike to regard black suffrage as the culmination of the sectional conflict.⁵⁷ The Fifteenth Amendment, a more positive grant of the electoral franchise to American blacks than the Fourteenth, passed both houses of Congress in 1869 with the backing of five members of Iowa's Republican delegation.⁵⁸ Hindsight reveals it to have been the bee sting of the abolitionist cause.

Other, more specific factors contributed toward the decline of Reconstruction as a political issue in Iowa. The first of these was the failure of radical Republicans to maintain the degree of pressure on party centrists that had hitherto yielded so many successes in the field of racial equality. What more could be done for the black man now that he was free and armed with the ballot? Many abolitionists turned their guns away from slavery and racism onto a range of unsolved moral problems (notably liquor drinking, capital punishment, and the oppression of women), thereby deflecting attention from the plight of Southern Unionists during Redemption.

By the early 1870s those radical leaders who might have been able to redirect the rusting antislavery artillery had surrendered their positions of power. Grinnell defected to the Liberals. Edward Russell retired temporarily as editor of the *Davenport Gazette.* John Teesdale and William Penn Clarke removed to Washington, D.C., to sing the praises of Senator Harlan. Into the breach stepped men who had little interest in the fate of Southern blacks. George Tichenor became Republican party chairman in 1868. A year later the Keokuk War Democrat William Worth Belknap was appointed secretary of war by President Grant. He quickly established himself as an influential figure in Iowa's Republican organization, his reputation undiminished by his refusal to recommend federal military intervention against the White Leagues in strife-torn Mississippi.[59] Equally harmful to the cause of equality was Judge George G. Wright's election to the U.S. Senate in 1870. A conservative who had recently advocated separate-but-equal education for blacks, Wright went to Washington a committed foe of the kind of civil rights legislation championed by Charles Sumner.[60] Like Belknap and Tichenor, his views on Reconstruction were by no means incompatible with those of the machine politicians who came to dominate the state in the last quarter of the nineteenth century.

Rampant factionalism did much to deflect attention away from Reconstruction, although the Southern question was not entirely unrelated to the power struggle that was now taking place within the state Republican organization. The decision of James W. Grimes to resign as U.S. senator after a second attack of paralysis in 1869 left his wing of the party in the hands of Congressmen James F. Wilson and William B. Allison, young, ambitious Republicans who had become close allies of the anti-Kasson leaders (principally Dodge, Tichenor, and Palmer) in the state's troubled fifth district. In April of that year Wilson informed General Dodge that Allison should run for the vacant Senate seat in the following year. "I don't think we ought to send an inexperienced man to succeed Grimes," he wrote.[61] By "inexperienced man," Wilson meant someone who could not be relied upon to further the private business interests of the incipient ring. Dodge, Allison, and he were all heavily involved in promoting western railroad development, particularly the Union Pacific project in which they held a sizable amount of stock. Judge Wright, who defeated Allison for the senatorship in January 1871, was no opponent of corporate capitalism. However, he was not a creature of the ring, and therefore Dodge and his friends redoubled their efforts to control the politics of the state.

During the course of 1871 the Dodge men began to move inexorably upon the works of Senator James Harlan.[62] They were aided, clandestinely at first, by the young editor of the Des Moines *Iowa State Register,* James S. Clarkson. Clarkson, the son of a prominent Iowa Republican, had earned the gratitude of Palmer and Wright by supporting their attempts to get to

Washington.[63] Now he became a key member of the ring by supporting its campaign to install Dodge's wartime colleague Cyrus Clay Carpenter as governor. In June this likeable Fort Dodge politician received the Republican gubernatorial nomination ahead of the outspoken radical and committed Harlanite, Henry O'Connor. Although Carpenter was thought by many to have been a neutral candidate, it is clear that the ring regarded him as something of a puppet.[64]

Well before Carpenter's election in October, Iowa's grand political showdown was underway. The prize was Harlan's U.S. Senate seat to be filled by the legislature in January 1872; the main protagonists: Harlan himself and Congressman William B. Allison. Although the senatorial fight had everything to do with power and very little with ideology, several issues played a part in what soon became the most bitter political campaign in the state's short history.

As the contest got underway, it rapidly became clear that Harlan's strategy was to assail Allison as a covert Liberal and opponent of evangelical forces in the state.[65] The Dubuque congressman was well placed to enlist reformist support because of his laissez-faire inclinations (which he may have inherited from Grimes). However, his friends insisted that he was a loyal Republican and counterattacked strongly by branding Harlan as a corruptionist. Particularly damaging to the Harlan cause were detailed reports about his shady activities as secretary of the interior. Some of these, published to the senator's chagrin in the *State Register* in December, were written by Fitz Henry Warren's longtime ally Hawkins Taylor. Seeking revenge on Harlan for failing to support Warren's efforts to secure the vacant short-term Senate place in 1866, Taylor alleged that the former cabinet member had lined his own pocket with large sums of money appropriated by Congress to feed starving Cherokee Indians.[66] Although Harlan dismissed his opponents as a ring of "sinister second or third rate men," the Allison campaign was both well orchestrated and ultimately successful in its design to besmirch the character of the incumbent senator.[67] On the night of 10 January 1872 the Republican legislative caucus gathered in Des Moines to decide the contest. The second formal ballot gave Allison victory by a majority of twenty-three over his opponent.[68] This left the state in the hands of a machine soon to be labeled the Des Moines Regency. Harlan's name was still being mentioned for high office until the end of the century, but by then his influence had long gone. The spoils belonged to Dodge, Allison, Wilson, Kirkwood, and Clarkson. When Allison died in 1908, he was still in possession of the Senate place he had snatched from Harlan thirty-six years previously.

Although the Regency leaders had played their part in the destruction of slavery, they were essentially pragmatic, business-orientated Republicans whose allegiance to consensus politics rendered them intensely suspicious of moralistic ideologues like Harlan's ambitious disciple and fellow Methodist James Baird Weaver. Under their control it was unlikely that the party would ever be ruled for long by the heart rather than the head.

The ease with which those uninterested in equal rights penetrated the upper echelons of Iowa's Republican organization should not be allowed to disguise the fact that the residue of the old abolitionist leaven continued to influence party policy after 1868. In that year the state supreme court ruled that black children could not be excluded from white schools because of their color.[69] Five years later the same tribunal struck at segregated transportation facilities by deciding that a mulatto woman had been unlawfully barred from eating at the same table as white passengers on a Mississippi River steamboat. "The doctrines of natural law and of christianity," ruled Chief Justice Joseph Beck, "forbid that rights be denied on the grounds of race or color."[70]

That slavery and institutional racism had withered so quickly under the fixed gaze of Republicanism was partly a tribute to the strength of evangelical influence within the anti-Southern coalition. Notwithstanding their perfectionist zeal, however, enlightened Northern Protestants could not entirely liberate themselves from the prejudices of the age. Justice Beck may have dealt segregation a powerful blow, but he undermined his case when he opined that in demanding recognition of her rights the mulatto plaintiff had "exhibited evidence of the Anglo-Saxon blood that flows in her veins." Much of the Christian humanitarian's sympathy for blacks—at home and in the South—was born of a sentimental feeling of kinship for the oppressed.[71] It was an attitude of mind encapsulated in the use of the term *darkies* by several radicals, including Edward Russell and Hiram Price.[72] Heavily imbued with the Victorian emphasis on individual self-improvement, Protestant paternalism was not ideally equipped to deal with the problems confronting American blacks during Reconstruction.

Other forces were at work sapping Republican resistance to Southern counterrevolution. Two of them in particular, a reaction to the centralizing tendencies of the war and a growing awareness of corruption within the party ranks, contributed toward the maturation of the Liberal revolt midway through Grant's first term.

The first western Republicans based much of their opposition to the Pierce and Buchanan administrations on the notion that well-defined areas of activity existed for state and federal governments. While their particularist stance was necessitated partly by Washington's perceived attempts to nationalize slavery, many of these men (ex-Whigs as well as former Democrats) were genuinely committed to the doctrine of state sovereignty and, though they agreed to abandon constitutional restraints for the sake of a Northern military victory, moved quickly to reassert the primacy of the antebellum polity after Appomattox. Naturally their enthusiasm was tempered by news of attacks on Southern Unionists and the need to prevent a Confederate resurgence, but by the end of the 1860s, the customary arguments against amnesty and readmission were beginning to wear thin.

Respect for state sovereignty ran deep in mid–nineteenth-century Iowa. In March 1869 Senator Thomas A. Hendricks, an Indiana Democrat, moved to strike out from an appropriation bill a provision for funding a federal department of education. Washington, he said, had no right to interfere with the educational interests of the states.[73] A recuperative James W. Grimes agreed. Iowans, he asserted, had built up their own public school system and imbibed "quite as much as I think we shall be apt to learn by an annual report from the Commissioner of Education located here at the capital of the nation, and at much less expense to ourselves."[74]

Justice Samuel F. Miller shared many of Grimes's fears about the growth of federal power. There were, it is true, differences between the opinions of the two antislavery Whigs. Whereas Grimes's retreat from Reconstruction was impelled partly by his growing predilection for laissez-faire thought and obsessive hatred of the radicals, Miller's belief that congressional policy portended "the eventual destruction of some of the best principles of our existing constitution" was balanced by his distrust of the South and continued commitment to Whig statism.[75] These latter emphases led the Keokuk judge to support most of the great national measures that required judicial interpretation during the 1860s. How ironic then that his opinion in the *Slaughter House Cases* of 1873 did far more damage to the cause of civil rights in America than Grimes's vote to acquit Andrew Johnson five years previously.

Miller's *Slaughter House* verdict was grounded partially in the antebellum Whig belief that state governments had a fundamental right to regulate their own societies and economies. In 1864, his second year at Washington, he had criticized the majority's decision to overturn an Iowa supreme court ruling in a case involving the legality of local tax aid to railroads. Miller's colleagues argued that Iowa's attempt to invalidate this form of economic investment impaired contracts entered into before the decision was handed down. The new associate justice denounced this reasoning as "a usurpation of the right, which belongs to the State courts, to decide as a finality upon the construction of State constitutions and State statutes."[76]

A decade later, when antimonopoly feeling at home was reaching its peak, Miller declared that the Fourteenth Amendment did not disencumber New Orleans butchers from a regulatory enactment of the general assembly. Although this statute appeared to be monopolistic, Miller's concern was to uphold the state's right to intervene in the local economy. "The power here exercised by the legislature of Louisiana is," he asserted, "in its essential nature one which has been up to the present period in the constitutional history of this country, always conceded to belong to the states."[77]

Had the Iowan left his argument here, *Slaughter House* would have constituted an unambiguous restatement of his dissent in the earlier railroad case and a powerful aid to Joseph Beck, a fellow Keokuk resident and ex-Whig, in his efforts to curb corporate influence west of the Mississippi. Miller, however, chose the occasion to use state sovereignty as a means of emasculating the Fourteenth Amendment—something he need not have done had his sole intention been to prevent federal encroachment on local police powers.[78] By distinguishing between state and national citizenship and ruling that the amendment protected only the *federal* rights of blacks, Miller undermined the entire fabric of congressional Reconstruction. Thus it must be assumed that the judge's fears concerning the erosion of the antebellum system had finally got the better of him. His decision left the freedmen at the mercy of local governments that were rapidly falling into the hands of white supremacists. "Even if Grant shall be elected for a second term," Miller had written privately in December 1870, "the carpet bag element of the South *must* subside as leaders."[79] *Slaughter House* helped to make this prediction a self-fulfilling prophecy.

Justice Miller's dismissive attitude toward Southern Unionists was consistent with the Republicans' traditional neglect of their colleagues south of the Mason-Dixon line. It also highlighted another important element in the waning of Reconstruction: corruption. Modern scholars have long recognized that reports of legislative fraud and black incompetence emanating from the South were grossly exaggerated, fueled more often than not by simple racism and a conservative dislike of taxation. Yet these stories were not entirely fictional. Individuals, white and black, did use radicalism as a smoke screen for their venal activities, especially in Louisiana and South Carolina, where the Republican regimes were undeniably corrupt.[80] Nor was carpetbag adventurism an invention of Southern white historians. In 1868 Grenville M. Dodge's army associate George Spencer, a former clerk of the Iowa house who had planned to make his fortune in Alabama after the war, was elected to the U.S. Senate by the Republican-controlled legislature in Montgomery. Two years later he could be found supporting a Democratic triumph in the state elections as part of his plan to monopolize the federal patronage for Alabama.[81] This cynical maneuver led Horace Greeley to blame Spencer for the Republican party's defeats in Alabama in 1870 and can thus be seen as having contributed directly to the process by which many Northern moderates became disillusioned with Reconstruction.[82]

Standards of political morality were no higher in the victorious section. Grant's administration was riven with corruption. So too were many Northern state governments. Iowa's was no exception. In 1866, for example, Governor Stone's private secretary was found guilty of having diverted swampland indemnity warrants worth $50,000 into his own funds.[83] Six years later, State Treasurer Samuel A. Rankin admitted stealing money belonging to Iowa's agricultural college.[84] Local politicians were heavily involved in a variety of dubious business activities: not only Harlan, whose peculations at Washington were public knowledge by 1871, but also Dodge, Wilson, and Allison (soon to be embroiled in the infamous Credit Mobilier scandal), and Secretary of War Belknap. Revelations of graft within and beyond the confines of the state helped to sap the Republican commitment to Reconstruction. Tales of carpetbag corruption and black misrule fed off Northern racism and reduced the party's opposition to a general amnesty for former rebels. Heightened public awareness of malfeasance at Des Moines and Washington intensified the reaction against machine politics and strengthened the case for a reform of the Republican organization.

The one man who might have made Liberalism a credible force in Iowa politics was James W. Grimes. In spite of suffering a second stroke in the summer of 1869, he had recovered sufficiently to tour extensively in Germany, Italy, and Great Britain. In London he took pleasure in writing to the London *Times* to deplore Charles Sumner's Anglophobe stance in the U.S. Senate.[85] He found Berlin "one of the very finest cities in Europe" and was impressed by the strength and discipline of the Prussian army. "I am filled with admiration of the German people," he reported in May 1870. "Such industry, such order, such sobriety, such neatness, such cultivation of everything that is beautiful and aesthetic, such schools, such freedom from poverty and misery is to be found nowhere else in the world."[86] If Prussia resembled the Whig paradise Grimes had once hoped to make of Iowa, he did not say so. On the contrary, his experiences during the Civil War and Reconstruction had helped to make him a committed foe of interventionist government. He was certainly no friend of radicalism, the nearest thing postbellum America had to Prussian statism. Glad that he was no longer active in political life, he told his fellow townsman Charles Mason: "[N]o man could be more happy to get into the Senate than I was to get out of it, after the inroad of the carpet-bag knights of the South."[87] If only the Democrats were to make "wise nominations," opined Grimes, "the republicans will be overthrown, and ought to be."[88]

Mason himself was again a key player on the Iowa political stage, for during 1871 he played a major role in redirecting his party's policy along the lines of the so-called New Departure.[89] Advocated first by Southern Democrats and then taken up by former midwestern Copperheads, the New Departure represented an attempt by old-line Democrats to regain the political initiative. This meant accommodating the party to the Reconstruction amendments and then formulating new issues with which to galvanize the electorate. In spite of being a prominent railroad man, Mason was keen to take advantage of grass-roots suspicion of monopoly capitalism and centralized power. He also realized that it was vital for men of his stamp to cooperate with dissident Liberals who were equally concerned with the dangers of government centralization. On 9 February 1871 the virulently racist Copperhead wrote to Grimes suggesting that he (Grimes) become a fusion candidate for governor. His hope, he told the exiled Iowan, was to effect a political organization on the following lines: universal amnesty for ex-Confederates, full recognition of states' rights, downward tariff revision, an end to the high premiums currently paid on U.S. bonds, the use of greenbacks rather than National Bank currency, and a general assault on "the worse than feudal system" then filling the country with "lordly corporations" and "poverty stricken vassals."[90]

Grimes, however, did not return home to Burlington until September and Mason was left to run against Cyrus Clay Carpenter himself. A crushing defeat ensued; one that was wholly predictable in the light of Mason's less-than-patriotic career during the Civil War. But by November both he and Grimes were working together to promote the aims of the reformers. The ex-governor was confident of electing Lyman Trumbull, one of the seven Republican senators who had voted against Andrew Johnson's impeachment, as president.[91] Yet the precise role Grimes would have taken in the 1872 election is uncertain. For on 7 February of that year he died of heart disease in Burlington at the age of fifty-five.[92]

The death of James Grimes signaled the premature demise of the state's Liberal movement. The mantle of reform passed into the hands of Fitz Henry Warren and Josiah B. Grinnell, powerful Republicans in their time, but men whose careers had been thwarted by others and whose defection from the party left them open to the charge of office seeking. In April these two former Whigs were prominent members of the modest gathering of Liberals that met in Davenport to elect delegates to the new party's national convention.[93] Subsequently Grinnell was present at Cincinnati where the reformers eventually nominated his longtime acquaintance Horace Greeley for president. A committed protectionist, temperance man, and original Republican, Greeley was far from popular in Democratic circles. However, their determination to defeat Grant meant that the Democrats had little choice but to endorse the New York editor's nomination.

On 5 May Fitz Henry Warren called at Mason's home in Burlington to propose a complete fusion of the elements hostile to the Grant administration.[94] The old Jacksonian leader welcomed this suggestion and traveled to Baltimore in July to lobby successfully for Greeley at the national Democratic convention. In August the two groups came together at Des Moines to draw up a ticket for the forthcoming state and congressional elections. Although fusion was symbolized by Copperhead Dennis A. Mahoney's overnight stay with Grinnell on the way to the capital (he slept in the same bed used by John Brown in 1858), the weakness of the reform movement in Iowa ensured that Democrats secured the lion's share of the nominations.[95]

As the campaign began in earnest, there were distinct signs of unease in the Republican camp. James F. Wilson bemoaned President Grant's fondness for the company of rich capitalists. "As the case stands today we are whipped," he told Dodge on 3 August.[96] Such pessimism was unwarranted. Wartime memories were still live enough to permit the Republicans to vaunt their past achievements to good effect. The preamble to their state platform recalled how the party had crushed "a gigantic rebellion," liberated four million human beings from bondage, and produced "a condition of individual and national prosperity heretofore unequalled." Resolutions affixed thereto gave notice that the Republican leadership took seriously the threat posed by the New Departure: one of them denounced preferential treatment for corporations; another opposed further land-grant aid to railroads.[97]

Persistent sectionalism was the key to the Republicans' easy triumph in November. Clarkson's *State Register* had defined Greeleyism as "an attempted diminution of the moral responsibility and guilt of the South for the rebellion," and it is clear from the election results that the vast majority of voters agreed.[98] With Greeley unable to shake off the stigma of his alliance with the Democrats, Grant carried the state (as he did the country) with ease. He won over two-thirds of the popular vote and lost heavily in only two counties: staunchly Democratic Dubuque and liberal Scott (where the influence of antiprohibition Germans may have been decisive).[99] The Republicans also triumphed comfortably in virtually every state and congressional race. Although the turnout in the presidential contest was well down (79 percent compared with 97.7 percent in 1868), this reflected a national trend and was probably due as much to Republican complacency as it was to apathy.[100] Certainly Charles Mason did not regard it as a crumb of comfort. "Am very despondent about the future of the republic," he noted in his diary on 9 November, "& am of the opinion that there is little hope short of a violent revolution which I think I see in the future."[101]

The late 1860s and early 1870s were transitional ones for the United States. Together with Southern intransigence and presidential obstructionism, wartime imperatives enabled Republicans not only to survive the postbellum challenge of the Democrats but also to persevere with their basically moderate plan of Reconstruction. While black suffrage, the party's major achievement at home and at large, might well have been enacted without the aid of unrepentant Confederates, it is doubtful whether Iowa's factionalized Republican organization could have maintained its impressive political hegemony without substantial reliance on past events. Yet the Liberal revolt of 1872, vapid though it was, clearly indicated that some Northerners were ready to question the sectional basis of American politics. The growing desire for peace and reconciliation was just one of several factors beginning to erode the Reconstruction consensus of 1866–67. Racism, war weariness, corruption, laissez-faire, and fears of overcentralization also played a role in the Republicans' gradual retreat from their original determination to remake the backward South in the image of the progressive North. However, as the architects of the New Departure Democracy were clearly aware, it was the reemerging primacy of economic issues that posed the gravest threat to Republican domination of the third party system. If Charles Mason had known that a damaging international depression was just around the corner, he might not have been quite so gloomy about the future.

11
The Railroad Question during the 1870s

s the Northern economy overheated in the aftermath of the war, Iowa Republicans struggled to confront the challenge posed by an aggressive Democracy eager to turn popular grievances against monopoly capitalism into an all-out revolt against greedy eastern financiers and manufacturers. Government bondholders, national banks, and the protective tariff were frequent targets for Democratic abuse, but as the most conspicuous symbol of the new industrialism in Iowa, it was the railroad corporation that once again became the focal point of political debate. While economic issues were not the only source of interparty competition during the 1870s—renewed evangelical calls for an effective prohibitory liquor law also proved significant in this respect—the overriding problems of the day were generated by the iron horse's continued penetration of the countryside.

Iowa prospered during the middle and late 1860s. Immigration picked up steadily after the war. By the end of the decade the population had increased to 1.2 million, giving rise to predictions that the state would soon become one of the most important in the Union.[1] Governor Samuel F. Merrill calculated that with the population density of Massachusetts, Iowa would contain 6.5 million inhabitants.[2] James Harlan foresaw a population greater than 10 million.[3] Demographic growth rates in the northwestern counties were spectacularly high as the wetlands of that region came under the plough for the first time.[4] Urbanization too proceeded apace. The federal census of 1870 listed six cities with populations over 10,000 (including the rapidly growing capital, Des Moines, now fourth in size behind Dubuque, Davenport, and Burlington), nineteen smaller but scarcely less ambitious towns such as Clinton and Cedar Rapids, and forty-four villages with between 1,000 and 2,500 inhabitants.[5]

Commercial farming was still the mainstay of the economy. Sixty-one percent of working Iowans were engaged in agricultural occupations, two-thirds of them farmers, the rest laborers.[6] Most of these people had benefited from the higher crop prices and farm wages induced by wartime demand and rural labor shortages. By 1870 Iowa was the second largest corn producer in the country, an impressive achievement in view of the fact that white settlement of the trans-Mississippi region had only begun forty years previously.[7] The cash value of farms in the state was well above the regional average, clearly indicative of the prosperity that soil fertility and the market had brought to the state.[8]

With the agricultural sector booming and America's people continuing to move westwards, there was every reason to suppose that the star of empire would eventually come to rest over the northwestern states. In October 1869 Iowa sent delegates to the National Capital Removal Convention in St. Louis. That body passed resolutions urging Congress to appoint commissioners to select a convenient site for the capital in the Mississippi Valley.[9] Governor Merrill advised the Des Moines legislature to accept these proposals, adding pointedly that the heart of the United States would soon be found close to the southeast corner of Iowa.[10]

Although Republican support for banks and infrastructural development had helped to lay the foundations for these dreams of grandeur, it had not yet produced the diversified economy looked upon by Whigs as essential to the maintenance of a healthy society. In 1870 the value of agricultural productions was over two and a half times as large as that for manufactured goods. In neighboring Illinois the ratio was nearly 1:1.[11] Most Iowa industry, moreover, involved the processing of farm products. Small-scale grist mills, lumber mills, distilleries, and pork-packing plants predominated. Machine shops had sprung up in some of the more-urbanized counties to serve the railroads, but the old Whig dream of a domestic textile industry had failed to materialize.

Several factors account for the weakness of Iowa's industrial base in the postbellum era. One of them was the sheer strength of manufacturing industry outside of the state. New England and the mid-Atlantic states were already highly industrialized in comparison with the trans-Mississippi West and were thus well placed to dominate the American market for finished goods. Unlike neighboring Illinois or Missouri, Iowa had no major city that could set itself up as a rival commercial-industrial center to Pittsburgh or New York. Dubuque and Davenport may have continued to grow during the 1860s but, as local merchants were quick to realize, they were rapidly becoming tributaries of Chicago.

There were also political and cultural reasons for the laggard progress of Iowa's manufacturing sector. Many farmers, particularly former Jacksonians, possessed an ingrained suspicion of industrial civilization. Even though they were now deeply enmeshed in the market, farm ownership remained in their eyes the only sure way of securing independence. Factory labor, on the other hand, bore the stigma of drudgery and dependence. So strong were these sentiments among the grass roots that when Iowa's free-soil Whigs came to power in 1854 they did not take immediate steps to build New England on the banks of the Cedar River. The Republican-controlled legislatures of the antebellum years failed to give specific encouragement to manufacturing industry. In early 1860 Republicans in the state senate did vote unanimously to instruct the ways and means committee "to enquire into the expediency of exempting machinery and other articles used in manufacturing, from taxation."[12] Nothing came of the resolution, however, almost certainly because the popular mood was inimical to "class" legislation and Republican leaders were wary of stirring up dissent among ex-Democrats in the party who had bought their economic baggage with them. As their largely rhetorical abuse of the railroads during the late 1850s revealed, Iowa Republicans were ambivalent allies of eastern capitalists.

Occasionally the state's ruling party did adopt a proindustrial stance on the tariff. Prior to the Civil War many local Republicans made no secret of their support for protection.[13] But while some of them, particularly ex-Whigs like William Penn Clarke and Josiah B. Grinnell, undoubtedly hoped that higher tariffs would help to build up home industries within Iowa, most championed protection on the patriotic grounds that it was necessary in order to prevent cheap foreign imports from undermining national manufactures and wages.[14] Although the state's congressional delegation voted for the higher Morrill Tariff of 1861, it soon became clear that sentiment in the party (particularly on the more liberal Grimes wing) was decidedly lukewarm on this issue.[15] As the Democrats repeatedly observed, protection aided existing manufacturers in the Northeast at the expense of western consumers.

If this was one of the prices to be paid for a political alliance with the industrial states, Iowa Republicans seemed prepared to pay it until the end of the Civil War. However, cognizant of Democratic criticisms and without a primary manufacturing constituency of their own, Grimes, Allison, Kasson, and others began to abandon protection during the late 1860s in favor of a more laissez-faire approach to economic problems.[16] In 1870 the state party modified its traditional stance on this question by declaring that any protective tariff "should be so adjusted as not to become prejudicial to the industrial interests of any class or sections of the country."[17] Just in case farmers were not convinced of their loyalty, the Republicans went one step further the following year by publicly recognizing agriculture's "pre-eminent claims for support, by legislation, or otherwise, as may be necessary to secure full development of our highly-favored State."[18]

The opposition's reluctance to come out fighting on the economy like the old Whig party made it even more difficult for Iowa Democrats to regain their lost prestige after Appomattox. There was, however, one area in which the Republicans had already proved vulnerable: railroad promotion. In 1858 Governor Ralph P. Lowe had endangered his party's hegemony by publicly endorsing state aid to railroad corporations. Twelve years later leading Democrats discerned a ground swell of popular antimonopoly feeling and began to ponder the feasibility of another assault on the enemy's Achilles' heel. On 12 November 1870 Charles Mason conferred with ex-Senator Augustus C. Dodge on the pros and cons of an anticorporate strategy. "He agrees with me in the policy of openly assailing railroad companies &c.," noted Mason after the meeting.[19] The problem was how to turn the greatest technological achievement of the age into the nemesis of a pragmatic ruling party still riding high on the back of past achievements.

There is no denying that Iowa Republicans were vulnerable on the railroad question. The close ties that existed between party leaders and eastern capitalists grew stronger during the 1860s. Harlan did the bidding of the Union Pacific. So did General Grenville M. Dodge, the transcontinental road's chief engineer after 1866.[20] Congressman William B. Allison was employed as an agent of the Dubuque & Sioux City, and the Burlington & Missouri relied heavily on James W. Grimes and James F. Wilson. Wartime inflation enabled Grimes to pay off his embarrassing debts, but circumspectly he continued to promote the Burlington & Missouri's interests in Washington.[21] In 1862 he advised James F. Joy to "select the right agents" to represent it at Des Moines. Were the legislature to meet at once, wrote Grimes, "any man of ordinary sagacity, of insight into the characters & motives of men & shrewdness in their management, could, in one week, secure just such legislation as you desire." The truth was, he continued, that "the state is at the mercy of the railroad companies. If they combine . . . they can control the legislation of the state."[22] After Appomattox the senator, a heavy investor in the stock of the Burlington road, labored to prevent the company from being prosecuted for nonpayment of federal taxes and to facilitate track construction in Iowa and Nebraska.[23] "Your extension bill has passed the Senate & Wilson says he will look after it in the House of Rep.," read a typical note to Joy in January 1866.[24]

Shortly before Grant's reelection in November 1872 the *New York Sun* broke the news of the Credit Mobilier affair. This, the most notorious scandal of the day, laid bare the incestuous nature of the Republicans' business links. Six Iowans were implicated. Two U.S. representatives,

Wilson and Allison, were found to have accepted gifts of tainted stock at a time when, during the winter of 1867–68, there was intense pressure on Congress to regulate Union Pacific rates. Wilson and Allison testified that they had subsequently returned their shares in the Credit Mobilier, a Pennsylvania corporation used by the Union Pacific as its private construction company, but not before receiving substantial dividends on them.[25] Both men had voted on the rate regulation motions, thereby infringing House Rule 29, which prohibited members from acting on measures in which they were personally involved.[26] Their friend Grenville M. Dodge, the road's postbellum chief engineer, was named several times in official reports. As well as holding Credit Mobilier stock, Dodge had been paid handsomely by the parent company for helping to steer important legislation through Congress. Reluctant to face the music, the general ignored a subpoena to attend the investigatory hearings and fled to St. Louis.[27]

Both of Iowa's Civil War senators had their names dragged into the affair. It was revealed that the late James Grimes had purchased 380 shares of Credit Mobilier stock after Oakes Ames offered to guarantee the principal and an interest rate of 10 percent.[28] Ames, a Boston financier, had saved the Union Pacific from collapse in 1865 and was looking to secure the support of respected public figures to enhance the company's image for investment purposes. In Grimes's defense, it should be emphasized not only that his involvement with the Credit Mobilier predated Ames's liberal distribution of stock during the regulation controversy but also that he was willing to disclose his interest in the Pacific road.[29]

There were no such mitigating circumstances in James Harlan's case. Thomas Durant, Ames's bitter rival on the Union Pacific board, testified that he had contributed $10,000 to the secretary of the interior's campaign for reelection to the U.S. Senate in late 1865.[30] Harlan admitted receiving the money but protested lamely that it was a purely personal donation.[31] So unconvinced were Mark Twain and Charles Dudley Warner that they chose to satirize Harlan as the corrupt and sanctimonious Methodist politician Reverend Orson Balaam in their classic indictment of the postwar era, *The Gilded Age: A Tale of Today,* published in 1873.[32]

A sixth Iowan escaped the full glare of publicity. In August 1864 H.M. Hoxie, then chairman of the Republican state central committee and a key member of the Dodge clique, signed a $50,000-per-mile deal with Thomas Durant to build the first section of the Union Pacific west of Omaha.[33] The arrangement was a sham because Hoxie had no engineering skills to recommend him, only his friendship with Dodge and a hankering to make money.[34] The former innkeeper and underground railroad operator was merely a cipher in Durant's plan to minimize his financial risks. By contracting with an agent on behalf of Credit Mobilier stockholders, Durant was able to ensure that the latter came into possession of thousands of Union Pacific shares and untold amounts of cash and securities. Soon afterwards Hoxie abandoned politics and became an employee of Durant.[35] By the end of 1872, when the scandal finally broke, he was working for the International Railroad Company in Texas. To the investigating committees he was just a name—"a person of little pecuniary responsibility."[36] Even George W. McCrary, the respected Keokuk Republican whose unpenetrating questions allowed Allison and Wilson to escape censure, had forgotten Hoxie's identity. It was all very convenient.

The men who found themselves in the dock during the early weeks of 1873 defended their past actions by arguing that they deserved praise not blame for helping to build the Union Pacific. They emphasized the impressive scale of the project, the enormous risks assumed by investors, the speed with which the tracks had been laid, and the tremendous social, economic, and military benefits the road had brought to the country. For Iowans, always in the vanguard of the transcontinental railroad movement, these were not empty claims. The Davenport congressman Hiram Price opined that the Union Pacific made the Appian Way look like a "cow path" and praised those "who have the money, the energy, and the nerve to prosecute an enterprise like this such as the world, up to the present time, has never seen, and never would see but for such men."[37]

Rhetoric like this was by no means unpopular during the middle decades of the nineteenth century, for most Iowans shared Price's faith in the railroad as a developmental tool. By 1870 all four of the original land-grant roads had reached the Missouri River, and no major urban center was without an iron link to the urban markets of the East. Over five thousand miles of track were built in the state in the decade and a half after the Civil War, giving Iowa more railroad mileage than Italy.[38] This prodigious feat testified to the citizenry's faith in the iron horse as a prime solution to the problems confronting a developing economy. Modern transportation facilities, it was argued by politicians, businessmen, and farmers alike, were an essential precondition for the various panaceas advanced to reduce Iowa's dependent status within the Union: for example, the building up of home manufactures and the exploitation of extensive coal deposits in the Des Moines valley. Farmers in the western counties (still largely deprived of railroad links with the market) joined civic-minded and probusiness politicians in demanding a rapid extension of the existing railroad network.

As the events of the late 1850s had revealed, however, the public attitude to the new technology was fundamentally ambivalent. Iowans wanted economic progress, but having impulsively authorized large-scale investment in corporate stock, they were not always willing to pay the higher taxes that ensued, nor were they ready for the clandestine attempts of railroad officers to influence public policy through lobbying, bribery, and the liberal distribution of travel passes. Legal conflicts between railroads and numerous social entities undermined complacent talk of mutual interests and increased the people's latent suspicion of monopoly and unbridled corporate power. After the bridging of the Mississippi, mercantile interests in Dubuque, Davenport, Burlington, and Clinton became disillusioned with the railroads as cheap through-rates encouraged farmers to send their produce direct to Chicago. By the close of the Civil War Illinois's bustling lakeside metropolis had established a strong hold over the commerce of eastern Iowa.[39] Far from promoting autarky and rescuing the state from eastern industrialists, the new technology showed every sign of delivering the prairies into the hands of an alternative western master.

Republican railroad policy in Iowa during the 1860s reflected a need to balance various developmental goals, political demands, and internal ideological tensions. For the most part growth-orientated measures tended to predominate over those likely to discourage capital investment in the local infrastructure. It is true that in June 1862 the state supreme court reversed its previous rulings and declared that the legislature had no legal authority to authorize municipalities to issue bonds for railroad construction.[40] But against this must be set the assembly's refusal to subject private corporations to the same rates of taxation as individuals or to exercise its uncertain right to regulate freight and passenger tariffs. Chicago's wartime grip on the trade of eastern Iowa, however, increased the pressure for legislative control of railroad tariffs in 1865–66. A maximum rate bill was only narrowly defeated in the senate that winter. Although their colleagues in the house had divided fifty-four to eighteen in favor of regulation, 45 percent of Republican senators voted to table a motion to take up a similar measure. Many of them were probably influenced by Attorney General Frederick Bissell's prior opinion that charter restrictions prevented rate fixing.[41] This counsel caused much unrest in the party's ranks. "I can in no just sense be caled anything but a RR man," wrote one troubled senator,

> that is I am exceeding anxious to have all the RRoads completed through the State and as many new ones as we can get untill every commercial want of our towns [is] fully suplied. I will not interpose any obstacle to their progress but will render them every proper assistance but if the doctrines now promulgated by the atorney General be even partially true it is of the

most vital importance to our Country that we arest their assumptions before they over shaddow all interest we hold dear in the State and concentrate all material and political Power.[42]

In spite of heavy business involvement in the upper echelons of the Republican organization, the action of the party's representatives in both chambers of the 1866 legislature revealed a continued responsiveness to interest-group pressure (in this instance to regulatory demands from hard-hit merchants in the river cities) and a genuine determination to prevent arrogant railroad corporations from eroding the rights of the state. So frustrated were some company officials at the assembly's willingness to interfere with the natural laws of trade that they began to look to Congress for redress.[43]

With northwestern Iowa eager for more railroads and eastern municipalities and merchants equally insistent on greater regulation, Republican politicians were on the horns of a very real dilemma. Postwar prosperity enabled them to skirt the problem by merely asserting the government's right to regulate the corporations, but by 1871 there was an urgent need to find a concrete solution to the railroad question.[44] Local farmers were now beginning to experience the effects of an uneven agricultural depression marked by falling crop prices and rising farm costs, land values, and tenancy. The railroads did little to alleviate the situation. Pooling and discriminatory freight charges infuriated agrarians and merchants alike and made a mockery of the familiar argument that competition (a euphemism for more railroads) would help to boost shrinking profit margins. As they had been in the past, pampered corporations became scapegoats for the ills afflicting the farming community—their seemingly arbitrary rates a focal point for antimonopoly dissent.

The Republican reaction was predictably ambivalent. In Congress Senators Harlan and James B. Howell criticized federal land-grant policy, much to the disgust of some of their western colleagues who accused them of switching horses in midstream. Occasionally their speeches were tinged with anticorporate rhetoric.[45] At home the legislators subjected railroads to heavier taxation and barred further municipal aid.[46] Opposition in the state senate, however, again prevented the enactment of a maximum rate bill, while Governors Merrill and Carpenter cautioned against hostile treatment of beneficent corporations.[47] What finally threw the Republicans into the antimonopoly camp were the events of 1872–73: the Credit Mobilier revelations, the defalcation of the state treasurer Samuel Rankin, a season of rock-bottom farm prices, and the sudden rise of the Granger movement.

A central figure in the Republican response to these developments was Cyrus Clay Carpenter, the former pro-Grimes Whig who had been elected governor in 1871. General Dodge and George C. Tichenor assumed that their former army comrade would assist them in their senatorial fight against Harlan and promote the various railroad interests that they represented. Both men underestimated Carpenter's ability to act independently of the ring. Largely self-educated, devout, and imbued with a refreshing sense of his own limitations, "Honest Cy" proved unwilling to see his party converted into a corrupt vehicle for the advancement of corporate aims.

The most pressing problem facing the pious Methodist governor in the months after Grant's reelection in November 1872 was how to react to Oliver Kelly's popular farmers' movement, the Patrons of Husbandry. By May 1873 there were 1,507 granges in Iowa, far more than in any other state in the Union.[48] Although it was not a neo-Populist organization as one historian has suggested, the Grange embraced a wide range of opinion.[49] In Iowa the leadership was conservative, preoccupied with market forces and more concerned with eliminating the middleman from the farm economy than denigrating the achievements of the iron horse.[50] On the whole its policies reflected the thinking of progressive farmers like the Republican editor, William Duane Wilson, not the utopian visions of agrarian radicals. A minority of Grangers, however, eschewed the apolitical stance of their officers and called for third-party action to promote the cause of the putatively downtrodden farmer.[51] Such demands, couched as they often were in fierce antimonopoly verbiage, caused consternation among fainthearted Republicans. "I went through the Know Nothing times," a worried journalist told Carpenter, "& know how clannishly men run wild on such matters. The leaders who get on the top wave ride it until it spends its force. They are making Grangers every day & they now have nearly 60000 voters enrolled."[52]

If hysterical comparisons between farmers and Communards were unwarranted, fears of independent political action were born out in the spring of 1873 when a group of third-party men nominated the retiring master of the Iowa Grange to oppose Carpenter in the fall elections. The governor responded to the press of events by joining his local grange—a move that was partly an exercise in public relations and yet also a genuine indication of his own sympathy with the social aims of the movement.[53] Carpenter evinced his determination to treat the complex railroad problem seriously by initiating a correspondence with liberal Massachusetts reformers and reading with interest the arguments of Charles Francis Adams, Jr., in favor of state ownership.[54] In August the independents merged with Iowa's embattled Democrats, ready at last to put their anticorporate policies into action, to form the Anti-Monopoly party. Two months later Carpenter, depressed by what he called the year's "crooked politics," was reelected with a severely reduced majority.[55] If this was not alarming enough, the election results also revealed that the fusionists had managed to obtain parity in the house of representatives—the first time ever that Republicans had lost control of that chamber. Shaken, party leaders including James S. Clarkson demanded that their brethren in the legislature pass a stringent rate bill to allay public suspicions that they were in league with the corporations. If they did not do so, warned the *Iowa State Register,* "The Republican party in Iowa may be written of as dead, and its last platform will prove its epitaph."[56]

During the winter a committee of the State Grange drew up a mild regulatory bill providing for the establishment of a railroad commission to oversee rates and prevent discrimination between short- and long-haul journeys.[57] Similar bodies had already been set up in Illinois and other states. Because their powers were generally limited, they were viewed with some suspicion by radical Grangers. Carpenter ignored the committee's recommendations and on 23 January 1874 announced his support for a maximum rate law modified by a classification system based on earnings.[58] It was an appeal above the heads of the Grange leadership, tailor-made to satisfy the inchoate antimonopoly demands of farmers and merchants in the eastern portion of the state.

A majority of Republican senators took their cue and fought off attempts by Dodge's ally John Y. Stone to substitute a commission amendment for the statutory rate bill under discussion. Only a quarter of Stone's copartisans voted against the measure's final passage (see fig. 11.1). In the house, where farmer-legislators were present in unprecedented numbers, the only real watering-down efforts were led by J.M. Dixon, the overseer of the State Grange and the defeated Anti-Monopoly candidate for speaker. Dixon, a Liberal Republican apparently worried about the bill's impact on future capital investment in Iowa railroads, introduced a substitute dealing solely with passenger fares. It was rejected by the bipartisan, proregulation core of the chamber, which then proceeded to pass the measure with only minor amendments (see fig. 11.2). When Carpenter signed the bill on 23 March, he did so with grave reservations. "I have doubted as to whether the people could reap all the benefits from this that they expect," he confided in his diary, "but I hope for the best."[59] In spite of his fears, the worthy governor must have been consoled by the knowledge that Republicans had outmaneuvered the enemy to preserve their political primacy in Iowa.

The railroads responded to the law by raising interstate charges and pursuing their case against it through the federal courts. They also launched a coordinated campaign to discredit regulation, blaming it for the cessation of track construction, but wisely failing to mention that the latter was primarily a consequence of the international depression. "Capital is prudent, conservative and timid," James F. Wilson told a group of legislators in February 1876. "It will not voluntarily submit itself to the control of those who do not own it."[60] The former congressman had survived the Credit

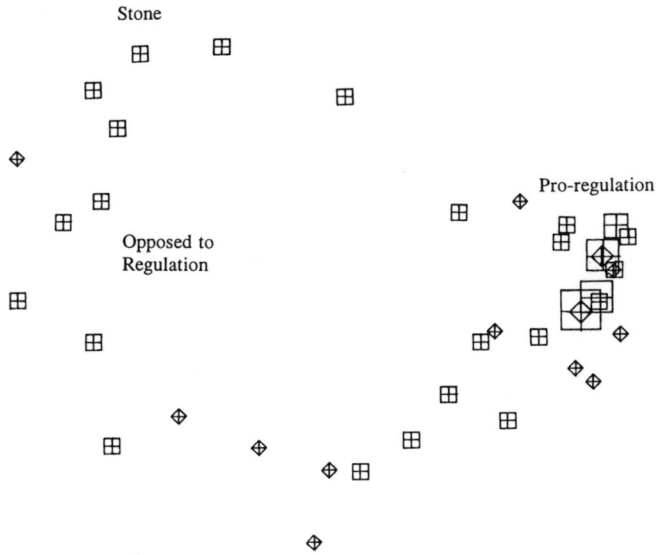

⊞ Republican

◆ Anti-Monopolist

MDS analysis (see Appendix); no. of motions = 15
SOURCE: *Ia. Sen. Jnl.* (1874), pp. 198, 203, 210–11, 214–15, 218–19, 292–95.

Fig. 11.1 Iowa Senate, 1874: Voting behavior on the Railroad Tariff Bill.

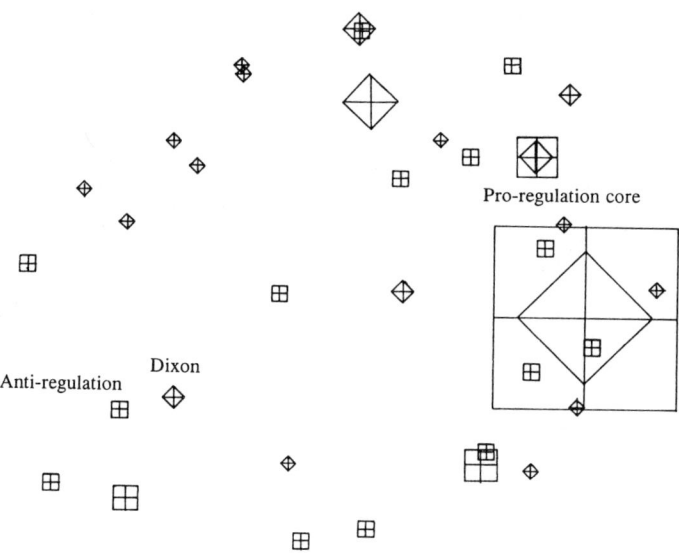

MDS analysis (see Appendix); no. of motions = 6
SOURCE: *Ia. Hse. Jnl.* (1874), pp. 346–47, 350–51, 402–4.

Fig. 11.2 Iowa House, 1874: Voting behavior on the Railroad Tariff Bill.

Mobilier scandal and was now lobbying on behalf of the Burlington & Missouri for repeal of the hated act. He would have secured that aim had not the Iowa house split three ways on the issue.

Differing regional objectives would appear to explain the configuration in fig. 11.3. Just over a third of delegates in the 1876 Iowa house supported a supervisory railroad commission bill designed to alleviate the burden of regulation on the corporations. Some of them hailed from counties along the Mississippi—a sign that the law had not brought unqualified benefits to the river merchants. Opposing the bill were two diametrically opposed groups, one of which refused to consent to any modification of the existing statute, and another that favored only minimal regulation. The former contained representatives from Dubuque, Muscatine, and the fiercely antimonopoly southeast. The laissez-faire bloc was dominated by men from western Iowa, where lack of market access was generally blamed for low growth. Together the two extremes united to defeat the commission bill, thus ensuring that Iowa remained the only midwestern state with a regulatory law on its statute books after 1876. Party affiliation played no role in its demise. All three groups contained roughly equal proportions of Republicans and Democrats. The index of likeness on its defeat was 95.5.[61]

When Governor Ralph P. Lowe failed to win renomination in 1859 because of his backing for state aid to local railroads, it may be significant that the sacrificial lamb went not to the slaughter but onto the Iowa supreme bench. For, if Morton Horwitz's thesis on the role of judges in promoting capitalist development in antebellum America can be extended into the Gilded Age, it is possible that apparent executive and legislative pragmatism on the railroad question merely veiled probusiness judicial activism.[62]

At the heart of Horwitz's interpretation of U.S. legal history is the notion that between 1780 and 1860, judges, not governors or assemblymen, took the lead in creating conditions favorable to economic development. Their main tool, he argues, was a redefinition of contract law by which the equitable eighteenth-century idea of fair exchange was transformed via "will" theory into a revolutionary "objective" conception of contract that fitted the needs of an aggressive commercial elite. Integral elements in this transformation were such water-rights cases as *Palmer* v. *Mulligan* (1805) in which a divided New York supreme court ruled that an upper riparian landowner could obstruct his neighbor's flow of water for mill purposes.[63] It is evident from this example that Horwitz owes (and surprisingly fails to acknowledge)

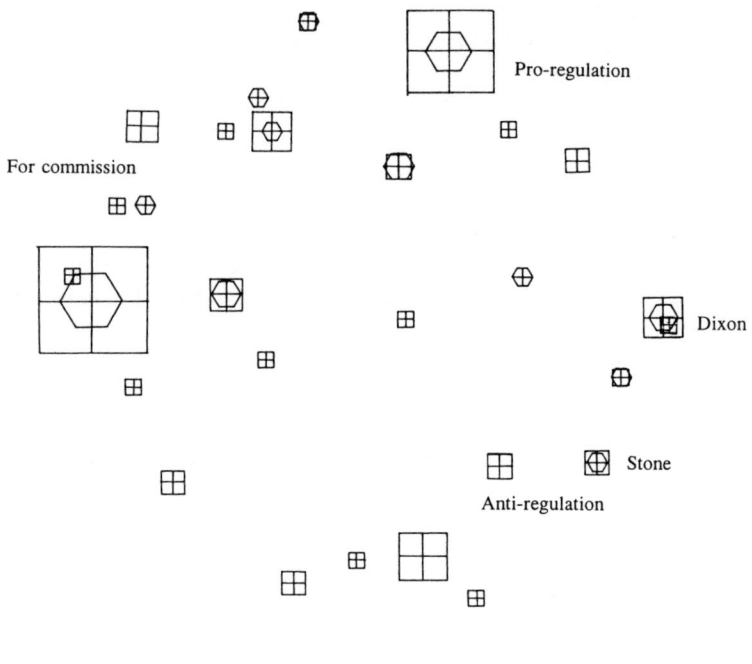

⊞ Republican

⊕ Democrat

MDS analysis (see Appendix); no. of motions = 5
SOURCE: *Ia. Hse. Jnl.* (1876), pp. 466, 475–76, 482, 531–32.

Fig. 11.3 Iowa House, 1876: Voting behavior on the Railroad Commission Bill.

a substantial debt to the pioneering work of James Willard Hurst. Hurst also contends that property was converted from a static to a creative institution by the expansion of contract.[64] What fundamentally divides the two scholars is the supposition that there was necessarily something sinister about capitalist development in the United States. In the words of one commentator: "For Horwitz, one feels, the Americans are divided into 'we' and 'they'; for Hurst, they are always 'we', and there is a strong sense that the community gained fairly distributed benefits from economic progress."[65] Both views are applicable to the early Iowa judiciary.

On 9 April 1856 Judge Norman W. Isbell overruled a decision of the Dubuque district court requiring a local railroad to fence its right-of-way. Pronounced the state supreme court justice in his summing up: "If verdicts of this character may be entailed upon railway companies, all along the lines of their roads, it requires no prophetic eye to see the discouraging effect they may have on such enterprises."[66] Given that most of Isbell's predecessors had already upheld the right of counties to assist in railroad construction in spite of a constitutional limitation on state indebtedness, it seems apparent that the higher echelons of the Iowa judiciary were reluctant to place restrictions on economic development.[67] Whether or not that wariness amounted to a conspiracy between the courts and commercial elites is a matter for debate, but evidence does exist to suggest that this may well have been the case.

Two Iowa judges warrant particularly close scrutiny. The first of these is Caleb Baldwin, the ambitious attorney who, with Dodge, Kasson, and Hoxie, was a key member of the acquisitive probusiness clique that quickly rose to power as the Des Moines Regency. After being elected to the supreme court in 1859 Baldwin was ideally placed to further the objectives of his colleagues. It does appear, however, that the Council Bluffs judge was not entirely comfortable in this position.[68] Early in 1861 Dodge asked him to put pressure on Chief Justice Lowe to decide in favor of the bondholders in a case involving the legality of local tax aid to railroads. His reply was that of a troubled man. "I would not dare to approach him in that way. I don't think it would suit him. And I do not desire to do such a thing. I think it is all wrong. I would do any thing I could to assist you except the one thing. I must not allow myself to be influenced nor would I do this."

It was a stout defense of judicial integrity, but one that was somewhat undermined by Baldwin's closing words, "I feel a deep interest in the welfare of our railroad interests, and will resign at any time I am in the way of their property."[69] In other words, as long as Dodge's eastern employers (principally Henry Farnam, president of the Mississippi & Missouri Railroad) were satisfied with his conduct, the judge would remain at his post. There is no direct proof that Baldwin ever molded a decision to suit corporate interests, but his later career as U.S. district attorney for Iowa casts further doubt on his earlier claims to independence. In March 1866 the federal employee was in Des Moines lobbying against the railroad tariff bill under discussion in the assembly. The house had ordered the measure to a third reading, he told Dodge: "It is a most infamous bill and if it became law and was enforced would stop all the roads in Iowa." Luckily, he added, "I think the Senate is all right."[70]

A second state supreme court justice similarly imbued with prorailroad sympathies was the Harvard-educated Des Moines lawyer Chester C. Cole.[71] Unlike Baldwin who was an original Republican, Cole's antebellum allegiance was to the Democracy. However, a publicly expressed conviction that tough actions were necessary to crush the Confederacy and perhaps a few private reflections on the partisan requirements for a successful judicial career in Iowa had made him a zealous Republican by the beginning of 1865. An astute readiness to cooperate with Dodge's friends brought him within the incipient Regency's sphere of influence. During the first half of 1867 he aided George C. Tichenor's efforts to split the rival Kasson faction in Polk County. Two years later he participated in an unsuccessful attempt to secure Dodge's appointment as U.S. secretary of war.[72]

Cole clearly expected some return on his political investment. Observing that Congress had recently passed a generous appropriation bill for the establishment of a post office building in Des Moines, he told Dodge in February 1867 that he wanted a place on any committee that might be set up to supervise the work. "To be entirely frank with you," he wrote, "my salary as Judge of Sup. Ct. does not support me & my family & I want something like above to help me out."[73] The impoverished jurist was subsequently confronted with charges of misappropriating funds belonging to the Iowa Soldiers' Orphans Home, but a Republican-dominated committee found no evidence to support them.[74]

Throughout his lengthy term of office on the supreme bench (1864–76) Cole, a director of the Iowa branch of the Union Pacific, revealed himself to be a true friend of the railroads.[75] He not only upheld the harsh common law doctrine of contributory negligence to the letter (thereby minimizing the sums paid out by the companies in damage assessment cases) but also, once he was convinced he had legislative backing, spearheaded judicial efforts to declare municipal bond issues constitutional.[76]

His most consistent stand was against local taxation of railroad property. As he indicated in a strongly worded dissent of 1874, he held Chief Justice John Marshall's *Dartmouth College* ruling to be decisive of the issue. The celebrated Virginia Federalist had maintained that private corporations were protected by the contract clause of the Constitution. Such reasoning was less than popular with antimonopoly voters after the war. Cole's dissent took this salient political fact into account by conceding the justice of the antimonopoly cause and then cleverly shifting the burden of guilt from private to public corporations. "Disguise it as we may," he opined,

> the practical effect of the Dartmouth College decision, is to exalt the rights of the few above those of the many. And it is doubtless true that, under the authority of that decision, more monopolies have been created and perpetuated, and more wrongs and outrages upon the people effectuated, than by any other single instrumentality in the government. Acknowledging the binding force of that decision . . . we have no purpose to deny or attempt to overrule it, yet, in full view of it and its damaging consequences, it well becomes us not to extend its doctrine of exemption from legislative authority to the numberless larger and lesser municipal corporations of the State, many of which have proved themselves very poor governmental agencies, and terribly exacting and bankrupting rulers.[77]

Here was a classic instance of populist rhetoric disguising the workings of contract and stare decisis as tools of developmental capitalism.

The judicial careers of Baldwin and Cole do much to support Horwitz's bleak interpretation of nineteenth-century American law. Both men were members of an opportunistic clique that was heavily involved in railroad construction, and neither of them was able to ignore that fact. Yet their very inability to transcend the political realities of their situation suggests one reason why the notion of a capitalist conspiracy should be treated with some caution. After 1857 Iowa supreme court judges were elected by the people for six-year terms. As a result the state's judiciary was constantly subject to democratic review. The effectiveness of that review was undoubtedly undermined by the use of legal jargon and the limited circulation of law reports. Nonetheless, accounts of major cases did appear sporadically in the press, thus giving the voters an opportunity to appraise the activities of the courts. Since most judges were successful partisan lawyers, they could hardly forget that, in the final analysis, they were representatives of a political organization. After Chief Justice Charles B. Lawrence of Illinois declared his state's railroad tariff law unconstitutional in 1873, he was not reelected.[78] The case was a notorious one for devotees of judicial independence, but Lawrence's removal from office was a clear sign that the demands of a mobilized electorate could not be taken lightly.

An analysis of 310 railroad cases decided in the Iowa supreme court during the first seven years of the 1870s indicates that there may have been a correlation between popular antimonopoly sentiment and judicial actions on the railroad question. From 1870 to 1872 the companies won 65.4 percent of all cases in which their interests were involved. The corresponding figure for the four subsequent years—those when antimonopoly feeling was at its peak—was 53.3 percent.

Equally significantly, the figures in table 11.1 appear to substantiate Hurst's conclusion that the judicial response to economic development in nineteenth-century America was pragmatic rather than conspiratorial. They certainly bear out his contention that the courts played an important role in creating favorable conditions for growth. The categories of cases in which the state supreme court seems to have been particularly well disposed toward railroads are those relating directly to track construction: real estate damages, investment, and taxation. The assertion of the right of eminent domain, for example, the ancient prerogative of the state to take private property for public use, was an essential precondition for the laying of rails across the prairies. The court acted positively to uphold that right (backed as it was by statute) and to limit the amount of damages incurred by the companies as a consequence of its operation.

Railroads won 61 percent of suits arising out of eminent domain proceedings, many of the decisions clearly reflecting the legislature's reluctance to hinder capital investment in the Iowa economy. Over 67 percent of cases relating to individual and community purchases of railroad stock were decided in favor of the private corporations. One of the most important of these verdicts was announced in October 1870 when the court, by a majority of three to one, upheld the general assembly's authority to enact a

Table 11.1. Analysis of railroad cases decided in the Iowa supreme court, 1870–76

Issue	N	W	L	O
Damages:				
Real estate (eminent domain)	59	36	19	4
Crops	10	4	6	0
Livestock	60	31	29	0
Personal injury:				
Employees	33	19	14	0
Passengers	13	5	6	2
Third parties	22	17	4	1
Investment in railroads	43	29	13	1
Public taxation of railroads	18	12	5	1
Common carrier	19	6	12	1
Conflicting land title	13	7	6	0
Miscellaneous	20	10	9	1
Total	310	176	123	11

Source: *Iowa Supreme Court Reports*, 1870–76.
Note: N = Number of cases surveyed.
    W = Number of cases won by railroads.
    L = Number of cases lost by railroads.
    O = Number of cases in which the decision was adjudged to have favored neither side.

law providing for popular referenda on local aid to internal improvements, thereby overturning a contrary ruling the previous year.[79] Judges were especially anxious to prevent investors from exploiting technicalities in order to escape from their contractual obligations. In a representative decision of 1871, Justice Joseph Beck, a former Henry Clay Whig who was one of the least avid supporters of business interests on the bench, declared that although part of a depot had been built more than one mile away from the Charles City post office (thereby contravening the terms of a subscription agreement) such a "trifling fact" would not be deemed to have annulled a "solemn contract."[80]

The transportation companies also won a sizable proportion (67 percent) of cases involving the right of municipalities to tax railroad property. In this field, however, the court proved qualitatively less eager to hear the business side of the argument. The important case of *City of Dubuque* v. *The Illinois Central Railroad Co.* (1874) was a prime example of judicial activism running counter to the demands of developmental capitalism and the expressed wishes of the legislature. Justice Beck's decision, which voided a statute exempting railroads from municipal taxation, was based not only on his reading of the state constitution (which he interpreted to mandate uniform taxation) but also on the decidedly nondevelopmental notion of taxation as contract. The assembly, he argued, could not discharge the obligation of railroads to pay municipal taxes because, by its very nature, a tax was a mutual obligation and therefore, by definition, a contract. The statute was thus an attempt to deprive local governments of their property and wholly unconstitutional.[81] Contract, it seems, could occasionally be a double-edged sword.

Although railroads had the best of development-related cases, they met with less success in appeals relating to crop and livestock damages, and their status before the law as common carriers. The issues here were only indirectly related to capital investment and were clearly of central importance to Iowa's vast farming community. Again, judicial actions tended to mirror prior legislative enactments. The statute of 1862 requiring railroads to fence their rights of way could have been perceived as an obstacle to construction, but although it was undoubtedly a response to popular pressure and worked a radical change in the common law, the court made no attempt to strike it down, always upholding the act as a proper exercise of the state's police power. In 1876 one company sought to have the act declared unconstitutional on the grounds that its double damages clause contravened the Fourteenth Amendment's equal protection clause. It was an interesting case, for if there had been a judicial conspiracy on behalf of American capitalism, one might have expected Justice Beck to seize on the notion (later propagated by Senator Roscoe Conkling of New York) that corporations were persons and rule that they were protected by the language of the amendment.[82] Evidently the judge was unaware that Conkling and his fellow members of the Joint Committee on Reconstruction had intended its meaning to include corporations as well as blacks. Failing to address that question at all, Beck simply averred that citizens were not liable under the fencing act's provisions "because within this State railroads are generally, if not always, operated by corporations. The law applies to all corporations operating railroads."[83]

If we recall Justice Isbell's ruling on the undesirability of compulsory fencing in 1856, it should be apparent that this later decision was part of an evolutionary process involving interest-group pressure (in this instance livestock owners living alongside rights of way) and legislative and judicial response. The same process was at work in cases of crop fires started by locomotive sparks. Justice Cole delivered a characteristically probusiness verdict in *Kespe* v. *The Chicago & N.W.R.R. Co.* (1870). Drawing upon his favorite doctrine of contributory negligence, Cole held that a farmer could not claim fire damages if he had stacked his hay in the vicinity of a railway line. "The instinctive sense of prudence innate in every reasonable person," he announced, "would say that such a use of one's own property was per se negligence—carelessness."[84] Decisions such as this resulted in a revision of the law. Section 1289 of the Code of 1873 made railroads liable for all fire damages caused by the operation of their trains. In October 1875 the Milwaukee & St. Paul attempted to nullify this statute by arguing that it impaired the contract (embodied in the road's charter) that existed between state and corporation. Once again the court displayed a marked reluctance to use contract to strike down a potentially counterdevelopmental statute. However, Justice Day's ruling, which maintained that the right to enact such a law derived from the state's police powers, did contain more than a hint of Hurst's release-of-energy thesis:

> What the policy of this legislation may be experience alone can show. It may be that it will prove to be unreasonably severe and to stand in the way of material progress and the best interests of the country at large. It may, upon the other hand, promote a high degree of skill and care, and stimulate the invention and use of improved appliances, lessening the dangers of fires and greatly increasing the safety of property, without any detriment to public interests.

Then, as if to caution those who would place too great an emphasis on judicial activism, the judge added: "With these questions we have nothing to do."[85]

The Republican court's response to the railroad question was no less a complex mixture of principle, pragmatism, and personal design than that of successive Republican executives and Republican-dominated legislatures. This was hardly surprising, given that the dividing line between judge and politician was frequently nonexistent. If this appears to corroborate Hurst's advantages-for-all interpretation (for growth was always popular with the majority of Iowans), there is no reason to reject outright Horwitz's darker thesis. Powerful probusiness forces were at work behind the scenes in Iowa, constantly seeking to influence legislation, judicial decisions, and public opinion. The none-too-impartial activities of Baldwin and Cole indicate that intimate connections did exist between members of the legal elite and the agents of corporate capitalism. And yet, for all their undeniable capacity to shape postbellum Republican economic policy, the railroad men could never be quite sure of always getting their way.

Late in 1874 Grenville M. Dodge was working as an engineer and lobbyist for the Texas & Pacific Railroad Company. On 15 December, as part of a coordinated campaign to secure federal aid for what was by then an ailing project, the general asked James S. Clarkson to write an article explaining the necessity of the road.[86] His colleague must have had deep reservations about this request, for it came at a time when antimonopoly feeling was still running high. These the young editor swallowed. In a lead editorial he called on Congress to give the Texas & Pacific serious attention as it was "too important to be dismissed by clamor, and embraces within the scope of its promise benefits too general to be defeated by prejudice."[87] Shortly after the appearance of these comments in the Des Moines *Iowa State Register* the U.S. House of Representatives dealt the enterprise a massive blow. Only one Iowa delegate supported the federal aid bill under discussion in a decisive test vote in early February 1875.[88] The rest confirmed Dodge's fears about the measure. "I think most of the Iowa members feel kindly towards it," he had told Clarkson shortly before Christmas, "but are afraid of Public Sentiment at home; they do not know whether they will be sustained or not."[89]

It was not only the antimonopoly demands of a fickle electorate that frustrated corporate interests. Businessmen and their political allies also came up against the formidable barrier of conflicting legal ideologies. The rulings of Joseph Beck, grounded as they were in prewar instrumentalism and Whig statism, must have been anathema to railroad officers. So too, in the short run, were formalist ideas about the primacy of judicial review over supposedly irresponsible legislative enactments.

In Iowa John F. Dillon, a son-in-law of Davenport Congressman Hiram Price and one of modernizing America's most-respected jurists, championed the right of appellate courts to strike down statutes that enabled railroad-crazed majorities to burden their communities with debt. His decision in *Hanson* v. *Vernon* (1869) negated a recent municipal tax aid law and anticipated similar rulings in other midwestern state courts.⁹⁰ Commenting favorably on one of these decisions, Dillon contended that "[t]he transcendent power to tax must be kept within its legitimate bounds, or else in these days of powerful combinations and monopolies, all security of property is undermined."⁹¹ This was hardly the stuff of developmental activism, although its laissez-faire implications would eventually play into the hands of American business. It is also true that *Hanson* v. *Vernon* was overturned by the Iowa court soon after Dillon had left to become a federal judge. Nevertheless, there remains a good deal of evidence to suggest that the supreme bench constituted a significant break on corporate designs. Why else would the Democratic strategist Charles Mason have supposed in March 1872 that the local judiciary offered Iowans their "only reliance" against railroad infiltration of the legislature or business representatives have fought for deregulation in federal rather than state courts later in the decade?⁹²

The fact that two-thirds of the Iowa house supported radical modification of the erroneously named Granger Law in 1876 hinted at a waning of the interventionist spirit. Ultimately Northerners responded in conservative fashion to the long, sapping economic slump of the 1870s.⁹³ They curtailed public expenditure, sought a return to specie payments, and surrendered their military grip on the defiant South. Iowans perceived crime to be on the increase and restored the death penalty (abolished in 1872).⁹⁴ They saw "tramps" in search of farm work infesting their streets and country roads and enacted a harsh vagrancy law that made a mockery of their previous angry reaction to Southern Black Codes.⁹⁵ The same sullen social climate that permitted these knee-jerk responses to unwelcome change enabled businessmen and their political allies to roll back some of the frontiers of the active state.

Assertions that the railroad tariff law was having a detrimental effect on the local economy sounded increasingly convincing to farmers who had not seen agricultural profits pick up as a result of regulation. Only the radical minority among them joined the Greenback party during the final years of the decade. In Iowa that organization campaigned with only limited success on inflationary and regulatory platforms, drawing its support mainly from the southern portion of the state where the soil was least fertile and the voters were traditionally more willing to endorse third-party activity.⁹⁶ Although fusion with the Democrats brought them a few notable political triumphs, the Greenbackers never captured more than around 15 percent of the state's electorate—this despite unfavorable economic conditions and, in the person of Bloomfield's renegade, pro-Harlan Republican James Baird Weaver, a local leader of national stature. The majority of Iowa farmers, isolated and relatively unpoliticized as many of them undoubtedly were, either remained politically apathetic or accepted the conservative economic arguments of the two main parties.

Deregulation came to be seen as a major panacea for the depression. The Republican-controlled legislature of 1876 removed the ban on municipal aid to internal improvements that had been established four years earlier.[97] In June 1877 the party's state convention ratified a plank calling for the encouragement of capital investment in Iowa "by wise and liberal legislation."[98] Notwithstanding a relatively poor showing in the fall elections, Republican leaders must have been encouraged by their continued domination of the legislature. Bolstered by another business-run repeal campaign and the "reform" utterings of Governor John H. Gear, a creature of the Regency, supporters of a supervisory railroad commission in the 1878 assembly finally succeeded in securing their aim.[99]

The opposition to repeal had not vanished entirely. In the house, where the commission bill originated, forty-three out of ninety-eight representatives voted against passage.[100] Most of them came from eastern counties that had benefited from a fall in short-haul rates to the river towns. Western delegates were almost unanimous in their desire for a commission. The bill met with more eastern opposition in the senate where it was finally passed by twenty-nine votes to twenty-one.[101] Low indices of cohesion testified to the measure's divisive impact on intraparty unity.[102] It was a triumph for the developmental strain of economic thought that had underlain state policy throughout the mid-nineteenth century, but for the railroads (which lost no time in trying to pack the government's supervisory commission with their own men) the new act constituted something of a Pyrrhic victory. The successful campaign for congressional regulation of interstate rates, the complexities of their own industry, and, in 1888, renewed hostility from the ruling Republican administration in Iowa ultimately ensured that the line between private and public interests remained more blurred than many American businessmen might have wished.[103]

The Republicans' flexible response to the railroad question during the troubled 1870s frustrated the efforts of Democratic policymakers to regain power with a program of opposition to monopolistic corporations. In spite of potentially embarrassing links with eastern businessmen, the majority party's continuing attachment to antebellum notions of state sovereignty and proven political agility on economic issues enabled it to ride out the slump with a surprising amount of ease. The fact that most Iowans opposed abuses of corporate power rather than railroads per se undoubtedly helped Republican leaders to steer a developmental course through the shoals of the depression, although clearly they were forced to make temporary concessions to popular antimonopoly sentiment along the way. The railroad tariff law of 1874 was the most significant of these. A remarkable instance of state intervention in the economy, it was a potent reminder that Jacksonian suspicions of monopoly and Whiggish and radical philosophies of active government retained their strength well into the Gilded Age—at least in straitened economic circumstances. Eventually, though, Reconstruction and recession combined to produce a conservative reaction to statism, and by the end of the decade the rate-fixing law had been modified to make it more acceptable to the corporations.

As already observed, the salience of sectional issues declined dramatically during the mid-1870s. However, they did not disappear entirely. Republicans were reluctant to let go of their past, particularly during a period when some observers were contending that the party of free soil and equal rights had outlived its usefulness. To many contemporaries it seemed that the presidential election of 1876 must decide not only this question but also the fate of the remaining radical regimes in the South. More than a decade after Appomattox Iowa's ruling partisans again prepared to defend the Union against Confederates abroad and Copperheads at home.

12
End of an Era, 1876–1877

amuel J. Kirkwood delivered his third inaugural address on 13 January 1876. A firm friend of the Regency, he was now in his sixty-third year and had recently been elected governor, much against his will, by a comfortable 57 percent majority over his Democratic–Anti-Monopoly opponent.[1]

He began his speech by reminding the legislature that 1876 was America's centennial year. He recalled Iowa's role in the preservation and development of the republic: its magnificent contribution to the Northern war effort and stunning economic progress (hampered only by a lack of investment in home manufactures). On the railroad question, Kirkwood argued that cheap transportation was vital if farmers were to make profits in these days of low commodity prices. Railroads had helped to raise transportation costs by forming combinations; therefore more perfect legislation was necessary to restore business competition. Whether or not the state's rate regulation law was an answer to the farmers' ills, Kirkwood was unsure. He described the statute as experimental and urged the lawmakers to examine the railroad problem "calmly and carefully, without passion and without prejudice." Iowans, he told his audience, "appreciate fully and concede freely the great benefits our state has gained from these works."[2] After admitting that it was the state's duty to ensure that corporations did not abuse their privileges, the governor returned to wider matters. Prominent among these was the forthcoming presidential campaign.

Kirkwood chose his language carefully when discussing the railroads, but he showed no desire to mince his words on the centenary election. Over recent years much of the bitterness arising out of the Civil War had subsided. This was all very well, contended the governor, but it was essential to make future generations aware "that in that terrible contest there was a right side and a wrong side."

We should make sure, so far as we can make sure, that their reverence and love shall be given to Lincoln and Grant and Sherman and Thomas and Sheridan, and not to Davis and Lee and Johnson and Beauregard and Forrest. To do this we must show them that our love and honor are given to the men who, in council and in action, labored for the preservation of the Union, and not for those who plotted and fought for its destruction. I have sometimes feared that in our extreme desire for peace and conciliation we have failed to keep this consideration properly in view.[3]

Kirkwood concluded his address by predicting that 1876 would see a determined struggle for control of the government "by a party composed of those who a few years ago used every effort to destroy it and those who fought to preserve it."[4]

The governor's peroration reflected a determination to shift the focus away from the troublesome state issues with which Republicans had been preoccupied for the past four years, to the safer ground of sectionalism. While cynical political reasons underlay this change in emphasis, there was a genuine feeling among many Northerners that the reconciliation process was proceeding too quickly. Radical Republican regimes had fallen prey to conservative Democrats (Redeemers) in several Deep South states during the 1870s, leaving only Louisiana, South Carolina, and Florida under Republican control by the beginning of 1876. Although the demise of these governments had prompted little adverse reaction among Northerners, members of the powerful veterans' group, the Grand Army of the Republic, were appalled to see their old battlefield adversaries returning to power. One Des Moines veteran complained that while the Republicans were "breaking up into squads with political womans rights[,] political temperance etc," the enemy was "solid on Washingtons Birthday & singing the war cry of state rights and white mans government. . . . [I]f we sleep much longer our pickets will be all captured and the main body routed."[5]

Having largely forgotten about Reconstruction since Grant's victory in 1872, Republican politicians hurried to rediscover it as a political issue. As well as offering them a respite from railroads and prohibition and a means of appealing to the vast constituency of veterans, it also served to dilute the significance of the continuing economic depression as a factor in the presidential campaign. Moreover, since this contest was likely to be much tighter than its predecessor, Republican leaders began to recognize that the electoral votes of the radical states might play a crucial role in the eventual result. For the first time since the early 1870s, developments in the South impinged upon the consciousness of Iowa voters.

Six days after his inaugural Kirkwood was elected to represent the state in the U.S. Senate. James Harlan had been a rival candidate for the office, but his last minute withdrawal left the opposition powerless to prevent the governor from securing his long-sought-after objective.⁶ In full control of Iowa's Republican organization, the Regency prepared to fend off the Democracy's challenge in the presidential election.

Although a majority of local Republican leaders remained loyal to President Grant throughout his term of office, most of them realized that a third nomination was impossible in view of the depressed state of the economy and the various scandals that had rocked the administration. Their favored candidate was James G. Blaine, a New England spoilsman with a solid record on the Southern question. Unfortunately for his many supporters Blaine had been involved in some questionable railroad dealings, and he was passed over at the national Republican convention in favor of Rutherford B. Hayes, an unprepossessing Ohioan with little to recommend him except a respectable war record and a reputation for honesty. To run against him the Democrats chose the wealthy governor of New York, Samuel J. Tilden, a fiscal conservative noted for his destruction of the Tweed Ring in his home state. Radical Iowa Democrats such as Henry Clay Dean denounced the choice of Tilden because it prevented them from making an issue of the Republicans' deflationary monetary policies.⁷ The majority, however, fell into line behind the nomination. Charles Mason confessed that there was "no essential difference between the two parties financially" but was optimistic about the Democrats' electoral chances. "I shall not be surprised to see a ground swell agitate the whole country," he mused, "& to find that a movement in favour of reform will spread everywhere."⁸

Iowa's Republican leaders swallowed their disappointment at Blaine's defeat and proceeded to quash Democratic hopes of a political revolution with a masterly campaign. Their main weapon was sectionalism.

Shortly after Tilden's nomination at St. Louis in July, the *Iowa State Register* gleefully reported that General James Tuttle, a prominent Des Moines veteran who had been the Democrats' gubernatorial nominee in 1863, had abandoned his party because of its alleged domination by former Confederates. According to Clarkson, the "ex-rebel array at St Louis" and their Northern trucklers had left the patriotic officer (once condemned by Republicans as a cotton speculator) with no alternative: "He sees in the old Democracy, revived only by the Southern element, and by it given its only hope, a menace to the Union."⁹ This was the rhetoric of 1856 and 1866, but it had paid dividends then and it would do so again.

Throughout the late summer and autumn of America's centenary year, Iowa Republicans returned again and again to their familiar denunciations of the Democrats as Copperheads and traitors. They warned that Tilden's election would result in the payment of Confederate claims against the United States. They pointed repeatedly to the sufferings of Southern Unionists at the hands of Redeemers. They urged that the fruits of the Civil War must not be surrendered. By election day a frustrated Charles Mason was resigned to yet another defeat. "I presume the republicans have succeeded in this district as well as in the country," he remarked on 7 November. "I have hoped for a different result but am fearful that the vengeful feelings out of which the war grew & which were fed & nurtured by the events of that war are not yet subdued."[10]

Mason was a little too pessimistic, though Hayes had certainly carried Iowa. While the Democrats made some inroads into Republican strength in the southeastern quarter of the state, only six counties were carried by Tilden. The New Yorker won 38.3 percent of the popular vote compared with Hayes's 58.6.[11] But elsewhere he performed rather better. First reports showed that he had carried key Northern states—New York, New Jersey, Indiana, and Connecticut—and was sweeping all before him in the South. Then came the news that Republicans were using reports of electoral fraud to discount sufficient Democratic votes in Louisiana, Florida, and South Carolina to give Hayes the presidency. Southern blacks were widely held to have delivered the nation from the hands of its enemies. A grateful Clarkson wrote on 17 November that "the man of bronze has now demonstrated that even in his weakness as a race, in his ignorance, in his dependence, he has a soul which equals in faithfulness, in gratitude, and in conviction that of the fairer race."[12]

During the winter of 1876-77 unemployed farm laborers, urban workers, and transients roamed the streets of Iowa's cities in search of food and warmth. The new vagrancy act empowered law enforcement officials to sentence such persons to hard labor in the county jail until they could pay off a statutory fine of not more than $50.[13] However, this harsh mandate proved unequal to the task before it, and the dangerous classes continued to impinge upon the lives of the local bourgeoisie. In the absence of substantive government help (retrenchment was the keynote of the times, just as it had been in 1857-58), most of the destitute relied heavily on private charity. The Des Moines *Iowa State Register* called on local Christians and businessmen to do more to help the unfortunates in their midst. Work was better than alms, urged an editorial on 9 February 1877: "Any other course in a city builds up professional mendicancy."[14] Disease and freezing temperatures compounded the hardships experienced by the indigent. Diphtheria was rife in the northern counties. One Fort Dodge resident reported that it had carried off several children in the area. "This is a terrible country and climate for poor people," he remarked. "The times are very hard indeed."[15]

If Iowa's unemployed were wondering what had become of the Republican strain of active government, they were no doubt consoled by the fact that the state's political leaders were preoccupied with the electoral crisis. Both sides claimed victory that winter, and there was widespread talk of another civil war to settle the issue. Behind the scenes complicated negotiations began involving representatives of Rutherford B. Hayes, Northern business interests, and Southern Whigs (generally thought by Republicans to be the party's best hope of establishing itself in the post-Reconstruction South). Iowa's onetime kingmaker, Grenville M. Dodge, was involved in the talks in his capacity as an employee of the Texas & Pacific.[16] Thomas A. Scott's railroad was still seeking federal aid, and both he and Dodge were keen that the offer of a generous subsidy for the Texas & Pacific should be held out to the Southerners as part of a deal leading to their acquiescence in Hayes's election. Although the precise nature of the concessions and incentives on offer remains unclear, the main element in the bargain was an assurance from the Republican candidate that his inauguration would be followed by the withdrawal of U.S. support from the remaining radical regimes in the South.

Meanwhile, in late January 1877, Congress finally agreed to set up an electoral commission to count the votes cast in the presidential contest. The decision of Iowa's U.S. senators, Allison and Wright, to support a commission was controversial because it seemed to offer the Democrats a chance of regaining power.[17] Allison, however, defended his action on the grounds that it was in the best interests of the party to provide some machinery for ending the crisis.[18] His judgment was vindicated the following month when the Electoral Commission decided by a majority of one to count the votes of South Carolina, Louisiana, and Florida for Hayes. Fears that Democratic filibustering might prolong the agony evaporated after further backroom negotiations confirmed that the carpetbag governments in the South would be abandoned. In truth neither party was eager to provoke a confrontation over this issue. The depressed economic state of the country and the yearning of Northern Democrats for political legitimacy had always pointed toward a compromise solution. Hayes was inaugurated peacefully at the beginning of March, and federal troops in the South were withdrawn to barracks shortly afterwards, thereby permitting the Redeemers to seize control in Baton Rouge and Columbia.

The realization that Reconstruction was finally over prompted different reactions among Iowa Republicans. Although the liberal element within the party tended to be in favor of the president's pacification policy, factional alignment appears to have had little impact on individual responses. Even the

Regency was split over the issue. Whereas Dodge, Allison, Kirkwood, and Grimes's former lieutenant, Jacob Rich, initially supported the "experiment" as the best means of nurturing Republican support among Southern white progressives, James S. Clarkson denounced Hayes for betraying the radicals.[19] So too did ex-governor Cyrus Clay Carpenter.

Carpenter was second comptroller in the U.S. Treasury Department early in 1877. Already unhappy with his anonymous existence in the federal bureaucracy, he found Hayes's policy impossible to stomach. One reason for this was his secondhand acquaintance with conditions in the Southern states. Former army comrades on duty below the Mason-Dixon line sent him graphic accounts of the illegal tactics pursued by the Redeemers in their search for power. One harrowing letter written in July 1876 reported the widespread intimidation and murder of blacks at Port Hudson and Mount Pleasant, Louisiana.[20] Another missive—from a Des Moines resident serving in the U.S. customhouse at New Orleans—reported that the local populace regarded Northerners "as Yankees & cowards fit only to be treated with the dirk & pistol."[21]

The Republican government of Daniel H. Chamberlain in South Carolina was the first to fall. Carpenter described this development as "a crime" and dispatched a letter of commiseration to the Harvard-educated governor. Chamberlain wrote back bemoaning the fact that so few men understood "the temper or spirit of the South."[22] When the radical regime of Stephen B. Packard in Louisiana collapsed at the end of April, the Iowan noted in his diary: "To-day was the day of days in New Orleans and leaves the South solidly Democratic forever. It seems to me the barest & most cowardly surrender the world ever witnessed."[23]

Although many Iowans shared Carpenter's belief that Hayes's policy was indefensible because it promoted the rehabilitation of disloyal Southern Democrats, few of them paused to reflect that their own lack of interest in Reconstruction had helped to undermine the Unionist cause in the South. The election crisis, however, had concentrated the mind wonderfully, and now many of them were ready once again to call for federal protection of black rights. It was too late, of course, for by this time Confederate heroes like Wade Hampton in South Carolina were back in power, and the Republicans were no longer in full control of Congress. But the crisis did prompt genuine feelings of outrage that loyal blacks were being betrayed by the party that had given them their freedom. The old antislavery spirit was not quite dead.

During the summer of 1877 Carpenter took time off from his irksome duties in Washington to compose two articles for the *Iowa State Register* back home. The first of these was a general piece criticizing the administration for being duped by Southerners into believing that the latter would respect the rights of the freedmen.[24] The second, entitled "The Negro," represented an attempt by a former Whig-Republican to counter the increasingly fashionable view that blacks were unworthy of the suffrage. Referring to a racist article that had recently appeared in the *New York Tribune,* Carpenter contended that "an insidious and well-directed movement is seeking to indoctrinate the public mind with the belief that any marked progress of the negro can only result from a direction of white forces." It was, he went on, wrong to suggest that blacks had made no progress since emancipation. If one took into account "the stupidity of the ignorant and thriftless whites in the North" and the minimal achievements of the emancipated Russian serf, "the halting progress" of American blacks could not, he insisted, be taken as "evidence of limitations in the African blood."[25]

Carpenter had been a progressive on racial issues since the last years of the Civil War. By no means all former radicals, however, joined in his criticism of the Hayes policy. Edward Russell, for example, the chief architect of black suffrage in Iowa, was convinced that it was time for the freedmen "to realize that their political salvation rests largely, if not entirely, in their own keeping," though he did insist on federal intervention if the blacks were forced to protect themselves against "the mad frenzy of the lower elements of Southern society."[26]

Such a view was not entirely typical. Six weeks before the Republican state convention was due to be held at Des Moines, Buren R. Sherman, a leading candidate for the gubernatorial nomination, observed that most Republican voters were "very much dissatisfied" with Hayes's policy and regarded it as "a square abandonment of principle, and the turning over of the Southern Republicans to the tender mercies of the Southern Guerrilla."[27] The truth of this remark was born out at the convention in June when Iowa Republicans endorsed a resolution demanding that Congress and the president act positively to secure "to every American citizen complete liberty and exact equality in the exercise of civil, political and public rights."[28] The strength of Regency control over the party, however, may have prevented an outright condemnation of Hayes. It certainly resulted in the nomination of John H. Gear for governor. Gear, a Burlington merchant and liberal Whig-Republican with close ties to the ring, was the railroads' choice for the governorship. He was also regarded as being more sympathetic to the administration's Southern policy than his rivals.

Even though prominent Iowa Republicans would continue to speak out in favor of black rights during the final decades of the nineteenth century, Gear's nomination confirmed his party's continued shift away from its antislavery origins. Local Republicans had always maintained links with American business, but these had never been the organization's raison d'être. Now sectionalism was in decline, and the party's capitalist proclivities were becoming more evident. In July 1877 a major strike by American railroad workers spread quickly eastwards along the nation's main trunk lines. While a thoughtful Cyrus Clay Carpenter pondered gloomily on this upsurge of "the mob spirit," Governor Joshua Newbold warned potential troublemakers "that the whole power of the State will, if necessary, be invoked for the support of the authorities and the execution of the law."[29] Although the militia did not in fact have to be called upon in Iowa, Newbold's proclamation indicated the Republicans' willingness to intervene on the side of the corporations. Together with the vagrancy act and the repeal of the railroad tariff law in 1878, it symbolized the redundancy of his party's faith in class harmony.

Conclusion

13
The Party of Progress and Humanity

The mid-nineteenth century has long been viewed as the era of the transforming, nationalist bourgeoisie. Although it is doubtful whether the United States circa 1860 was dominated by a well-defined industrial middle class along the lines of that which existed in Britain and France, one does not have to be a cultural Marxist or a proponent of the modernization synthesis to agree that the early Republican party was a purveyor of values and policies that from our vantage point appear to have fostered economic change, national unity on a basis of commercial-industrial capitalism, and the growth of an unmistakably bourgeois *mentalité*. Even on one of the peripheries of the developing world, amidst a fluid postfrontier society that was neither wholly middle class nor modern, its leading figures were fervent champions of moral and material progress along capitalist lines.

An examination of the party's origins and development in Iowa, however, suggests that its role was somewhat more complex than some historians have led us to believe. While the local organization did help to preserve the territorial integrity of the American republic, its blatantly sectional policies undoubtedly contributed toward the breakup of the Union in 1860-61. To describe men like James W. Grimes and William Penn Clarke as nationalists is thus to ignore the part they played in obstructing the power of the central government and inducing the cotton South to secede. Moreover, although Republican politicians had close ties with eastern capitalists and were themselves relatively wealthy by local standards, it must be debatable that men who failed to sponsor the growth of manufacturing industry in the state and who took positive steps to rein in the power of the railroad corporations can really be said to have masterminded the triumph of industrialism. Quite simply there were too many tensions within Republican ideology to denote it nationalist, bourgeois, or industrializing with any degree of confidence.

Monocausal interpretations of political parties and tangled historical events are seldom persuasive. Recent works by scholars such as Eric Foner and William E. Gienapp attempt to examine Republicanism in the widest possible context and to take full account of the social basis of political activity in what was clearly a nation in flux.[1] The preceding chapters reveal the wisdom of this approach. Nineteenth-century Iowa Republicans were products of their changing times. They responded creatively to the great demographic, economic, and intellectual shifts that were transforming America, appreciative of the benefits of commercial-industrial capitalism, but generally cognizant of the strains that economic progress placed on midwestern society.

The historian who seeks to locate the soul of the early Republican party is confronted with many difficulties, not least the coalitional nature of the organization, its flexible response to a variety of issues, and the problem of determining the motivation of men long since passed from the earth.

Manifestly personal ambition was a prime determinant of political action in mid-Victorian Iowa. The recurring significance of U.S. senatorial elections, the persistence of factionalism, and the constant jockeying for position of leading politicians all testified to the attraction that power and place held for members of Iowa's political elite. But while it is essential to recognize the significance of power seeking as a dynamic of intra- and interparty competition, we should be wary of dismissing Civil War–era politics as venal, faction ridden, and elite dominated. Men of wealth and professional status certainly dominated the governance of Iowa—even during the region's territorial phase—and corruption there was aplenty. Close, often clandestine, ties linked many politicians with the commercial giants of the day: witness the railroad activities of Harlan, Grimes, and Dodge. Nepotism was far from uncommon, and there were even hints of inbreeding: Harlan's daughter, Mary, married Lincoln's eldest son, Robert; William B. Allison married Grimes's niece. Yet in spite of certain similarities, nineteenth-century Iowa was not Georgian England. By the 1840s no self-respecting American politician could ignore the fact that he lived in a democratic age, and once it was apparent that the masses could no longer be excluded from participation in government and that electoral success was dependent on skillful coalition building, deference to the will of the people became the sine qua non of local politics. Inevitably that deference was often rhetorical (amounting, in many cases, to outright demagoguery), but even lip service to the notion of popular sovereignty helped to preclude the establishment of a narrow and largely unresponsive political elite such as that which still existed on the other side of the Atlantic in the mid-Victorian period.

The need to be seen to respond positively to grass-roots demands inside and outside the party forced Iowa politicians to reconcile their own interests with those of their constituents. This did not prevent them from using politics to further personal or corporate objectives, but it did act as a break on untrammeled greed. Majoritarian democracy also stymied attempts by radicals to impose their will on party policy. Political abolitionists, temperance activists, and locofoco Democrats frequently discovered their support for controversial policies obstructed by the overriding desire of party leaders not to alienate specific interest groups in local society. Only when events or economic conditions eroded consensus at the center did radicals find enough support from swing groups to enable them to convert their rhetoric into action.

While none of Iowa's leading politicians could have survived in power for long without being bound in some way to the people they represented, the nature of that bond was complicated. Republicans and Democrats alike certainly took note of voter demands (as expressed through election results, legislative petitions, spontaneous rallies, and well-organized conventions) when formulating policy. But there were other inputs too. Individual businessmen exerted a direct influence on legislation through backstage political contacts and the activities of corporate lobbyists. Moreover, strategic goals could counteract the most vocal popular opinion. The Republican determination to attract liberal German Protestants into the fold helped to soften the party's stance on prohibition after the mid-1850s, even though evangelicals within the anti-Southern coalition became increasingly frustrated with the lack of government action on this subject. Grass-roots views did help officeholders to make decisions, but they were not the sole element in the political process.

The factors linking voters to leaders were clearly diverse. Ethnocultural historians have suggested that the primary determinants of party affiliation in this period were those arising out of the growing ethnic and religious divisions in American society. Works on Iowa in the late nineteenth century indicate that pietistic Yankees and northern European Protestants evinced a much greater fondness for Republicanism than foreign Catholics and American-born liturgicals.[2] This cleavage had its origins in the immediate antebellum era when the failure of the major parties to respond adequately to voter concerns about nativism and temperance helped to undermine the second party system. Tables 13.1, 13.2, and 13.3 contain data on the ethnoreligious makeup of Republican and Democratic parties in the Iowa state legislature during the middle decades of the nineteenth century.

In table 13.1 Southerners and continental Europeans are shown to have played a greater role in the Democratic organization than they did in that of the opposition, while the reverse was true of New Englanders and Britons. On the other hand, there does not seem to have been any major polarization between Yankee and Southern party affiliation, and both coalitions contained predictably large numbers of westerners, New Yorkers, and Pennsylvanians.

Table 13.2 is more supportive of the ethnocultural argument. Evangelicals of all types constituted over half of the legislative population. Yet only 32.1 percent of Democrats declared themselves to be devotees of pietistic religion, compared with over 60.1 percent of Republicans. At least one in three Democrats were nonevangelical Christians.[3]

Table 13.1. Iowa general assembly, 1854–78: Ethnic composition of parties

Region of birth	Republican		Democrat	
	N	%	N	%
New England	109	17.0	24	11.3
Mid-Atlantic states	208	32.3	69	32.4
West	206	32.0	56	26.3
South	69	10.7	35	16.4
Europe	43	6.7	29	13.6
Germany	(10)	(1.6)	(10)	(4.7)
Ireland	(7)	(1.1)	(12)	(5.6)
England, Scotland	(22)	(3.4)	(2)	(0.9)
Canada	8	1.2	—	—
Total	643	99.9	213	100.0

Source: See Appendix.
Note: Including 1854 Anti-Nebraska delegates; excluding 1864 Unionists, and excluding 1874 Anti-Monopolists.

Table 13.2. Iowa general assembly, 1854–72: Religious composition of parties

Religious category	Republican		Democrat	
	N	%	N	%
Revival Calvinist	119	30.2	19	14.5
Evangelical Arminian	118	29.9	23	17.6
Nonevangelical Christian	47	11.9	44	33.6
Nondenominational Protestant	19	4.8	11	8.4
Liberal	71	18.0	28	21.4
Unclassified	20	5.1	6	4.6
Total	394	99.9	131	100.1

Source: See Appendix.
Note: Including 1854 Anti-Nebraska delegates; excluding 1864 Unionists.

Table 13.3. Iowa general assembly, 1854–72: Party affiliation for individual religious denominations

Denomination	% Republican		% Democrat	
Congregational	100.0	(90)	—	(10)
Free-Will Baptist	100.0	(95)	—	(5)
Methodist	83.5	(90)	16.5	(10)
Presbyterian	83.3	(70)	16.7	(30)
Universalist	81.5		18.5	
Baptist	80.0		20.0	
Quaker	80.0	(85)	20.0	(15)
Liberal	77.8		22.2	
None	55.9		44.1	
Episcopalian	53.3		46.7	
Lutheran	42.9	(45)	57.1	(55)
Unitarian	40.0		60.0	
Old School Presbyterian	28.6		71.4	
Roman Catholic	—	(5)	100.0	(95)

Source: Paul Kleppner's figures (in parentheses) are taken from *The Cross of Culture: A Social Analysis of Midwestern Politics, 1850–1900* (New York, 1970), p. 70. His percentages are for Northern Presbyterians, New York Methodists, German Lutherans, and Irish Catholics.

The figures in table 13.3 provide further evidence that religion was a prime determinant of partisanship, for they reveal a strong similarity between Paul Kleppner's 1971 estimates of party strength for selected denominations across the Midwest and those calculated from the Iowa data. Combined with qualitative evidence about the nature of the Republicans' social base in Iowa and William E. Gienapp's regression statistics on the 1854 and 1856 elections, these tables support the view that the third party system was grounded in ethnocultural conflict. As described, the Republicans absorbed the majority of Iowa nativists during the years immediately preceding the Civil War and frequently used negative ethnic referents (principally Irish Catholics and Southerners) as weapons in their assaults on the Democracy. Prohibition, voter registration law reform, and the use of the Bible in public schools were important issues in mid-nineteenth-century Iowa, all of them testifying to the strength of the ethnoreligious fault lines in local society.

In contrast, the figures in table 13.4 do little to indicate that there were strong class divisions between the parties. Indeed, the occupational statistics for both organizations are remarkably similar, with farmers and professionals constituting over three-quarters of their respective legislative populations. These results, however, should not be taken to preclude the possibility that class was a factor in the politics of this era. Most historians have generally recognized that there was little to choose between Whig, Democratic, and Republican leaders in terms of wealth and occupation.[4] Quite clearly class

Table 13.4. Iowa general assembly, 1854–78: Occupational composition of parties

Occupational category	Republican		Democrat	
	N	%	N	%
Farmers	453	41.6	173	44.8
Farm elite	141	12.9	46	11.9
Proprietors	53	4.8	15	3.9
Professionals	381	35.0	130	33.7
Capitalists	38	3.5	12	3.1
Artisans	20	1.8	9	2.3
Unclassified	4	0.4	1	0.3
Total	1,090	100.0	386	100.0

Source: See Appendix.
Note: Including 1854 Anti-Nebraska delegates; excluding 1864 Unionists, and excluding 1874 Anti-Monopolists. This table is based on a survey of legislative places rather than individuals because of the variable nature of occupational data.

tensions did exist in the wider society even though many politicians sought to deny their existence.

Evidence that Republicanism was strongest in the market-orientated wheat-exporting counties of eastern Iowa during the 1850s and among the prosperous farmers and small towns of Indiana in the 1870s hints at something more than an ethnocultural explanation for party behavior.[5] In fact, because ethnicity and class frequently overlapped in all the Northern states, it seems reasonable to suggest a dual explanation, part cultural, part economic, for Gilded Age linkage. Party rhetoric and actions on ethnic and religious issues did have crucial resonance for specific groups but so too did Democratic efforts to mobilize lingering Jacksonian class prejudices. Attempts by men like Charles Mason to brand the opposition as friends of monopoly capitalism cemented the hard-pressed Irish Catholic community's attachment to an organization already attractive to it by dint of its opposition to prohibition, tighter voting registration laws, and equal rights for blacks. Similarly, Republican support for banks and railroads may have proved particularly appealing to the more well-to-do sectors of society (for example, commercial farmers, urban professionals, and native-born or British artisans) who were also drawn to the organization by its compelling anti-Catholic and anti-Southern image. The unpopularity of the slaveholders, of course, enabled the Republicans to draw on popular class prejudices of their own. Attacks on power-hungry Southern "aristocrats" helped to neutralize pseudo-Jacksonian rhetoric and further the ruling party's efforts to promote class harmony at home.

Because certain issues were of vital symbolic and practical importance to Iowa voters, it is logical to regard policy as a useful indicator of linkage.

Provided in table 13.5 are indices of partisan cohesion on a wide range of topics dealt with by the Iowa legislature. Manifestly Republicans and Democrats were most comfortable when they were voting on matters arising out of the sectional crisis. Even though the assemblymen were elected primarily to deal with problems of direct concern to their constituents, they exhausted a great deal of time debating the national issues that provided the parties with their fundamental raisons d'être. This suggests that we should be wary of placing too much emphasis on local issues. Sensitivity to Northern rights meant that key events such as the Kansas-Nebraska Act, the Lecompton crisis, and John Brown's raid on Harpers Ferry agitated voters at the grass-roots level because they were important in themselves and not just concomitants of parochial group conflicts. One simple reason why the Republicans' slave power thesis proved so potent a political force was that many Northerners genuinely felt that the South *was* aggressive, expansionistic, and determined to ram black slavery down the throats of an unwilling populace. Ethnocultural and economic factors increased the force of sectional issues (most notably race, which was inextricably bound up with the North-South conflict), but they should not allow us to conclude that the desire to curb Southern power within the framework of the federal Union was not a primary dynamic of the third party system.

Table 13.5. Iowa general assembly, 1856–62, 1866–78: Mean indices of likeness and cohesion for selected issues

Issue	N	R	D	IL
Sectional crisis	34	91.4	85.5	15.0
Reconstruction	22	88.5	85.7	26.9
Nativism	24	74.5	83.5	36.7
Black rights	41	72.5	83.9	39.7
Temperance	112	55.8	70.5	41.3
Banking	73	71.3	61.0	41.3
Social policy	43	69.5	57.2	41.8
Women's rights	15	49.8	64.9	70.0
Expenditure	36	51.0	40.7	70.2
Local government	22	40.4	35.0	73.1
Education	39	48.6	28.9	74.5
Morality	72	46.0	42.3	76.1
Economic development	24	60.1	58.8	78.3
Railroads	260	52.1	53.3	82.5
Conservation	35	47.9	39.2	87.3

Source: See Appendix (which also contains an explanation of terms).
Note: N = Number of motions per issue.
    R = Mean Rice Index of cohesion for Republican votes.
    D = Mean Rice Index of cohesion for Democrat and Anti-Monopoly votes.
    IL = Mean index of likeness.

The figures in table 13.5 suggest that while some local issues did help to promote party competition in Iowa others undermined intraparty unity or were the subjects of political consensus. Banking, equal rights for Iowa blacks, and nativism were topics on which Republicans and Democrats were less polarized than the sectional crisis, but still divided along party lines. Economic, ethnocultural, and sectional concerns, as well as persistent partisan prejudices rooted in the Jacksonian era, fueled the debates over these issues producing relatively high indices of cohesion and low indices of likeness. Significantly, however, temperance—an issue on which ethnocultural historians lay great stress—promoted much less unity in the Republican ranks than one might have expected. Democrats generally favored licensing liquor stores as an alternative to prohibition, for most of their foreign-born constituents were opposed to state interference with traditional drinking habits. After an initial burst of enthusiasm, Republicans backed off from prohibition and sought to balance liberal and evangelical demands by acquiescing in local option. Banking had a similar (though less divisive) effect on the opposition during the late 1850s when many conservative Democrats supported reform of the state constitution to liberalize Jacksonian financial restrictions.

A third class of issues failed to generate interparty competition. Railroad problems dominated the legislature throughout the mid-nineteenth century, but the divisions they created were based on geography rather than party. In spite of the Democracy's sporadic attempts to pin the label of monopoly capitalism on its opponents, most of that organization's leading figures were as heavily involved in railroad promotion as the Republican chieftains. Generally the reaction of both groups to such problems as rate discrimination and track construction was dependent on the demands of the local constituency. Eastern Iowa Democrats and Republicans tended to favor tougher treatment of business corporations than their counterparts in the northwest, where farmers were still crying out for better transportation facilities in the mid-1870s.

Similar internal fissures were caused by reform issues not related directly to the sectional crisis or ethnocultural tensions within society. Moves to confer the suffrage on women after the Civil War prompted an equivocal response from members of both parties. Support often came from antislavery Republicans keen to extend their equal rights philosophy to women and a minority of racist Democrats determined to embarrass the opposition at a time when female suffrage was regarded as ridiculous by most Northerners. Few party leaders on either side, however, showed much real enthusiasm for this controversial issue, and when sensational revelations about the free-love activities of women's rights campaigners began to circulate during the early 1870s, Republicans and Democrats swiftly let it sink into oblivion.[6] Efforts to abolish the death penalty in Iowa also promoted intraparty disunity with antislavery Republicans again in the vanguard of the movement. While the reformers accomplished their objective in 1872, hanging was restored as the ultimate deterrent six years later when majorities in both parties responded to voter concerns about rising crime during the depression.

Governor James W. Grimes's Whiggish inaugural address of December 1854 appeared to herald the coming to power of a new interventionist philosophy at odds with the laissez-faire approach of the Democracy. In fact Iowa Republicans did display a greater attachment to the notion of active government. They backed the establishment of state-supported institutions to care for the disadvantaged in society (the deaf and dumb, the blind, and the insane), sponsored important educational reforms (such as the erection of a state agricultural school), and, during the late 1860s and early 1870s, passed legislation to regulate dangerous machinery in the workplace and protect child labor and coal miners. Whig paternalism and Democratic suspicions of corporate capital did give hybrid Republicanism, particularly radical Republicanism, an interventionist thrust. The high indices of likeness in table 13.5 for such issues as education and expenditure, however, indicate a certain amount of bipartisan agreement on many of these issues. There were, moreover, severe limits to Republican statism. Retrenchment, for example, was the watchword of both parties during times of economic hardship. The poor were thus left heavily dependent on private charity throughout the Civil War period and were little helped by the passage of the harsh Vagrancy Act of 1876. Constitutional conservatism and internal laissez-faire sentiment also hindered the Republicans' ability to respond adequately to the economic (as opposed to political) needs of emancipated Southern blacks during Reconstruction.

These findings cast doubt on claims that the Republican party was a comprehensive reform vehicle, although the existence within its ranks of large numbers of perfectionist evangelical Protestants undoubtedly impelled its leaders to look more kindly on social engineering than their Jacksonian predecessors. It was the sectional crisis, however, that breathed life into the third party system and underlay the division between the two major parties for much of the period in question. At the root of that crisis lay the North's changing moral and material attitudes to the peculiar institution brought on by the South's increasingly belligerent response to the abolitionist threat.

In spite of the unsurprising fact that its adherents failed to promote a just solution to the race question, there seems little reason to doubt the view that Republicanism was a product of the last and most effective metamorphosis of the political antislavery movement in the United States. Republican activities in Iowa (as in many other parts of the Midwest and New England) bespoke a strong commitment to immediatist objectives. Prior to April 1861 radical members of the anti-Southern coalition displayed a willingness to undermine the peculiar institution, not only by supporting nonextension but also by harboring runaway slaves from neighboring Missouri and abetting revolutionary abolitionists like John Brown and Thomas Wentworth Higginson. Although most Douglas Democrats were themselves inimical to slavery expansion, their constitutional and racial beliefs usually prevented them from condoning actions that played into the hands of Southern separatists. Like the majority of their western colleagues, Iowa Republicans were genuine nationalists, but their fealty to the Union was largely conditional on depriving the South of its grip on the federal government. When war finally came, the party of Abraham Lincoln moved slowly but with increasing determination to crush the rebellion and destroy the pernicious forced labor system that had spawned it.

Eric Foner has contended that the fundamental achievement of the antebellum Republicans was "the creation and articulation of an ideology which blended personal and sectional interest with morality so perfectly that it became the most potent political force in the nation."[7] This is a sensitive judgment and one with which it is hard to disagree. Northern sectionalism was the gel that held together what was essentially a popular front to contain slavery expansion and thereby counteract Southern influence within the Union. Fueled constantly by the actions of the plantocracy and its Northern Democratic allies, this powerful sentiment gave antislavery Republicans the leverage they needed to influence men less committed to equal rights than themselves. Had it not been for wartime imperatives and the constant pressure exerted by radicals on their copartisans, Republicanism would never have been so successful in the field of equal rights. For the 1860s witnessed the attainment of racial goals far beyond the reach of abolitionists in the previous two decades.

Long after the passage of the Fifteenth Amendment, Iowa Republicans continued to view the world through a sectional lens. They did so partly because they knew that the evocation of war memories won votes and obscured troublesome local issues such as rate regulation and temperance. Yet their motives were by no means entirely cynical. As the response of Cyrus Clay Carpenter and many other Half-Breeds to the ending of Reconstruction revealed, they had few doubts that the South remained unregenerate in spirit. Some of them even regretted the abandonment of Southern Republicans during the early 1870s and worked to improve conditions for blacks in that benighted region until the end of the century. In short, despite all the self-seeking and corruption, there was just enough evidence in the organization's cumulative support—in Iowa and in several other "safe" Northern states—for black rights to substantiate the belief of a Corydon radical that the early Republican party was "the party of progress & humanity, contending for the rights of [the] oppressed & downtrodden."[8]

Appendix

The preceding chapters make substantial use of an extensive computer-assisted roll-call survey of the thirteen regular sessions of the Iowa state legislature that convened between 1854 and 1878. This project was carried out in four stages.

1. The names and related biographical variables of 1,217 senators and representatives, together with their aggregate total of 69,233 votes cast on 1,045 selected motions, were inputted into an ICL 2988 mainframe computer using ICL's Personal Data System (PDS) software package. Although the choice of motions was entirely subjective, it was guided by informed qualitative research and designed to embrace as comprehensive a range of issues as possible. These issues can be found in table 13.5. A rudimentary statistical analysis of this data was then undertaken employing ICL's Querymaster retrieval facility. This yielded a composite picture of the legislature over time.

Biographical information—not uniformly available for each session—was drawn from the following sources: *Iowa Senate Journal* (1855), Appendix, pp. 520–21; *Iowa House Journal* (1855), Appendix, pp. 246–48; *Iowa Senate Journal* (1857), pp. 592–93; Des Moines *Tri-Weekly Citizen,* 28 Jan. 1858 (house); Des Moines *Tri-Weekly Iowa State Journal,* 3 Mar. 1858 (senate); *Rules and Statistics of the Senate and House of Representatives, Adopted by the Tenth General Assembly* . . . (Des Moines, 1864), pp. 21–24 (house), pp. 25–26 (senate); *Rules and Statistics of the Senate and House of Representatives* (Des Moines, 1866), pp. 13–16 (house), pp. 25–27 (senate); *Rules of the Twelfth General Assembly of the State of Iowa and List of Standing Committees and Members* (Des Moines, 1868), pp. 21–23 (senate), pp. 24–27 (house); *Rules of the Thirteenth General Assembly* . . . (Des Moines, 1870), pp. 21–23 (senate), pp. 24–27 (house); *Rules of the Fourteenth General Assembly* . . . (Des Moines, 1872), pp. 21–23 (senate), pp. 24–27 (house); *Rules of the Sixteenth General Assembly* . . . (Des Moines, 1876), pp. 23–24 (senate), pp. 25–28 (house); *Rules of the Seventeenth General Assembly* . . . (Des Moines, 1878), pp. 26–27 (senate), pp. 28–31 (house).

Partisan affiliation was not listed in the official documents until 1878. This information was gleaned from several sources: T. Eagal and R. Sylvester, eds., *The Iowa State Almanac and Statistical Register for 1860* (Davenport, 1860), pp. 22-24, 28-29 (1854-60); Des Moines *Iowa State Register,* 16 Oct. 1861; ibid., 24 Nov. 1863; ibid., 5 Dec. 1865; ibid., 16 Jan. 1868; ibid., 6 Jan. 1870; ibid., 31 Oct. 1871; ibid., 22 Oct. 1873; ibid., 7 Jan. 1876.

2. The second stage of the project was an evaluation of partisanship in the assembly. Rice indices of cohesion and indices of likeness were calculated from totals produced by the crosstabulation program contained in Norman H. Nie, C. Hadlai Hull, Jean G. Jenkins, Karin Steinbrenner, and Dale H. Bent, *SPSS: Statistical Package for the Social Sciences* (2nd ed., New York, 1975), pp. 214-48. The Rice index of cohesion, a measure of intraparty unity on separate motions, is obtained by subtracting the percentage of party x voting nay from the percentage of the same party voting in the affirmative. Any minus signs can be ignored. The index of likeness is designed to quantify the extent of interparty agreement on individual motions. It is calculated by the formula $100 - (\%x \text{ or } y - \%y \text{ or } x)$, where $\%x$ and $\%y$ are the percentages of parties x and y voting yea on a single roll call and the smaller figure is always subtracted from the larger, i.e., 100 = total agreement; 0 = complete disagreement. A full discussion of these elementary procedures appears in L.F. Anderson et al., *Legislative Roll Call Analysis* (Evanston, 1966), pp. 32-34, 44-45.

3. The value of Yules Q, a variation of chi-square, was ascertained for each pair of roll calls in a session in order to provide prima facie evidence of interrelated issues—a useful means of detecting hidden strands of the Republican world view. The formula for calculating Q is:

$$\frac{ad - bc}{ad + bc}$$

where $a, b, c,$ and d are four segments of a two-motion square:

	Yea	Nay
Yea	a	b
Nay	c	d

My understanding of this statistic was enhanced by the discussion contained in the appendix to Edward Countryman, *A People in Revolution: The American Revolution and Political Society in New York, 1760-1790* (Baltimore and London, 1981). Dr. Countryman's own experiences with quantitative techniques as recounted to me in conversation played an important part in directing my approach to the Iowa data.

4. The next step was to conduct a statistical analysis of the voting data. After conversations with Professor Morgan Kousser of California Technical Institute, Dr. Valerie Cromwell of Sussex University, and Dr. Clive Osmond of the MRC Environmental Epidemiology Unit, Southampton University, I decided to make use of those multidimensional scaling (MDS) techniques that have been applied not only in several areas of political science but also, in a specifically historical context, by Dr. Cromwell herself.[1]

The principal aim of this sophisticated form of multivariate analysis is to generate from mathematical dissimilarities a geometric configuration of points reflecting the proximity values of certain objects.[2] This configuration takes the form of a map in which the objects—in this case, Iowa legislators—are represented by points, the distances between which are in good agreement with the dissimilarity values. Legislators voting the same way on most motions will therefore be close together on the map; those voting antagonistically will be distant from each other. For the purpose of this study the dissimilarity value for a pair of legislators was defined as the ratio

$$\frac{\text{Number of motions in which both voted antagonistically}}{\text{Number of motions in which both voted}}$$

Using a program written by Dr. Osmond and adapted for use on the Oxford computer by Paul Salotti, a database consultant at the Oxford University Computing Centre, two-dimensional MDS maps were produced for many sets of roll calls. Abstentions and absentees were unfortunately, but necessarily, discarded, and a legislator was excluded from the analysis if he had voted in fewer than half the motions in a set. When the small number of roll calls included in a set resulted in two or more legislators sharing the same coordinates (i.e., having the same voting pattern), the map points were inflated in direct proportion to the number of men on that position.

The end result of this survey is a detailed picture of intra- and interparty reaction to a wide range of issues—some of them related—over a long period of time. The visual output format provided by MDS reduced the need for turgid explanatory prose and indigestible tabular information. To those like myself who believe that history should be a basically literary (but not innumerate) discipline, this particular form of statistical analysis is a potent quantitative tool.

Abbreviations Used in Notes and Bibliography

AHR	*American Historical Review*
AI	*Annals of Iowa*
CG	*Congressional Globe*
CWH	*Civil War History*
IaCJ	*Journal of the Iowa Council*
IaHJ	*Journal of the Iowa House of Representatives*
IaSJ	*Journal of the Iowa Senate*
IHR	*Iowa Historical Record*
IJH	*Iowa Journal of History*
IJHP	*Iowa Journal of History and Politics*
JAH	*Journal of American History*
JAS	*Journal of American Studies*
JEH	*Journal of Economic History*
JSH	*Journal of Southern History*
LC	Library of Congress
MVHR	*Mississippi Valley Historical Review*
RAH	*Reviews in American History*
SHSI	State Historical Society of Iowa
WMQ	*William and Mary Quarterly*
WRHS	Western Reserve Historical Society

Notes

1 / Republicanism in the Civil War Era: Iowa as a Test Case

1. *Appletons' Hand-Book of American Travel: Western Tour* (New York and London, 1873), 202.
2. The concept of the market revolution has been developed most fully by C.G. Sellers, *The Market Revolution and Jacksonian America, 1815–1846* (New York and Oxford, 1991).
3. C.A. and M.R. Beard, *The Rise of American Civilization* (London, 1927), II, 53.
4. R.L. McCormick, *The Party Period and Public Policy: American Politics from the Age of Jackson to the Progressive Era* (New York and Oxford, 1986), 98.
5. E. Foner, *Politics and Ideology in the Age of the Civil War* (New York and Oxford, 1980); S. Wilentz, *Chants Democratic: New York City and the Rise of the American Working Class, 1788–1850* (New York and Oxford, 1984); B. Laurie, *Working People of Philadelphia, 1800–1850* (Philadelphia, 1980).
6. D.B. Davis, *The Problem of Slavery in the Age of Revolution 1770–1823* (Ithaca and London, 1975), and *Slavery and Human Progress* (New York and Oxford, 1984).
7. J. Leach, "A New Manifesto for Responsible Republicanism," *Des Moines Register*, 27 September 1981, 3C.
8. E.g., K.M. Stampp, *The Era of Reconstruction: America after the Civil War, 1865–77* (London, 1965).
9. S.P. Hays, "Politics and Society: Beyond the Political Party," in P. Kleppner et al., *The Evolution of American Electoral Systems* (Westport, Conn., and London, 1981), 243–67; R.D. Brown, *Modernization: The Transformation of American Life, 1600–1865* (New York, 1976); R. Wiebe, *The Opening of American Society: From the Adoption of the Constitution to the Eve of Disunion* (New York, 1984).
10. Hays, "Politics and Society," 254.
11. L. Benson, *The Concept of Jacksonian Democracy: New York as a Test Case* (Princeton, 1961); R.P. Formisano, *The Birth of Mass Political Parties: Michigan, 1827–1861* (Princeton, 1971); P. Kleppner, *The Cross of Culture: A Social Analysis of Midwestern Politics, 1850–1900* (New York and London, 1970).
12. Brown, *Modernization*, 131, 167.
13. Hays, "Politics and Society," 257.
14. J. Atack and F. Bateman, "Self-Sufficiency and the Marketable Surplus in the Rural North, 1860," *Agricultural History*, LVIII (July 1984), 298.
15. E. Dicey, *Six Months in the Federal States* (London and Cambridge, England, 1863), II, 163–64.
16. Quoted in A.C. Cole, *The Era of the Civil War, 1848–1870* (*Centennial History of Illinois*, vol. III, Springfield, Ill., 1919), 65.
17. J.M. Clubb et al., *Partisan Realignment: Voters, Parties, and Government in American History* (Beverly Hills and London, 1980).

18. F.J. Sorauf, *Political Parties in the American System* (Boston and Toronto, 1964), 2.

2 / The Second Party System on the Frontier, 1838–1846

1. Iowa Secretary of State, *Historical and Comparative Census of Iowa for 1880* (Des Moines, 1883), 168.
2. T. Le Duc, "History and Appraisal of U.S. Land Policy to 1862," in H.W. Ottoson, ed., *Land Use Policy and Problems in the United States* (Lincoln, Nebr., 1963), 3–27.
3. A.G. Bogue, "The Iowa Claim Clubs: Symbol and Substance," *MVHR*, XLV (September 1958), 231–53.
4. L.L. Sage, *A History of Iowa* (Ames, Iowa, 1974), 71–72.
5. R.P. Swierenga, *Pioneers and Profits: Land Speculation on the Iowa Frontier* (Ames, Iowa, 1968), 35–36.
6. Iowa Secretary of State, *Comparative Census, 1880*, 168.
7. On the rapid development of commercial farming in the antebellum Midwest see M. Throne, "Southern Iowa Agriculture, 1833–1890: The Progress from Subsistence to Commercial Farming," *Agricultural History*, XXIII (April 1949), 124–30, and J. Atack and F. Bateman, *To Their Own Soil: Agriculture in the Antebellum North* (Ames, Iowa, 1987).
8. M.F. Holt, "The Election of 1840: Voter Mobilization and the Emergence of the Second American Party System: A Reappraisal of Jacksonian Voting Behavior," in W.J. Cooper et al., *A Master's Due: Essays in Honor of David Herbert Donald* (Baton Rouge and London, 1985), 16–58.
9. *Laws of the Territory of Iowa* (Burlington, Iowa, 1840), 158.
10. *IaHJ*, 1839–40, 239.
11. L. Pelzer, "The History and Principles of the Whigs of the Territory of Iowa." *IJHP*, V (January 1907), 50.
12. Ibid., 51–52.
13. Holt, "Election of 1840," 23.
14. Pelzer, "History and Principles," 52.
15. Sage, *History of Iowa*, 80–91.
16. John Catlin to George W. Jones, 13 December 1836, in J.P. Bloom, ed., *Wisconsin Territory, The Territorial Papers of the United States*, vol. XXVII (Washington, D.C., 1969), 686.
17. E.A. Erickson, *Banking in Frontier Iowa, 1836–1865* (Ames, Iowa, 1971), 27.
18. Ibid., 33; *IaHJ*, 1845, 49.
19. For biographical details on Clarke see E.M. Eriksson, "William Penn Clarke," *IJHP*, XXV (January 1927), 3–61.
20. B.F. Shambaugh, ed., *Fragments of the Debates of the Iowa Constitutional Conventions of 1844 and 1846* (Iowa City, 1900), 349–51.
21. Ibid., 68–69.
22. Ibid., 70.
23. Ibid., 74–75.
24. Ibid., 75–76.
25. Ibid., 76.
26. Erickson, *Banking in Frontier Iowa*, 47.
27. J. Ashworth, *"Agrarians" & "Aristocrats": Party Political Ideology in the United States, 1837–1846* (London, 1983), 7–51, 87–111, 132–46.
28. Shambaugh, *Debates*, 191.
29. *Du Buque Visitor*, 13 July 1836.

30. Bloom, *Wisconsin Territory,* illustration following p.74.
31. *IaHJ,* 1838-39, 63.
32. Ibid., 234; *IaCJ,* 1838-39, 196.
33. *IaHJ,* 1842-43, 39-40, 43-44, 103.
34. Ibid., 258.
35. Ibid., 252.
36. Ibid.
37. U.S. Census Office, *Seventh Census of the United States: 1850* (Washington, D.C., 1853), lvii-lix.
38. *IaCJ,* 1838-39, 9
39. *IaHJ,* 1842-43, 190.
40. Ibid., 134-35.
41. Ibid., 134.
42. Shambaugh, *Debates,* 21-22.
43. Ibid., 19.

3 / Defeat of the Democracy, 1846-1854

1. H.S. Fairall, *The Iowa City Republican Manual of Iowa Politics* (Iowa City, 1881), 22-23.
2. Ibid., 19.
3. Washington, D.C., *National Era,* 15 April 1847.
4. *The Statute Laws of the Territory of Iowa . . . 1838-39,* 65-67; the bill passed the house without a roll call and the council nine to three, *IaCJ,* 1838-39, 164.
5. R.R. Dykstra, "White Men, Black Laws: Territorial Iowans and Civil Rights, 1838-1843," *AI,* 3rd Series, XLVI (Fall 1982), 409-10.
6. My discussion of abolitionist communities in early Iowa relies heavily on ibid., 411-20.
7. G.F. Magoun, *Asa Turner: A Home Missionary Patriarch and His Times* (Boston, 1889), 290.
8. Kleppner, *Cross of Culture,* 71-75.
9. Dykstra, "White Men," 422, 424-25.
10. Ibid., 437.
11. See esp. J.B. Stewart, "Abolitionists, Insurgents, and Third Parties: Sectionalism and Partisan Politics in Northern Whiggery, 1836-1844," in A.M. Kraut, ed., *Crusaders and Compromisers: Essays on the Relationship of the Antislavery Struggle to the Antebellum Party System* (Westport, Conn., and London, 1983), 25-43.
12. *National Era,* 4 February 1847, 10 February 1848.
13. Ibid., 17 August 1848.
14. F.H. Warren to W.P. Clarke, 29 March 1848, William Penn Clarke Papers, SHSI, Des Moines.
15. W.D. Burnham, *Presidential Ballots, 1836-1892* (Baltimore, 1955), 412-30.
16. Fairall, *Manual,* 23.
17. F.H. Warren to W.P. Clarke, 8 July 1849, Clarke Papers.
18. Ibid.
19. T.C. Smith, *The Liberty and Free Soil Parties in the Northwest* (New York, London, and Bombay, 1897), 217.
20. Fairall, *Manual,* 28.
21. *CG,* 31 Cong., 1 Sess., Appendix, 1716.

22. Ibid., 910.
23. *Acts, Resolutions, and Memorials Passed at the Regular Session of the Third General Assembly, of the State of Iowa . . . 1850* (Iowa City, 1851), 172–73.
24. F.H. Warren to W.P. Clarke, 17 August 1851, Clarke Papers.
25. Iowa Secretary of State, *Comparative Census, 1880,* 168.
26. *National Era,* 23 June 1853.
27. M.M. Rosenberg, *Iowa on the Eve of the Civil War: A Decade of Frontier Politics* (Norman, Okla., 1972), 25.
28. *CG,* 30 Cong., 1 Sess., 986–87.
29. *Laws of Iowa,* 1850–51, 22–24, 70–72, 75–77, 127–31, 164–65, 202–4.
30. Fairall, *Manual,* 33.
31. *Acts, Resolutions, and Memorials Passed at the Regular Session of the Fourth General Assembly of the State of Iowa . . . 1852* (Iowa City, 1853), 58–62.
32. Fairall, *Manual,* 32.
33. Erickson, *Banking in Frontier Iowa,* 64–65.
34. See esp. R.A. Billington, *The Protestant Crusade, 1800–1860* (Quadrangle ed., Chicago, 1964), chaps. 2–10.
35. E. Adams, *The Iowa Band* (Boston, 1870).
36. Iowa Secretary of State, *Comparative Census, 1880,* 168–69.
37. D.E. Clark, "The History of Liquor Legislation in Iowa, 1846–1861," *IJHP,* VI (January 1908), 57–64.
38. On Price's early temperance activities see B.F. Gue, "The Public Services of Hiram Price," *AI,* 3rd Series, VIII (January 1895), 587–91.
39. W. Salter, *The Life of James W. Grimes, Governor of Iowa, 1854–1858; A Senator of the United States, 1859–1869* (New York, 1876), 26.
40. Fairall, *Manual,* 32–33.
41. Ibid., 33.
42. R.C. Bain and J.H. Parris, *Convention Decisions and Voting Records* (2nd ed., Washington, D.C., 1973), Appendix C.
43. Ibid., Appendix C.
44. G. Shedd to W.P. Clarke, 21 January 1852, Clarke Papers.
45. *National Era,* 26 August 1852.
46. S. Petersen, *A Statistical History of the American Presidential Elections* (New York, 1963), 31.
47. On the genesis of Kansas-Nebraska see R.F. Nichols, "The Kansas-Nebraska Act: A Century of Historiography," *MVHR,* XLIII (September 1956), 187–212; R.W. Johannsen, *Stephen A. Douglas* (New York, 1973), chap. 17.
48. Iowa senator A.C. Dodge's role in the formulation of the Kansas-Nebraska bill is recounted in L. Pelzer, *Augustus Caesar Dodge: A Study in American Politics* (Iowa City, 1909), 181–93.
49. Fairall, *Manual,* 37–38.
50. Keokuk *Des Moines Valley Whig,* 2 March 1854; on Frances Waters see *National Era,* 21 November 1850, and her obituary in *National Era,* 22 July 1852.
51. S. Waters to J.A. Reed, 3 October 1854, Julius A. Reed Papers, Grinnell College Library.
52. Sage, *History of Iowa,* 127.
53. Salter, *Grimes,* is the standard life.
54. Ibid., 153.
55. Ibid., 26.
56. Ibid., 115; Sage, *History of Iowa,* 127–28.

57. Magoun, *Turner*, 287.
58. F.H. Warren to W.P. Clarke, 8 April 1854, Clarke Papers.
59. Salter, *Grimes*, 34–50; according to Magoun, a draft of this address had been used to influence the Free-Soil convention at Crawfordsville. Magoun, *Turner*, 287.
60. Salter, *Grimes*, 47.
61. Ibid., 48.
62. C.C. Carpenter, "James Grimes, Governor and Senator," *AI*, 3rd Series, I (1894), 511.
63. J.W. Grimes to E.B. Washburne, 13 July 1854, Elihu B. Washburne Papers, LC.
64. The official source for state election results is Iowa Secretary of State, *Election Returns, 1839–1890* (microfilm copy, University of Iowa Library, Iowa City), reel 1.
65. W.E. Gienapp, *The Origins of the Republican Party, 1852–1856* (New York and Oxford, 1987), 122, 502.
66. Ibid., 499.
67. Rosenberg, *Eve of Civil War*, 13, 26.

4 / Formation of the Republican Party in Iowa, 1854–1856

1. J.W. Grimes to C. Mason, 21 October 1854, Charles Mason Papers, SHSI, Des Moines.
2. Salter, *Grimes*, 54.
3. Ibid., 55.
4. Ibid., 56.
5. B.F. Shambaugh, ed., *Messages and Proclamations of the Governors of Iowa* (Iowa City, 1903–5), II, 13.
6. Salter, *Grimes*, 63n.
7. D.E. Clark, *History of Senatorial Elections in Iowa* (Iowa City, 1912), 73.
8. J. Brigham, *James Harlan* (Iowa City, 1913), 87.
9. Initially thirteen Whigs refused to vote for Harlan, but this total quickly dwindled to seven, *IaHJ*, 1854–55, 106, 109.
10. Salter, *Grimes*, 63.
11. Ibid., 63.
12. Ibid., 64.
13. Ibid.
14. The evangelical total does not include two committed abolitionists, Thomas Turner of Quasqueton and Jacob W. Rogers of West Union.
15. F.H. Warren to E.B. Washburne, 23 November 1860, Washburne Papers.
16. *IaHJ*, 1854–55, 330–31; *IaSJ*, 1854–55, 201.
17. *IaHJ*, 1854–55, 244–45.
18. *IaSJ*, 1854–55, 208.
19. *Proceedings of the Iowa Baptist Convention . . . 1851* (Burlington, Iowa, 1851), 11.
20. J.B Chase, ed., *Minutes of the General Association of Congregational Churches and Ministers of the State of Iowa . . . 1840 to 1865* (Hull, Iowa, 1889), 79.
21. *Addresses Delivered upon the Installation of Rev. Lucien W. Berry, D.D., as President of the Iowa Wesleyan University . . . 1856* (Mount Pleasant, Iowa, 1856), 14, 35.
22. Salter, *Grimes*, 69.
23. *National Era*, 5 April, 4 October 1855.
24. R.F. Matthias, "The Know Nothing Movement in Iowa" (University of Chicago Ph.D. thesis, 1965), 38.
25. Ibid., 29–31.

26. M.F. Holt, *The Political Crisis of the 1850s* (New York, 1978), 158–69.
27. Matthias, "Know Nothing Movement," 27–28.
28. E. Foner, *Free Soil, Free Labor, Free Men: The Ideology of the Republican Party before the Civil War* (New York, 1970), 259.
29. W.E. Gienapp, "Salmon Chase, Nativism, and the Formation of the Republican Party in Ohio," *Ohio History,* XCIII (Winter-Spring 1984), 5–39.
30. *National Era,* 4 October 1855.
31. Ibid.
32. Matthias, "Know Nothing Movement," 113.
33. Burlington *Weekly Hawk-Eye and Telegraph,* 14 November 1855.
34. W. Spicer to W.P. Clarke, 11 November 1855, Clarke Papers.
35. L. Pelzer, "The Origin and Organization of the Republican Party in Iowa," *IJHP,* IV (October 1906), 500. It is equally likely that James W. Grimes was the author of the call for a Republican state convention. See the memo in William Salter Papers, SHSI, Des Moines.
36. Pelzer, "Origin," 501n.
37. Keokuk *Daily Gate City,* 27 February 1856.
38. *National Era,* 6 March 1856.
39. J.W. Grimes to W.P. Clarke, 3 April 1856, Clarke Papers.
40. Keokuk *Daily Gate City,* 27 February 1856, contains convention minutes and a list of delegates.
41. Fairall, *Manual,* 40–41.
42. Pelzer, "Republican Party," 512–13.
43. Salter, *Grimes,* 79. The only concession to Know Nothings in the Republican platform was a plank lauding the election of Nathaniel P. Banks as speaker of the U.S. House of Representatives.
44. Matthias, "Know Nothing Movement," 137.
45. Ibid., 146.
46. J.W. Grimes to W.P. Clarke, 3 April 1856, Clarke Papers.
47. Salter, *Grimes,* 80.
48. G.G. Rice to J.A. Reed, 10 July 1854, Reed Papers.
49. G.G. Rice to J.A. Reed, 22 August 1854, ibid.
50. *CG,* 34 Cong., 1 Sess., Appendix, 270–76.
51. Ibid., 274–75.
52. J. Harlan to M. Simpson, 5 January 1856, Matthew Simpson Papers, LC.
53. J. Harlan to M. Simpson, 11 February 1856, ibid.
54. Ibid.
55. *Weekly Hawk-Eye and Telegraph,* 13, 20 February 1855.
56. J. Harlan to M. Simpson, 11 February 1856, Simpson Papers, LC.
57. S. Pomeroy to W.P. Clarke, 14 June 1856; J.H. Lane to W.P. Clarke, 30 June 1856, Clarke Papers; Eriksson, "William Penn Clarke," 40–41.
58. B. Walsh to W.P. Clarke, 30 June 1856, Clarke Papers.
59. H. Price to W.P. Clarke, 6 August 1856, ibid.
60. J.W. Grimes to W.P. Clarke, June 1856, ibid.
61. J. Connor, "The Antislavery Movement in Iowa," *AI,* 3rd Series, XL (Summer and Fall 1970), 455.
62. J. Todd, *Early Settlement and Growth of Western Iowa or Reminiscences* (Des Moines, 1906), chap. 7; J. Todd to W. Salter, 17 September 1856, William Salter Papers, SHSI, Des Moines.
63. G. Lewis to W. Salter, 12 July 1856; E. Jones to W. Salter, 2 August 1856, ibid.
64. J.C. Knapp to L. Summers, 14 July 1856, Laurel Summers Papers, SHSI, Des Moines.

65. T.W. Higginson to W.P. Clarke, 14 August 1856, Clarke Papers.

66. See F.D. Sanborn, *Recollections of Seventy Years* (Boston 1909), I, 53–55, 59–63, for an account of the Yankee's activities in Iowa.

67. Ibid., I, 67.

68. J. Rossbach, *Ambivalent Conspirators: John Brown, the Secret Six, and a Theory of Slave Violence* (Philadelphia, 1982), chaps. 5–8.

69. Salter, *Grimes*, 86.

70. Ibid., 87.

71. For an enlightening discussion of the slave power thesis see W.E. Gienapp, "The Republican Party and the Slave Power," in R.H. Abzug and S.H. Maizlish, eds., *New Perspectives on Race and Slavery in America: Essays in Honor of Kenneth M. Stampp* (Lexington 1986), 51–78.

72. H. Greeley to W.M. Chase et al., 9 May 1856, Horace Greeley Papers, LC.

73. *Economist* (London), 24 December 1859.

74. Shambaugh, *Messages*, II, 130.

75. See *AI*, 3rd Series, IV (October 1899), 233–34, for a sketch of James.

76. *Burlington Weekly Hawk-Eye and Telegraph*, 25 June 1855.

77. Salter, *Grimes*, 73.

78. Ibid., 73.

79. Ibid.

80. *The Debates of the Constitutional Convention of the State of Iowa . . . 1857* (Davenport, Iowa, 1857), II, 910.

81. J. Davis, *The Rise and Fall of the Confederate Government* (London, 1881), I, 33.

82. W.W. Hamilton to C. Aldrich, 16 February 1861, Charles Aldrich Papers, SHSI, Des Moines.

83. C.C. Nourse, *Autobiography of Charles Clinton Nourse* (Cedar Rapids, Iowa, 1911), 41.

84. Ibid., 32.

85. C. Fairman, *Mr. Justice Miller and the Supreme Court, 1862–1890* (Cambridge, Mass., 1939), 30.

86. Salter, *Grimes*, 5, 196; J.W. Grimes to Rev. C.C. Shackford, 20 March 1852, Salter Papers. Shortly before his marriage in November 1846 Grimes summed up his religious views thus: "[T]he only safe course for a man in this life is to be a christian. Even if the Bible is false, the man who believes in it, & follows its precepts, is a happier & a better man & the man who does not believe in the Bible, should it prove to be true, is not so happy, or so useful in this life, & his future will be a most unhappy one." G.A. Thomas to W. Salter, 6 August 1877, ibid.

87. Salter, *Grimes*, 239.

88. See Nourse, *Autobiography*, 34–36, for an account of Phillips's speech.

89. Salter, *Grimes*, 42–43.

90. Petersen, *Presidential Elections*, 35.

91. Burnham, *Presidential Ballots*, 412–34.

92. Gienapp, *Origins*, 429.

93. Quoted in ibid., 429.

94. Ibid., 539.

95. Ibid., 537.

96. Ibid., 543.

97. Ibid., 545; E. Magdol, *The Antislavery Rank and File: A Social Profile of the Abolitionists' Constituency* (New York, Westport, Conn., and London, 1986); S. Drescher, *Capitalism and Antislavery* (Basingstoke and London, 1986).

5 / The Race Question in the Campaign of 1857

1. Rosenberg, *Eve of the Civil War*, 149.
2. Ibid., 149.
3. See chap. 6.
4. Iowa Secretary of State, *Comparative Census, 1880*, 168, 170.
5. The remarks that follow are based on my own analysis of the U.S. MS Census, 1860: Iowa (SHSI, Des Moines).
6. *Past and Present of Fayette County, Iowa* (Indianapolis, 1910), I, 131-32.
7. For a sketch of Clark see *The History of Muscatine County, Iowa*, . . . (Chicago, 1879), 597-98.
8. *CG,* 34 Cong., 1 Sess., Appendix, 407.
9. Ibid., 408.
10. *IaHJ,* 1854-55, 319.
11. Iowa, Fifth General Assembly, Senate, Bills, S.F. 141, State Archives, SHSI, Des Moines.
12. *IaHJ,* 1854-55, 380.
13. Ibid., 395.
14. My contention that Grimes did not sign the bill is based on (1) the fact that it was not published along with the other acts of 1855, (2) an American Colonization Society report that alluded to an executive veto of the measure, *The Annual Reports of the American Society for Colonizing the Free People of Color of the United States* (reprinted, New York, 1969), XXXIX, 6.
15. See Appendix for sources of legislative data.
16. *IaHJ,* 1854-55, 229-30.
17. *IaSJ,* 1856-57, 127-29.
18. *IaHJ,* 1856-57, 466.
19. E.H. Stiles, *Recollections and Sketches of Notable Lawyers and Public Men of Early Iowa* (Des Moines, 1916), 112.
20. *Burlington Weekly Hawk-Eye and Telegraph,* 11 July 1855.
21. *Constitutional Convention, 1857,* I, 101.
22. *National Era,* 4 December 1856.
23. *Constitutional Convention, 1857,* I, 102.
24. Ibid., II, 736.
25. Ibid., II, 737.
26. Ibid., II, 738-39.
27. Ibid., II, 741.
28. Ibid., II, 681-82.
29. Ibid., II, 690.
30. Ibid., II, 700, 703.
31. Ibid., II, 888-905.
32. Ibid., I, 129.
33. Stiles, *Recollections,* 672-73; on Clarke's links with Warren see Clark, *Senatorial Elections,* 73-74; on his nativist past see *Constitutional Convention, 1857,* II, 862.
34. *Constitutional Convention, 1857,* I, 181; Clarke's subsequent advocacy of Indian extermination casts serious doubts on his claim to be "a friend of the whole human race." See R.L.B. Clarke to W.B. Allison, 18 October 1875, William Boyd Allison Papers, SHSI, Des Moines.
35. *Constitutional Convention, 1857,* I, 130.
36. Ibid., I, 133.

37. Ibid., I, 132–33.
38. Ibid., I, 135, 138.
39. Ibid., I, 172.
40. Ibid., I, 177.
41. Ibid., I, 180.
42. Ibid., I, 180.
43. Ibid., I, 185.
44. Ibid., I, 187.
45. Ibid., I, 189.
46. Ibid., I, 191–94.
47. Ibid., I, 196, 198.
48. Ibid., I, 200, II, 734.
49. Ibid., I, 45.
50. Ibid., I, 46.
51. Ibid., I, 216, 219.
52. Ibid., II, 641.
53. Ibid., II, 650.
54. Ibid., II, 660.
55. Ibid., II, 663.
56. Ibid., II, 675–76.
57. Ibid., II, 699–700.
58. Ibid., II, 673.
59. Ibid., II, 679.
60. Ibid., II, 672.
61. J.W. Grimes to C.C. Carpenter, 30 November 1857, Cyrus Clay Carpenter Papers, SHSI, Des Moines.
62. *Constitutional Convention, 1857,* II, 912.
63. L. Fishel, "Wisconsin and Negro Suffrage," *Wisconsin Magazine of History,* XLVI (Spring 1963), 184–85.
64. *Constitutional Convention, 1857,* II, 917.
65. Clark, "Liquor Legislation, 1846–61," 73–74.
66. Fairall, *Manual,* 45.
67. This survey of West Union is based on my own analysis of U.S. MS Census, 1860: Iowa, Fayette County, West Union Township (SHSI, Des Moines).
68. *Portrait and Biographical Album of Fayette County, Iowa* (Chicago, 1891), 181–83.
69. *Past and Present of Fayette Co.,* I, 143.
70. J.W. Rogers Diary, 11 July 1857, Jacob Wentworth Rogers Papers, SHSI, Iowa City.
71. Ibid., 13 July 1857; West Union *Fayette County Pioneer,* 20 July 1857.
72. J.W. Rogers Diary, 20 July 1857, Rogers Papers.
73. Ibid., 29 July 1857.
74. *Fayette County Pioneer,* 10 August 1857.
75. Ibid., 20 July 1857.
76. J.W. Rogers Diary, 16 July 1857, Rogers Papers.
77. Ibid., 19 February 1878.
78. Ibid., 30 July 1857; *West Union Republican Gazette,* 22 December 1871.
79. R. Eddy, "History of Universalism," in R. Eddy and J.H. Allen, *A History of the Unitarians and Universalists in the United States* (*The American Church History,* vol. X, New York, 1894), 255–493.
80. *National Era,* 8 November 1849.
81. *Fayette County Pioneer,* 16 February 1857.

82. J.W. Rogers Diary, 9 July 1857, Rogers Papers.
83. Ibid., 10 July 1857; *Fayette County Pioneer,* 29 June 1857.
84. L.J. Friedman, *Gregarious Saints: Self and Community in American Abolitionism, 1830-1870* (Cambridge, England, 1982), chap. 4.
85. J.W. Rogers Diary, 1 February 1857, Rogers Papers.
86. Ibid., 3 February 1857.
87. *The History of Fayette County, Iowa* (Chicago, 1878), 366.
88. *Fayette County Pioneer,* 27 July 1857.
89. J.W. Rogers Diary, 4 July 1857, Rogers Papers; *History of Fayette Co.,* 542, identifies Moulton.
90. J.W. Rogers Diary, 1 August 1857, Rogers Papers.
91. Ibid., 3 August 1857.
92. *Fayette County Pioneer,* 10 August 1857.
93. J.W. Rogers Diary, 15 August 1857, Rogers Papers.
94. Rosenberg, *Eve of the Civil War,* 154.
95. R.R. Dykstra, "The Issue Squarely Met: Toward an Explanation of Iowans' Racial Attitudes, 1865-1868," *AI,* 3rd Series, XLVII (Summer 1984), 432n.
96. Fairall, *Manual,* 43.
97. Ibid., 45.
98. R.R. Glashan, *American Governors and Gubernatorial Elections, 1775-1978* (London, 1979), 92.

6 / The Impact of Recession on Local Politics, 1858-1859

1. Iowa Secretary of State, *Comparative Census, 1880,* 168.
2. Ibid., 169.
3. E.H. Hall, *Ho! For the West!! The Traveller and Emigrants' Hand-Book to Canada and the North-West of the American Union . . .* (London, 1858), 22-23.
4. Ibid., 22.
5. *Agriculture of the United States in 1860: Compiled from the Original Returns of the Eighth Census* (Washington, D.C., 1864), 51.
6. Ibid., 51.
7. U.S. Bureau of the Census, *Historical Statistics of the United States: Colonial Times to 1970* (Washington, D.C., 1975), I, 462.
8. Atack and Bateman, *To Their Own Soil,* 223, 250.
9. C. Mason Diary, 14 July 1855, Mason Papers.
10. A. Fishlow, "Antebellum Interregional Trade Reconsidered," *American Economic Review,* LIV (May 1964), 352-64.
11. J.L. Larson, *Bonds of Enterprise: John Murray Forbes and Western Development in America's Railway Age* (Cambridge, Mass., and London, 1984), 53-82.
12. Rosenberg, *Eve of the Civil War,* 72, 77.
13. L.F. Ralston, "Railroads and the Government of Iowa, 1850-1872," (University of Iowa Ph.D. thesis, 1960), 26-28.
14. Shambaugh, *Messages,* II, 17.
15. Ibid., II, 17-18, 38.
16. Ralston, "Railroads," 35.
17. Erickson, *Banking in Frontier Iowa,* 81-82.
18. Ibid., 86.
19. *Constitutional Convention, 1857,* I, 350.

20. Ibid., I, 350.
21. Ibid., I, 375-77.
22. Ibid., I, 367.
23. Ibid., I, 364.
24. Ibid., I, 349, 354, 387.
25. Ibid., I, 355-56.
26. Ibid., II, 794; Erickson, *Banking in Frontier Iowa*, 88-89.
27. *Dubuque Co. v. Dubuque & Pacific RR Company*, 4 G. Greene 1 (1853); Shambaugh, *Messages*, II, 37.
28. *Constitutional Convention, 1857*, I, 337.
29. Ibid., I, 316-17.
30. Ibid., I, 418.
31. Ibid., I, 305.
32. Ibid., II, 812, 1024-25.
33. E.g., *Fayette County Pioneer*, 27 July 1857.
34. See the letter from J.C. Hall in Des Moines *Iowa State Journal*, 1 August 1857.
35. Shambaugh, *Messages*, II, 117-18, 121.
36. Ibid., II, 126.
37. Ibid., II, 45.
38. *IaHJ*, 1858, 600, 587.
39. *IaSJ*, 1858, 419, 510.
40. *IaHJ*, 1858, 242, 246, 249, 697, 746.
41. H. Taylor to S.J. Kirkwood, 29 June 1859, Samuel J. Kirkwood Papers, SHSI, Des Moines.
42. Larson, *Bonds of Enterprise*, 74-75.
43. *Constitutional Convention, 1857*, II, 862.
44. Ibid., I, 322.
45. J.B. Grinnell to J. Grinnell, 3 May 1854, Josiah B. Grinnell Papers, Grinnell College Library.
46. J. Harlan to E. Clark, 17 November 1856, James Harlan Papers, SHSI, Iowa City.
47. D.S. Sparks, "Iowa Republicans and the Railroads, 1856-1860," *IJH*, LIII (July 1955), 276, 278.
48. Larson, *Bonds of Enterprise*, 58.
49. Ibid., 67.
50. J.W. Grimes to J.F. Joy, 18 December 1857, James F. Joy Papers, Detroit Public Library.
51. J.W. Grimes to J.F. Joy, 11 March 1858, ibid.
52. J.W. Grimes to J.F. Joy, 18 February 1858, ibid.
53. J.W. Grimes to J.F. Joy, 11 March 1858, ibid.
54. J.W. Grimes to J.F. Joy, 18 March 1858, ibid.
55. J.W. Grimes to J.F. Joy, 22 March 1858, ibid.
56. J.W. Grimes to J.F. Joy, 11 January 1859, ibid.
57. Smith's maneuvers and Lowe's response are detailed in L.F. Ralston, "Governor Ralph P. Lowe and State Aid to Railroads: Iowa Politics in 1859," *IJH*, LVIII (July 1960), 207-18.
58. G. Shedd to W.P. Clarke, 19 April 1858, Clarke Papers.
59. Erickson, *Banking in Frontier Iowa*, 93.
60. Ralston, "State Aid," 215.
61. T.F. Withrow to C.C. Carpenter, 8 November 1858, Cyrus Clay Carpenter Papers, SHSI, Iowa City.
62. Ralston, "State Aid," 215.

63. J. Bowen to W.P. Clarke, 20 October 1858, Clarke Papers.
64. J. MacBride, "'The Hard Times' of '58-'60 or Reminiscences of Southeastern Iowa," *IHR*, XIII (October 1897), 173.
65. See, e.g., S.M. Langworthy Diary, January 1859, Solon M. Langworthy Papers, SHSI, Iowa City.
66. W.W. Hamilton to S.J. Kirkwood, 12 April 1859, Samuel J. Kirkwood Papers, SHSI, Des Moines.
67. J.A. Kasson to S.J. Kirkwood, 1 May 1859, ibid.
68. J.W. Grimes to S.J. Kirkwood, 29 May 1859, ibid.
69. J. Harlan to W.P. Clarke, 12 May 1859, Clarke Papers.
70. J. Harlan to S.J. Kirkwood, 4 July 1859, Kirkwood Papers, SHSI, Des Moines.
71. Fairall, *Manual*, 50.
72. F.E. Herriott, "Germans in the Gubernatorial Campaign of Iowa in 1859," reprinted (1915) from *Deutsch-Amerikanische Geschichtsblatter Jahrbuch der Deutsch-Amerikanischen Historischen Gesellschaft von Illinois*, XIV (1914).
73. Fairall, *Manual*, 51.
74. Ibid., 52-53.
75. D.E. Clark, *Samuel Jordan Kirkwood* (Iowa City, 1917), 139-40.
76. Pelzer, *Dodge*, 246.
77. Rosenberg, *Eve of the Civil War*, 205.
78. Sparks, "Iowa Republicans and the Railroads," 274 and ff.; Rosenberg, *Eve of the Civil War*, 125.

7 / Iowa and the Coming of the Civil War, 1859-1861

1. *IaHJ*, 1858, 107-8.
2. Ibid., 311-13.
3. J.W. Grimes to S.J. Kirkwood, 11 March 1858, Kirkwood Papers, SHSI, Des Moines.
4. F. Springer to R.P. Lowe, 24 February 1858, ibid.
5. *Fairfield Ledger*, 6 January 1859.
6. C.C. Carpenter, "Speech on Freedom and Slavery, 1859," Carpenter Papers, Iowa City.
7. Foner, *Free Soil*, 136.
8. J.W. Grimes to S.P. Chase, 30 May 1859, Salmon P. Chase Papers, LC.
9. Webster City *Hamilton Freeman*, 29 October 1859.
10. On Brown's exploits in Iowa see J. Connor, "The Antislavery Movement in Iowa," *AI*, 3rd Series, XL (Fall 1970), 462-63, 465, 467-71; S. Oates, *To Purge This Land with Blood: A Biography of John Brown* (New York, Evanston, and London, 1970), 210, 221-23, 242-43, 265; F. Lloyd, "John Brown among the Pedee Quakers," *AI*, 1st Series, IV (April-October 1866), 665-70, 712-19, 759-64.
11. J.B. Grinnell, *Men and Events of Forty Years: Autobiographical Reminiscences of an Active Career from 1850 to 1890* (Boston, 1891), 214.
12. Eriksson, "William Penn Clarke," 43.
13. Iowa City *Iowa Republican*, 30 November 1859.
14. H. Taylor to A. Lincoln, 8 November 1859, Abraham Lincoln Papers, LC.
15. *Iowa Weekly Republican*, 21 December 1859.
16. B.F. Gue, "John Brown and His Iowa Friends," *Midland Monthly*, VII (March 1897), 273-76.
17. A.C. Dodge to L. Summers, 16 December 1859, Summers Papers.

18. *IaSJ*, 1860, 345–46.
19. Shambaugh, *Messages*, II, 229–47.
20. Ibid., II, 246.
21. *Special Acts and Resolutions Passed at the Regular Session of the Eighth General Assembly of the State of Iowa . . . 1860* (Des Moines, 1860), 145–46.
22. *IaSJ*, 1860, 423.
23. T.C. Cochran, *Railroad Leaders, 1845–1890: The Business Mind in Action* (Cambridge, Mass., 1953), 332.
24. Des Moines *Iowa State Register*, 23 February 1860. The letter first appeared in the Republican *Chicago Tribune*.
25. Des Moines *Iowa State Register*, 20 February 1860.
26. J. Harlan to S.J. Kirkwood, 12 February 1860, Kirkwood Papers, Des Moines.
27. F.H. Warren to J.S. Pike, 2 February 1860, in J.S. Pike, *First Blows of the Civil War* (New York, 1879), 484.
28. C.C. Nourse, "The Iowa Delegation in the Republican National Convention of 1860," *IHR*, XI (July 1895), 295.
29. F.H. Warren to E.B. Washburne, 6 February 1860, Washburne Papers.
30. K.F. Millsap, "The Election of 1860 in Iowa," *IJH*, XLVIII (April 1950), 103; Rosenberg, *Eve of the Civil War*, 211.
31. Nourse, "Iowa Delegation," 294–95. William Penn Clarke, denoted a Seward supporter by Nourse, may well have voted for Cameron in a bid to secure a greater share of the spoils. (See the denunciation of Clarke's opportunism in G.W. Ells to S.P. Chase, 13 April 1860, Chase Papers.)
32. "A Delegate's Memories of the Chicago Convention of 1860: An Interview with Hon. Charles C. Nourse . . . 1907," *AI*, 3rd Series, XII (October 1920), 455.
33. Ibid., 459–60.
34. Millsap, "Election of 1860," 104.
35. Fairall, *Manual*, 55–56.
36. D. Rorer to C. Mason, 7 September 1860, Mason Papers.
37. *Dubuque Herald*, 17 October 1860.
38. Petersen, *Presidential Elections*, 39.
39. Burnham, *Presidential Ballots*, 412–34.
40. G.H. Daniels, "Immigrant Vote in the 1860 Election: The Case of Iowa," in F.C. Luebke, *Ethnic Voters and the Election of Lincoln* (Lincoln, Nebr., 1971), 146–62.
41. A. Turner to E. Adams, 9 November 1860, Ephraim Adams Papers, SHSI, Iowa City.
42. Quoted in Fairman, *Miller*, 36.
43. Ibid.
44. Millsap, "Election of 1860," 115–16; Davenport *Democrat and News*, 30 July 1860.
45. J.C. Savery to S.J. Kirkwood, 26 November 1859, Kirkwood Papers, SHSI, Des Moines.
46. E. Younger, *John A. Kasson: Politics and Diplomacy from Lincoln to McKinley* (Iowa City, 1955) is the standard biography.
47. S.P. Hirshson, *Grenville M. Dodge: Soldier, Politician, Railroad Pioneer* (Bloomington, Ind., and London, 1967), chap. 3.
48. J.A. Kasson to G.M. Dodge, 16 December 1859, Grenville M. Dodge Papers, SHSI, Des Moines.
49. J.C. Savery to S.J. Kirkwood, 26 November 1859, Kirkwood Papers, Des Moines.
50. C. Baldwin to G.M. Dodge, 9 December 1860, Dodge Papers.
51. E. Sells to S.J. Kirkwood, 22 March 1861, Kirkwood Papers, Des Moines.
52. H. Taylor to D. Davis, 27 December 1860; F. Springer to A. Lincoln, 22 January

1861; E. Sells et al. to A. Lincoln, 10 January 1861, Lincoln Papers.
   53. W. Vandever to A. Lincoln, 29 December 1860; J. Harlan to A. Lincoln, 17 January 1861, ibid.
   54. F.H. Warren to H. Taylor, 2 January 1861, ibid.
   55. *Cedar Falls Gazette,* 16 November 1860.
   56. Fairman, *Miller,* 36; J.A. Kasson to W.P. Clarke, 25 January 1861, Clarke Papers.
   57. G.M. Dodge to J. Dodge, 16 December 1860, Dodge Papers; W.W. Hamilton to S.J. Kirkwood, 19 December 1860, Kirkwood Papers, Des Moines.
   58. *CG,* 36 Cong., 2 Sess., 1.
   59. D.M. Potter, *Lincoln and his Party in the Secession Crisis* (New Haven and London, 1942), 95–98.
   60. *CG,* 36 Cong., 2 Sess., Appendix, 45.
   61. Potter, *Secession Crisis,* 294.
   62. Ibid., 288; Salter, *Grimes,* 132.
   63. K. Colton, ed., "'The Irrepressible Conflict of 1861': The Letters of Samuel Ryan Curtis," *AI,* 3rd Series, XXIV (July 1942), 18.
   64. J. Harlan to W.P. Clarke, 26 January 1861, Clarke Papers.
   65. Colton, "'Irrepressible Conflict'," 18.
   66. *Iowa State Register,* 23 January 1861.
   67. Iowa City *Iowa Weekly State Reporter,* 23 January 1861.
   68. "Letters of a War Governor," *IHR,* II (October 1886), 377–78.
   69. J.W. Grimes to S.J. Kirkwood, 28 January 1861, in *Iowa Weekly Republican,* 13 February 1861.
   70. L.E. Chittenden, *A Report of the Debates and Proceedings in the Secret Sessions of the Conference Convention, for Proposing Amendments to the Constitution of the United States . . . 1861* (New York, 1864), 71–73 (Curtis); *CG,* 36 Cong., 2 Sess., 1405 (Harlan).
   71. Ibid., 1422.
   72. Ibid., 1403.
   73. W.W. Belknap to C. Mason, 11 March 1861, Mason Papers.
   74. C. Mason Diary, 13 April 1861, ibid.
   75. H.C. Perkins, *Northern Editorials on Secession* (Gloucester, Mass., 1964), I, 488.
   76. Salter, *Grimes,* 132.

8 / The Union in Peril, 1861–1865

   1. Fairall, *Manual,* 57–58.
   2. Stiles, *Recollections,* 879.
   3. E. Price to S.J. Kirkwood, 8 August 1861, Kirkwood Papers, Des Moines.
   4. *Minutes of the [Congregational] General Association of Iowa at Its Session in Waterloo, June, 1861* (Des Moines, 1861), 7–8.
   5. Salter, *Grimes,* 146–47.
   6. Ibid., 153.
   7. S.R. Curtis to A. Lincoln, 12 October 1861, Lincoln Papers.
   8. J.W. Grimes to W.P. Fessenden, 13 November 1861, William Pitt Fessenden Papers, Bowdoin College Library.
   9. H.H. Wubben, *Civil War Iowa and the Copperhead Movement* (Ames, Iowa, 1980), 46.
   10. Glashan, *Gubernatorial Elections,* 92.
   11. S. Oates, *With Malice toward None: The Life of Abraham Lincoln* (Mentor ed., New

York and Scarborough, Ont., 1978), 290.

12. Shambaugh, *Messages,* II, 305.
13. C. Clarke to S.J. Kirkwood, 20 March 1862, Kirkwood Papers, Des Moines.
14. *CG,* 37 Cong., 2 Sess., 1333, 1522-23, 1526.
15. Ibid., 1357, 1359.
16. A.G. Bogue, *The Earnest Men: Republicans of the Civil War Senate* (Ithaca and London, 1981), 102.
17. Salter, *Grimes,* 143.
18. Ibid., 193.
19. Ibid., 196.
20. Ibid., 197.
21. *Daily State Register,* 24 May 1862.
22. Bogue, *Earnest Men,* 161.
23. *Daily State Register,* 7 June 1862.
24. N.H. Brainerd to A. Clark, 8 August 1862, Governor's Letterbook, 1861-63, Samuel J. Kirkwood Papers, SHSI, Iowa City.
25. S.J. Kirkwood to H. Halleck, 5 August 1862, Kirkwood Papers, Iowa City.
26. *Daily State Register,* 10 July 1862.
27. *CG,* 37 Cong., 2 Sess., Appendix, 319.
28. Fairall, *Manual,* 64.
29. C. Baldwin to G.M. Dodge, 25 July 1862, Dodge Papers.
30. *Minutes of the Nineteenth Session of the Iowa Annual Conference of the Methodist Episcopal Church Held at Washington, Iowa, September 10th to 15th, 1862* (Burlington, Iowa, 1862), 17.
31. *Daily State Register,* 24 September 1862.
32. C. Baldwin to G.M. Dodge, 24 September 1862, Dodge Papers.
33. *Daily State Register,* 6 January 1863.
34. Ibid., 7 January 1863.
35. Ibid., 31 January, 10 April 1863.
36. An account of Webb's arrest appeared in ibid., 21 January 1863.
37. Ibid., 21, 22 January 1863.
38. *Laws of Iowa,* 1851, 172-73.
39. *Daily State Register,* 3 February 1863.
40. Ibid., 3 February 1863.
41. But note that attempts by Democrats to prosecute a black domestic in Fayette County under the exclusion act were foiled by local Republicans after Gray's decision. N.N. Sykes to A. Brown, 23 February 1863, Aaron Brown Papers, SHSI, Iowa City.
42. J.S. Griffing to W.P. Fessenden, 1 October 1864, William Pitt Fessenden Papers, WRHS.
43. *Daily State Register,* 31 January 1863.
44. E.D. Ross, *Iowa Agriculture: An Historical Survey* (Iowa City, 1951), 54.
45. On minstrelsy see J.H. Baker, *Affairs of Party: The Political Culture of Northern Democrats in the Mid-Nineteenth Century* (Ithaca and London, 1983), 212-58.
46. T.L. Hoffman Diary, 25 October 1863, Thomas L. Hoffman Papers, SHSI, Des Moines. I have retained the original spelling in this and subsequent quotations from soldiers' letters.
47. J.S. Woolson to T.W. Woolson, 13 July 1862, John S. Woolson Papers in possession of Julia Gentleman, Des Moines.
48. A.A. Rigby Diary, 28 October 1862, Alfred A. Rigby Papers, SHSI, Des Moines.
49. M.M. Crocker to E. Sells, 6 January 1862, in *Daily State Register,* 19 January 1862.

50. C.C. Carpenter to R.E. Carpenter, 6 August 1862, Carpenter Papers, SHSI, Iowa City.
51. J. Sharp to M. Sharp, 8 October 1862, John Sharp Papers, SHSI, Des Moines.
52. J. Ruckman to E.B. Ruckman, 10 October 1862, John L. Ruckman Papers, SHSI, Des Moines.
53. A.A. Abernethy Diary, 8 April 1863, Alonzo A. Abernethy Papers, SHSI, Des Moines.
54. C.C. Carpenter to R.E. Carpenter, 13 September 1863, Carpenter Papers, Iowa City.
55. J. Ruckman to A. Ruckman, 26 April 1863, Ruckman Papers.
56. See Kasson's speech (January 1863) in *Colonization Society Reports,* XLVI, 28-33.
57. *Cedar Falls Gazette,* 13 February 1863.
58. S.J. Kirkwood to J.W. Grimes et al., 3 February 1863, Iowa Governor, Executive Correspondence (War Matters: Miscellaneous), State Archives, SHSI, Des Moines.
59. J.W. Rankin to W.P. Clarke, 9 May 1863, Clarke Papers.
60. See *Roster of Iowa Soldiers in the War of the Rebellion* (Des Moines, 1911), V, 1585-87, for a historical sketch of the regiment.
61. *Daily State Register,* 9 August 1863.
62. C. Sumner to J. Bright, 21 July 1863, John Bright Papers, British Library, f. 43390.
63. Glashan, *Gubernatorial Elections,* 92.
64. J. Harlan to S.P. Chase, 24 May 1862, Chase Papers.
65. R.L.B. Clarke to S.P. Chase, 21 October 1863, ibid.
66. R.L.B. Clarke to S.P. Chase, 5 November 1863, ibid.
67. *IaHJ,* 1864, 231.
68. Ibid., 308.
69. D.V. Smith, *Chase and Civil War Politics* (Columbus, 1931), 122.
70. *IaSJ,* 1864, 520-21.
71. *CG,* 38 Cong., 1 Sess., 641.
72. Ibid., 636.
73. Ibid., 1361.
74. Ibid., 2543.
75. Ibid., 2971-75, 3299-3300, 3350.
76. *CG,* 38 Cong., 1 Sess., 2353, 2424.
77. Ibid., 2972, 2974.
78. Ibid., 2972.
79. J.W. Grimes to W.P. Fessenden, 3 August 1864, Fessenden Papers, Bowdoin.
80. J. Harlan to W.P. Clarke, 2 April 1864, Clarke Papers.
81. See Dykstra, "Issue Squarely Met," 449.
82. *Acts and Resolutions Passed at the Regular Session of the Tenth General Assembly of the State of Iowa* (Des Moines, 1864), 6, 41.
83. *CG,* 38 Cong., 1 Sess., 2108, 3461.
84. Wubben, *Copperhead Movement,* 170-71.
85. Fairall, *Manual,* 68-69.
86. Wubben, *Copperhead Movement,* 173; *Guide to U.S. Elections,* 613.
87. Burnham, *Presidential Ballots,* 415-35.
88. S.M. Langworthy Diary, 20 November 1864, Langworthy Papers.
89. *Davenport Gazette,* 18 March 1865.
90. *Daily Iowa State Register,* 12 February 1865.
91. G.C. Tichenor to G.M. Dodge, 14 April 1865, Dodge Papers.
92. *Daily Gate City,* 4 May 1865.
93. *Daily State Register,* 4 February 1865.

9 / Black Suffrage and the Intraparty Crisis of 1865-1866

1. Rules for the apportionment of delegates appeared in *Daily Iowa State Register,* 13 June 1865.
2. For the convention minutes and a list of delegates see ibid., 15 June 1865.
3. M.B. Hoxie to G.M. Dodge and G.C. Tichenor, 16 June 1865, Dodge Papers.
4. *Daily Iowa State Register,* 16 June 1865.
5. C.E. Russell, *A Pioneer Editor in Early Iowa: A Sketch of the Life of Edward Russell* (Washington, D.C., 1941), 7.
6. J.M. Dixon, *The Valley and the Shadow* (New York, 1868), 72.
7. *Daily Iowa State Register,* 16 June 1865.
8. This account of the debate follows that which appeared in *Davenport Daily Gazette,* 16 June 1865.
9. B.F. Gue, *History of Iowa: From the Earliest Times to the Beginning of the Twentieth Century* (New York, 1903), III, 1.
10. *Davenport Daily Gazette,* 16 June 1865.
11. Gue, "Hiram Price," 598.
12. Ibid., 601.
13. On the cynical use of radicalism in other states see M.L. Benedict, *A Compromise of Principle: Congressional Republicans and Reconstruction, 1863-1869* (New York, 1974), 59, 113-14.
14. *Burlington Daily Hawk-Eye,* 23 May 1865; Stiles, *Recollections,* 63-64.
15. Mount Pleasant *Home Journal,* 15 September 1865. Impartial suffrage would have involved certain restrictions (e.g., literacy and loyalty tests) on the franchise of both blacks and whites.
16. *Daily Iowa State Register,* 16 June 1865.
17. *Minutes of the [Congregational] General Association of Iowa at Its Session in Grinnell, June 1864* (Dubuque, Iowa, 1864), 10.
18. *Davenport Daily Gazette,* 30 May 1865.
19. L.N. Green Diary, 27 January 1865, Levi N. Green Papers, SHSI, Des Moines.
20. L.D. Ingersoll, "Brigadier General Samuel A. Rice of Iowa," *AI,* 1st Series, III (January 1865), 399.
21. Benedict, *Compromise of Principle,* 111.
22. R. Robinson to L. Summers, 17 July 1865, Summers Papers.
23. *Burlington Daily Hawk-Eye,* 21 June 1865.
24. H.H. Wubben, "The Uncertain Trumpet: Iowa Republicans and Black Suffrage, 1860-1868," *AI,* 3rd Series, XLVII (Summer 1984), 412.
25. Glashan, *Gubernatorial Elections,* 92.
26. R.R. Dykstra, "Iowa: 'Bright Radical Star,'" in James C. Mohr, ed., *Radical Republicans in the North: State Politics during Reconstruction* (Baltimore and London, 1976), 177.
27. M. Throne, *Cyrus Clay Carpenter and Iowa Politics, 1854-1898* (Iowa City, 1974), 61; C.C. Carpenter to R.E. Carpenter, 24 May 1863, Carpenter Papers, Iowa City.
28. C.C. Carpenter to K. Carpenter, 30 April 1865, Carpenter Papers, ibid.
29. Fort Dodge *Iowa North West,* 9 January 1866.
30. T.H. Benton, Jr., to A. Johnson, 16 September 1865, Andrew Johnson Papers, LC.
31. J. Harlan to E.B. Washburne, 12 June 1865, Washburne Papers.
32. *Daily Iowa State Register,* 29 August 1865.
33. Fairall, *Manual,* 70.
34. C. Mason Diary (1863-67), 31 December 1865, Mason Papers.

35. *Daily Burlington Hawk-Eye,* 17 November 1865.
36. Shambaugh, *Messages,* III, 86.
37. *IaHJ,* 1866, 147–49.
38. Ibid., 186, 227.
39. Ibid., 322.
40. Ibid., 545.
41. Ibid., 643–47.
42. *IaSJ,* 1866, 635–36.
43. See Appendix for source of biographical data.
44. Dykstra, "'Bright Radical Star'," 179–80.
45. Ibid., 179.
46. Fairall, *Manual,* 69–70.
47. *IaHJ,* 1866, 65, 96–97, 648.
48. Fairman, *Miller,* 128.
49. *Daily Iowa State Register,* 22 February 1866.
50. *IaSJ,* 1866, 250–51.
51. *IaHJ,* 1866, 284–85.
52. *IaSJ,* 1866, 335.
53. Ibid., 424.
54. *IaHJ,* 1866, 756–75.
55. Clark, *Senatorial Elections,* 138.
56. For speculation that Stone had his eyes on the Senate place see W.E. Shepherd to J.F. Lacey, 14 March 1865, John F. Lacey Papers, SHSI, Des Moines; A.B.F. Hildreth to S.J. Kirkwood, 1 April 1865, Kirkwood Papers, Des Moines.
57. G.C. Tichenor to G.M. Dodge, 29 November 1865, Dodge Papers; M. Crocker to P. Casady, 7 June 1861, Simon Casady Papers, SHSI, Des Moines.
58. It is quite likely that Harlan had always regarded the cabinet position as a means of improving his reelection chances. See, e.g., H.M. Hoxie to G.M. Dodge, 3 March 1865, Dodge Papers.
59. J.W. Grimes to S.J. Kirkwood, 12 October 1865, Kirkwood Papers, Des Moines.
60. Brigham, *Harlan,* 275–77; J. Harlan to M. Simpson, 28 October 1865, Simpson Papers, LC; J. Lyman to J.F. Lacey, 14 January 1866, Lacey Papers; J. Harlan to W.P. Clarke, 18 January 1866, Clarke Papers; Clark, *Senatorial Elections,* 140–41.
61. G. Shedd to S.J. Kirkwood, 27 February 1866, Kirkwood Papers, Des Moines.
62. *CG,* 39 Cong., 1 Sess., 943, 3842, 3850 (Freedmen's Bureau bill); ibid., 1809, 1861 (Civil Rights bill). Kasson joined the majority to override the vetoes even though he had been the only Iowan not to register a vote on the Civil Rights Act in March.
63. Benedict, *Compromise of Principle,* 109.
64. Ibid., 184–86.
65. W.M. Stone to J.F. Wilson and H. Price, 24 February 1866, Iowa Governor, Governor's Letterbook, 1866–68, State Archives, SHSI, Des Moines.
66. Shambaugh, *Messages,* III, 74.
67. *CG,* 39 Cong., 1 Sess., 3149.
68. On Harlan's involvement in the Cherokee deal see P.W. Gates, *Fifty Million Acres: Conflicts over Kansas Land Policy, 1854–1890* (Ithaca, 1954), 140, 156.
69. Ibid., 140.
70. *New York Times,* 27 January 1866.
71. *Diary of Gideon Welles, Secretary of the Navy under Lincoln and Johnson* (New York and Boston, 1911), II, 425, 481.
72. J. Harlan to A. Johnson, 27 July 1866, Johnson Papers.

73. See Younger, *Kasson,* 188, 191-92, 195, 200-202.
74. Hirshson, *Dodge,* 134-37.
75. J. Hedrick to W.P. Clarke, 25 June 1866, Clarke Papers.
76. Ibid.; W.E. Shepherd to J.F. Lacey, 20 January, 14 March 1865, Lacey Papers.
77. C. Mason Diary (1863-67), 8 April 1866, Mason Papers.
78. G. Gillaspy to C. Mason, 2 July 1866, ibid.
79. F.H. Warren to W.W. Belknap, 7 August 1866, William Worth Belknap Papers, Princeton University Library.
80. J.A. Kasson to M. Blair, 28 August 1866, Johnson Papers.
81. H.M. Wead to C. Mason, 28 May 1866, Mason Papers; F.H. Warren to H. McCulloch, 31 October 1866, Assessors Records, Iowa, 1st District, National Archives, R.G. 56.
82. C. Mason Diary (1863-67), 30 September 1866, Mason Papers.
83. *Davenport Daily Gazette,* 1 August 1866.
84. *Daily Iowa State Register,* 11 August 1866.
85. *Guide to U.S. Elections,* 616.

10 / The Waning of Reconstruction, 1867-1872

1. T. Saunders to W.P. Clarke, 11 November 1866, Clarke Papers.
2. J. Harlan to W.P. Clarke, 7 November 1866, ibid.
3. J. Grimes to G. Welles, 14 October 1866, Gideon Welles Papers, LC.
4. Fairman, *Miller,* 192-93.
5. *Daily State Register,* 15 November 1866.
6. Ibid., 11 December 1866.
7. *CG,* 39 Cong., 2 Sess., 124-25.
8. Ibid., 198.
9. Ibid.
10. Ibid., 46.
11. *Davenport Daily Gazette,* 27 December 1866.
12. *Daily State Register,* 29 December 1866.
13. G.C. Tichenor to S.J. Kirkwood, 10 January 1867, Kirkwood Papers, Des Moines.
14. G.G. Wright to S.J. Kirkwood, 29 January 1867, ibid.
15. J.N. Dewey to S.J. Kirkwood, 1 January, 28 January 1867, ibid.
16. G.M. Dodge to S.J. Kirkwood, 7 January 1867, ibid.
17. Hirshson, *Dodge,* 8-9.
18. *CG,* 39 Cong., 2 Sess., 360.
19. *CG,* 39 Cong., 2 Sess., 817; W.R. Brock, *An American Crisis: Congress and Reconstruction, 1865-1867* (London and New York, 1963), 70-72, has described this vote as a decisive test of radicalism.
20. *CG,* 39 Cong., 2 Sess., 1215.
21. Ibid., 1469.
22. Ibid., 1316.
23. Ibid., 1319.
24. Ibid., 1340.
25. Benedict, *Compromise of Principle,* 238.
26. Ibid., 1399-1400.
27. Ibid., 1645.
28. C. Mason Diary (1867-69), 24 February 1867, Mason Papers.

29. E. Foner, *Nothing but Freedom: Emancipation and Its Legacy* (Baton Rouge and London, 1983), 6.
30. Fairall, *Manual,* 77.
31. G.C. Tichenor to G.M. Dodge, 28 August 1867, Dodge Papers.
32. J.W. Grimes to W.P. Fessenden, 7, 29 September 1867, Fessenden Papers, Bowdoin.
33. J.W. Grimes to W.P. Fessenden, 29 September 1867, ibid.
34. J.W. Grimes to W.P. Fessenden, 7 September 1867, ibid.
35. Glashan, *Gubernatorial Elections,* 92.
36. J.W. Grimes to W.P. Fessenden, 24 October 1867, Fessenden Papers, Bowdoin.
37. *CG,* 40 Cong., 2 Sess., 68.
38. On the high correlation between impeachment and the currency question see M.L. Benedict, *The Impeachment and Trial of Andrew Johnson* (New York, 1973), 81–85.
39. F.H. Warren to E.B. Washburne, 29 November 1867, Washburne Papers.
40. *Daily State Register,* 15 November 1867.
41. C. Dudley to J.F. Lacey, 22 January 1868, Lacey Papers.
42. *CG,* 40 Cong., 2 Sess., 1400.
43. *IaHJ,* 1868, 310.
44. *IaSJ,* 1868, 191, 199.
45. See *Proceedings of the Iowa State Colored State Convention, Held in the City of Des Moines, Wednesday and Thursday, February 12th and 13th, 1868* (Muscatine, Iowa, 1868).
46. *IaSJ,* 1868, 265, 385; *IaHJ,* 1868, 133, 514–15.
47. H. Price to S.J. Kirkwood, 4 January 1868, Kirkwood Papers, Des Moines.
48. Fairman, *Miller,* 140.
49. *Daily State Register,* 8 May 1868.
50. C. Mason Diary, 30 March 1868, Mason Papers.
51. *CG,* 40 Cong., 2 Sess., Supplement, 423–24.
52. Sage, *History of Iowa,* 177.
53. *Daily State Register,* 22 October 1868.
54. Dykstra, "'Bright Radical Star,'" 185.
55. *Davenport Western Soldiers' Friend,* 24 October 1868, quoted in ibid., 184.
56. G.G. Berrier, "The Negro Suffrage Issue in Iowa, 1865–1868," *AI,* 3rd Series, XXXIX (Spring 1968), 258–60.
57. See, e.g., Governor Merrill's first biennial message to the legislature in January 1870 in Shambaugh, *Messages,* III, 321.
58. *CG,* 40 Cong., 3 Sess., 1563–64, 1641. The five members of the Iowa delegation who supported the Fifteenth Amendment were Harlan, Wilson, Price, Allison, and Dodge. Representative William Loughridge voted against. Grimes and Kasson did not register an opinion.
59. W.W. Belknap to U.S. Grant, 30 July 1874, Ulysses S. Grant Papers, LC.
60. See Wright's dissent in *Clark* v. *Board of Directors, etc.,* 24 Iowa 266, 279–80 (1868).
61. J.F. Wilson to G.M. Dodge, 22 April 1869, Dodge Papers.
62. Hirshson, *Dodge,* 61.
63. C.F. Clarkson to J.S. Clarkson, 12 February 1870; F.W. Palmer to J.S. Clarkson, 29 January 1870; G.G. Wright to J.S. Clarkson, 1 November 1870, James S. Clarkson Papers, LC.
64. Throne, *Carpenter,* 106, 111.
65. For a detailed account of the Harlan–Allison Senate battle see Clark, *Senatorial Elections,* 152–67.
66. *Daily Iowa State Register,* 27 December 1871; H. Taylor to S.J. Kirkwood, 21 November 1871, Kirkwood Papers, Des Moines.
67. J. Harlan to M. Simpson, 13 October 1871, Matthew Simpson Papers, Drew

University.
  68. Clark, *Senatorial Elections,* 166–67.
  69. *Clark v. The Board of Directors, etc.,* 24 Iowa 266 (1868).
  70. *Coger v. The North West Union Packet Co.* 37 Iowa 145, 154 (1873).
  71. Ibid., 149.
  72. H. Price to S.J. Kirkwood, 29 August 1876; E. Russell to S.J. Kirkwood, 8 May 1877, Kirkwood Papers, Des Moines.
  73. *CG,* 40 Cong., 3 Sess., 1795.
  74. Ibid., 1797.
  75. Fairman, *Miller,* 191.
  76. Quoted in E.P. Allen, "Gelpcke v. The City of Dubuque," *IJHP,* XXVIII (April 1930), 192.
  77. *Slaughter House Cases* 83 U.S., 394, 404 (1873).
  78. Loren P. Beth, "The Slaughter-House Cases Revisited," *Louisiana Law Review,* XXIII (1963), 501–3.
  79. Fairman, *Miller,* 405.
  80. E. Foner, *Reconstruction: America's Unfinished Revolution 1863–1877* (New York, 1988), 385–86.
  81. S.W. Wiggins, *The Scalawag in Alabama Politics, 1865–1881* (University, Ala., 1977), 57.
  82. W.L. Fleming, *Civil War and Reconstruction in Alabama* (New York, 1905), 737; Wiggins, *Scalawag in Alabama,* 69.
  83. Gue, *History of Iowa,* III, 6–7.
  84. Ibid., 53–54.
  85. *Times* (London), 12 May 1869.
  86. Salter, *Grimes,* 380.
  87. Ibid., 385.
  88. M. Throne, "The Liberal Republican Party in Iowa, 1872," *IJH,* LIII (April 1955), 127.
  89. See, e.g., C. Mason, *A Review of the New Departure* (Burlington, Iowa, 1871).
  90. C. Mason to J.W. Grimes, 9 February 1871, Mason Papers.
  91. C. Mason Diary, 22 November 1871, ibid.
  92. Salter, *Grimes,* 387.
  93. Throne, "Liberal Republican Party," 134–36.
  94. C. Mason Diary, 5 May 1872, Mason Papers.
  95. Throne, "Liberal Republican Party," 142–43.
  96. J.F. Wilson to G.M. Dodge, 3 August 1872, Dodge Papers.
  97. Fairall, *Manual,* 88–89.
  98. *Daily Iowa State Register,* 11 October 1872.
  99. Burnham, *Presidential Ballots,* 413–35.
  100. Throne, "Liberal Republican Party," 148.
  101. C. Mason Diary, 9 November 1872, Mason Papers.

11 / The Railroad Question during the 1870s

  1. Iowa Secretary of State, *Comparative Census, 1880,* 168, 170.
  2. Shambaugh, *Messages,* III, 127.
  3. *Proceedings of the First Iowa Methodist State Convention . . . 1871* (Burlington, Iowa, 1871), 75.

4. Decennial growth rates for Iowa counties were calculated using the standard formula: $r = (m\sqrt{(Xn/Xr)} - 1)$. Rates for 1860–70 included O'Brien 56.7, Sioux 50, and Palo Alto 26. Southeastern Iowa rates were much lower, e.g., Lee 2.4, Louisa 2.2, and Henry 1.4.

5. U.S. Census Office, *Ninth Census* (Washington, D.C., 1872), I, 131–42.

6. Ibid., III, 812–23.

7. U.S. Census Office, *Report of the Productions of Agriculture as Returned at the Tenth Census* (June 1, 1880) . . . (Washington, D.C., 1883), 17.

8. *Historical Statistics,* I, 463.

9. Shambaugh, *Messages,* III, 421–24.

10. Ibid., III, 418–21.

11. U.S. Census Office, *Ninth Census,* III, 81, 392.

12. *IaSJ,* 1860, 534.

13. Fairall, *Manual,* 47.

14. *CG,* 38 Cong., 1 Sess., 307.

15. *CG,* 36 Cong., 1 Sess., 2056, 2 Sess., 1065.

16. Salter, *Grimes,* 334; L.L. Sage, *William Boyd Allison: A Study in Practical Politics* (Iowa City, 1956), 78; Younger, *Kasson,* 212.

17. Fairall, *Manual,* 84.

18. Ibid., 87.

19. C. Mason Diary, 12 November 1870, Mason Papers.

20. Hirshson, *Dodge,* 132.

21. J.W. Grimes to J.F. Joy, 16 April 1864, Joy Papers.

22. J.W. Grimes to J.F. Joy, 25 November 1862, ibid.

23. J.W. Grimes to J.F. Joy, 21 March, 24 September 1864, 26 February 1865, 20 January, 31 January, 7 February, 8 March 1866, ibid.

24. J.W. Grimes to J.F. Joy, 24 January 1866, ibid.

25. *Report of the Select Committee to Investigate the Alleged Credit Mobilier Bribery* . . . (Washington, D.C., 1873), 29–30, 34, 39–41, 111, 211–20, 242, 289–93, 309, 333–34, 356–59, 361, 408, 421, 424, 428–29, 453, 457, 462.

26. *CG,* 40 Cong., 2 Sess., 2130, 2428–29.

27. Ibid., 42 Cong., 3 Sess., Appendix, 109, 111; Hirshson, *Dodge,* 191–93.

28. *Credit Mobilier,* 19, 220.

29. J.W. Grimes to W.M. Evarts, 19 October 1868, Johnson Papers.

30. *Credit Mobilier,* 178.

31. Brigham, *Harlan,* 277.

32. B.M. French, *Mark Twain and "The Gilded Age": The Book That Named an Era* (Dallas, 1965), 89.

33. R. Fogel, *The Union Pacific Railroad: A Case in Premature Enterprise* (Baltimore, 1960), 61.

34. H.M. Hoxie to G.M. Dodge, 12 August 1864, Dodge Papers.

35. Harlan, desirous of getting the powerful and Machiavellian U.S. marshal out of the state before the 1865 senatorial campaign, may have prevailed upon Durant to find Hoxie a position with the Union Pacific, H.M. Hoxie to G.M. Dodge, 3 March 1865, Dodge Papers. Hoxie would almost certainly have thrown his weight behind Kasson's candidacy.

36. *CG,* 42 Cong., 3 Sess., Appendix, 107.

37. Ibid., 40 Cong., 2 Sess., 2111.

38. Iowa Secretary of State, *Comparative Census, 1880,* 126–29; B.R. Mitchell, *European Historical Statistics,* 1750–1970 (London and Basingstoke, 1978), 317.

39. G.H. Miller, *Railroads and the Granger Laws* (Madison, Milwaukee, and London, 1971), 99–100.

40. *The State of Iowa, ex. rel. The Burlington and Missouri River Railroad Company* v. *The County of Wapello* 13 Iowa 388 (1862).
41. *IaHJ,* 1866, 163-64; *IaSJ,* 1866, 661; *IaHJ,* 1866, 124-29, contains Bissell's opinion.
42. E. Clark to S.J. Kirkwood, 10 February 1866, Kirkwood Papers, Des Moines. I have retained the original spelling.
43. J.N. Dennison to J.F. Joy, 23 March 1866, in Cochran, *Railroad Leaders,* 306.
44. P.A. Dey, "Railroad Legislation in Iowa," *IHR,* IX (October 1893), 553-54.
45. *CG,* 41 Cong., 2 Sess., 1609-11, 2480-82, 2493, 2575, 2578-84, 2838-39.
46. *General and Public Acts Passed at the Regular Session of the Fourteenth General Assembly of the State of Iowa . . . 1872* (Des Moines, 1872), 29-32, 59.
47. Miller, *Granger Laws,* 111; Shambaugh, *Messages,* III, 309, IV, 21, 23.
48. S.J. Buck, *The Granger Movement: A Study of Agricultural Organization and Its Political, Economic, and Social Manifestations, 1870-1880* (Cambridge, Mass., 1913), 58.
49. Ibid., 308.
50. On Grange objectives see Ross, *Iowa Agriculture,* 97-100. Ross fails to emphasize the conservative aspects of the movement that are highlighted in its annual session reports, e.g., *Report of Proceedings of the Fifth Annual Session of the Iowa State Grange . . .* (Des Moines, 1874), 39-44.
51. M. Throne, "The Anti-Monopoly Party in Iowa, 1873-1874," *IJH,* LII (October 1954), 289-91.
52. C. Aldrich to C.C. Carpenter, 1 April 1873, Carperter Papers, Iowa City.
53. C.C. Carpenter Diary, 11 April 1873, ibid.
54. Ibid., 27 March, 29 March 1873.
55. Ibid., 15 September 1873.
56. *Daily Iowa State Register,* 30 October 1873.
57. Miller, *Granger Laws,* 114. Miller contends that Iowa's rate law was primarily a result of mercantile pressure, but manuscript evidence clearly indicates that popular antimonopoly sentiment had a determining impact on Republican and Democratic policy during the 1870s.
58. Shambaugh, *Messages,* IV, 87-91.
59. C.C. Carpenter Diary, 23 March 1874, Carpenter Papers, Iowa City.
60. *Iowa State Register,* 24 February 1876.
61. See Appendix for explanation of terminology.
62. M. Horwitz, *The Transformation of American Law, 1780-1860* (Cambridge, Mass., and London, 1977).
63. Ibid., 27.
64. J.W. Hurst, *Law and the Conditions of Freedom in the Nineteenth-Century United States* (Madison, 1956).
65. J.R. Pole, *Paths to the American Past* (New York and Oxford, 1979), 192.
66. *Henry* v. *The Dubuque & Pacific R.R. Co.* 2 Iowa 234, 246 (1856).
67. *Dubuque Co.* v. *Dubuque & Pacific R.R. Company* 4 G. Greene 1 (1853).
68. For a biographical sketch see G.G. Wright, "Chief Justice Caleb Baldwin," *AI,* 3rd Series, I (October 1893), 209-14.
69. C. Baldwin to G.M. Dodge, 13 March 1861, Dodge Papers.
70. C. Baldwin to G.M. Dodge, 16 March 1866, ibid.
71. Stiles, *Recollections,* 472-81.
72. C.C. Cole to G.M. Dodge, 1 April 1867, Dodge Papers.
73. C.C. Cole to G.M. Dodge, 26 February 1867, ibid.
74. *IaSJ,* 1868, 550-51.
75. Cole was elected a director in December 1865, *Daily Iowa State Register,* 17 December 1865.

76. *Dewey* v. *The Chicago & N.W.R.R.* 31 Iowa 373 (1871); *Murphy* v. *C., R.I. & P.R.R. Co.* 38 Iowa 539 (1874).
77. *The City of Dubuque* v. *The Illinois Central Railroad Company* 39 Iowa 56, 95–96 (1874).
78. Buck, *Granger Movement,* 85.
79. *Steward* v. *Board of Supervisors of Polk County* 30 Iowa 9 (1870).
80. *Cedar Falls and Minnesota R.R. Co.* v. *Rich* 33 Iowa 113, 116 (1871).
81. *City of Dubuque* v. *The Illinois Central Railroad Co.* 39 Iowa 56 (1874).
82. H.J. Graham, "The 'Conspiracy Theory' of the Fourteenth Amendment," *Yale Law Journal,* XLVII (January 1938), 371–403.
83. *Tredway* v. *The S.C. & St. P.R. Co.* 43 Iowa 527, 528 (1876).
84. *Kespe* v. *The Chicago & N.W.R.R. Co.* 30 Iowa 78, 83 (1870).
85. *Rodemacher* v. *The Mil. & St. P. R'y Co.* 41 Iowa 297, 309 (1875).
86. G.M. Dodge to J.S. Clarkson, 15 December 1874, Dodge Papers.
87. *Daily Iowa State Register,* 29 December 1874.
88. Ibid., 25 February 1875.
89. G.M. Dodge to J.S. Clarkson, 15 December 1874, Dodge Papers.
90. *Hanson* v. *Vernon* 27 Iowa 28 (1869).
91. J.F. Dillon, "Comments on the People v. Township Board," *American Law Register,* XVIII (August 1870), 503.
92. C. Mason Diary, 31 March 1872, Mason Papers.
93. M. Keller, *Affairs of State: Public Life in Late Nineteenth Century America* (Cambridge, Mass., and London, 1977), 126–27.
94. *Laws of Iowa,* 1872, 139; although minorities in both parties opposed the death penalty in 1878, a bill to restore capital punishment passed house and senate with bipartisan support, *IaHJ,* 1878, 606; *IaSJ,* 1878, 506.
95. *Acts and Resolutions Passed at the Regular Session of the Sixteenth General Assembly of the State of Iowa . . . 1876* (Des Moines, 1876), 56.
96. Fairall, *Manual,* 100–101, 105, 108–9 contains Greenback platforms, 1876–78.
97. *Laws of Iowa,* 1876, 110–13.
98. Fairall, *Manual,* 104.
99. Shambaugh, *Messages,* V, 10–12.
100. *IaHJ,* 1878, 345.
101. *IaSJ,* 1878, 367.
102. See Appendix for explanation of terminology.
103. J.B. Workman, "Governor William Larrabee and Railroad Reform," *IJH,* LVII (July 1959), 231–66.

12 / End of an Era, 1876–1877

1. Glashan, *Gubernatorial Elections,* 92; Clark, *Kirkwood,* chap. 28.
2. Shambaugh, *Messages,* IV, 297–98.
3. Ibid., 300.
4. Ibid., 300–301.
5. R.N. Ankeny to G.G. Wright, 22 February 1875, George G. Wright Papers, SHSI, Des Moines.
6. Clark, *Senatorial Elections,* 177.
7. C. Mason Diary, 24 June 1876, Mason Papers.
8. Ibid., 30 June 1876.

9. *Iowa State Register,* 2 July 1876.
10. C. Mason Diary, 7 November 1876, Mason Papers.
11. Petersen, *Presidential Elections,* 47.
12. *Iowa State Register,* 17 November 1876.
13. *Laws of Iowa,* 1876, 56.
14. *Iowa State Register,* 9 February 1877.
15. R.E. Carpenter to C.C. Carpenter, 8 January 1877, Carpenter Papers, Iowa City.
16. G.M. Dodge to R.B. Hayes, 15 February 1877; G.M. Dodge to T.A. Scott, 20 February 1877; G.M. Dodge to H.V.N. Boynton, 2 April 1877, Dodge Papers.
17. *Congressional Record,* 44 Cong., 2 Sess., 913.
18. W.B. Allison to C.C. Carpenter, 30 January 1877, Carpenter Papers, Iowa City.
19. Sage, *Allison,* 150; B.F. Gue to G. Parker, 18 May 1877, letter in possession of James Leonardo, Des Moines; *Iowa State Register,* 7 March, 22 April 1877.
20. I.O. Shelby to C.C. Carpenter, 29 July 1876, Carpenter Papers, Iowa City.
21. J.M. Griffiths to C.C. Carpenter, 20 January 1877, ibid.
22. C.C. Carpenter Diary, 2 April 1877, ibid.; D.H. Chamberlain to C.C. Carpenter, 14 April 1877, Carpenter Papers, Des Moines.
23. C.C. Carpenter Diary, 24 April 1877, Carpenter Papers, Iowa City.
24. *Iowa State Register,* 20 July 1877; C.C. Carpenter Diary, 23 June 1877, Carpenter Papers, Iowa City.
25. *Iowa State Register,* 23 August 1877; C.C. Carpenter Diary, 26 August 1877, Carpenter Papers, Iowa City.
26. *Davenport Gazette,* 5 April 1877.
27. B.R. Sherman to C.C. Carpenter, 14 May 1877, Carpenter Papers, Iowa City.
28. Fairall, *Manual,* 104.
29. C.C. Carpenter Diary, 27 July 1877, Carpenter Papers, Iowa City; Shambaugh, *Messages,* iv, 375.

13 / The Party of Progress and Humanity

1. Foner, *Free Soil;* Gienapp, *Origins.*
2. B.C. Campbell, *Representative Democracy: Public Policy and Midwestern Legislatures in the Late Nineteenth Century* (Cambridge, Mass., and London, 1980); B.G. Kelley, "Ethnocultural Voting Trends in Rural Iowa, 1890-1898," *AI,* 3rd Series, XLIV (Fall 1978), 441-61.
3. I am well aware of the hazards involved in pigeonholing religious groups, particularly as the evidence provided by T.L. Smith, *Revivalism and Social Reform in Mid-Nineteenth Century America* (New York and Nashville, 1957), indicates that by 1860 revivalism had transformed American Protestantism into a synthesis of Calvinist and Arminian beliefs. Notwithstanding the pitfalls, I believe that some attempt at categorization is better than none at all, and to this end I have used Smith's loosely defined divisions (pp. 32-33) as a basis for my own analysis. This resulted in six separate categories: (1) Revival Calvinists—including Presbyterians, Congregationalists, and Baptists; (2) Evangelical Arminians (Methodists, Free-Will Baptists, and Quakers); (3) Nonevangelical Christians (a fusion of Smith's "traditionalists" and "orthodox Calvinists" composed largely of Episcopalians, Catholics, Lutherans, and Old School Presbyterians); (4) Nondenominational Protestants; (5) Liberals—mostly nonbelievers and those who actually described themselves as "liberals"; (6) unclassifiable groups, e.g., those who listed their religious affiliation as "antislavery."
4. E.g., Benson, *Jacksonian Democracy,* chap. 4.

5. M. Hammarberg, *The Indiana Voter: The Historical Dynamics of Party Allegiance during the 1870s* (Chicago and London, 1977).

6. L.R. Noun, *Strong-minded Women: The Emergence of the Woman Suffrage Movement in Iowa* (Ames, Iowa, 1969), 178–79, 199–200, 218. The Senate defeated a woman's suffrage amendment in March 1872 by twenty-four votes to twenty-two. Six Democrats and eighteen Republicans voted against its passage, *IaSJ*, 1872, 421.

7. Foner, *Free Soil*, 309.

8. W. Hartshorn to G.M. Dodge, 9 November 1867, Dodge Papers.

Appendix

1. V. Cromwell, "Mapping the Political World of 1861: A Multidimensional Analysis of House of Commons' Divisions Lists," *Legislative Studies Quarterly*, VII (May 1982), 281–87.

2. The technical aspects of MDS are discussed in J.B. Kruskal and M. Wish, *Multidimensional Scaling*, Sage University Papers: Quantitative Papers in the Social Sciences, No. 11 (London, 1978).

Bibliography

Manuscript Sources

Bowdoin College Library, Brunswick, Maine
    William Pitt Fessenden Papers

British Library, London
    John Bright Papers

Detroit Public Library
    James F. Joy Papers (microfilm)

Drew University Library, Madison, N.J.
    Matthew Simpson Papers (photocopies)

Grinnell College Library, Grinnell, Iowa
    Josiah B. Grinnell Papers
    Julius A. Reed Papers

Library of Congress, Washington, D.C.
    Salmon P. Chase Papers (microfilm)
    James S. Clarkson Papers
    William Pitt Fessenden Papers (microfilm)
    Joshua Giddings–George W. Julian Papers
    Ulysses S. Grant Papers (microfilm)
    Horace Greeley Papers
    Andrew Johnson Papers (microfilm)
    Abraham Lincoln Papers (microfilm)
    Matthew Simpson Papers
    Elihu B. Washburne Papers
    Gideon Welles Papers

National Archives, Washington, D.C.
    Secretary of the Interior, Office of Indian Affairs, Letters Sent, 1824–82, Record Group 48 (microfilm, reels 77–79)
    Secretary of the Treasury, Assessors/Collectors Records, Iowa, Record Group 56

Princeton University Library, Princeton, N.J.
    William Worth Belknap Papers (microfilm copy in SHSI, Iowa City)

Private Collection
John S. Woolson Papers in possession of Julia Gentleman, Des Moines

State Historical Society of Iowa
Des Moines
Alonzo A. Abernethy Papers
Charles Aldrich Papers
William B. Allison Papers
William Anderson Papers
Lewis Bolton Papers
Allen Boyd Papers
Jacob de Witt Brewster Papers
Cyrus Clay Carpenter Papers
Simon Casady Papers
William Penn Clarke Papers
Marcellus Crocker Papers
Grenville M. Dodge Papers
William G. Donnan Papers
William H. Fleming Papers
Levi N. Green Papers
Benjamin F. Gue Papers
Thomas L. Hoffman Papers
John A. Kasson Papers
Nathan D. King Papers
Samuel J. Kirkwood Papers
John F. Lacey Papers
Henry Clay McArthur Papers
Charles Mason Papers
John S. Morgan Papers
Hiram Pratt Papers
Alfred A. Rigby Papers
Charles R. Riggs Papers
John L. Ruckman Papers
William Salter Papers
John Sharp Papers
Benjamin F. Stevens Papers
Laurel Summers Papers
Hawkins Taylor Papers
Seneca B. Thrall Papers
John Todd Papers
George W. Towne Papers
U.S. MS Census 1860, 1870: Iowa
James Baird Weaver Papers
James A. Williamson Papers
George G. Wright Papers

Iowa City
Ephraim Adams Papers
Aaron Brown Papers
Cyrus Clay Carpenter Papers

I.N. Carr Papers
James Harlan Papers
Nathan Isbell Papers
Samuel J. Kirkwood Papers
Solon M. Langworthy Papers
William Larrabee Papers (photocopies)
Jacob Wentworth Rogers Papers
David Rorer Papers
Secretary's Book, Doyle Township, Clarke County, Iowa Grange 964
James Thorington Papers

State Archives, Des Moines
Iowa, General Assembly, House of Representatives, Bills/Resolutions
Iowa General Assembly, Senate, Bills/Resolutions
Iowa Governor, Executive Correspondence

University of Iowa Library, Iowa City
Iowa Secretary of State, Election Returns, 1839-90 (microfilm copy, reel 1)
Lee County, Jackson Township, Board of Trustees Minutes, April 1847-January 1868

Western Reserve Historical Society, Cleveland, Ohio
William Pitt Fessenden Papers

Newspapers

Burlington Hawk-Eye
Cedar Falls Gazette
Washington, D.C., *Chronicle*
Des Moines *Citizen*
Clinton Herald
Davenport Gazette
Davenport *Democrat and News*
Keokuk *Des Moines Valley Whig*
Dubuque Herald
Dubuque Times
Du Buque Visitor
Fairfield Ledger
West Union *Fayette County Pioneer*
Keokuk *Gate City*
Webster City *Hamilton Freeman*
Mount Pleasant *Home Journal*
Fort Dodge *Iowa North West*
Iowa City *Iowa Republican*
Des Moines *Iowa State Journal*
Des Moines *Iowa State Register*
Iowa City *Iowa State Reporter*
Marshalltown *Iowa Temperance Standard*

Mount Pleasant *Iowa True Democrat*
Muscatine Journal
Washington, D.C., *National Era*
New York Times
Council Bluffs *Nonpareil*
McGregor *North Iowa Times*
Oskaloosa Herald
Ottumwa Courier
Sioux City Journal
Waterloo Courier
West Union Republican Gazette

Printed Primary Sources

Adams, Charles Francis, Jr., "The Granger Movement," *North American Review*, CXX (April 1875), 394-424.
Adams, Ephraim, *The Iowa Band* (Boston, 1870).
Addresses Delivered upon the Installation of Rev. Lucien W. Berry, D.D., as President of the Iowa Wesleyan University, July 2, A.D. 1856 (Mount Pleasant, Iowa, 1856).
Aldrich, Charles, "Early Journalism in Iowa: The Founding of the *Hamilton Freeman* at Webster City in 1857," *IHR*, VIII (October 1892), 394-414.
_____, "The Repeal of the Iowa Granger Law in Iowa," *IJHP*, III (April 1903), 256-70.
Andreas, A.T., *Illustrated Historical Atlas of the State of Iowa 1875* (Chicago, 1875).
The Annual Report of the Colonization Society of the State of Iowa, with the Proceedings of the Second Anniversary, in the Capitol, 1857 (Iowa City, n.d.).
The Annual Reports of the American Colonization Society for Colonizing the Free People of Color of the United States (reprinted, New York, 1969).
Appletons' Hand-Book of American Travel: Western Tour (New York and London, 1873).
Bates, Edward, *The Diary of Edward Bates, 1859-1866*, ed. Howard K. Beale (Washington, D.C., 1933).
Bloom, John Porter, ed., *Wisconsin Territory: The Territorial Papers of the United States*, vol. xxvii, (Washington, D.C., 1969).
Broderick, James L., *The Character of the Country: The Iowa Diary of James L. Broderick, 1876-1877*, ed. Loren Horton (Iowa City, 1976).
Browning, Orville H., *The Diary of Orville Hickman Browning*, eds. Theodore C. Pease and James G. Randall (2 vols., Springfield, Ill., 1927-33).
Burrows, John M.D., *Fifty Years in Iowa: Being the Personal Reminiscences of J.M.D. Burrows, Concerning the Men and Events, Social Life, Industrial Interests, Physical Development, and Commercial Progress of Davenport and Scott County, during the Period from 1838 to 1888* (Davenport, Iowa, 1888).
Caird, James, *Prairie Farming in America with Notes by the Way on Canada and the United States* (London, 1859).
Carpenter, Cyrus C., "James Grimes, Governor and Senator," *AI*, 3rd Series, I (October 1894), 505-24.
Chase, Salmon P., *Inside Lincoln's Cabinet: The Civil War Diaries of Salmon P. Chase*, ed. David Donald (New York, London, and Toronto, 1954).

Chittenden, L.E., *A Report of the Debates and Proceedings in the Secret Sessions of the Conference Convention, for Proposing Amendments to the Constitution of the United States, Held at Washington, D.C., in February, A.D. 1861* (New York, 1864).
Clark, Samuel M., "Hon. James Harlan," *Midland Monthly*, I (March 1894), 227–43.
———, "Senator James B. Howell," *AI*, 3rd Series, I (April 1894), 345–54.
Clute, O., "George W. McCrary," *IHR*, VI (October 1890), 557–62.
The Code of Iowa Passed at the Session of the General Assembly of 1850-1 (Iowa City, 1851: reprinted, Des Moines, 1912).
Curtis, Samuel Ryan, "'The Irrepressible Conflict of 1861': The Letters of Samuel Ryan Curtis," ed. Kenneth E. Colton, *AI*, 3rd Series, XXIV (July 1924), 14–58.
Davis, Jefferson, *The Rise and Fall of the Confederate Government* (2 vols., London, 1881).
Davis, John M., "Elijah Sells," *AI*, 3rd Series, II (October 1896), 518–30.
The Debates of the Constitutional Convention; of the State of Iowa, Assembled at Iowa City, Monday, January 19, 1857 . . . (2 vols., Davenport, Iowa, 1857).
Dey, Peter A., "John Henry Gear," *IHR*, XVIII (July 1902), 497–509.
———, "John F. Duncombe," *IHR*, XVIII (October 1902), 587–97.
Dicey, Edward, *Six Months in the Federal States* (2 vols., London and Cambridge, England, 1863).
Dillon, John F., "The Homestead Exemption," *American Law Register*, X (September 1862), 641–56.
———, "Comments on the The People v. Township Board," *American Law Register*, XVIII (August 1870), 501–3.
Dixon, J.M., *The Valley and the Shadow* (New York, 1868).
Eagal, T.D., and Sylvester, R.H., eds., *The Iowa State Almanac and Statistical Register for 1860* (Davenport, Iowa, 1860).
Fairall, Herbert S., *The Iowa City Republican Manual of Iowa Politics* (Iowa City, 1881).
Fessenden, Francis, *Life and Public Services of William Pitt Fessenden* (2 vols., Boston and New York, 1907).
Fleming, William H., "The Autobiography of a Private Secretary," *AI*, 3rd Series, XV (July 1925), 3–46.
Frazee, George, "Clark Dunham, Sometime Editor of the *Burlington Hawk-Eye*," *AI*, 3rd Series, IV (October 1899), 209–18.
Garretson, O.A., "Travelling on the Underground Railroad in Iowa," *IJHP*, XXII (July 1924), 418–53.
Greeley, Horace, *Recollections of a Busy Life* (New York and Boston, 1868).
Grimes, Elizabeth, "Letters by Mrs. James W. Grimes," *IJHP*, I (July 1903), 329–33.
Grimes, James W., "Letters of James W. Grimes," *AI*, 3rd Series, XXII (October 1940), 469–504; XXII (January 1941), 556–88.
Grinnell, Josiah B., *Men and Events of Forty Years: Autobiographical Reminiscences of an Active Career from 1850 to 1890* (Boston, 1891).
Gue, Benjamin F., "The Public Services of Hiram Price," *AI*, 3rd Series, I (January 1895), 585–602.
———, "John Brown and His Iowa Friends," *Midland Monthly*, VII (February 1897), 103–13; (March 1897), 267–77.
———, "Judge George G. Wright," *AI*, 3rd series, IV (October 1900), 483–93.

Hall, Edward H., *Ho! For the West!! The Traveller and Emigrants' Hand-Book to Canada and the North-West of the American Union* . . . (London, 1858).
Howe, Timothy O., "Is the Republican Party in Its Death-Struggle?" *North American Review,* CXXVI (May–June 1878), 381–403.
Ingersoll, Lurton D., "Brigadier General Samuel A. Rice of Iowa," *AI,* 1st Series, III (January 1865), 385–403.
_____, "General James A. Williamson," *AI,* 1st Series, VIII (April 1870), 170–84.
Iowa Board of Immigration, *Iowa: The Home for Immigrants, Being a Treatise on the Resources of Iowa, and Giving Useful Information with Regard to the State, for the Benefit of Immigrants and Others* (Iowa City, 1970; 1st ed., Des Moines, 1870).
Iowa Census Board, *The Census Returns of the Different Counties of the State of Iowa, for 1856* (Iowa City, 1857).
_____, *The Census of Iowa as Returned in the Year 1875* . . . (Des Moines, 1875).
Iowa General Assembly, *Journal of the House of Representatives,* 1839–78.
_____, *Journal of the Council/Senate,* 1839–78.
_____, *Statistics upon Railways,* prepared in accordance with a joint resolution of the adjourned session of the Fourteenth General Assembly (Des Moines, 1874).
Iowa Secretary of State, *Historical and Comparative Census of Iowa for 1880* (Des Moines, 1883).
Journal of the Joint Committee of Fifteen on Reconstruction: 39 Congress, 1865–1867, ed. Benjamin B. Kendrick (New York, 1914).
Julian, George W., "The Death-Struggle of the Republican Party," *North American Review,* CXXVI (March–April 1878), 262–92.
_____, *Political Recollections, 1840 to 1872* (Chicago, 1884).
Kasson, John A., "Municipal Reform," *North American Review,* CXXXVII (September 1883), 218–30.
_____, "Otto von Bismarck, Man and Minister," *North American Review,* CXLIII (August 1886), 105–18.
Larrabee, William, *The Railroad Question: A Historical and Practical Treatise on Railroads, and Remedies for their Abuses* (10th ed., Chicago, 1898).
Lincoln, Abraham, *The Collected Works of Abraham Lincoln,* ed. Roy Basler (9 vols., New Brunswick, 1953–55).
Lloyd, Frederick, "John Brown among the Pedee Quakers," *AI,* 1st Series, IV (April 1866), 665–70; IV (July 1866), 712–19.
MacBride, James, "'The Hard Times' of '58–'60 or Reminiscences of Southeastern Iowa," *IHR,* XIII (October 1897), 169–80.
Magoun, George F., *Asa Turner: A Home Missionary Patriarch and His Times* (Boston and Chicago, 1889).
Mason, Charles, *A Review of the New Departure* (Burlington, Iowa, 1871).
Messages and Proclamations of the Governors of Iowa, ed. Benjamin F. Shambaugh (7 vols., Iowa City, 1903–05).
Mills, Frank Moody, *Something about the Mills Family and Its Collateral Branches with Autobiographical Reminiscences* (Sioux Falls, S.D., 1911).
Minutes of the Des Moines Annual Conference of the Methodist Episcopal Church, 1865–69, 1871–77.
Minutes of the General Association of Congregational Churches and Ministers of the State of Iowa . . . *1840 to 1855,* ed. J.B. Chase (Hull, Iowa, 1889).
Minutes of the General [Congregational] Association of Iowa, 1861, 1862, 1864.
Minutes of the Iowa Annual Conference of the Methodist Episcopal Church, 1854–56,

1858-62, 1865-67, 1869, 1873-77.
Minutes of the Iowa Baptist State Convention, 1846, 1850-51, 1855, 1860-61, 1863, 1865-66.
Minutes of the Upper Iowa Annual Conference of the Methodist Episcopal Church, 1857, 1859-61, 1865-66.
Minutes of the Western Iowa Annual Conference of the Methodist Episcopal Church, 1861-63.
Northern Editorials on Secession, ed. Howard Cecil Perkins (2 vols., Gloucester, Mass., 1964).
Nourse, Charles C., "The Iowa Delegation in the Republican National Convention of 1860," *IHR,* XI (July 1895), 293-96.
_____, *Autobiography of Charles Clinton Nourse* (Cedar Rapids, Iowa, 1911).
_____, "A Delegate's Memories of the Chicago Convention of 1860," *AI,* 3rd series, XII (October 1920), 454-66.
Parvin, Theodore S., "Enoch Worthen Eastman," *IHR,* I (April 1885), 49-57.
_____, "Hon. John Abbott Parvin," *IHR,* IX (July 1893), 481-89.
_____, "Thomas Hart Benton, Jr.," *IHR,* XVI (January 1900), 1-14.
Pike, James S., *First Blows of the Civil War* (New York, 1879).
Price, Hiram, "The Government and the Indians," *Forum,* X (February 1891), 708-15.
_____, "Recollections of Iowa Men and Affairs," *AI,* 3rd Series, I (April 1893), 1-14.
Proceedings of the First Iowa Methodist State Convention Held at Iowa City, Iowa, July 11th, 12th, and 13th, 1871 (Burlington, Iowa, 1871).
Report of the Commissioner of Indian Affairs, 1865, House Executive Documents, I, 39 Congress, 1 Session, No. 1248.
Report of the Commissioner of Indian Affairs, 1866, House Executive Documents, I, 39 Congress, 2 Session, No. 1284.
Report of the Debates and Proceedings of the Convention for the Revision of the Constitution of the State of Ohio, 1850-51 (2 vols., Columbus, Ohio, 1851).
Report of Proceedings of the Fourth Annual Session of the Iowa State Grange of the Patrons of Husbandry (Des Moines, 1873).
Report of Proceedings of the Fifth Annual Session of the Iowa State Grange of the Patrons of Husbandry (Des Moines, 1874).
Report of the Secretary of the Interior 1865, House Executive Documents, I, 39 Congress, 1 Session, No. 1248.
Richman, Irving B., "Congregational Life in Muscatine, 1843-1893," *IJHP,* XXI (July 1923), 347-72.
Salter, William, *The Life of James W. Grimes, Governor of Iowa, 1854-1858; A Senator of the United States, 1859-1869* (New York, 1876).
Sanborn, Franklin D., *Recollections of Seventy Years* (2 vols., Boston, 1909).
Springer, Francis, "Recollections of Judge Francis Springer," *AI,* 3rd Series, II (January 1897), 569-85.
Springer, John, "Theodore Sutton Parvin," *IHR,* XVII (July 1901), 335-44.
Stiles, Edward H., *Recollections and Sketches of Notable Lawyers and Public Men of Early Iowa* (Des Moines, 1916).
Throne, Mildred, ed., "Iowa Farm Letters, 1856-1865," *IJH,* LVIII (January 1960), 37-88.
Todd, John, *Early Settlement and Growth of Western Iowa or Reminiscences* (Des Moines, 1906).

U.S. Census Office, *Seventh Census of the United States: 1850* (Washington, D.C., 1853).
____, *The Eighth Census of the United States: 1860* (3 vols., Washington, D.C., 1864-65).
____, *The Ninth Census of the United States: 1870* (3 vols., Washington, D.C., 1872).
____, *The Tenth Census of the United States: 1880* (22 vols., Washington, D.C., 1883-88).
____, *Compendium of the Tenth Census* (June 1, 1880) . . . (Washington, D.C., 1880).
Welles, Gideon, *Diary of Gideon Welles: Secretary of the Navy under Lincoln and Johnson* (3 vols., Boston and New York, 1911).
Wilson, James F., "Christian W. Slagle," *IHR,* III (October 1887), 529-43.
Wright, George G., "Chief Justice Caleb Baldwin," *AI,* 3rd Series, I (October 1893), 209-14.

Published Secondary Sources

Abzug, Robert H., and Maizlish, Stephen E., eds., *New Perspectives on Race and Slavery in America: Essays in Honor of Kenneth M. Stampp* (Lexington, 1986).
Agnew, Dwight L., "The Mississippi & Missouri Railroad, 1856-1860," *IJH,* LI (July 1953), 211-32.
Alcorn, Richard S., "Leadership and Stability in Mid-Nineteenth-Century America: A Case Study of an Illinois Town," *JAH,* LXI (December 1974), 685-702.
Alexander, Thomas B., *Sectional Stress and Party Strength: A Study of Roll-Call Voting Patterns in the United States House of Representatives, 1836-1860* (Nashville, 1967).
Allen, Ethan P., "Gelpcke v. The City of Dubuque," *IJHP,* XXVIII (April 1930), 177-93.
Anderson, L.F., Watts, M.W., and Wilcox, A.R., *Legislative Roll Call Analysis* (Evanston, 1966).
Appleby, Joyce, "Commercial Farming and the 'Agrarian Myth' in the Early Republic," *JAH,* LXVIII (March 1982), 833-49.
____, "Republicanism in Old and New Contexts," *WMQ,* XLIII (January 1986), 20-34.
Ashworth, John, *"Agrarians" & "Aristocrats": Party Political Ideology in the United States, 1837-1846* (London, 1983).
____, "The Relationship between Capitalism and Humanitarianism," *AHR,* XCII (October 1987), 813-28.
Atack, Jeremy, and Bateman, Fred, "Self-Sufficiency and the Marketable Surplus in the Rural North," *Agricultural History,* LVIII (July 1984), 296-313.
____, *To Their Own Soil: Agriculture in the Antebellum North* (Ames, Iowa, 1987).
Aydelotte, William D., Bogue, Allan G., and Fogel, Robert W., eds., *The Dimensions of Quantitative Research in History* (London, 1972).
Bain, Richard C., and Parris, Judith H., *Convention Decisions and Voting Records* (2nd ed., Washington, D.C., 1973).
Baker, Jean H., *Affairs of Party: The Political Culture of Northern Democrats in the Mid-Nineteenth Century* (Ithaca and London, 1983).

Banner, Lois, "Religious Benevolence as Social Control," *JAH*, LX (June 1973), 23-41.
Baum, Dale, "Know-Nothingism and the Republican Majority in Massachusetts: The Political Realignment of the 1850s," *JAH*, LXIV (March 1978), 959-86.
Beard, Charles A., and Beard, Mary R., *The Rise of American Civilization* (2 vols., London, 1927).
Belz, Herman, *Reconstructing the Union: Theory and Policy during the Civil War* (Ithaca, 1969).
_____, *A New Birth of Freedom: The Republican Party and Freedmen's Rights, 1861 to 1866* (Westport, Conn., and London, 1976).
Benedict, Michael Les, *The Impeachment and Trial of Andrew Johnson* (New York, 1973).
_____, *A Compromise of Principle: Congressional Republicans and Reconstruction, 1863-1869* (New York, 1974).
_____, "Southern Democrats in the Crisis of 1876-1877: A Reconsideration of 'Reunion and Reaction,'" *JSH*, XLVI (November 1980), 489-524.
_____, "Free Labor Ideology and the Meaning of the Civil War and Reconstruction," *RAH*, IX (June 1981), 179-85.
Benson, Lee, *The Concept of Jacksonian Democracy: New York as a Test Case* (Princeton, 1961).
Bergmann, Leola N., "The Negro in Iowa," *IJHP*, XLVI (January 1948), 3-90.
Berrier, G. Galin, "The Negro Suffrage Issue in Iowa—1865-1868," *AI*, 3rd series, XXXIX (Spring 1968), 241-61.
Berwanger, Eugene H., *The Frontier against Slavery: Western Anti-Negro Prejudice and the Slavery Extension Controversy* (Urbana, 1967).
_____, *The West and Reconstruction* (Urbana, Chicago, and London, 1981).
Beth, Loren P., "The Slaughter-House Cases Revisited," *Louisiana Law Review*, XXIII (1963), 501-3.
Bickel, Alexander, "The Original Understanding and the Segregation Decision," *Harvard Law Review*, LXIX (November 1955), 1-65.
Billington, Ray A., *The Protestant Crusade, 1800-1860* (Quadrangle ed., Chicago, 1964).
Black, Paul Walton, "Lynchings in Iowa," *IJHP*, X (April 1912), 151-254.
Blue, Frederick J., *The Free Soilers: Third Party Politics, 1848-54* (Urbana, Chicago, and London, 1973).
Blumin, Stuart M., *The Urban Threshold: Growth and Change in a Nineteenth-Century American Community* (Chicago and London, 1976).
_____, "The Hypothesis of Middle-Class Formation in Nineteenth-Century America," *AHR*, XC (April 1985), 299-338.
Bogue, Allan G., "The Iowa Claim Clubs: Symbol and Substance," *MVHR*, XLV (September 1958), 231-53.
_____, *From Prairie to Corn Belt: Farming on the Illinois and Iowa Prairies in the Nineteenth Century* (Chicago and London, 1963).
_____, *The Earnest Men: Republicans of the Civil War Senate* (Ithaca and London, 1981).
Bonadio, Felice, *North of Reconstruction: Ohio Politics, 1865-1870* (New York, 1970).
Bowers, William L., "Crawford Township, 1850-1870: A Population Study of a Pioneer Community," *IJH*, LVIII (January 1960), 1-30.
Brigham, Johnson, *James Harlan* (Iowa City, 1913).

Brock, W.R., *An American Crisis: Congress and Reconstruction, 1865-1867* (London and New York, 1963).
_____, *Parties and Political Conscience: American Dilemmas, 1840-1850* (New York, 1979).
Brown, Richard D., *Modernization: The Transformation of American Life, 1600-1865* (New York, 1976).
Buck, Solon J., *The Granger Movement: A Study of Agricultural Organization and Its Political, Economic, and Social Manifestations, 1870-1880* (Cambridge, Mass., 1913).
Burnham, Walter Dean, *Presidential Ballots, 1836-1892* (Baltimore, 1955).
Campbell, Ballard C., *Representative Democracy: Public Policy and Midwestern Legislatures in the Late Nineteenth Century* (Cambridge, Mass., and London, 1980).
Clark, Dan Elbert, "The History of Liquor Legislation in Iowa, 1846-1861," *IJHP*, VI (January 1908), 55-87.
_____, "The History of Liquor Legislation in Iowa, 1861-1878," *IJHP*, VI (July 1908), 339-74.
_____, *History of Senatorial Elections in Iowa* (Iowa City, 1912).
_____, *Samuel Jordan Kirkwood* (Iowa City, 1917).
Clark, Robert D., *The Life of Matthew Simpson* (New York, 1956).
Clubb, Jerome M., Flanigan, William H., and Zingale, Nancy, *Partisan Realignment: Voters, Parties, and Government in American History* (Beverly Hills and London, 1980).
Cochran, Thomas C., *Railroad Leaders, 1845-1890: The Business Mind in Action* (Cambridge, Mass., 1953).
Cole, Arthur C., *The Era of the Civil War, 1848-1870* (*Centennial History of Illinois*, vol. III, Springfield, Ill., 1919).
Collins, Bruce, "The Ideology of Ante-bellum Northern Democrats," *JAS*, XI (April 1977), 103-21.
_____, "Economic Issues in Ohio's Politics during the Recession of 1857-1858," *Ohio History*, LXXXIX (Winter 1980), 46-64.
_____, *The Origins of America's Civil War* (London, 1981).
_____, "The Lincoln-Douglas Contest of 1858 and Illinois' Electorate," *JAS*, XX (December 1986), 391-420.
Congressional Quarterly's Guide to U.S. Elections (Washington, D.C., 1975).
Connor, James, "The Antislavery Movement in Iowa," *AI*, 3rd Series, XL (Summer and Fall 1970), 343-76, 450-79.
Conzen, Michael P., "Local Migration Systems in Nineteenth-Century Iowa," *Geographical Review*, LXIV (July 1974), 339-61.
Cooper, William J., *Liberty and Slavery: Southern Politics to 1860* (New York, 1983).
Cooper, William J., Holt, Michael F., and McCardell, John, eds., *A Master's Due: Essays in Honor of David Herbert Donald* (Baton Rouge and London, 1985).
Countryman, Edward, *A People in Revolution: The American Revolution and Political Society in New York, 1760-1790* (Baltimore and London, 1981).
Cox, LaWanda, *Lincoln and Black Freedom: A Study in Presidential Leadership* (Columbia, 1981).
Cox, LaWanda, and Cox, John H., *Politics, Principle, and Prejudice, 1865-1866: Dilemma of Reconstruction America* (London, 1963).
_____, "Negro Suffrage and Republican Politics: The Problem of Motivation in

Reconstruction Historiography," *JSH,* XXXIII (August 1967), 301-30.
Cromwell, Valerie, "Mapping the Political World of 1861: A Multidimensional Analysis of House of Commons' Division Lists," *Legislative Studies Quarterly,* VII (May 1982), 281-97.
Curry, Richard O., "The Civil War and Reconstruction, 1861-1877: A Critical Overview of Recent Trends and Interpretations," *CWH,* XX (September 1974), 215-38.
Dahl, Robert, "A Critique of the Ruling Elite Model," *American Political Science Review,* LII (June 1958), 463-69.
Danhof, Clarence, *Change in Agriculture: The Northern United States, 1820-70* (Cambridge, Mass., 1969).
Davis, David Brion, *The Slave Power Conspiracy and the Paranoid Style* (Baton Rouge, 1969).
_____, *The Problem of Slavery in the Age of Revolution, 1770-1823* (Ithaca and London, 1975).
_____, *Slavery and Human Progress* (New York and Oxford, 1984).
_____, "Reflections on Abolitionism and Ideological Hegemony," *AHR,* XCII (October 1987), 797-812.
Dawley, Alan, *Class and Community: The Industrial Revolution in Lynn* (Cambridge, Mass., and London, 1976).
Donald, David, *Charles Sumner and the Rights of Man* (New York, 1970).
_____, *Charles Sumner and the Coming of the Civil War* (New York, 1974).
Downey, Matthew T., "Horace Greeley and the Politicians: The Liberal Republican Convention in 1872," *JAH,* LIII (March 1967), 727-50.
Doyle, Don Harrison, *The Social Order of a Frontier Community: Jacksonville, Illinois, 1825-70* (Urbana, Chicago, and London, 1978).
Drescher, Seymour, *Capitalism and Antislavery* (Basingstoke and London, 1986).
Duberman, Martin, ed., *The Antislavery Vanguard: New Essays on the Abolitionists* (Princeton, 1965).
Dumond, Dwight, *Antislavery Origins of the Civil War in the United States* (Ann Arbor and London, 1939).
Duverger, Maurice, *Political Parties: Their Organization and Activity in the Modern State* (London and New York, 1964).
Dykstra, Robert R., "White Men, Black Laws: Territorial Iowans and Civil Rights, 1838-1843," *AI,* 3rd series, XLVI (Fall 1982), 403-40.
_____, "The Issue Squarely Met: Toward an Explanation of Iowans' Racial Attitudes, 1865-1868," *AI,* 3rd Series, XLVII (Summer 1984), 430-50.
Eddy, Richard, and Allen, Joseph H., *A History of the Unitarians and Universalists in the United States* (*The American Church History,* vol. X, New York, 1894).
Edelstein, Tilden G., *Strange Enthusiasm: A Life of Thomas Wentworth Higginson* (New Haven and London, 1968).
Erbe, Carl H., "Constitutional Provisions for the Suffrage in Iowa," *IJHP,* XXII (April 1924), 163-216.
_____, "Constitutional Limitations on Indebtedness in Iowa," *IJHP,* XXII (July 1924), 363-417.
Erickson, Charlotte, *American Industry and the European Immigrant, 1860-1885* (Cambridge, Mass., 1957).
Erickson, Erling A., *Banking in Frontier Iowa, 1836-1865* (Ames, Iowa, 1971).
Eriksson, Erik McKinley, "William Penn Clarke," *IJHP,* XXV (January 1927), 3-61.

Fairman, Charles, *Mr. Justice Miller and the Supreme Court, 1862-1890* (Cambridge, Mass., 1939).
Farnham, Wallace D., "Grenville Dodge and the Union Pacific: A Study of Historical Legends," *JAH,* LI (March 1965), 632-50.
Field, Phyllis F., *The Politics of Race in New York: The Struggle for Black Suffrage in the Civil War Era* (Ithaca and London, 1982).
Fishlow, Albert, "Antebellum Interregional Trade Reconsidered," *American Economic Review,* LIV (May 1964), 352-64.
Fite, Gilbert, *The Farmers' Frontier* (New York, 1966).
Fogel, Robert W., *The Union Pacific Railroad: A Case in Premature Enterprise* (Baltimore, 1960).
Foner, Eric, *Free Soil, Free Labor, Free Men: The Ideology of the Republican Party before the Civil War* (New York, 1970).
_____, *Politics and Ideology in the Age of the Civil War* (New York and Oxford, 1980).
_____, *Reconstruction: America's Unfinished Revolution, 1863-1877* (New York, 1988).
Formisano, Ronald P., *The Birth of Mass Political Parties: Michigan, 1827-1861* (Princeton, 1971).
Fredrickson, George, *The Black Image in the White Mind: The Debate on Afro-American Character and Destiny, 1817-1914* (New York, 1971).
_____, "A Man but Not a Brother: Abraham Lincoln and Racial Equality," *JSH,* XLI (February 1975), 39-58.
_____, *White Supremacy: A Comparative Study in American and South African History* (New York and Oxford, 1981).
Friedman, Lawrence J., *Gregarious Saints: Self and Community in American Abolitionism, 1830-1870* (Cambridge, England, 1982).
Galenson, David W., and Pope, Clayne L., "Economic and Geographic Mobility on the Farming Frontier: Evidence from Appanoose County, Iowa, 1850-1870," *JEH,* XLIX (September 1989), 635-55.
Gates, Paul Wallace, *Fifty Million Acres: Conflicts over Kansas Land Policy, 1854-1890* (Ithaca, 1954).
Genovese, Eugene G., *The Political Economy of Slavery: Studies in the Economy and Society of the Slave South* (New York, 1965).
Gerteis, Louis S., *From Contraband to Freedman: Federal Policy toward Southern Blacks, 1861-1865* (Westport, Conn., and London, 1973).
Gienapp, William E., "Salmon Chase, Nativism, and the Formation of the Republican Party in Ohio," *Ohio History,* XCIII (Winter-Spring 1984), 5-39.
_____, *The Origins of the Republican Party, 1852-1856* (New York and Oxford, 1987).
Gillette, William, *The Right to Vote: Politics and the Passage of the Fifteenth Amendment* (Baltimore, 1965).
_____, *Retreat from Reconstruction, 1869-1879* (Baton Rouge and London, 1979).
Glashan, Roy R., *American Governors and Gubernatorial Elections, 1775-1978* (London, 1979).
Gold, David M., "Redfield, Railroads, and the Roots of 'Laissez-Faire Constitutionalism,'" *American Journal of Legal History,* XXVII (July 1983), 254-68.
Graham, Howard Jay, "The 'Conspiracy Theory' of the Fourteenth Amendment," *Yale Law Journal,* XLVII (January 1938), 371-403.
Grodinsky, Julius, *The Iowa Pool: A Study in Railroad Competition, 1870-84*

(Chicago, 1950).
Gue, Benjamin F., *History of Iowa, From the Earliest Times to the Beginning of the Twentieth Century* (4 vols., New York, 1903).
Hammarberg, Melvyn, *The Indiana Voter: The Historical Dynamics of Party Allegiance during the 1870s* (Chicago and London, 1977).
Hampel, Robert L., *Temperance and Prohibition in Massachusetts, 1813–1852* (Ann Arbor, 1980).
Hansen, Stephen L., *The Making of the Third Party System: Voters and Parties in Illinois, 1850–1876* (Ann Arbor, 1980).
Hartog, Hendrik, ed., *Law and the American Revolution and the Revolution in the Law: A Collection of Review Essays on American Legal History* (New York and London, 1981).
Haskell, Thomas L., "Capitalism and the Origins of the Humanitarian Sensibility," *AHR*, XC (April 1985), 339–61; (June 1985), 547–66.
Haynes, Fred E., *James Baird Weaver* (Iowa City, 1919).
Herriott, F.E., "Iowa and the First Nomination of Abraham Lincoln," *AI*, 2nd series, VIII (July 1907), 81–115; VIII (July 1908), 444–66; IX (April 1909), 45–64.
_____, "Germans in the Gubernatorial Campaign of Iowa in 1859," reprinted from *Deutsch-Amerikanische Geschichtsblätter Jahrbuch der Deutsch-Amerikanischen Historischen Gesellschaft von Illinois*, XIV (1914).
Hill, James L., "Migration of Blacks to Iowa, 1820–1960," *Journal of Negro History*, LXVI (Winter 1981–82), 289–303.
Hirshson, Stanley P., *Grenville M. Dodge: Soldier, Politician, Railroad Pioneer* (Bloomington, Ind., and London, 1967).
_____, *Farewell to the Bloody Shirt: Northern Republicans and the Southern Negro, 1877–1893* (Chicago, 1968).
Holt, Michael F., *Forging a Majority: The Formation of the Republican Party in Pittsburgh, 1848–60* (New Haven and London, 1969).
_____, *The Political Crisis of the 1850s* (New York, 1978).
Horwitz, Morton J., *The Transformation of American Law, 1780–1860* (Cambridge, Mass., and London, 1977).
Howe, Daniel Walker, *The Political Culture of the American Whigs* (Chicago, 1979).
Hurst, James Willard, *Law and the Conditions of Freedom in the Nineteenth-Century United States* (Madison, 1956).
Huston, James L., "Abolitionists and an Errant Economy: The Panic of 1857 and Abolitionist Economic Ideas," *Mid-America*, LXV (January 1983), 15–27.
_____, "Western Grains and the Panic of 1857," *Agricultural History*, LVII (January 1983), 14–32.
Hutchinson, William K., and Williamson, Samuel H., "The Self-Sufficiency of the Antebellum South: Estimates of the Food Supply," *JEH*, XXXI (September 1971), 591–612.
Jellison, Charles, *Fessenden of Maine: Civil War Senator* (Syracuse, 1962).
Jensen, Richard, *The Winning of the Midwest* (Chicago and London, 1971).
Johannsen, Robert W., *Stephen A. Douglas* (New York, 1973).
Johnson, Hildegard Binder, "German Forty-Eighters in Davenport," *IJHP*, XLIV (January 1946), 3–53.
Jordan, Philip D., *William Salter: Western Torchbearer* (Oxford, Ohio, 1939).
_____, *Catfish Bend, River Town and County Seat: An Informal History of Burlington, Iowa, 1836–1900* (Burlington, Iowa, 1975).
Jupp, James, *Political Parties* (London and New York, 1968).

Keller, Morton, *Affairs of State: Public Life in Late Nineteenth Century America* (Cambridge, Mass., and London, 1977).
Kelley, Bruce Gunn, "Ethnocultural Voting Trends in Rural Iowa, 1890–1898," *AI*, 3rd Series, XLIV (Fall 1978), 441–61.
Kleppner, Paul, *The Cross of Culture: A Social Analysis of Midwestern Politics, 1850–1900* (New York and London, 1970).
———, *The Third Electoral System, 1853–1892: Parties, Voters, and Political Cultures* (Chapel Hill, N.C., 1979).
Kleppner, Paul, Burnham, Walter Dean, Formisano, Ronald P., Hays, Samuel P., Jensen, Richard, and Shade, William G., *The Evolution of American Electoral Systems* (Westport, Conn., and London, 1981).
Klingman, David C., and Vedder, Richard K., eds., *Essays in Nineteenth Century Economic History: The Old Northwest* (Athens, Ohio, 1975).
Kraut, Alan M., ed., *Crusaders and Compromisers: Essays on the Relationship of the Antislavery Struggle to the Antebellum Party System* (Westport, Conn., and London, 1983).
Kruskal, Joseph, and Wish, Myron, *Multidimensional Scaling*, Sage University Papers: Quantitative Applications in the Social Sciences, No. 11 (London, 1978).
Larson, John Lauritz, *Bonds of Enterprise: John Murray Forbes and Western Development in America's Railway Age* (Cambridge, Mass., and London, 1984).
Laurie, Bruce, *Working People of Philadelphia, 1800–1850* (Philadelphia, 1980).
Lebergott, Stanley, "The Demand for Land: The United States, 1820–1860," *JEH*, XLV (June 1985), 181–212.
Lee, Robert Edson, "Politics and Society in Sioux City, 1859," *IJH*, LIV (April 1956), 117–30.
Lendt, David L., *Demise of the Democracy: The Copperhead Press in Iowa, 1856–1870* (Ames, Iowa, 1973).
Lewellen, Fred B., "Political Ideas of James W. Grimes," *IJHP*, XLII (October 1944), 339–404.
Lindstrom, Diane, "American Economic Growth before 1840: New Evidence and New Directions," *JEH*, XXXIX (March 1979), 289–301.
Lipset, Seymour M., and Rokkan, Stein, eds., *Party Systems and Voter Alignments: Cross National Perspectives* (New York and London, 1967).
Litwack, Leon, *North of Slavery: The Negro in the Free States, 1790–1860* (Chicago, 1961).
Loving, Jerome M., "Whitman and Harlan: New Evidence," *American Literature*, XLVIII (May 1976), 219–22.
Lucas, Henry S., "The Political Activities of the Dutch Immigrants from 1847 to the Civil War," *IJHP*, XXVI (April 1928), 171–203.
Luebke, Frederick C., *Ethnic Voters and the Election of Lincoln* (Lincoln, Nebr., 1971).
McClain, Emlin, "The Iowa Codes," *Iowa Law Bulletin*, I (January 1915), 3–28.
McCormick, Richard L., *The Party Period and Public Policy: American Politics from the Age of Jackson to the Progressive Era* (New York and Oxford, 1986).
McCormick, Richard P., *The Second American Party System: Party Formation in the Jacksonian Era* (Chapel Hill, N.C., 1966).
McCrary, Peyton, "The Party of Revolution: Republican Ideas about Politics and Social Change, 1862–1867," *CWH*, XXX (December 1984), 330–50.
McFeeley, William S., *Grant: A Biography* (New York and London, 1981).

McGerr, Michael E., "The Meaning of Liberal Republicanism: The Case of Ohio," *CWH*, XXVIII (December 1982), 307-23.
McKitrick, Eric L., *Andrew Johnson and Reconstruction* (Chicago, 1960).
McLaughlin, Tom L., "Grass-Roots Attitudes Toward Black Rights in Twelve Non-Slaveholding States, 1846-1869," *Mid-America*, LVI (July 1974), 175-81.
Magdol, Edward, *The Antislavery Rank and File: A Social Profile of the Abolitionists' Constituency* (New York, Westport, Conn., and London, 1986).
Mak, James, "Intraregional Trade in the Antebellum West: Ohio, a Case Study," *Agricultural History*, XLVI (October 1972), 489-97.
Malone, Wex S., "The Formative Era of Contributory Negligence," *Illinois Law Review*, XLI (July-August 1946), 161-82.
Marshall, Lynn L., "The Strange Stillbirth of the Whig Party," *AHR*, LXXII (January 1967), 445-68.
Mathews, Donald G., *Slavery and Methodism: A Chapter in American Morality, 1780-1845* (Princeton, 1965).
Mayhew, Anne, "A Reappraisal of the Causes of Farm Protest in the United States, 1870-1900," *JEH*, XXXII (June 1972), 464-75.
Miller, George H., *Railroads and the Granger Laws* (Madison, Milwaukee, and London, 1971).
Millsap, Kenneth F., "The Election of 1860 in Iowa," *IJH*, XLVIII (April 1950), 97-120.
Mohr, James C., *The Radical Republicans and Reform in New York during Reconstruction* (Ithaca and London, 1973).
_____, ed., *Radical Republicans in the North: State Politics during Reconstruction* (Baltimore and London, 1976).
Montgomery, David, *Beyond Equality: Labor and the Radical Republicans, 1862-1872* (New York, 1967).
Moore, Barrington, *Social Origins of Dictatorship and Democracy: Lord and Peasant in the Making of the Modern World* (London, 1967).
Nichols, Roy F., "The Kansas-Nebraska Act: A Century of Historiography," *MVHR*, XLIII (September 1956), 187-212.
Noun, Louise R., *Strong-minded Women: The Emergence of the Woman Suffrage Movement in Iowa* (Ames, Iowa, 1969).
Oates, Stephen, *To Purge This Land with Blood: A Biography of John Brown* (New York, Evanston, and London, 1970).
_____, *With Malice toward None: The Life of Abraham Lincoln* (New York and Toronto, 1977).
Ottoson, Howard W., ed., *Land Use Policy and Problems in the United States* (Lincoln, Nebr., 1963).
Overton, Richard C., *Burlington West: A Colonization History of the Burlington Railroad* (Cambridge, Mass., 1941).
Paludan, Philip S., "Law and the Failure of Reconstruction: The Case of Thomas Cooley," *Journal of the History of Ideas*, LIII (1972), 597-614.
_____, "The American Civil War: Triumph through Tragedy," *CWH*, (September 1974), 239-50.
Payne, Charles E., *Josiah Bushnell Grinnell* (Iowa City, 1938).
Pelzer, Louis, "The Origin and Organization of the Republican Party in Iowa," *IJHP*, IV (October 1906), 487-525.
_____, "The History and Principles of the Whigs of the Territory of Iowa," *IJHP*, V (January 1907), 46-90.

Perman, Michael, *Reunion without Compromise: The South and Reconstruction, 1865-1868* (Cambridge, England, 1973).
Perry, Lewis, and Fellman, Michael, eds., *Antislavery Reconsidered: New Perspectives on the Abolitionists* (Baton Rouge and London, 1979).
Peskin, Allan, "Was There a Compromise of 1877?" *JAH*, LX (June 1973), 63-75.
Petersen, Svend, *A Statistical History of American Presidential Elections* (New York, 1963).
Plamenatz, John, *Ideology* (London, 1970).
Pole, J.R., *The Pursuit of Equality in American History* (Berkeley, Los Angeles, and London, 1978).
Potter, David M., *Lincoln and His Party in the Secession Crisis* (New Haven and London, 1942).
Powell, Clifford, "History of the Codes of Iowa II: The Code of 1851," *IJHP*, X (January 1912), 3-69.
Power, Richard Lyle, *Planting Corn Belt Culture: The Impress of the Upland Southerner and Yankee in the Old Northwest* (Indianapolis, 1953).
Ralston, Leonard F., "Governor Ralph P. Lowe and State Aid to Railroads: Iowa Politics in 1859," *IJH*, LVIII (July 1960), 207-18.
Ratcliffe, Donald J., "Politics in Jacksonian Ohio: Reflections on the Ethnocultural Interpretation," *Ohio History*, LXXXVIII (Winter 1979), 5-36.
Riley, Glenda, *Frontierswomen: The Iowa Experience* (Ames, Iowa, 1981).
Roberts, George E., "The Career of Jacob Rich," *IJHP*, XIII (April 1915), 165-74.
Rosenberg, Morton M., *Iowa on the Eve of the Civil War: A Decade of Frontier Politics* (Norman, Okla., 1972).
Ross, Earle D., *Iowa Agriculture: An Historical Survey* (Iowa City, 1951).
Rossbach, Jeffery, *Ambivalent Conspirators: John Brown, the Secret Six, and a Theory of Slave Violence* (Philadelphia, 1982).
Rothstein, Morton M., "America in the International Rivalry for the British Wheat Market, 1860-1914," *MVHR*, XLVII (December 1960), 401-18.
Russel, Robert R., *Improvement of Communication with the Pacific Coast as an Issue in American Politics, 1783-1864* (Cedar Rapids, Iowa, 1948).
Russell, Charles Edward, *A Pioneer Editor in Early Iowa: A Sketch of the Life of Edward Russell* (Washington, D.C., 1941).
Rutland, Robert, "Iowans and the Fourteenth Amendment," *IJH*, LI (October 1953), 289-300.
Sage, Leland L., "The Clarksons of Indiana and Iowa," *Indiana Magazine of History*, L (December 1954), 429-46.
_____, *William Boyd Allison: A Study in Practical Politics* (Iowa City, 1956).
_____, *A History of Iowa* (Ames, Iowa, 1974).
Schmidt, Louis B., "Internal Commerce and the Development of National Economy before 1860," *Journal of Political Economy*, XLVII (December 1939), 798-822.
Schob, David E., *Hired Hands and Plowboys: Farm Labor in the Midwest, 1815-60* (Urbana, Chicago, and London, 1975).
Sellers, C. G., *The Market Revolution and Jacksonian America, 1815-1846* (New York and Oxford 1991).
Sewell, Richard, *Ballots for Freedom: Antislavery Politics in the United States, 1837-1860* (New York, 1976).
Shade, William G., *Banks or No Banks: The Money Issue in Western Politics, 1832-1865* (Detroit, 1972).
Sharkey, Robert P., *Money, Class, and Party: An Economic Study of Civil War and*

Reconstruction (Baltimore, 1959).
Silag, William, "Gateway to the Grasslands: Sioux City and the Missouri River Frontier," *Western Historical Quarterly*, XIV (October 1983), 397-414.
Silbey, Joel, "Proslavery Sentiment in Iowa, 1838-1861," *IJH*, LV (October 1957), 289-318.
_____, *The Shrine of Party: Congressional Voting Behavior, 1841-1852* (Pittsburgh, 1967).
_____, *A Respectable Minority: The Democratic Party in the Civil War Era, 1860-1868* (New York, 1977).
Smith, Theodore Clarke, *The Liberty and Free Soil Parties in the Northwest* (New York, London, and Bombay, 1897).
Smith, Timothy L., *Revivalism and Social Reform in Mid-Nineteenth-Century America* (New York and Nashville, 1957).
Sobel, Robert, and Raimo, John, eds., *Biographical Directory of the Governors of the United States, 1789-1978* (2 vols., Westport, Conn., 1978).
Soltow, Lee, *Men and Wealth in the United States, 1850-1870* (New Haven and London, 1975).
Sorauf, Frank J., *Political Parties in the American System* (Boston and Toronto, 1964).
Sparks, David S., "Iowa Republicans and the Railroads, 1856-1860," *IJH*, LIII (July 1955), 273-86.
_____, "The Birth of the Republican Party in Iowa, 1854-1856," *IJH*, LIV (January 1956), 1-34.
Sproat, John G., *"The Best Men": Liberal Reformers in the Gilded Age* (New York, 1968).
Stampp, Kenneth M., *And the War Came: The North and the Secession Crisis, 1860-1861* (Baton Rouge, 1950).
Strand, Norman V., *Prices of Farm Products in Iowa, 1851-1940*, Agricultural Experiment Station Research Bulletin No. 303 (Ames, Iowa, 1942).
Swierenga, Robert P., *Pioneers and Profits: Land Speculation on the Iowa Frontier* (Ames, Iowa, 1968).
_____, *Acres for Cents: Delinquent Tax Auctions in Frontier Iowa* (Westport, Conn., and London, 1976).
Temperley, Howard, "Capitalism, Slavery, and Ideology," *Past and Present*, LXXV (May 1977), 94-118.
Thornborough, Emma Lou, *Indiana in the Civil War Era, 1850-1880* (Indianapolis, 1965).
Thornton, J. Mills, III, *Politics and Power in a Slave Society: Alabama, 1800-1860* (Baton Rouge and London, 1978).
Thorp, Robert K., "The Copperhead Days of Dennis Mahoney," *Journalism Quarterly*, XLIII (Winter 1966), 680-86, 696.
Throne, Mildred, "Southern Iowa Agriculture, 1833-1890: The Progress from Subsistence to Commercial Corn-Belt Farming," *Agricultural History*, XXIII (April 1949), 124-30.
_____, "Southern Iowa Agriculture, 1865-1870," *IJH*, L (July 1952), 209-24.
_____, "The Repeal of the Iowa Granger Law, 1878," *IJH*, LI (April 1953), 97-130.
_____, "The Anti-Monopoly Party in Iowa, 1873-1874," *IJH*, LII (October 1954), 289-326.
_____, "The Liberal Republican Party in Iowa, 1872," *IJH*, LIII (April 1955), 121-52.

———, *Cyrus Clay Carpenter and Iowa Politics, 1854–1898* (Iowa City, 1974).
Tyrell, Ian R., *From Temperance to Prohibition in Antebellum America, 1800–1860* (Westport, Conn., and London, 1979).
Unger, Irwin, *The Greenback Era: A Social and Political History of American Finance, 1865–1879* (Princeton, 1964).
U.S. Bureau of the Census, *Historical Statistics of the United States: Colonial Times to 1970* (2 vols., Washington, D.C., 1975).
Van Deusen, Glyndon G., *William Henry Seward* (New York, 1967).
Voegeli, V. Jacques, *Free but Not Equal: The Midwest and the Negro during the Civil War* (Chicago and London, 1967).
Wallace, Anthony F.C., *Rockdale* (New York, 1978).
Walsh, Margaret, *The American Frontier Revisited* (London and Basingstoke, 1981).
———, *The Rise of the Midwestern Meat Packing Industry* (Lexington, Ky., 1982).
White, Edward G., *The American Judicial Tradition: Profiles of Leading American Judges* (New York, 1976).
Wiggins, Sarah Woolfolk, *The Scalawag in Alabama Politics, 1865–1881* (University, Ala., 1977).
Wilentz, Sean, *Chants Democratic: New York City and the Rise of the American Working Class, 1788–1850* (New York and Oxford, 1984).
Winters, Donald L., *Farmers without Farms: Agricultural Tenancy in Nineteenth Century Iowa* (Westport, Conn., and London, 1978).
Woodward, C. Vann, *Reunion and Reaction: The Compromise of 1877 and the End of Reconstruction* (Boston, 1951).
———, "Yes, There Was a Compromise of 1877," *JAH,* LX (June 1973), 215–23.
Workman, J. Brooke, "Governor William Larrabee and Railroad Reform," *IJH,* LVII (July 1959), 231–66.
Wright, Luella M., *Peter Melendy: The Mind and the Soil* (Iowa City, 1943).
Wubben, Hubert H., "Copperhead Charles Mason: A Question of Loyalty," *CWH,* XXIV (March 1978), 46–65.
———, *Civil War Iowa and the Copperhead Movement* (Ames, Iowa, 1980).
———, "The Uncertain Trumpet: Iowa Republicans and Black Suffrage, 1860–1868," *AI,* 3rd Series, XLVII (Summer 1984), 409–29.
Younger, Edward, *John A. Kasson: Politics and Diplomacy from Lincoln to McKinley* (Iowa City, 1955).

Unpublished Secondary Sources

Boeck, George A., "An Early Iowa Community: Aspects of Economic, Social, and Political Development in Burlington, Iowa, 1833–1866" (University of Iowa Ph.D. thesis, 1961).
Gallagher, Mary Annette, "John F. Lacey: A Study in Organizational Politics" (University of Arizona Ph.D. thesis, 1970).
Harris, Fay Erma, "A Frontier Community: The Economic, Social, and Political Development of Keokuk, Iowa, from 1820 to 1866" (University of Iowa Ph.D. thesis, 1965).
Matthias, Ronald F., "The Know Nothing Movement in Iowa" (University of Chicago Ph.D. thesis, 1965).
Ralston, Leonard F., "Railroads and the Government of Iowa, 1850–1872" (University of Iowa Ph.D. thesis, 1960).

Sparks, David S., "The Birth of the Republican Party in Iowa, 1848 to 1860" (University of Chicago Ph.D. thesis, 1951).
Toussaint, Willard I., "Biography of an Iowa Businessman: Charles Mason, 1804–1882," (University of Iowa Ph.D. thesis, 1963).

Index

Abernethy, Alonzo A., 168, 169, 172
Abolitionists. *See also* Brown, John; Liberty party
 in Civil War, 140, 145, 146
 and colonization, 77–78
 and Kansas, 63
 and politics, 35–36, 38, 53, 66, 90–92, 121, 127
 postwar influence, 193, 196
 and race, 35
 in territorial Iowa, 28, 30, 33–35, 115
Act to Regulate Blacks and Mulattoes (1839), 33, 35, 255 n. 4
Adams, Charles F., Jr., 211
African-Americans. *See also* Black suffrage; Democrats; Racism; Reconstruction; Republicans
 general, 4, 12, 37, 38, 68, 78, 129, 136, 247
 in Iowa, 33, 65, 76–77, 82, 94, 141, 143–45, 161–62, 164, 191, 196
 in North, 32–33
 and Reconstruction, 159–60, 164, 174–75, 183, 187, 188, 190, 194, 198, 222, 230, 232, 245
 and wartime enlistment, 141, 148–49, 156
Agriculture, in Iowa, 4, 17, 96–97, 139, 143, 145, 149, 204, 205–6, 210
Aldrich, Charles, 119
Allison, William B.
 as congressman, 142, 153, 187, 194, 272 n. 58
 elected to Senate, 195
 and 1876–77 election crisis, 231–32
 laissez-faire views of, 205
 marries, 238
 and railroads, 205, 206, 207–8
American Colonization Society, 77

American Emigrant Company, 179
American Home Missionary Society, 34, 42
Ames, Oakes, 207
Amnesty. *See* Confederates
Antietam, battle of, 148
Anti-Masonry, 90
Anti-Monopoly party, 211–12
Antimonopoly sentiment, 99, 100, 101, 105, 106, 109–10, 123, 152, 191, 198, 200, 203, 206, 209, 218–20, 223, 226, 275 n. 57
Artisans, 70, 105, 242
Ashley, James, 119, 187, 189
Atack, Jeremy, 96
Atlanta, battle of, 154

Baldwin, Caleb, 129, 141, 142, 217–18, 219, 223
Baldwin, John T., 129
Banks, Nathaniel P., 58, 258 n. 43
Banks and banking
 and capitalism, 4, 6
 and 1857 constitutional convention, 75, 80, 98–101
 and Iowa politics, 22–26, 28, 44, 47, 49, 102, 103, 111, 115, 126, 203, 204, 242, 244
 in national politics, 18–20
Baptists, 28, 49, 147, 168. *See also* Evangelical protestants and protestantism
Barnburners, 36
Bateman, Fred, 96
Bates, Edward, 124, 125
Beard, Charles A., 6, 8
Beard, Mary R., 6, 8
Beauregard, Pierre G. T., 228
Beck, Joseph, 196, 198, 221–22, 223

Beecher, Lyman, 42
Belknap, William W., 134, 194, 199
Bell, John, 126
Benton, Thomas Hart, 18
Benton, Thomas Hart, Jr., 166
Berry, Lucien W., 55
Bismarck, Otto von, 129
Bissell, Frederick, 209
Black Hawk Purchase, 15
Blacks. *See* African-Americans
Black suffrage
  in Civil War, 151, 154–55
  in 1857 constitutional convention, 80, 81, 85–87
  in 1857 election, 92–94
  and Reconstruction, 159–60, 166–75, 178, 182, 183, 184–93, 269 n. 15
  and 1865 Republican convention, 160–66
Blaine, James G., 229
Blair, Montgomery, 181
Bloomfield, Iowa, 224
Blue laws, 29
Bogue, Allan G., 140
Boston Advertiser, 189
Boutwell, George, 188
Bowen, Jesse, 120
Breckinridge, John C., 125, 126
Brown, B. Gratz, 185
Brown, John, 61, 63, 115, 116, 119–22, 132, 134, 201, 243, 246
Brown, Richard D., 7
Browning, Milton, 54
Buchanan, James, 68, 69, 70, 97, 103, 110, 111, 113, 115, 116, 117, 129, 130, 196
Bull Run, first battle of, 137–38
Burlington, Iowa, 17, 82, 96, 97, 103, 107, 108, 109, 126, 130, 140, 150, 151, 161, 167, 168, 180, 189, 192, 200, 201, 204, 209, 233
Burlington and Des Moines Transportation Company, 26
Burlington fugitive slave case, 65–66, 67, 81
Burlington Hawk-Eye, 163, 165, 167, 176
Burlington & Missouri Railroad, 63, 98, 107, 109, 110, 206, 215
Butler, Benjamin F., 184

Butler, Jacob, F., 125, 150

Cameron, Simon, 125
Capital punishment, 90, 193, 224, 245, 276 n. 94
Carpenter, Cyrus C.
  and Des Moines Regency, 195
  elected governor, 200
  and Granger law, 210–12
  and Hayes policy, 232–33, 246
  and labor, 234
  and race, 118, 165–66, 232–33
Cass, Lewis, 36, 38, 44
Cattell, Jonathan W., 121, 160, 169
Cedar Falls Gazette, 148
Cedar Rapids, Iowa, 39, 204
Centerville, Iowa, 69
Chamberlain, Daniel H., 232
Chambers, John, 21
Chancellorsville, battle of, 148
Charles City, Iowa, 221
Chase, Salmon P., 36, 48, 52, 53, 55, 57, 60, 66, 119, 125, 138, 150
Cherokee Neutral Tract, 179
Chicago
  1860 convention, 124–25
  dominates Iowa trade, 149, 204–5, 209
Chickamauga, battle of, 149
Cincinnati, nativist riots in, 57
City of Dubuque v. *The Illinois Central Railroad Co.* (1874), 221
Civil War, 3, 11, 34, 134, 135, 136–56, 159, 182, 227–28
Clark, Alexander, 76, 77, 94, 141
Clark, Ezekiel, 169
Clark, John T., 81, 84, 86
Clarke, Charles, 139
Clarke, Rufus, 57, 82–86, 94, 100, 101, 150, 152, 260 n. 33, 260 n. 34
Clarke, William Penn
  and John Brown, 120
  at Chicago convention, 124, 125, 265 n. 31
  in 1857 constitutional convention, 81, 82, 84, 86, 87, 99–100, 101
  economic views of, 23–24, 205
  feud with Kirkwood, 113, 128
  as Free-Soiler, 36, 37, 39, 44
  and Harlan, 184, 194

and Kansas, 62, 63
and Know Nothings, 56, 58
railroad links, 107
and secession, 132-33
as sectionalist, 134, 237
Clarkson, Coker F., 151
Clarkson, James F., 194, 195, 201, 212, 223, 232
Class, as basis of partisanship, 70, 241-42
Clay, Henry, 36, 165
Clinton, Iowa, 17, 204, 209
Clubb, Jerome M., 10
Code of 1851, 89, 108
Code of 1873, 222
Cole, Chester C., 218-19, 222, 223
Colonization, 77-78, 83, 86, 91, 122, 139, 165, 260 n. 14
Committee of Thirty-Three, 131, 132
Compromise of 1850, 37, 38, 39, 43, 44, 45, 50, 53, 65, 81, 133
Confederates, status of during Reconstruction, 165, 172, 178, 180, 188, 197, 199, 200
Congregationalists, 28, 29, 60, 90, 106, 177. *See also* Evangelical protestants and protestantism
and black suffrage, 164
missionary activity of, 42, 55
and political involvement, 46, 67
and slavery, 33, 34, 62, 132, 137, 161
Congressional elections, 111, 142, 154, 182
Conkling, Roscoe, 221
Constitution
of 1846, 39, 43, 75, 244
of 1857, 87-89, 91-94, 102, 103, 110, 119, 155, 161, 164, 167, 168, 169, 182, 185, 186, 221
Constitutional Convention
of 1844, 21, 23, 24-25, 29
of 1846, 22, 23, 25
of 1857, 80-87, 94, 98-102, 105, 106, 188
Constitutional Union party, 125
Contributory negligence, 218, 222
Cook, Lyman, 108
Coolbaugh, William, 44, 97, 108, 109, 110
Cooley, Dennis N., 179

Copperheads. *See* Peace Democrats
Coppoc, Barclay, 121-22, 123, 134
Coppoc, Edwin, 121
Corruption, 95, 107, 110-11, 113, 179, 195, 196-97, 202, 206-8, 210, 238
Corydon, Iowa, 244
Council Bluffs, Iowa, 39, 60, 85, 128, 129, 180, 217
Cowles, William F., 162
Crawfordsville, Iowa, 34, 36, 47, 66
Credit Mobilier scandal, 199, 206-8, 210
Crimean War, 40, 49
Crittenden Compromise, 133-34, 135
Crocker, Marcellus, M., 65, 146
Cuba, 114, 118
Curtis, Samuel R., 124, 131, 133, 134, 138, 148

Dartmouth College v. *Woodward* (1819), 218-19
Darwin, Charles Ben, 168
Davenport, Iowa, 17, 56, 62, 97, 120, 125, 127, 164, 200, 204, 208, 209, 223
Davenport Gazette, 155, 164, 186, 194
Davis, David, 129
Davis, David Brion, 6
Davis, Jefferson, 37, 66, 172, 228
Davis, Timothy, 54
Dean, Henry Clay, 229
Deering, Nathaniel C., 161
Democrats, 8, 10. *See also* Buchanan, Factionalism; Peace Democrats
and banks, 22-26, 41, 98-101, 102, 103, 105
and black suffrage, 85-86, 168, 169, 171, 191
and John Brown raid, 124-26
and Civil War, 138, 142, 143, 146, 153-54, 156, 164
and 1857 constitutional convention, 75, 81-87, 98-102
and corporations, 26-28
and 1848 election, 36
and 1876 election, 229-30
and ethnocultural issues, 28-30, 42, 43, 44, 55, 56, 88, 114, 242, 244
ethnoreligious composition of party, 239-41
and fusion with Anti-Monopolists,

Democrats (*continued*)
  211
  ideology of, 18
  and Kansas, 11, 62, 113
  and Kansas-Nebraska Act, 45, 47–48
  and laissez-faire, 25, 27–28, 29, 30, 38, 40, 71, 101, 105, 114, 123, 245
  and Mexican War, 31
  and protection, 205
  and race, 32, 33, 76–77, 78, 80, 83, 84, 91, 114, 126, 144, 154, 189, 228, 242, 267 n. 41
  and railroads, 40, 97, 101–2, 103, 108–10, 111, 206, 215, 224, 225, 244
  and Reconstruction, 174, 180–81, 192
  and role in Republican party, 59, 67, 71, 75, 86–87, 98, 100–101, 112, 145, 149, 152, 160, 185, 187, 194, 197, 205, 218
  and secession, 143
  and 1854 senate election, 53–54
  and slavery expansion, 31–32, 36, 38, 44, 50, 66
  and South, 44, 114
  and territorial politics, 5, 15, 18–30
Denmark, Iowa, 33–34, 47, 81, 177
Depression of 1870s, 11, 202, 210, 224–26, 228, 229, 230–31, 245
Des Moines, Iowa, 39, 48, 56, 75, 98, 107, 108, 109, 111, 112, 113, 117, 121, 123, 124, 125, 128, 129, 130, 148, 150, 153, 155, 160, 163, 167, 169, 176, 179, 180, 182, 185, 186, 188, 189, 195, 199, 201, 203, 204, 206, 218, 233
Des Moines Regency, 128–30, 176, 194–95, 196, 217, 218, 225, 231–32, 233
Dewey, John N., 186
Dillon, John F., 223–24
District of Columbia
  black suffrage in, 151, 186
  emancipation in, 139
Dixon, J.M., 212
Dodge, Augustus C., 22, 32, 37, 38, 44, 53, 97, 114, 122, 139, 181, 206
Dodge, Grenville M.
  and black suffrage, 186–87, 272 n. 58
  in Civil War, 142
  and Credit Mobilier, 199, 206–7
  and Des Moines Regency, 129, 194–95, 210–11
  and Hayes policy, 232
  and Kasson, 176, 180, 182, 194
  and Texas & Pacific, 223, 231
Douglas, Stephen A., 7, 22, 38, 44, 45, 48, 97, 113, 116, 118, 124, 125, 126, 138
Dred Scott v *Sanford* (1857), 91, 93, 103, 114, 118
Dubuque, Iowa, 17, 49, 54, 69, 76, 93, 97, 101, 102, 112, 114, 126, 154, 195, 204, 209, 215, 217
Dubuque Herald, 138
Dubuque & Pacific Railroad, 98, 101, 110, 206
Dubuque Times, 134
Dudley, Charles, 167
Duncan, L.A., 121
Durant, Thomas, 176, 207, 274 n. 35
Dykstra, Robert R., 171, 172, 193

Economic development of Iowa, 4, 8, 15, 16, 17, 39, 41, 95–98, 101, 109, 203–5, 208–9, 274 n. 4. *See also* Banks and banking; Railroads
Edwards, John, 82, 84
Ells, George W., 66, 81, 86, 100, 106
Emancipation Proclamation, 6, 142, 143, 146–47, 165
Emerson, J. H., 101
Eminent domain, 220
Episcopalians, 34
Ethnocultural foundations. *See also* Nativism; Temperance
  of second party system, 28–30, 41, 43, 49, 50, 68, 239
  of third party system, 10–11, 70, 239–44
Evangelical protestants and protestantism. *See also* names of individual denominations
  and abolitionism, 34–35, 43
  and capitalism, 6
  categorization of, 277 n. 3
  and national Whig party, 20
  and nativism, 42, 55, 57
  and radical Republicanism, 172, 245
  and state politics, 10, 49, 54, 195,

239–41, 257 n. 14
and territorial politics, 28–30

Factionalism, 88–89, 95, 97, 112–13, 116, 125, 128–30, 153, 162–63, 175–77, 184, 186, 194–95, 238
Fairfield, Iowa, 139, 145, 188
Fairfield Ledger, 118
Farnam, Henry, 129, 217
Fayette, Iowa, 89
Fayette County Pioneer, 89–90, 91
Fessenden, William Pitt, 138, 151, 160, 178, 189, 192
Fifteenth Amendment, 193, 246, 272 n. 58
Fillmore, Millard, 38–39, 43, 44, 59, 60, 68, 69, 71
Finkbine, Robert, 169
First Military Reconstruction Act, 188, 189
Flanigan, William H., 10
Foner, Eric, 6, 238, 246
Foote, John G., 151
Forbes, John M., 107, 108, 123
Foreign-born, 4, 7, 39, 41–43, 47, 49, 55, 56, 57, 69, 70, 71, 78, 95, 112, 113, 127, 244. *See also* Germans; Irish; Nativism
Fort Dodge, Iowa, 118, 146, 165, 195, 230
Fort Madison, Iowa, 17
Fort Sumter, 4, 94, 134
Fourteenth Amendment, 6, 178, 181, 182, 183, 184, 185, 187, 191, 193, 198, 221
Frazier, Thomas, 34
Freedmen's Bureau, 152, 174, 177
Freedmen's Bureau bill, veto of, 169, 172, 174, 175, 178, 179
Free labor, 3, 64, 67, 71, 145, 183
Freeport doctrine, 126
Free-Soilers and Free-Soil party
  Buffalo convention, 36
  and Compromise of 1850, 39
  and fusion, 37, 44–47, 56–59, 71, 257 n. 59
  and role in Republican party, 59, 65, 66, 81, 161, 177
  and 1854 senatorial election, 53
  and temperance, 43

Free Will Baptists, 90, 92, 125
Frémont, John C., 68, 69, 70, 93, 123, 138
Fugitive Slave Law of 1850, 37, 38, 46, 54, 65, 66, 77, 81, 119, 120, 133

Garrison, William L., 35
Gate City (Keokuk), 59, 155
Gear, John H., 225, 233
Gehon, Francis, 25
General assembly
  and blacks, 33, 35, 38, 78, 80, 81, 83, 84, 153, 167–69
  and black suffrage, 167–69, 171–72, 191
  composition of, 239–42
  and economic development, 26–27, 40, 97, 98, 103, 105, 107–8
  and Kansas resolutions, 117
  and 1860 legislation, 123, 124, 127, 128–130
  and Lincoln's reelection, 150–51
  and manufacturing, 205
  and "moral" legislation, 29, 55, 87–88
  and public policy, 244–45
  and railroads, 209–10, 212, 215, 223–24, 225
  Republican domination of, 5
Germans, 41, 42, 43, 55, 57, 59, 69, 87, 110, 113, 114, 127, 161, 201, 239
Gettysburg, battle of, 149
Gibson, H.D., 100
Giddings, Joshua, 48, 53, 119
Gienapp, William E., 49, 69, 70, 238, 241
Gillaspy, George, 83, 84, 99
Goodell, William, 91
Granger movement, 210–12, 234, 275 n. 50
Grand Army of the Republic, 228
Granger Law (1874), 212, 215, 224–25, 226, 227, 275 n. 57
Grant, Ulysses S., 147, 148, 155, 190, 192, 193, 194, 196, 198, 199, 200, 201, 206, 211, 228, 229
Gray, John H., 144–45
Great Britain, 149
Greeley, Horace, 64, 124, 198–99, 200, 201
Greenback party, 224–25

Griffing, Josephine S., 145
Grimes, Elizabeth N., 46–47, 65, 67, 68, 135, 138, 140, 192
Grimes, James W., 20, 43, 75, 81, 87, 100, 101, 111, 116, 127, 128, 161, 174, 190
  and 1854 campaign, 46–51
  as centrist, 66–68, 80, 125, 137, 151, 177–78
  and Civil War, 137–38, 139–41, 150, 151, 152, 153
  and colonization, 78, 260 n. 14
  dies, 200
  and 1859 election, 103, 112–14
  and federal government, 64, 109, 197
  and formation of Republican party, 52–60, 69, 70, 257 n. 59, 258 n. 35
  and Harlan, 176–77
  and Kansas, 61–64, 117
  and laissez-faire, 151–52, 189, 195, 197, 205
  and Liberal Republicanism, 199–200
  and nationalism, 237
  and railroads, 97, 98, 107–10, 123, 152, 206, 207, 238
  and Reconstruction, 160, 163–64, 177–78, 184, 187, 188, 189, 191–92, 272 n. 58
  and religion, 67, 259 n. 86
  resigns, 194
  and secession, 131–34
  and slavery, 65–66, 119, 137–38, 139–41
Grinnell, Josiah B., 67, 106, 107, 120, 121, 142, 160, 180, 188, 205
  and black suffrage, 162, 165
  and Liberal Republicanism, 194, 200, 201
  and Reconstruction, 163, 187, 188
Gubernatorial elections, 5, 48–49, 93, 102, 112–115, 138–39, 149–50, 165, 189, 211, 227
Gue, Benjamin F., 121, 161, 162

Hale, John P., 44
Hale, William, 168
Hall, Jonathan C., 25, 82, 83, 85, 86, 99
Halleck, Henry, 141, 148
Hamilton, William W., 59, 66, 112

Hampton, Wade, 232
Hanson v. *Vernon* (1869), 223–24
Harlan, James, 59, 111, 116, 124, 125, 128, 143, 146, 210, 238
  as centrist, 66–68, 80, 93, 151
  and Civil War, 139–41, 150, 151, 152, 153
  and corruption, 107, 179, 195, 199, 207
  and Grimes, 176–77
  and Kansas, 60–61
  loses power, 194–95, 228–29
  and Reconstruction, 163, 166, 184, 187, 192, 272 n. 58
  and secession, 131–34
  as secretary of the interior, 162–63, 166, 178–79
  in Senate elections, 54, 78, 113, 123, 176, 194–95, 211, 274 n. 35
  and slavery, 54, 77, 139–41
Harpers Ferry, 63, 119–22, 243
Harris, Amos, 69, 83, 99
Harrison, William H., 19, 20, 21
Hayes, Rutherford B., 229–33
Hays, Samuel P., 7
Hempstead, Stephen, 24, 26, 41, 48, 98
Hendricks, Thomas A., 197
Higginson, Thomas W., 63, 64, 246
Horwitz, Morton, 215, 217, 219, 223
Howard, Jacob W., 178
Howell, James B., 59, 210
Hoxie, H. M., 129, 130, 142, 207–8, 217, 274 n. 35
Hunter, David, 140
Hurst, James W., 217, 220, 222, 223
Hoffman, Thomas L., 145–46
Hubbard, Nathaniel, 153

Impeachment, of Andrew Johnson, 181, 189–92, 197, 200
Indiana Exclusion Law (1831), 33
Indians, American, 3, 4, 15–16, 65, 85, 95, 129, 172, 179, 195
Ingersoll, Lurton D., 128, 164
International Railroad Company, 208
Iowa Central Air Line Railroad, 98
Iowa City, Iowa, 23, 32, 46, 56, 59, 62, 67, 68, 71, 75, 98, 101, 102, 111, 112, 113, 120, 125, 128, 153
Iowa City Republican, 121, 128

INDEX

Iowa Maine Law (1855), 55, 59, 70, 90, 110, 114
Iowa State Register (Des Moines), 66, 140–41, 142, 144, 145, 149, 155, 156, 174, 181, 185, 186, 190, 194, 195, 201, 212, 223, 229, 232
Iowa State Reporter (Iowa City), 128, 132–33
Iowa Wesleyan University, 54, 55
Irish, 41, 42, 43, 69, 78, 88, 147, 154, 162, 241, 242
Isbell, Norman W., 54, 217, 222

Jackson, Andrew, 4, 18, 23, 41, 122
James, Edwin, 65
Jenkin's Ferry, battle of, 164
Johns, John, 125
Johnson, Andrew, 159–60, 166, 167, 169, 172, 174, 175, 177, 178, 179, 180, 181, 182, 183, 184, 185, 188. *See also* Impeachment
Joint Committee on Reconstruction, 178, 187, 221–22
Jones, George W., 32, 37, 38, 44, 77, 97, 116, 125, 138
Jordan, James C., 160
Joy, James F., 107–10, 206

Kansas
  guerilla war in, 60, 68, 95, 162
  as political issue, 11, 58, 59, 60–64, 70–71, 103, 111, 113, 116–19
Kansas-Nebraska Act, 45–51, 52, 53, 55, 56, 60, 68, 71, 83, 243
Kasson, John A.
  at Chicago convention, 125
  eclipse of, 176, 180, 218
  elected to Congress, 142
  and laissez-faire, 205
  and National Union movement, 181
  and Reconstruction, 187, 188, 270 n. 62, 272 n. 58
  and Regency, 129, 217
  as Republican party chairman, 112
  and secession, 130
Kelly, Oliver, 211
Keokuk, Iowa, 17, 56, 76, 97, 98, 105, 107, 121, 124, 126, 138, 148, 149, 162, 174, 194, 198, 208
Keokuk Evening Times, 86

Keosauqua, Iowa, 68
Kespe v. *The Chicago & N.W.R.R.* (1870), 222
Kirkwood, Samuel J., 59, 111, 113, 114, 117, 128, 129, 160, 169
  as centrist, 68, 93, 121–22, 124, 125
  and Civil War, 137, 139, 141, 145, 148, 149
  and Hayes policy, 232
  and Reconstruction, 166, 177, 185–87, 188, 191
  and Regency, 195, 227
  and secession, 133, 134
  senatorial ambitions of, 163, 176, 228–29
  and third inaugural, 227–28
Kleppner, Paul, 241
Knapp, Joseph C., 62
Know Nothings, 56–60, 68, 71, 275 n. 43. *See also* Nativism

Land policy, of U.S., 3, 15, 97, 210
Lane, James H., 61–62
Langworthy, Solon M., 154
Laurie, Bruce, 6
Lawrence, Charles B., 219
Lawrence, Kansas, sack of, 61
Lecompton, 61, 113, 117–18, 122, 126, 243
Lee, Robert E., 155, 228
Letcher, John, 121–23
Liberal Republicans, 194, 195, 196, 199–201, 202, 213
Liberty party, 35–36, 53, 65, 66, 71, 81, 91
Lincoln, Abraham, 3, 6, 124, 125, 126, 127, 128, 130, 131, 134, 137, 156, 163, 165, 184, 228, 246
  as president, 138, 139, 140, 141, 142, 148, 150–53, 154, 155
Lloyd, Frederick, 128
Loughridge, William, 180, 190, 272 n. 58
Lowe, Ralph P., 29, 64–65, 93, 103, 110–14, 117, 206, 215, 217
Lucas, Robert, 21, 24, 29, 43
Lyons, Iowa, 97

McClellan, George B., 148, 153–54
McClintock, William, 89

McCormick, Richard L., 6
McCrary, George W., 161, 208
McDill, James W., 161
McGregor, Iowa, 137
McLean, John, 47
McNutt, Samuel, 168
Madison, James, 64
Mahoney, Dennis A., 138, 201
Market revolution, 4, 6
Marshall, John, 218
Marvin, A.H., 86–87
Marx, Karl, 5
Mason, Charles, 96, 97, 134, 242
  in Civil War, 138
  and 1870s politics, 199–201, 202, 206, 224, 229, 230
  and Reconstruction, 167, 180, 181, 188, 192
Melendy, Peter, 192
Memphis massacre, 189, 190
Merrill, Samuel F., 189, 203, 204, 210
Methodists and Methodism, 28, 179, 207. *See also* Evangelical protestants and protestantism
  and black suffrage, 162, 165–66
  and slavery, 34, 35, 65, 67, 120, 139, 142, 143, 145
  and state politics, 49, 54, 61, 78, 176
  and temperance, 43
Mexican War, 21, 31, 50, 131
Miller, Samuel F., 67, 127, 130, 174, 185, 191, 197–98
Milwaukee & St. Paul Railroad, 222
Miners' Bank of Dubuque, 22–25
Mississippi & Missouri River Railroad, 62, 98, 101, 106, 107, 108, 109, 129, 217
Missouri Compromise, 45, 48
Mitchell, Thomas, 160
Moderate Republicans. *See also* Republicans; Radical Republicans
  and black suffrage, 161–75
  and Civil War, 137–38, 139–42, 143–45, 146, 148, 151–52, 153, 156
  in 1857 constitutional convention, 80–87
  and 1857 election, 92–94
  and 1860 election, 123–27
  radicalization of, 116, 118–19, 121–22, 138

  and Reconstruction, 159–60, 163, 166–67, 172–75, 177–78, 180–82, 183–93, 197–99
  and secession crisis, 130–35
  and slavery, 66–68
Modernization synthesis, 7, 237
Montana, black suffrage in, 151
Morrill Tariff, 205
Moulton, A.K., 92
Mount Pleasant, Iowa, 46, 54, 63, 100, 107, 124, 139, 146, 150, 176
Mount Pleasant Observer, 58
Muscatine, Iowa, 17, 19, 56, 64, 76, 82, 93, 109, 125, 215

National Capital Removal Convention, 204
National Era (Washington, D.C.), 57
Nationalism, 3, 131, 135, 136, 237, 246
National Union party, 179–82, 184
Nativism, 11, 41–42, 44, 49, 123. *See also* Ethnocultural foundations; Know Nothings
  and conservative Republicans, 68
  and 1859 election, 113, 114
  and 1860 election, 127
  as political force, 55–61, 71
  and racism, 78
  and temperance, 43
  and third party system, 239, 241, 242, 244
Nebraska, black suffrage in, 185–87
Negro Exclusion Act (1851), 38, 77–78, 143–44, 153
Newbold, Joshua, 234
Newcomb, Carmen A., 89–92
New England and New Englanders, 8, 34, 46–47, 49, 63, 69, 88, 106, 240
New Orleans massacre, 181, 189, 190
New York City, draft riots in, 149
New York Sun, 206
New York Tribune, 233
Northwest Ordinance, 48
Nourse, Charles C., 67, 125, 143

O'Connor, Henry, 125, 160, 162, 192, 195
Oskaloosa, Iowa, 162, 164, 180
Ossawatamie massacre, 61
Ottumwa, Iowa, 17, 83, 99, 162

INDEX

Packard, Stephen B., 232
Painter, John H., 120
Palmer, Frank W., 140–41, 144, 149, 161, 190, 194
Palmer v *Mulligan* (1805), 215
Panic of 1837, 19, 20
Parvin, John A., 82, 85, 86, 102, 169
Patronage, 18, 21, 128, 152, 163, 175–76, 179, 180–81, 198
Peace Democrats (Copperheads), 138, 145, 147, 153–54, 155, 156, 165, 181, 200, 201
Personal liberty laws
  in Iowa, 81–82, 94, 119
  in U.S., 132, 133, 135
Phillips, Wendell, 67, 68
Pierce, Franklin, 44, 60, 61, 63, 71, 96, 97, 196
Political culture, 7–8, 9–11, 238–45
Polk, James K., 31, 32, 40
Popular sovereignty, 9, 38, 60, 82, 113, 114, 116, 117, 126
Presbyterians, 28, 29, 47, 86, 90, 103. *See also* Evangelical protestants and protestantism
  and abolitionism, 24, 78
Presidential election
  of 1840, 19, 20
  of 1844, 35
  of 1848, 36
  of 1852, 44–45
  of 1856, 68–70, 93
  of 1860, 93, 125–27
  of 1864, 154
  of 1868, 193
  of 1872, 201
  of 1876, 229–30
Price, Daniel, 85, 86
Price, Eliphalet, 137
Price, Hiram, 62, 107, 120, 142, 153, 160, 208, 223
  and black suffrage, 162
  and prohibition, 42–43, 59
  and race, 196
  and Reconstruction, 178, 187, 188, 190, 191, 272 n.58
Pritchard, Reasin, 77
Prohibition. *See* Temperance
Protection, 6, 20, 44, 70, 200, 203, 205

Quakers, 28, 90, 144
  and abolition, 34, 120–22

Racism. *See also* African-Americans; Black suffrage; Democrats; Radical Republicans; Republicans
  and demise of Reconstruction, 198, 199, 202
  impact of Civil War on, 145–47, 165
  in Iowa, 68, 141, 196
  in U.S., 32–33, 38, 193
Radical Republicans, 7, 66–68, 71. *See also* Republicans
  and black suffrage 161–75
  and John Brown, 120–22
  and Civil War, 137, 138, 139–40, 142, 147, 149, 150–53, 156
  and colonization, 78, 80
  in 1857 constitutional convention, 81–87, 106
  in 1857 election, 88–94
  and 1860 election, 123–27
  and Hayes policy, 233
  and paternalistic racism, 196
  as pressure group, 246
  and Reconstruction, 159–60, 166, 167, 172–75, 177–78, 180–82, 183–94, 197, 198, 199, 231–32
  and secession, 130–35
  and statism, 172, 245
Railroads, 4, 11, 16, 40, 45, 50, 75, 96–98, 101–2, 103, 152, 242. *See also* Antimonopoly sentiment; Corruption; Democrats; Republicans
  in 1859 election campaign, 110–15
  and 1877 election, 233
  and judiciary, 215, 217–24
  and partisanship, 244
  and politics of 1870s, 201, 203, 206
  and rate regulation, 123, 172, 209–10, 212, 215, 218, 224–25, 246
Rankin, John W., 148
Rankin, Samuel A., 199, 210
Recession of 1850s, 102–115, 117
Reconstruction, 11, 153, 155, 159–60, 166–75, 177–202, 228, 231–32, 245, 246
Redemption, 193, 228, 230, 231–32. *See also* Reconstruction

Republicans. *See also* Factionalism; Moderate Republicans; Radical Republicans
  as ambivalent nationalists, 237, 246
  and banks, 98–101, 103, 105, 115, 242
  and black suffrage in Iowa, 85–87, 92–94, 115, 154–55, 159–75, 192–93
  and capitalism, 5
  and Civil War, 136–56
  in 1857 constitutional convention, 75, 80–87, 98–102
  and corruption, 107, 110–11, 179, 198–99, 206–8, 210
  and 1860 election, 123–27
  and 1876 election, 229–30
  ethnoreligious composition of party, 239–41
  and genesis of party, 52–71
  and Grangers, 212–13, 215
  and Harpers Ferry, 120–22
  and Hayes policy, 231–33
  and Kansas, 60–64, 111, 113, 117–18
  and manufacturing, 205, 237
  and nativism, 55–60, 68, 78, 94, 113, 241, 258 n. 43
  and prohibition, 53, 55, 59, 87–88, 90–91, 94, 110, 115, 161, 172, 228, 239, 242, 244, 246
  and protection, 70, 205
  and race, 60–61, 68, 75–94, 139–45, 149, 155, 196, 232–33, 247
  and railroads, 98, 101–102, 103, 105, 106–15, 148, 206–26, 227, 233–34, 238, 242, 244, 246
  and Reconstruction, 159–60, 166–75, 180–94, 196–99, 202, 245, 286
  and secession, 127, 128, 130–35
  and slave power, 11, 51, 64, 67, 71, 82, 93, 94, 109, 113, 115, 116, 126, 132–35, 242, 243
  and slavery, 6, 11–12, 53, 64–68, 83, 90–92, 94, 106, 119, 134–35, 137–43, 146, 165, 246
  and state sovereignty, 63–64, 93, 94, 119, 196–97, 225
  Whiggish character of, 112, 245
Rice, George G., 60
Rice, Samuel A., 164
Rich, Jacob, 161, 232

Rigby, Alfred A., 146
Robinson, Charles, 61
Rock Island Railroad, 120, 129
Rogers, Jacob W., 78, 88–92, 93, 257 n. 14
Rogers, Thomas, 27, 29
Roman Catholics and Catholicism, 7, 41–42, 55, 56, 114, 127, 239, 241. *See also* Foreign-born; Irish; Germans; Nativism; Know Nothings
Rorer, David, 65, 126
Ruckman, Joseph, 147
Rusch, Nicholas, 113, 114
Russell, Edward
  and black suffrage 155, 160–65
  and Hayes policy, 233
  racial views of, 196
  and Reconstruction, 166, 181
  retires, 194

Sabbatarianism, 29, 55
Salem, Iowa, 34
Salter, William, 46
Sample, Hugh, 162
Samuels, Benjamin, 93, 116
Sanborn, Franklin D., 63, 64
Saulsbury, Willard, 139–40
Saunders, Alvin, 59, 124, 125
Saunders, Thomas F., 151
Savery, James C., 128–29, 179
Scott, Thomas A., 231
Scott, Winfield, 31, 43, 44, 49
Scott County Hydraulic Company, 27
Secession crisis, 127, 128, 130–35
Second party system, 5, 19, 22, 28, 30, 56, 70, 76, 109, 239. *See also* Democrats; Whigs
Sectionalism, 5, 9, 10–11, 30, 47, 50, 57, 58, 59, 61, 64, 68, 70, 71, 81–82, 93, 94, 113, 115, 124, 193, 237, 243. *See also* Civil War; Republicans; South
  as basis of political conflict, 244–46
  persistence of, 201, 226, 227–33
Sells, Elijah, 146, 179
Senatorial elections, 53–54, 107, 123, 163, 176, 194–95, 228–29, 238
Seward, William H., 123, 124, 125, 131, 132, 138, 149
Sharp, John, 147

Shedd, George, 35, 44, 46, 47, 110–11, 177
Shellabarger, Samuel, 188
Sheridan, Philip H., 189, 228
Sherman, Buren R., 233
Sherman, William T., 228
Simpson, Matthew, 61
Sioux City, Iowa, 39
Slagle, Christian, 161
Slaughter House Cases (1873), 107–8
Slave code, for U.S. territories, 113, 119, 134
Slavery expansion. *See also* Republicans; Secession crisis; South
 as basis of Republicanism, 246
 opposition to in Congress, 31–32
 opposition to in Iowa, 36, 37
 as political issue, 47–48, 50, 53, 56, 57
Slave trade, reopening of, 113, 114, 118, 134
Smith, Platt, 110, 112
Sons of Temperance, 42
Sorauf, Frank, 11
Soulé, Pierre, 38
South. *See also* Republicans; Secession crisis; Sectionalism; Slavery expansion
 and defeat, 154, 146
 as negative referent, 11, 53, 58, 61, 64, 67, 68, 71, 94, 113, 115, 116, 126, 131, 132, 134, 147, 165, 201, 241, 243
 and Reconstruction, 159, 166, 174, 175, 179, 182, 185, 190, 202, 231
Southern-born, in Iowa, 16, 69–70, 71, 78, 88, 127, 240
Spencer, George, 198–99
Springdale, Iowa, 120–22
Springer, Francis, 19, 22, 59, 117–18, 130, 150
Stanton, Edwin M., 189, 190
Starr, William H., 65
Statehood controversy, 21–22
Stephens, Alexander H., 48
Stevens, Thaddeus, 153, 159, 160, 187, 189
Stewart, Alvan, 91
Stiles, Edward H., 162, 165, 169
Stone, John Y., 212

Stone, William M., 145, 149, 165, 167, 168, 169, 176
Sumner, Charles, 147, 151, 152, 178, 182, 185–87, 189, 193, 194, 199
Supreme Court
 of Iowa, 91, 101, 112, 113, 129, 137, 196, 197–98, 209, 215, 217–24
 of U.S., 91, 127, 197–98

Tabor, Iowa, 62, 120
Tannehill, Harvey, 161
Taxation, 21, 101–2, 108, 114, 197, 198, 205, 206, 209, 210, 217, 218, 220, 221, 223–34
Taylor, Hawkins, 105, 121, 130, 195
Taylor, Samuel, 147
Taylor, Zachary, 31, 32, 35, 36, 37, 38
Teesdale, John, 66, 120, 123, 132, 133, 194
Temperance. *See also* Democrats; Ethnocultural foundations; Nativism; Republicans
 and antislavery, 78
 as political issue, 11, 42–43, 46, 47, 49, 53, 55, 56, 59, 87–88, 110, 113, 201, 203, 228, 239, 242, 244
 in territorial Iowa 28, 30
Templeton, LeRoy, 89
Tenure of Office Act, 190, 192
Texas & Pacific Railroad, 223
Third party system, 5, 8, 10–12, 109, 202, 239–47. *See also* Democrats; Republicans
Thirteenth Amendment, 155, 159, 172
Thorington, James, 57
Tichenor, George C., 176, 186, 189, 194, 210–11, 218
Tilden, Samuel G., 229, 230
The Times (London), 199
Topeka government, 61, 62
Tracey, Joshua, 162
Trumbull, Lyman, 200
Turner, Asa, 34, 35, 46, 47, 67, 81, 127
Turner, Frederick J., 10
Tuttle, James, 229
Twain, Mark, 207
Tyler, John, 21

Union Pacific Railroad, 176, 194, 206, 207, 218

Unitarians, 67, 90, 162
Universalists, 90
Urban growth, in Iowa, 17, 39, 96–97
Usury, 27

Vagrancy act, 224, 230, 234
Van Buren, Martin, 15, 18, 20, 36
Vandever, William, 131, 134
Veterans, in postwar politics, 165, 168, 169, 175, 180, 189, 193, 228
Vicksburg, Mississippi, 9, 147, 148, 149

Wade, Benjamin F., 189, 192
Wade-Davis bill, 153
Wapello, Iowa, 19
Warner, Charles D., 207
Warren, Fitz Henry
  and cabinet post, 128, 130
  and 1860 election, 124
  and Grimes, 54, 111
  and Kansas, 63
  postwar political career, 169, 174, 176, 180, 181, 190, 200–201
  as Whig politician, 36, 39, 47, 59
Washburne, Elihu B., 190
Washington, Iowa, 34
Washington, D.C., peace conference, 133
Waterloo, Iowa, 39
Waters, Frances, 46
Waters, Simeon, 46
Watrous, George, 76, 92
Weaver, James B., 196, 224
Webb, Archie P., 143–45
Webster City, Iowa, 119
Welles, Gideon, 140, 184
West
  as distinct section, 8–9
  missionary activity in, 29, 34, 42, 55
West Union, Iowa, 88–92
Whigs
  and banks, 22–26, 41
  as bourgeois party, 6
  and Compromise of 1850, 38, 39
  and constitutional reform, 40
  and Constitutional Union party, 125
  and corporations, 26–27
  and ethnocultural issues, 28–30, 42, 43, 46, 56
  Free-Soil criticism of, 111
  and fusion, 37, 44–47, 57, 59, 77
  ideology of, 20, 29–30
  and Kansas-Nebraska Act, 47
  and manufacturing, 204–205
  and Mexican War, 31
  and race, 32, 33, 35, 76–77, 78
  and railroads, 40, 97
  in Republican party, 59, 64, 66, 67, 68, 71, 100, 101, 103, 152, 160, 174, 197, 198, 205, 210, 221, 223, 233, 245
  and slavery, 31–32, 35, 36, 37, 47, 50, 61, 66
  and territorial politics, 18–30
Wiebe, Robert, 7
Wilentz, Sean, 6
Williams, Elias H., 137
Williamson, James A., 185
Wilmot, David, 31
Wilmot Proviso, 31, 32, 36, 38, 50
Wilson, Henry, 141
Wilson, James F.
  as congressman, 142, 153, 161, 178, 187, 188, 190, 194, 195, 199, 201, 206, 272 n. 58
  in 1857 constitutional convention, 80–81, 83, 84, 100, 120
  and Granger Law, 212–13
Wilson, William D., 211
Wisconsin, black suffrage in, 87, 193
Withrow, Thomas, 111, 141
Wolf, William, 161
Women, 10, 85, 143, 193, 228
  and suffrage 244, 278 n. 6
Woolson, Theron W., 146, 151, 169
Wright, Ed, 121, 144, 169, 182, 186
Wright, George G., 68, 194, 231

Yellow Springs, Iowa, 34, 35

Zingale, Nancy, 10